MW01505191

American Policy Toward Israel

American Policy Toward Israel explains the institutionalization of nearly unconditional American support of Israel during the Reagan administration, and its persistence in the first Bush administration in terms of the competition of belief systems in American society and politics.

The book explains policy changes over time and provides insights into what circumstances might lead to lasting changes in policy. It identifies the important domestic social, religious and political elements that have vied for primacy on policy toward Israel and, using case studies, such as the 1981 AWACS sale and the 1991 loan guarantees, argues that policy debates have been struggles to embed and enforce beliefs about Israel and about Arabs. It also establishes a framework for better understanding the influences and constraints on American policy toward Israel. An epilogue applies the lessons learned to the current Bush administration.

This book will be of interest to students of U.S. Foreign Policy, Middle Eastern Politics and International Relations.

Michael Thomas is a former military lawyer and civilian litigator who is concerned with the formulation of American policy in the Middle East. He holds a PhD in International Relations from the London School of Economics, U.K.

LSE international studies series

Series editors: John Kent, Christopher Coker, Fred Halliday, Dominic Lieven and Karen Smith

1 **American Policy Toward Israel**
The power and limits of beliefs
Michael Thomas

American Policy Toward Israel

The power and limits of beliefs

Michael Thomas

Routledge
Taylor & Francis Group

LONDON AND NEW YORK

First published 2007
by Routledge
2 Park Square, Milton Park, Abingdon, Oxon OX14 4RN

Simultaneously published in the USA and Canada
by Routledge
270 Madison Ave, New York, NY 10016

Routledge is an imprint of the Taylor & Francis Group, an informa business

Transferred to Digital Printing 2009

© 2007 Michael Thomas

Typeset in Garamond by Wearset Ltd, Boldon, Tyne and Wear

British Library Cataloguing in Publication Data
A catalogue record for this book is available from the British Library

Library of Congress Cataloging in Publication Data
Thomas, Michael Tracy.
American policy toward Israel : the power and limits of beliefs /
Michael Thomas.
p. cm.
Includes bibliographical references and index.
 1. United States–Military policy. 2. United States–Foreign
relations–Israel. 3. Israel–Foreign relations–United States. 4. United
States–Foreign relations–1981–1989. 5. United States–Foreign
relations–1989– I. Title.
UA23.T44 2006
355'.033573095694–dc22

                                                        2006034565

ISBN10: 0–415–77146–3 (hbk)
ISBN10: 0–415–54517–X (pbk)
ISBN10: 0–203–08887–5 (ebk)

ISBN13: 978–0–415–77146–7 (hbk)
ISBN13: 978–0–415–54517–4 (pbk)
ISBN13: 978–0–203–08887–6 (ebk)

This book is dedicated to Dorothy O. Thomas

Contents

Acknowledgments

I acknowledge with gratitude the wise counsel and constructive criticism of Professor Christopher Coker and Dr. John Kent of the London School of Economics and Political Science. A number of participants in the process of making U.S. policy toward Israel, including but not limited to those quoted as interviewees, were very generous with their time and insights. The final product benefited greatly from the review of Sheridan Strickland. Remaining errors of fact or judgment are entirely my own.

1 Explaining the extra-special relationship

The battle of beliefs

The relationship between the United States and Israel is in many ways unlike any other bilateral relationship of the United States. That much is agreed by all knowledgeable observers. Americans and their officials also agree that the United States has undertaken, and will always honor, an obligation to insure the continued existence and security of the State of Israel. As to nearly any other statement about the relationship, disagreements are numerous and often rancorous.

When you listen to participants in the policy process, you are always struck by the wide divergence in relevant beliefs, and the intensity of advocates' efforts to establish their beliefs as predominant. To understand the policies as well as the rancor, it is necessary to identify the beliefs of important participants in the policy-making process, and to study how the competition among those beliefs is conducted. Most important are beliefs, both moral and strategic, about the identity and role of Israel. Also relevant are beliefs about Arabs and Palestinians, Islam and terrorism and (during the Cold War) Soviet communism.

Advocates seek to establish their beliefs as predominant in part by identifying them with prevailing American cultural, normative and ideological preferences. Salient pro-Israel conceptualizations have been: Israel as religious or eschatological imperative; moral obligee; Western democratic cultural sibling; and finally as strategic asset in American efforts to contain Soviet communism and Islamist terrorism. Most Americans understand Israel to be the land of their Bible and the country in the Middle East most like the United States in important ways: democratic, open and populated by fiercely independent and courageous people. That vision of Israel, and empathy with its founding after the Holocaust, have formed the basis of broad popular support. Those Jews and Christians for whom Israel fulfills an eschatological role argue there is a religious duty to support those who seek to reconstitute the land God gave Abraham. Others, including but not limited to Jews whose self-identification is tied up with Israel, argue that Israel is America's cultural sibling and moral obligee, and that it must always be favored over its neighbors as the region's only Western-style democracy. Many, including those for whom the principal reason for support is really religion or affinity, make a strategic case for maintaining Israel as a regional hegemon. On the other side are realists and others not driven by religion or affinity, who deny some or all of the proffered justifications and argue that policies uniquely and overwhelmingly favoring Israel have been not just wrong, but destructive of American interests.

Personal belief systems also explain divergent characterizations of the process by which policy toward Israel has come to be what it is. Realists and other critics of American policy, frustrated by the perceived irrationality of their opponents, sometimes claim that a small, mostly Jewish, pro-Israel lobby has American policy in a "stranglehold," and has caused the United States to abandon its own national interests in favor of Israel's interests by means of political leverage, intimidation and control of public discourse. This implied accusation of dual loyalty or worse is sometimes made explicitly. Those who support ever-stronger ties argue that such ties not only facilitate a rational pursuit of American national security interests but also affirm American political and moral values. They tend to view the critics as blind to America's true interests, or even as anti-Semitic. Each of these positions, and their many permutations and combinations, reflect sets of beliefs about Israel, about Arabs and Palestinians, and ultimately about what America is or should be.

Most analysts of international relations use rationalist models, in which actors' interests, preferences and causal beliefs are given and ideas are relegated to minor roles. However, one's beliefs shape how he defines goals and understands cause and effect. They provide filters and blinders as he seeks and considers evidence. They provide default positions when strategic analysis yields only ambiguous answers. And by defining policies over time and becoming embedded in political institutions, beliefs can shape policy long after the evidence originally relied upon is obsolete or discredited (Goldstein and Keohane 1993: 3). Beliefs can be "world views" (fundamental normative, cosmological, ontological and ethical beliefs), "principled" beliefs about justice or causal beliefs.[1]

American policy makers often "default" to policies based upon cultural ideology, a "structure of meaning" that defines the American collectivity, its morality, and its friends and enemies (Mansour 1994: 261). When in doubt, "political actors follow the strategy most in conformity with their identity and ideology." Such a strategy can be stable in the absence of substantial material interests (ibid.: 276–7).[2] When in most cases a policy of strong and unconditioned support does not appear to damage U.S. interests, the policy maker is reassured that optimism and following his "conscience" are warranted.

Beliefs held strongly by leaders tend to stifle debate and chill the production of variant approaches to policy; as such ideas become embedded as "conventional wisdom," the quality and variety of policy papers declines, and career decisions are affected. Beliefs become "institutional roadmaps." Even

if individual officials can identify viable policy options based upon different
beliefs, they are often not given a full hearing because to do so would force
rethinking basic assumptions about values or causation. An example is the
relatively insignificant impact of the regional specialists ("Arabists") of the
State Department in the years under study.[3]

Ideas or ideology have other functions in policy-making: mobilizing
support; structuring information; obscuring alternative facts and policy
options; and creating momentum or inertia, among others. Whatever the
origin of ideas or their continuing connection to interests, they persist in
influence when they become embedded in institutions and in the terms of
policy debate, particularly when they have affected institutional design.
Political institutions – agency organization and staffing, laws, rules, norms,
operating procedures, and budgets – mediate between ideas and policy outcomes (Goldstein and Keohane 1993: 20–1). As ideas become predominant
and embedded institutionally, they change political institutions so that
policy makers thereafter have a different set of enabling and constraining
structures within which to work.[4] Changes in policy – here, we posit a
"ratcheting" of support for Israel – must take into account, not just external
events and the contemporaneous preferences of the president and other
participants in the process, but also the institutional changes that have been
produced in part by the cementing of ideas central to prior policy decisions.[5]

This book will seek to explain the elements and dynamics of the "special
relationship" and how it has shaped and constrained American policy toward
Israel and the Palestinians. To do so, it will focus on groups holding different sets of beliefs about Israel and Palestinians, and their efforts to establish
their beliefs as predominant and thereby limit and define policy options. In
each administration, the president and the key advisers on whom he relies
bring their beliefs and leadership skills to a contest in congressional and
electoral politics with groups possessing their own skills and sets of beliefs.
We will look in depth at the administrations of presidents Ronald Reagan
and George H. W. Bush, 1981–1993. During Reagan's two terms, proponents of ever-deeper ties and nearly unconditional support of Israeli policies,
led by the American Israel Public Affairs Committee (AIPAC), had a receptive audience, and succeeded in embedding their beliefs in policy and institutions to an unprecedented degree. During "Bush I," it became evident
that this process of ratcheting support had limits, and was conditional on
developments in the region and the degree to which the president and his
chief advisers shared their predecessors' deep emotional affinity toward
Israel. Drawing on the lessons learned in the two administrations, we will
summarize the important determinants of American policy toward Israel
and the Palestinians. In an epilogue, we will examine how the elements
described and analyzed in earlier administrations have changed during the
administration of George W. Bush, and how the dynamics of change played
out through 2006. We will find that some advocates, and some sets of
beliefs, grew in influence, and some receded at least temporarily.

How special is it?

Generally, those who speak of a "special relationship" between the United States and Israel are referring to the cultural, religious, moral, historical and emotional ties between the peoples of the two nations. It is a phrase often used to refer to one set of explanations for favorable American policies toward Israel, in contradistinction to strategic arguments for cooperation and support. Often, arguments for support of Israel cast in terms of affinities and moral or religious obligations are more effective with target audiences than arguments based on Israel's asserted strategic value. However, the resulting policies are not limited to moral or emotional support or guarantees of Israel's security, but involve very real economic, military and political assistance, often of Israeli governments which then pursue policies not favored, or even actively opposed, by the United States. Some of that support can be quantified, and compared with how the United States treats other states, including strategic and ideological allies.

Israel has been the largest recipient of U.S. foreign aid in the period since World War II; it was the largest recipient for the years 1976–2004, when Iraq began to account for more aid.[6] Total economic and military aid, including loans and grants, amounted to over $146 billion (in constant 2004 dollars) in the period 1946 through 2004. Most of that aid was given after 1970, and all loan programs were converted to grant programs in 1981 (Economic Support Funds, or ESF) and 1985 (Foreign Military Financing, or FMF). At Israel's request, ESF funds are being phased out by 2008, partially offset by increased FMF funds; however, the FY2007 budget request for aid to Israel totals $2.59 billion, about 30 million more than FY2006.[7] Unlike other aid recipients, whose funds are parceled out over the fiscal year and allocated to audited programs, Israel by law receives its aid money within 30 days of the start of the fiscal year, and ESF funds are unallocated and essentially unaudited. Also unlike other recipients, Israel can use approximately one-quarter of its FMF funds to purchase from Israeli, rather than American, manufacturers.[8] FMF constitutes approximately 23 percent of the Israeli defense budget.

These direct aid figures measure only a part of the total economic benefit of the relationship. Israel is one of three countries (the others being Canada and Mexico) that benefit from laws permitting tax deductions for contributions to foreign charities. Such contributions are thought to exceed $1 billion per year; some go to settler organizations and others who could not under United States law be the beneficiaries of ESF or other aid funds. In 1985, the two countries signed a Free Trade Agreement that resulted in the elimination of all customs duties between the countries and a 200 percent increase in Israeli exports to the United States.[9]

The military support given by the United States, including FMF, is intended to allow Israel to maintain a "Qualitative Military Edge" (QME) over all neighboring militaries.[10] In April 1988, Israel was declared a "major

non-NATO ally" of the United States, which gave Israel preferential treat-
ment as a bidder on U.S. defense contracts and allowed it to acquire surplus
American equipment at reduced or no cost. Israel participates in several
Mediterranean-based NATO programs. It also participates in major United
States research and development programs: Israel is developing the Arrow
antiballistic missile for the Strategic Defense Initiative at a cost to the
United States of over $1 billion, and participating in development of the F-
35 Joint Strike Force fighter aircraft. Under Memoranda of Understanding
from 1981 and 1983, Israel and the United States coordinate strategic planning and war-fighting capabilities in biannual meetings of a Joint Political
and Military Group. Joint military exercises and U.S. stockpiling of materiel
in Israel began in 1984. Since 2001, annual multi-agency meetings have
addressed long-term strategic issues.

These programs are visible signs of a much more dramatic truth: over the
years since 1970, and particularly since 1981, Israel has increasingly been
able to depend upon the United States in maintaining an unassailable security position. The Israel Defense Forces have married their logistics, planning
and technology development to those of the American Defense Department,
and achieved interoperability not matched by any other ally of the United
States. A policy of mutual assistance has become embedded in habits of
thinking, institutional design, programs, staffing and budgets. Israel's
potential adversaries have either been brought on side, as with Egypt and
Jordan, or have long come to understand that even without commitment of
American troops, Israel cannot be defeated militarily.

Similarly, the United States has given Israeli governments political
support unlike that afforded any other ally. Some has come in the form of
added money: when Israel spun into deep recession in the 1980s, the United
States converted all aid to grants and added $1.5 billion in one-time aid;
when Israel kept out of Desert Storm as requested in 1991, it received $650
million and Patriot missiles; faced with an influx of Soviet immigrants in
1992, Israel received $10 billion in housing loan guarantees; in the after-
math of the 2003 Iraq invasion Israel received $9 billion in loan guarantees
and $1 billion in added FMF grants; and even as Israel's implementation of
the Wye Agreement stalled in 1999, President Clinton insisted on $1.2
billion in added grants. Beginning with Kissinger's shuttle diplomacy in
1973 and accelerating after the Camp David accords under President Carter,
the costs of implementing agreements favored by the United States have
been underwritten in large part by the United States.

Often U.S. support comes in the form of political protection against the
rest of the international community. The United States has vetoed 39
United Nations Security Council Resolutions criticizing or making demands
upon Israel, out of a total of 181 resolutions vetoed by all permanent
members of the Security Council in the period 1946 to May 2006.[11] Many
other resolutions were withdrawn because of the certainty of a veto by the
United States. President George W. Bush supported Israel's refusal to allow

a U.N. investigation of Israel's 2002 incursion into Ramallah in spite of Israel's earlier consent to the investigation and Bush's own criticism of the operation. Because of the relationship between the U.S. and Israel, no peace process is possible without the participation of the American administration. Since with few exceptions American presidents have allowed the Israeli government to determine whether the security situation permitted concessions on land or the conditions of the occupation, Israel's position on when to engage in negotiations and how to structure negotiations is immeasurably strengthened.

Just as the justifications for this unique level of bilateral support are seen as admirable or malign, depending upon the beliefs of the observer, so are policy results. As noted, there is near universal public support for policies that are seen to guarantee Israel's continued existence and security, and security includes some level of economic security. Further, there is no question that during the Cold War, Israel provided valuable services in providing intelligence, developing and demonstrating war-fighting techniques with American arms against Soviet systems, and more generally devaluing alliances with the Soviet Union. Even during the Cold War period, however, realist critics argued that the empowering of Israel encouraged a dangerous and costly impunity when Israel did not in fact share American policy interests or goals. Its military was superior to those of Soviet client states which were Israel's adversaries, but not very useful against overt Soviet use of force, and not capable of being integrated into regional efforts involving Arab states.[12] Richard Nixon was greatly impressed by Israel's value in discouraging a Soviet-backed Syria in 1970; but Henry Kissinger had all he could do to prevent Israel's destruction of the Egyptian army in the desert in 1973, and a damaging Arab oil embargo followed that war. Ronald Reagan had mixed feelings about Israel's pre-emptive destruction of the Iraqi nuclear facilities at Osirak, but was chagrined to be pulled involuntarily into strategic, domestic and moral dilemmas by Ariel Sharon's war of choice in Lebanon. Israel pursued its own interests, first and foremost security as defined by Israelis. As it did so, it repeatedly raised questions about whether American empowerment of and identification with Israel created a powerful and reliable ally, or a free agent that was a principal cause of Middle East crises that damaged relations with Arab states and Muslim populations, and that fueled resentment boiling over into terrorism.

After 1989, any strategic advantage Israel provided against Soviet ambitions was gone, and the 1991 Gulf War demonstrated that Israel's relationships with the United States and with its neighbors could impede or complicate American policy goals, even goals shared by Israel. However, Israel's domestic advocates argued that Israel's role in American policy – as a democratic example in a region of autocracy and theocracy, and as a uniquely effective ally against rogue states, terrorism and weapons proliferation – was more important than ever. Those who had been skeptical of Israel's value in the Cold War were at least as skeptical that Israel presented solutions to these issues rather than being a cause of them. After the terrorist attacks of 11 September 2001, these arguments became central to American foreign policy, and once again those favoring support of Israel and of Israel's policy choices broadly prevailed.

A little realism about the national interest

All policy makers claim to act in the national interest, and much of the debate concerning America's relationship with Israel has been cast in terms of American national security interests. Hans Morgenthau joined his famous dictum that the central goal of every state's foreign policy is to achieve "the national interest in terms of power" with his assurance that the true states-man would know the security needs of the country, and thus the national interest.[13] Morgenthau's complaint was that there had been few such states-men after the first century of American nationhood (Morgenthau 1951). Kenneth Thompson, E. H. Carr and Kenneth Waltz also demonstrated the dangers of inattention to vital security interests defined in terms of power in the international system. However, when national survival is not at stake, the struggle among executive, legislative and interest group actors sharing power over decision making is likely to dominate foreign policy formulation (Milner 1997: 4, 14).

Like the "general welfare" and the "public interest," the national interest is typically defined either so broadly in terms of core values as to be useless in rigorous policy analysis (e.g. survival and security of the state, sover-eignty, economic subsistence) or so specifically in terms of policy "sub-goals" as to represent the subjective beliefs and priorities of advocates (George 1987).[14] Power, the measure used by realists, is a means to a funda-mental goal, security; security is always context dependent. Policy prefer-ences will be defined by leaders and advocates in light of their principled and causal beliefs, their affiliations and the character of their constituencies (Milner 1997: 15). Preferences may be "wrong," in that they misjudge other international actors and lead to adverse results. The United States is suffi-ciently powerful to approximate its major policy goals even if it makes mis-judgments concerning regional and systemic alignments and reactions; it can therefore often afford to continue debating its national interests in the face of what are arguably poor or unexpected outcomes of particular policies.[15] We will be more interested in the uses made of national interest and national security arguments than in their objective results as policy.[16]

In arguments about the national interest, nearly all members of the American policy community fell into one of two groups: those who saw Israel as a strategic asset, and those who accepted a moral obligation to guar-antee Israel's security but saw Israel in strategic terms as a burden (Mansour 1994).[17] Strategic asset advocates argued for exclusive support of Israel, as the Arabs could have only a "temporary convergence of interests" with the United States (Indyk *et al.* 1983: 13). They relied upon shared values as assurance of reliability, but not as the basis of support, as that would imply dependence and vulnerability (see, Tucker 1981). They tended not to address problems of Israeli dissent from U.S. positions or its adventurism, and saw any diminution of Israel's capabilities or freedom of action as a threat to its value as an asset.[18] During the Cold War, they believed all enemies of Israel were under Soviet influence; thereafter, radical Arab states and Islamic fundamentalism were the common enemies (e.g. Spiegel 1990–1991).[19]

Strategic asset advocates were opposed by skeptics who doubted Israel could ever fight the Soviet Union because of concern for the welfare of some two million Soviet Jews, because the 1973 war experience exposed the limits of sustained Israeli operations and because likely Soviet targets (the Gulf, Iran) were beyond effective Israeli operating range.[20] Skeptics were concerned about the fragility of Arab regimes with which the U.S. wanted better relations but with which Israel was hostile. They were not impressed by what Israel could offer beyond weapons evaluation and intelligence, which they considered the least Israel should do in return for massive aid. They were prepared to offer security guarantees, but linked to progress toward settlement of the Arab–Israeli conflict.[21] Such conditionality was anathema to strategic asset advocates, both because it would invite tests by Israel's enemies and because America's guarantees after Vietnam were not thought reliable. In fact, Israel's advocates knew that there was an unwritten guarantee, the advantage of which was that it did not cost Israel anything.

One need not doubt the sincerity of any of these advocates to appreciate that each understood the advantage, and perhaps the necessity, of casting arguments in terms of the national interest. Henry Kissinger acknowledged that "Israel's security could be preserved in the long run only by anchoring it to a strategic interest of the United States, and not to the sentiments of individuals" (Kissinger 1982: 203–4). Moral and cultural ties were insufficient to generate the economic, military and political support that the United States has provided since 1967; an image of Israel as key ally and possible strategic asset, made feasible by the events of 1967 and 1970, was necessary (Bar-Siman-Tov 1998).

The actors: the president

The theory and reality of presidential power in foreign affairs have been debated since before the republic was founded. Alexander Hamilton argued that the "[d]ecision, activity, secrecy and dispatch" required for effective diplomacy required a preponderance of power in the chief executive (Federalist No. 70, in Hamilton *et al.* 1937 (1787): 455).[22] During the early years of the Cold War, the "imperial" presidency amassed more power in foreign affairs than even Hamilton could have dreamed; the people and the Congress generally conceded the need for secrecy and instantaneous response, signified by the president's "nuclear football." The Constitution gave little of this power expressly; most of it accreted through custom, tradition, perceived necessity, presidential assertiveness, judicial interpretation and legislative acquiescence. Accordingly, much of the power was subject to dissipation as conditions changed.

Before the end of the Cold War, the excesses of Vietnam and Watergate undercut the willingness of the American people, and of the Congress, to entrust unobserved and nearly unconditional power to the chief executive. "Intermestic" issues such as trade involved domestic players and consequences, exploding the number of domestic groups, and Congressional committees, with vital concerns in foreign policy. Presidential prerogative was increasingly subject to congressional oversight, budget restrictions and "legislative vetoes." Ideological polarization occurred concurrently with this increased competition for control. Experienced practitioners worried that a pragmatic "Establishment" in foreign affairs had been replaced by an ideological and often irresponsible "professional elite," seeking power in the White House as "courtiers" and firing partisan shots from nearby policy institutes (Destler *et al.* 1984). In 1966, Aaron Wildavsky had posited "two presidencies," one in domestic affairs enmeshed in politics and one in foreign affairs where presidential power was pre-eminent; by 1991 he conceded that "as ideological and partisan divisions have come to reinforce each other . . ." foreign policy has become more like domestic policy – a realm marked by serious partisan division in which the president cannot count on a free ride" (Oldfield and Wildavsky 1991).

As institutional presidential pre-eminence in foreign policy receded, the personal beliefs, leadership skills and credibility of the president and his principal advisers grew in importance. As ideology increasingly drove policy debates, the building of political networks based on ideology as well as interests became necessary and prevalent.

Accordingly, the elements which are critical to understand are the belief system of the president – his principled and causal beliefs as they relate to the principal players and issues in the Middle East – and his ability to translate those beliefs into policy and to embed them institutionally. Whatever the ideas and skills of the president, there will always be limits on his ability to frame and implement policy. Exogenous events may make announced policy totally impracticable, or even change some of the president's assumptions. Forces engaged in the Congress, in public and media opinion and in electoral politics may make policy impossible, or too costly given other parts of the president's agenda. However, the personal leadership qualities of the president, including his commitment and consistency, communication skills, organizational capacity, and political and coalition-building skills, can be decisive if brought to bear on a particular issue. As many have noted, persistent personal attention by the president can overcome substantial political and bureaucratic opposition or inertia and even change institutional structure and policy assumptions; as Richard Neustadt would warn, choosing one's battles wisely is critical to marshalling the essential prestige of the office (Neustadt 1990).

Throughout his several excellent studies of American policy in the Arab–Israeli conflict, William Quandt's opinion has been constant: domestic politics and the lobbies can occasionally be influential, particularly during election years; the national interest perspective can support diametrically opposed policies; bureaucratic politics explains uninspired staff work and implementation problems, but not major policy choices; and the most important element is always the policy view of the president and his closest advisers (Quandt 1977; Quandt 1986a; Quandt 2001). However, while Quandt notes times when presidential policy preferences were explicitly or implicitly informed by a political cost–benefit analysis, and occasions when presidential initiatives were frustrated, he does not use such events to test his operating assumptions. When presidents choose policies in line with Israeli preferences, it is often difficult to judge the extent to which that is due to cultural or ideological conditioning, unwillingness to pay the political price for bucking Israel or pure strategic analysis. However, changes in announced policies in the face of Israeli or domestic opposition call for more careful parsing. We will examine cases where the effects of domestic pressure and constraint seem clear.

The perceived power of a lobby is sometimes more useful to presidents than limiting. It can be used as cover for policies chosen for other reasons or used as a bargaining tool with those opposing the lobby's position; and the lobby can be called on for help or political credit when the president's policies match those of the lobby. If the power of the president is the power to persuade and to negotiate, such uses of domestic political players as helpers, foils, excuses and threats must be tools of the trade (Neustadt 1990). However, proponents of presidential power such as Steven Spiegel overreach their evidence when they in effect argue that those are the only or primary roles of the pro-Israel lobby.[23] A 1990 article suggests that in spite of his earlier insistence that Israel's role as a strategic asset was a result of presidential calculation, he recognized that a positive moral image was central to the cultural affinity many Americans feel toward Israel, and thus to the relationship (Spiegel 1990–1991).[24]

Presidential leadership is a principal factor in the setting of policy toward Israel. However, presidential leadership in directions not desired by Israel or its supporters has been episodic, and "victories" over the lobby have been notable for their rarity and impermanence. We must take due account of the president's power. In each case, however, we should ask: is this change in policy better accounted for by adjustments in the ideas embraced by the president, or by his inability effectively to embed and implement his ideas?

We will be examining three Republican presidents, who were very different men in terms of their beliefs and abilities, and who found themselves in substantially different political and geopolitical contexts.

The actors: the lobby's place in domestic politics

The United States has developed a peculiarly open form of democratic pluralism, allowing groups with shared interests and values to access many points in the policy-making process and to compete for influence over national policy (Truman 1971; Risse-Kappen 1991). Generally, such dynamics are more important in setting policy on domestic issues, where constituencies are energized by more immediate impacts and act through their congressional delegations, than in foreign policy, where the impacts are generally more diffuse and the president is invested with substantial authority. Policy toward Israel is an exception. As we will see, it is either an exception to, or a particularly powerful example of, nearly every general rule about foreign policy formulation.

All observers of American foreign policy note both pragmatic and moralistic or value-laden elements.[25] Americans are said to combine pragmatism with an optimistic belief in the possibility of solutions, through technological means or by negotiation and conciliation. Belief in the universal validity of American values encourages identification with those thought to share them. In the Middle East, only Israel is said to have a democratic form of government, something approaching a free-market economy, and ideals of freedom and individualism. From the founding of the republic, American leaders have at least rhetorically identified their country with "Zion," often explicitly asserting that the United States was the heir of biblical ideals associated with the ancient Jewish kingdom, the "chosen people."[26] The somewhat idealized image many Americans have had of modern Israelis, based upon conflation of modern Israel with biblical Israel, popular cultural portrayals and the efforts of advocates, is of Western-style liberal democrats, pragmatic problem solvers and fierce but highly moral pioneers and fighters. These images form the core of a powerful cultural affinity, as well as the cause of disillusionment when Israelis seem not to live up to the values attributed to them.

Public opinion is said to "influence public policy, but often in very indirect ways" (Quandt 1977: 17). Realists, from Hamilton to Niebuhr to Lippmann, Morgenthau and Kennan,[27] have feared the pernicious effects of public opinion on foreign policy, believing the public to have little interest, less knowledge, short attention spans and quixotic emotional swings between aggressiveness and self-righteous isolationism (Hoffmann 1968: Chs 4–6; Holsti 1996: 5; Holsti 2002: 344–8).[28] Surveys generally confirm that Americans do not follow foreign affairs in any detail, and that therefore their opinions on particular issues or regional actors tend to have shallow roots; on most issues they will follow the leadership of the president (Waltz 1971; Kegley and Wittkopf 1996: 265–6, 288–9). There are relatively few region-specific issues on which public opinion has been tracked with any regularity, much less where opinion has remained stable.[29]

The Arab–Israeli dispute is again a significant exception to these generalities. Polls since the declaration of the State of Israel consistently showed that Americans identified with, or empathized with, Israel in preference to Arabs in ratios that usually ranged from 3:1 to 7:1 (Moughrabi 1987; Newport and Carroll 2006). The support, while strong, has always been conditional: the ratios increased after acts of terrorism attributed to Arabs, and decreased both when Arabs acted "against type" (Sadat's trip to Jerusalem, for example) and when Israel appeared to have violated values or norms of behavior attributed to them (after the 1982 Beirut camp massacres). Few supported use of American troops, and some who "supported" Israel opposed arms sales and favored aid cuts. Polls also consistently showed support for a negotiated settlement based on land for peace, and recognition of the Palestine Liberation Organization conditioned on rejection of terror and recognition of Israel's right to exist – positions consistent with values said to be American.

One study holds that only when opinion has been consistently and dominantly (over 80 percent) on one side of an issue are conflicting policy choices effectively ruled out politically; preponderant opinions (70–79 percent) have substantial impact on policy trends, but bare majorities have little or no effect, usually not even registering with policy makers (Graham 1994).[30] The president is also likely to have substantial difficulty initiating a policy that involves diffuse potential gains but costs that are borne by a concentrated group that is highly organized and "disproportionately enfranchised" (Evans 1993: 412–14 and chapters cited). That is the circumstance when a president undertakes an Arab–Israeli peace process involving assumptions about Israel's needs different from those of Israel's advocates. There is broad but shallow public support for even-handed policies encouraging a peace process and Palestinian rights; those who participate actively fight with single-minded intensity against forcing Israel to compromise.

Nearly all Americans have opinions about Israel and American policy relating thereto, but as is the case with most issues, most do not devote much time, effort or money trying to affect policy. The principal sources of committed and uncompromising supporters of Israel are the Jewish and evangelical Christian communities.

Jewish Americans have a long tradition of effective social and political organization. Although initially much of the organized Jewish community was not Zionist, identification with and anxiety about Israel solidified after 1947 and intensified after the 1967 war. As American Jews increasingly defined their Jewishness in terms of Israel, leadership within the community became defined by involvement in efforts to support Israel. Nevertheless, there has always been tension between those who support Israel as a safe home for the world's Jews and an expression of idealistic Judaism, and those who support the hard-line policies of particular Israeli governments. The great majority of American Jews are non-Orthodox liberal or progressive Democrats, and they favor a negotiated peace process and recognition of Palestinian human and political rights when consistent with Israeli security. However, those who have supported the maximalist Revisionist Zionist program of the Likud in Israel, involving the retention and settlement of biblical Israel, have increasingly controlled the organizations that wield effective political power in the Congress and in executive departments. How that happened will be a significant part of our story.

The American Israel Political Affairs Committee (AIPAC) is the most effective and powerful of the entities influencing policy toward Israel in the Congress. Starting in the Reagan years, it also has been effective in the executive branch, although it suffered a setback with the 2005 criminal indictment of AIPAC policy director Steve Rosen. The Conference of Presidents of Major American Jewish Organizations (Presidents Conference) was formed to represent organized American Jewry to the executive branch; in spite of the fact that the majority of the individual Jews who belong to the conference's member organizations are progressives, its executive director has effectively used its masthead of 52 national organizations to support the Likud. Other organizations usually aligned with AIPAC and the Presidents Conference include the Zionist Organization of America and the Anti-Defamation League. This group of organizations, or sometimes AIPAC alone, is referred to as "the lobby."

The lobby started with a strong base of national empathy for Israel; its first challenge was to reinforce the image of Israel as America's cultural, religious and democratic sibling, and to persuade the public and American officials that Israel was entitled to support against adversaries whose culture and values were antithetical to those shared with Israel. Often, Israel's conduct complicated that task. In part, the problem was that the "values" thought to be shared were not in fact identical, something often not well understood even by American Jews.[31] In part, the problem was confusion between broadly stated values and the way in which the respective societies translated them into norms of behaviour. Criticism of behavioral norms does not necessarily mean disagreement with the lasting values of the society (Windsor 2002: 86–7). The policies of Menachem Begin, Yitzhak Shamir and Ariel Sharon toward Palestinians and the Occupied Territories implemented particularist Zionist, not universalist, values; and the methods used were sometimes jarring to liberal American (including American Jewish) sensibilities. Those who fervently supported Israel as an important part of their self-identity sought bases on which to reduce that cognitive dissonance. The lobby provided those arguments, and mobilized efforts to sell and defend the resulting images of Israel in the Jewish community, the media and academe, as well as in the Congress and the White House. Generally, there was no organized effort opposing AIPAC, so that the competition for policy dominance was more often between AIPAC and the president than among competing interest groups.

The second challenge for the lobby was to translate broadly shared positive images and affinity into affirmative policy. The methods used by the lobby until the Reagan administration centered on the Congress, using traditional lobbying, directed campaign financing and networking with media and other organizations. Beginning with Reagan, the lobby added extensive executive branch lobbying, both at the White House and in departments such as defense. Also beginning in the Reagan years, the evangelical Christian community mobilized politically and became allied with the established lobby in supporting Israel. Not until the second Bush administration, however, did Christian conservatives, many of them strongly Zionist, combine substantial power in the Congress with access to the White House.

One part of the explanation for Israel's success in achieving American support is its separate penetration, with the help of its domestic allies, of all levels of the policy-making process.[32] It does so directly, as posited by Keohane in his study of the influence of small allies (diplomatic relations, working relationships inside relevant bureaucracies and organized domestic group support in the Congress), but also indirectly through labor, eleemosynary and religious organizations, the media and policy institutes, the political parties and political campaign organizations (Keohane 1971). Many of these activities were increasingly coordinated by AIPAC, but there continued to be direct relationships in most if not all of the named areas.

In the 1970s and 1980s, new domestic political institutions and alignments were used effectively by the lobby, although sometimes to the considerable discomfiture of the Jewish community out of which it had grown.[33] The Reagan administration was the first to combine fervent anticommunism, affinity-based support of Israel, and ties to the neoconservative movement and the Christian Right. Reagan drew on, and strengthened, conservative policy institutes and the new "professional elite" in foreign policy. The Congress had since 1974 restructured itself substantially, in large part to be able to compete for control of foreign policy. Campaign finance laws had created powerful new tools for interest groups that were prepared to use them aggressively. It had long been noted that policy related to the Middle East (or other areas of significant political controversy) became quiescent during presidential election years, as presidents avoided the passions and risks of failure inherent in those issues.[34] In the 1980s, AIPAC coordinated political action committee donations to insure that issues relating to Israel became the basis of national campaigns for, and particularly against, sitting members of Congress.

The growing assertiveness of Congress was important, because Congress is institutionally more politically responsive to interest group pressure than is the executive. Its most tangible role in foreign policy is control over expenditures; it is institutionally incapable of diplomatic initiatives or ongoing management of foreign affairs.[35] However, in the Middle East, most active (as opposed to declaratory) diplomacy has been defined in terms of military and economic aid and arms sales, issues over which the Congress has considerable authority. If the president could neither condition aid to Israel nor sell arms to Arabs because of congressional opposition, he could be more than embarrassed; he could be thwarted. During the second Bush administration, the leadership of Congress and the president's own political base were disproportionately populated by conservative Christians who would not tolerate pressure on Israel; the question then was whether the Congress constituted a constraint on or an echo of the policies set in the Oval Office.

A recent paper by two prominent realists, Professor John Mearsheimer of the University of Chicago and then-Dean Stephen Walt of Harvard's Kennedy School of Government, demonstrates how the nature of "the lobby" can be misunderstood and its influence overstated (Mearsheimer and Walt 2006a).[36] The authors are sure they know the national interest, and find that policies favoring Israel have ill-served that interest. They attribute the diversion of policy from the true path to the "Israel Lobby." However, they define that lobby so broadly that it includes nearly everyone who generally supports Israel, including persons and entities who have heatedly attacked each other on what support should mean. They sometimes conflate "Jews" with "the lobby," a serious mistake. They argue that Israel is a strategic liability and does not deserve support on moral grounds; both arguments can be made, but these authors rely too much upon crude generalizations and badly analyzed sources to do so persuasively.[37] They are correct, as shown by countless polls and other measures, that American identification with Israel has cost the United States dearly in Arab and Muslim opinion, but that does not clinch their broader argument that there is no justification for American policy.

Mearsheimer and Walt claim that "AIPAC, which is a *de facto* agent for a foreign government, has a stranglehold on the U.S. Congress." That is a remarkable statement for at least two reasons. (1) The beliefs of AIPAC's leaders have increasingly made it more nearly the agent of a party – the Likud – than of the Israeli government. AIPAC has had serious disputes with prime ministers Rabin, Barak and Sharon when they advocated either negotiated or unilateral concessions. (2) AIPAC reinforces images of Israel, provides data and arguments, and enforces political discipline through various means, but its power is derivative of, and dependent on, the degree to which it reflects politically popular and feasible policies. When there is a credible Palestinian negotiating partner and an Israeli government prepared to negotiate, AIPAC is essentially powerless to prevent American support of such efforts.

The authors make the dubious assertion that pressure from Israel and the "Israel Lobby" was a "critical element" in the Bush administration's decision to invade Iraq in 2003.[38] After 9/11, President Bush was empowered to act in almost any way he saw fit. Neoconservative advisers such as Paul Wolfowitz and Douglas Feith urged invasion and, as strong supporters of Israel, undoubtedly believed it would benefit Israel. However, the evidence is that most Israeli leaders saw Iran as a greater threat to Israel than Iraq, and simply found it impolitic to press that view in the face of the administration's determination to oust Saddam (*WP* 7 Feb. 2002: A22; Brom 2003).[39]

Those in the Jewish community who supported the war and the democratization of the Middle East argued that the leadership of mainstream Jewish pro-Israel groups, including AIPAC, were too wedded to Democratic New Deal politics to do what was required in Israel's interest: fight for the neoconservative agenda (e.g. Schwartz 2006).

The Mearsheimer–Walt paper is a strangely sloppy product of respected if frustrated scholars. However, the reaction to their paper demonstrates the tendency for argument on these issues to escalate quickly beyond analysis to *ad hominem* attacks meant to silence rather than advance debate. Alan Dershowitz of Harvard Law School led dozens to the attack with a lengthy rebuttal on the Kennedy School website. He picked at many statements (most of them peripheral) and exposed several misuses of sources, but the burden of his criticism was that those who made such arguments were paranoid purveyors of views found in the Protocols of the Elders of Zion, Nazi and Soviet propaganda and the rantings of white supremacist David Duke (Dershowitz 2006).[40] Elsewhere, he repeatedly called the authors "liars" and "bigots" (*HCrim* 21 Mar. 2006). Neoconservative Max Boot compared the paper to a pamphlet by demagogue Senator Joe McCarthy as an example of paranoid American politics (Boot 2006). Johns Hopkins professor Eliot Cohen, wrote an opinion column entitled "Yes, It's Anti-Semitic," in which he accused the authors of "systematically select[ing] everything unfair, ugly or wrong about Jews" (Cohen 2006). Even some who did not hurl epithets strained mightily to neutralize the Mearsheimer–Walt argument. David Gergen, who served four presidents, stated that with the exception of the profane Nixon, he never heard any discussion of the Israel lobby in the White House, although there was discussion of evangelicals and other pressure groups (Gergen 2006). Given that Gergen was in the Reagan White House, this book will demonstrate that either his memory is faulty or his access was remarkably circumscribed.

Others have offered more nuanced analysis of domestic constraints on the president than Mearsheimer and Walt. William Quandt concluded that Congress could set limits on presidential authority and require respect for Israel's interests, but could not set policy, and normally respected presidential arguments on national security grounds (Quandt 1977: 22). So broadly stated, the conclusions are sound. However, the question we seek to answer is whether limits on presidential authority became progressively so constraining as to make declaratory policy opposed by the lobby impracticable.

Steven Spiegel claimed to have disproven the idea that the lobby significantly affected policy. For example, he argued that arms sales to Arabs became more difficult by 1985 not because of the strength of the pro-Israeli lobby, but because Arabs had not produced the movement toward settlement with Israel that congressmen had expected. Reagan could have had his way if he had wanted to sell more arms; "Congress has been largely irrelevant to U.S. participation in the Middle East peace process" (Spiegel 1986: 388). That is unsustainable: as we will see, President Reagan could not deliver arms sales he had promised, which derailed Reagan's plan to rely on Jordan to represent Palestinians; Congress increased aid to Israel over Reagan's heated objections in 1982; and the administration concluded that it had to work with AIPAC thereafter. Spiegel does not seriously address the possibility that Congress, whether responding to a lobby or to their own calculation of the national interest, had deprived Reagan of options.

American policy toward Israel is unusually, perhaps uniquely, subject to constraints reflecting broad public affinity with the Jewish state and enforced by an energized and effective network of advocates. Once the origins and limitations of such constraints are studied, the course of U.S. policy cannot be considered unexpected.

2 The pro-Israel community prior to 1981

Introduction

By 1981, the American pro-Israel lobby advocated a conception of Israel not just as a fellow democracy sharing Western and biblical values, but as America's exclusive regional strategic partner against Soviet and other threats to American interests. The lobby worked to suppress beliefs inconsistent with those concepts.

From the perspective of a few decades earlier, that was not a predictable role for American Jewish leaders. Although Israeli officials had had major roles in establishing the principal organizations constituting the lobby, the organizations grew out of a Jewish community that, unlike Israel's, was largely universalist and socially liberal. The policies of Likud-led Israeli governments made many Jews uncomfortable. Yet pro-Israel, and pro-Likud, advocacy became the core requirement of public leadership among American Jews. This chapter will analyze how that happened, how relationships among the lobby, Jewish organizations and Israel developed, and what explained the political effectiveness of the resulting lobby.

Early organized American Jewry

Traditions of organizing, federations and defense agencies

The American Jewish experience was always different from that of other diaspora Jews. In August 1790, President George Washington wrote to assure descendants of Portuguese Marrano Jews in Rhode Island that his government gave "to bigotry no sanction, to persecution no assistance." America was unlike other countries because all citizens "possess alike liberty of conscience and immunities of citizenship" (Goldberg 1996: 83). The assurance was welcome. Freedom and equality, however, carried new challenges: there being no state-sanctioned religion, all were free to disassociate and, unlike in Europe where a *shtadlan* ("court Jew") would be appointed, anyone could claim to speak for a community. America's five synagogues could not decide in 1790 who should speak for them, and Washington received letters from three synagogues (ibid.: 84–6). A felt need for protection and support, concern about assimilation and loss of heritage, and a struggle to maintain cohesion, would remain distinctive themes of American Jewish community life; and fear would remain "the greatest single factor accounting for Jews' high level of political activity" (Isaacs 1974: 15).

Jews in the Pale of Settlement always had a *pushke* (alms box) in their home, collecting money for the poor. This tradition of welfare translated into philanthropic organizations and social norms requiring Jewish leaders to demonstrate generosity. German Jews began organizing charitable societies in the 1840s, and Jewish hospitals, fraternal organizations and educational institutions thereafter (Chanes 2001). It was a short step to political fundraising, to secure through politics the welfare they had supported through philanthropy.

Jewish social service agencies in each community formed federations to engage in joint fundraising, allocation of funds and coordination of services. The federations also had advocacy functions, largely seeking government funding. The federation movement had a central role in local Jewish community life, serving to identify community leaders. An umbrella body, the Council of Jewish Federations (CJF), guided local federations in planning and budgeting and represented approximately 200 federations to the governments of Canada, the United States and (since 1948) Israel. The annual General Assembly of the CJF served as a forum for Jewish leaders to sort out national and international priorities.

There are three "defense" agencies, originally formed to fight anti-Semitism. The oldest, the American Jewish Committee (AJC), was formed by the German Jewish establishment in 1906 to respond to issues including anti-Jewish pogroms in czarist Russia. It was for years a self-selected group; by 1918 Eastern European Jews critical of the AJC's exclusivity and lack of popular mandate formed the American Jewish Congress (AJCongress). The AJC eschewed confrontational tactics as risking unwanted attention; the more blue-collar and leftist AJCongress pioneered the use of protest and litigation in combating discrimination. The AJCongress was formed by Zionists, while the AJC reflected the establishment Jewish view before World War II that Zionism was dangerous to Jews in America. The Anti-Defamation League of B'nai B'rith (ADL) was created in 1913 in reaction to a notorious lynching. ADL's agenda expanded over the years from discrimination to civil rights, church–state separation, Holocaust education and Israel. It was the most aggressive and litigious of the three.

Between World Wars I and II, local community relations councils (CRCs) were established, often funded by the AJC and ADL, as "fire brigades" against anti-Semitism. In 1944, these councils were included in a National Community Relations Advisory Council (NCRAC), formed under the aegis of CJF as a national coordinating and planning council including the three defense agencies.[1] NCRAC grew to include the three main synagogue unions, the three largest Jewish women's groups and over 100 local councils. NCRAC negotiated an annual *Joint Program Plan* covering the largely liberal causes to which the groups were jointly committed.

American Judaism, American Zionism

"American values and culture have helped forge a Judaism that is, in many respects, unlike its counterpart(s) in Israel" (Cohen and Liebman 2000: 12). Cohen and Liebman show that "adaptionist" American Judaism has been marked by universalism, moralism, personalism/individualism and voluntarism. By this they mean, *inter alia*, that American Jews believe that Judaism's message is for all, that they value ethical behavior over ritual and that they accept the individual's right to identify as a Jew or not and to personalize religious experience. Only about a quarter of American Jews are strictly observant, and the great majority who claim affiliation with a synagogue identify with the Conservative or Reform traditions rather than the Orthodox. There has for decades been anxious study of Jewish assimilation; it is generally accepted that generations with no personal experience of the Holocaust or overt anti-Semitism are more loosely connected to synagogues or to traditional Jewish causes.

Zionism was very slow to find support in America, especially among the successful and assimilated, but even among the newly arrived poor. Rabbi I. M. Wise, founder of American Reform Judaism and a dominant Jewish leader early in the last century, said, "We are unalterably opposed to political Zionism ... Zion was a precious possession of the past ... but it is not our hope for the future. America is our Zion" (Grose 1983: 44). The first breakthrough was the conversion of Louis Brandeis, prominent lawyer, confidant of President Wilson and future Supreme Court Justice, in 1912. Brandeis advocated Zionism as embracing both American and Jewish ideals, by helping oppressed Jews abroad. Zionism was, then, a duty of all loyal Americans who were Jews. He persuaded his friend President Wilson to support the British Balfour Declaration. However, the American role was to be philanthropic, not ideological (Rosenthal 2001: 14–16). On the day the Balfour Declaration was issued in 1917, Brandeis said that "Jewish statehood" would be "a most serious menace" (Auerbach 1996: 336). Henry Morgenthau, Sr., American ambassador to Turkey, and Adolph Ochs, publisher of the *New York Times*, joined 28 others, mostly prominent Jews, in a petition to Wilson warning that it was contrary to the principles on which World War I was waged to found a nation on race or religion (Glick 1982: 48).

In the 1930s, both Christian pro-Zionist groups and Jewish anti-Zionist groups were active. In May 1942, the major secular, religious and labor Zionist organizations adopted the "Biltmore Program," setting as a goal a Jewish commonwealth in Palestine to be achieved under American Zionist leadership.[2] This shift reflected changed leadership in Israel and in the United States, and surging membership in the Zionist Organization of America (ZOA) and Hadassah, the women's Zionist organization. Once the horrors of the Holocaust were known and the State of Israel proclaimed, support for the existence and security of Israel was nearly universal among American Jews, the exceptions being traditional Orthodox who still believed that an Israel created by man was blasphemy.

Nevertheless, there was always tension between American Jews and Israelis as to the meaning of Zionism. David Ben-Gurion, when asked what American Jews should do for Israel, said "What we need is Jews" (Tivnan 1987: 29). He pressed for *aliyah* ("going up," or immigration to Israel) by American Jews. In August 1950, Jacob Blaustein, then head of the AJC, traveled to Jerusalem to tell Ben-Gurion that American Jews did not consider themselves in *galut* (exile), and that an America strong in democratic values and safe for Jews was essential for the continued well-being of Israel. Ben-Gurion apologized, and thereafter the role of American Jews was to support Israel financially and politically (ibid.: 32). However, Israeli disdain for diaspora Jews, and for their advice, remained a source of recurring tension.

American Jewish liberalism

Most American Jews are descendants of those who fled oppression and the Holocaust in the period 1881–1948. They identified their worst persecutors with right-wing nationalists and monarchists, and many were committed to socialism. Most arrived in America destitute, and were greeted with hostility by earlier immigrants who feared for their jobs. Their self-interest and prior political associations favored the left.

Jews were essential to every American liberal political movement in the twentieth century. Jews led the National Association for the Advancement of Colored People (NAACP), the leading civil rights organization, from 1915 through 1975; Jews joined with black leaders to push for fair employment practices; Jews were the first presidents of the American Federation of Labor and the National Organization for Women; the first two (and the only serving) Socialist members of Congress have been Jews; and Jews founded the most influential liberal action groups after the Vietnam War, Human Rights Watch and People for the American Way. Most Jews persisted in strongly supporting liberal causes, and the Democratic Party, long after their access and affluence seemingly aligned their interests with conservatives. There were inroads: the ratio of Democratic votes fell from 3:1 to about 2:1 between the 1930s and mid-1960s, rising again after Reagan's first election in 1980 (Table 2, Goldberg 1996: 34). And there were exceptions: Jews split with Blacks over quotas, and the neoconservative movement was led by Jews. Israeli government policies have also led to splits with Blacks and traditional Christian churches over human rights. However, both the leadership of major Jewish organizations and the wider Jewish community remained more liberal, and more Democratic, than the rest of the population (Greenberg and Wald 2001).[3]

American Jews have always supported separation between church and state and minimal state interference in moral matters; they have been internationalist at least to the extent of supporting policies protecting their co-religionists. Those preferences meant support of Jeffersonian and Jacksonian Democrats, regional splits after the Civil War and splits among major parties and Socialists from 1900 to 1932 (Forman 2001). After 1916, however, only in the 1920 and 1980 elections did less than a majority of Jews vote for the Democratic presidential candidate. In both cases the Jewish community was angry at an outgoing Democratic administration, and defections were primarily to liberal third-party candidates rather than to Republicans (Goldberg 1996: 33–5).

Many see this persistent liberalism as "applied Judaism," a natural expression of Jewish values including a belief in *tzedakeh*, the injunction to assist the poorest in the community (Greenberg and Wald 2001: 163–4). However, most observant Jews are conservative. Most Israeli Jews are not social liberals, and there is no Hebrew word for what Americans mean by "liberalism" (Liebman and Cohen 1990: 114). The Jewish state is not egalitarian for non-Jews. If liberalism is applied Judaism, it is American Judaism.

Principal pro-Israel organizations

The Presidents Conference

The Conference of Presidents of Major Jewish Organizations allegedly resulted from the complaint in 1953 of Assistant Secretary of State Henry Byroade to Nahum Goldmann, president of the World Zionist Organization (WZO)[4] that too many Jewish groups sought his time. He wanted a single spokesman (Sachar 1992: 726). Goldmann and Abba Eban persuaded 12 major groups to allow Goldmann to chair an umbrella organization. He enlisted Philip Klutznick, president of B'nai B'rith International, as chair; Klutznick hired Yehuda Hellman, recently arrived from Israel, as director. Hellman, working with Goldmann and Eban, gained unofficial recognition in the executive branch as the voice of the Jewish community on Israel (Goldberg 1996: 152–3).[5]

The Presidents Conference was really the voice of the Israeli government. After American Jews questioned Israeli pronouncements on American policy in Vietnam and Israeli policy in the Territories, several organizations including NCRAC, AJC and the Presidents Conference studied the limits of dissent. All concluded that American Jews had the right to debate Israeli policy privately, but not in public. Working with Israeli Ambassador Simcha Dinitz, the Conference and NCRAC developed tenets to guide American Jews: only Israelis could decide Israeli policy; American Jews must publicly support Israel (ibid.: 207–8).

It became common for former chairs of the Conference to question the policies of Likud-led governments, only to be admonished by the current chair to abide by the agreed *omerta*. In July 1980, 56 prominent American Jews, including three former chairs of the Conference, publicly condemned "[e]xtremists in ... the [Israeli] Government" who endangered and isolated Israel, "undermining the ethical basis for our claims to a life of peace and security." New Conference chair Howard Squadron promptly called such public statements "always unjustified and divisive"; Morris Amitay of AIPAC said American Jews had "more important things to do," namely fighting for Israeli aid and against arms sales to Arabs (Rosenthal 2001: 55).

For many years, the informal agreement was that the Presidents Conference would lobby the State Department and White House, and AIPAC would lobby the Congress. The effectiveness of the Conference was limited by a lack of independent staff and its rule that all policy decisions would be by consensus. As the Conference grew to include over three dozen major Jewish organizations, its procedures grew increasingly unwieldy. Its major functions often seemed to be providing authoritative statements on noncontroversial issues; enforcing discipline on public discourse; carrying any criticism of Israeli policies quietly to Jerusalem; and appearing on the letterhead of AIPAC to increase AIPAC's credibility.

The Israeli origins and early development of AIPAC

When Abba Eban arrived in 1950 to take up dual posts as Israel's permanent representative to the United Nations and ambassador to the United States, he found that "America's relationship with Israel was not institutionalized" (Melman and Raviv 1994: 52). It depended upon aides to President Truman and Truman's relationship with the ailing Zionist leader Chaim Weizmann. Major American Jewish organizations were not focused on Israel. Aid to the struggling infant state was miniscule as compared with that from Europe.

Eban at first lobbied Congress directly, but found that awkward for an ambassador. It also did not address the legislators' primary interest, which was re-election. Eban and fellow Israeli official Teddy Kollek accessed American Jewish political activists and contributors directly, including Barney Balaban of Paramount Pictures and Henry Morgenthau, Jr., Roosevelt's treasury secretary (Melman and Raviv 1994: 54–6). However, what was needed was a permanent and knowledgeable advocate in Congress, and that person was at hand. I. L. ("Si") Kenen had been public relations aide to Rabbi Abba Hillel Silver, Zionist movement leader after the Biltmore Conference. In 1951 he worked for Eban in a similar capacity. Eban asked him to set up a Washington lobbying office for the Zionist movement.[6] He was to be there for months; he headed the office, which eventually became AIPAC, until 1975, and was active in AIPAC and its publications until his death in 1988.

Issues of agency and of dual loyalty have dogged AIPAC. Kenen and his successors always insisted that AIPAC, like Brandeis, supported American values and interests, which would be advanced by a strong democratic ally in Israel. The vast majority of American Jews have generally believed that a secure democracy in Israel is in America's national interest. Formally, AIPAC always represented Americans. Within eight years, the name was changed from American Zionist Committee to American Israel Public Affairs Committee, to reflect the fact that both Zionist and non-Zionist organizations supported the effort. AIPAC and the Presidents Conference soon were represented on each other's boards; by the late 1980s, the AIPAC Executive Committee numbered well over 100, including presidents of 38 major Jewish organizations with memberships of over 4.5 million American Jews (O'Brien 1986: 159).

However, issues of agency persisted. There was close coordination between AIPAC and the government of Israel, if only to avoid embarrassing each other.[7] At times, AIPAC made a point of differentiating its position from that of Israel, but it was not always clear the differences were intended.[8] AIPAC Executive Committee members sometimes stated flatly that they would support Israeli government policies even when those policies changed radically. AIPAC asserted that it spoke for the vast majority of organized American Jewry as represented on its letterhead, but it did not consult those "represented." It could move quickly and aggressively precisely because it was not shackled by requirements of formal consensus within the community. Its leaders came to see its relationship with the larger Jewish community as one of education and training, and of enforcing discipline on public discourse, not of measuring or reflecting the community's sometimes sharply divided views.

Thus, there is a second agency issue: among American Jewry, whom did AIPAC represent? It is plausible to argue that generally it represented the substantial majority of American Jews for whom Israel and her security constituted a core value of their Jewish identity; such persons were generally willing to delegate authority to knowledgeable advocates and to self-censor any doubts about Israeli government policy. It is also plausible to argue that such reliance on the "experts" made AIPAC's executive director and staff free agents, unless major conflicts with other core values or relationships resulted. Such limits began to be felt during the Israeli siege of Beirut in 1982 and the 1987 Intifada; unease was also felt by many liberal Jews over links with the Christian Right. Finally, the role of "Likudniks" within the organization can be seen as determinative, effectively denying those with conflicting views access to the levers of influence.

These issues did not gel until the election of Menachem Begin in 1977. Particularly between 1951 and 1967 the task before Si Kenen and AIPAC was straightforward: to build a relationship with the Congress that would, year after year, increase economic and political support for Israel. Aid to Israel increased from $35 million in 1951 to $126.8 million in 1966; of the $1.12 billion total, some $367.4 million were grants, the remainder being loans on favorable terms. The Export–Import Bank granted $126.2 million in loans during the same period (Mark 2002). Those numbers should however be compared to reparations paid by Germany, which averaged $125 million per year during the same period (90 percent of which were grants), and contributions from world Jewry, predominantly American Jews, which averaged $200 million per year before 1967 (Safran 1978: 123).

Harder to measure, but in the long term more important, was Kenen's quiet success in building a solid base of supporters in Congress, and in coordinating with other pro-Israel organizations and the Israeli government to ensure access as issues arose. Kenen had many friends in Congress, including Hubert Humphrey, who "stood guard" for Israel in the Senate for 25 years, and Humphrey's aide Max Kampelman (Kenen 1981: 80). Kenen worked closely with NCRAC's staff in New York, and with Yehuda Hellman, executive director of the Presidents Conference. Ambassador Eban was "an invisible fourth partner," involved in planning, lobbying and mediating with prickly Jewish leaders (Goldberg 1996: 154).

AIPAC was a shoestring professional operation with five employees, including a secretary in a New York office (where major Jewish organizations were headquartered) and a former Ben-Gurion aide "looking for cooperative local leaders" (Kenen 1981: 70). Until 1966, Kenen often went without his meagre salary, and even lent money to the operation.

The Amitay era of AIPAC

In December 1974, Morris Amitay, aide to Senator Ribicoff, replaced Kenen. With Richard Perle, aide to Senator Jackson, Amitay had just engineered the Jackson–Vanik amendment conditioning trade benefits to the Soviet Union on treatment of Soviet Jews. Amitay, a lawyer and former Foreign Service officer, evoked some resentment with confrontational and retributive methods. He saw that after the 1973 war, prevailing aid levels and the $250 million pledged to the United Jewish Appeal would not suffice; "Israel required billions" (Tivnan 1987: 83). After the 1974 organizational changes in Congress, he needed to be able to educate members and staff outside the small network of key chairmen and staff with whom Kenen had worked. He wanted more staff, more research capability and credible capacity to reward and punish.

In 1975, AIPAC's ability to block the president was tested. Secretary of State Kissinger, frustrated by the Rabin government's positions in Sinai withdrawal negotiations, had President Ford send Rabin a blunt letter, expressing "profound disappointment" with "Israel's attitude" and announcing "a reassessment of United States policy in the region, including our relations with Israel" (Rabin 1996: 256). Arms awaiting delivery were suspended. Within days, AIPAC obtained the signatures of 76 senators on a letter to Ford, supporting economic aid to Israel and urging Ford to base any reassessment on the premise that the United States "stands firm with Israel in the search for peace" (Spiegel 1986: 296).[9] Signed by senators on the right (Thurmond, Goldwater) and the left (Kennedy, McGovern), the letter seemed a promise of trouble for any policy of pressure on Israel. However, President Ford did not attempt to dissuade the senators, and might have succeeded; it is much easier to sign a vague "warning shot" letter than to refuse a president's personal request for latitude in foreign policy, and even strong supporters of Israel were uncomfortable with what they had done.[10]

Steven Spiegel asserts that the "letter of 76" did not explain the resumption of shuttle diplomacy and aid delivery thereafter (Spiegel 1986: 387). He relies upon a statement in Ford's memoirs that the letter made him determined to resist pressure. Such statements in political memoirs carry little weight. Amitay, who wrote the letter, had it reprinted in the *New York Times*, which also reported that "senior Israeli officials ... buoyed by recent demonstrations of congressional support" would now "ignore repeated United States requests" for negotiating proposals (O'Brien 1986: 178). If so, the letter had significantly affected government-to-government relations. Amitay was showcasing the letter for what it was: evidence of AIPAC's strength.

Amitay built a tightly run professional organization. When he hired Douglas Bloomfield, former aide to Senator Humphrey and Representative Rosenthal, as legislative director in January 1980, there were four lobbyists and about 20 researchers and staff. The 1980 budget was a modest $1.2 million (Goldberg 1996: 202). That meant contributions were relatively small, and the "strings" that come with large contributions were avoided. Amitay had close relationships with AIPAC officers and substantial discretion (Bloomfield interview). The misnamed Executive Committee, an unwieldy and scattered group of heads of major organizations, did not determine legislative strategy. Although there were contacts in the executive branch, AIPAC concentrated on Congress, where Amitay believed their leverage was. They prided themselves on reliable research, delivered quickly where it would do the most good (ibid.).[11] They had daily contact with members and staff, and attended all relevant committee meetings. A key to their effectiveness was their ability to obtain intelligence concerning administration initiatives well in advance of their publication, allowing them to arrange amendments or blocking maneuvers, often before the administration had made its case. Sometimes AIPAC's speed and autonomy meant taking positions with little or no input from Israel.

In February 1978, President Carter announced a sale of 60 F-15 aircraft to Saudi Arabia. Amitay took the initiative to block the sale under a law that then allowed a congressional veto. He was supported by the Presidents Conference, organized labor and an *ad hoc* interfaith group, but all deferred to AIPAC. The government of Israel was initially split, with Foreign Minister Dayan urging opposition to the sale and Defense Minister Weizman arguing they should seek compensation. Prime Minister Begin vacillated, but finally favored the opponents (Goldberg 1990: 68). AIPAC approached the administration to discuss compromise, but antagonism between the lobby and the administration had by 1978 minimized access (ibid.: 66). The administration avoided a legislative veto, in part by adding 20 F-15s to the package for Israel.

The fallout was bitter. Mark Siegel, White House Jewish liaison, resigned, telling reporters that the sale had been intended to break the lobby (Tivnan 1987: 125). Carter's chief of staff was quoted saying they had intended "to break the back of the Jewish lobby"; that was denied (ibid.: 126). Amitay was intent on retribution. He angrily announced a Jewish boycott of Senator George McGovern's re-election campaign for opposing the lobby. McGovern, a liberal with few Jewish constituents, had previously been supported by Jews for his usually loyal support of Israel. He was now targeted by the National Conservative Political Action Committee (NCPAC), and the withdrawal of support by nearly all of his old Jewish friends was disabling (ibid.: 126–7). He might well have lost anyway, but it became known that AIPAC's Amitay had done what he could to guarantee his defeat.

The Dine era at AIPAC begins

The fallout over the 1978 arms sales may have convinced Lawrence Weinberg, AIPAC's president,[12] that Amitay should be replaced.[13] In late 1980, AIPAC hired Thomas A. Dine, a long-time Democratic congressional aide, former Peace Corps volunteer and research fellow at the Brookings Institution. Dine was Jewish, but not observant, was married to a non-Jew and had no history of affiliation with Jewish organizations. But he had worked closely with pro-Israeli groups for senators Muskie and Church, and had a reputation for intelligence and skill. He taught a course at Harvard's Kennedy Institute of Politics on the effective exercise of congressional powers in foreign policy, and wrote a piece for the *New York Times* summarizing his views (Dine 1975). There, he described eight methods by which Congress could compete effectively with the president in setting policy, including developing expertise and independent bases of information, using staff as political actors, using the appropriation power to curtail executive options, linking external and domestic interests, and using special-interest groups to mobilize support and provide legitimacy (ibid.). Dine set out to implement these ideas for AIPAC.

Dine believed that foreign policy should be generated by grassroots action, and intended to expand greatly AIPAC's contact network and educational outreach in order to mobilize the grassroots (Dine interview). He sought to turn a "small agency, run by the national Jewish organizations, into an independent mass-membership powerhouse run by its wealthiest donors" (Goldberg 1996: 201). He led expansion of the officers' group, adding people based on five criteria: geographic representation, community involvement, articulateness, money contributed and political connections (Dine interview). He would add substantially to the research staff.

As staff and budget grew, and as active and well-connected people were added to the "officers' group," the effect was to put more power into the hands of a small group of wealthy contributors who were principal officers, and to weaken AIPAC's ties to other organizations. When asked who he thought of as AIPAC's constituency, Dine says that there were three groups: the Zionist organizations that had supported AIPAC originally (ZOA and Hadassah), "leadership Jews," and non-Jewish supporters of Israel, including the Christian Right (Dine interview). None of those groups had meaningful input into positions AIPAC took, nor the tactics used to pursue them. Further, other pro-Israel groups were tax exempt, meaning that they were legally prohibited from committing any major portion of their efforts to lobbying. They were in no position to mount a sustained challenge if they did disagree. AIPAC was becoming a self-sustaining, self-referential, independent force.

Tom Dine took over a potent advocacy organization in October 1980. Partly through its efforts, aid to Israel had grown from $778 million in FY1975, when Amitay began, to $4.888 billion in FY1979 (including one-time compensation) and $2.121 billion in FY1980 (Mark 2002). AIPAC had begun to use congressional support to limit presidential policy choice.

Strength multipliers: political demographics, skill and affinity

The Jewish population of the United States peaked as a proportion of the whole population in the 1920s and 1930s, when anti-Semitic politics and discrimination were prevalent, and when the influence of the Jewish community on immigration and other matters of vital interest was minimal. The proportion of Jewish population fell from under 4 percent in the 1930s to under 3 percent in the 1980s, even as discrimination ended and the community began to exercise disproportionate influence on foreign policy. Basic demographic, cultural and political factors enabled that result.

The Jewish population was historically concentrated in states important in national elections. In New York, Jews were approximately 14 percent of the population during the 1970s, although that proportion fell steadily thereafter (Isaacs 1974: 6; Smith 2000: 99). Jews participated at much higher rates than others; in the 1980 elections, 92 percent of registered Jewish voters voted, compared to a general rate of 53 percent (Novik 1986: 59). The states in which Jewish voters concentrated were Democratic strongholds, and Jewish voters voted disproportionately Democratic – on average four to one – so that they made up nearly 30 percent of the New York State Democratic primary electorate, and nearly half of the electorate in New York City. Smaller but important concentrations were located in New Jersey and Florida, and significant concentrations in Connecticut, Massachusetts, California, Maryland and Pennsylvania. Nationally, Jewish voters cast over 4 percent of the votes when they constituted less than 3 percent of the eligible population, meaning over 750,000 additional votes concentrated in key Electoral College states (Isaacs 1974: 6–7). The Jewish community's skill and experience in organizing their political environment generally, and their network of community-based organizations (some 300 national organizations, 230 local federations of agencies, and 5,000 synagogues) meant that there were many familiar channels of political intelligence. Armed with information about issues and candidates, Jewish voters were accustomed to fundraising, targeting important races and voting as a bloc. President Carter, a relative unknown to the Jewish community in 1976 and a born-again Christian, nevertheless received 70 percent of the Jewish vote; but in 1980, reacting to his policies toward Israel, those voters gave him less than 50 percent of their votes (Novik 1986: 64).

Dedication to education – over 80 percent attended university – and skill in political organizing meant that by the 1960s, Jews were prominent in all aspects of political life, except elected office. Jews were among the most important historians, political scientists, political journalists, pollsters, trade unionists, campaign managers, speech-writers, fundraisers and party chairmen; but Episcopalians and Presbyterians, together about 2.8 percent of the population, made up nearly 27 percent of the Congress, while Jews barely matched their proportion of the population at 2.8 percent (Isaacs 1974: 6–13). That changed by the 1980s, as Jews overcame fear of prejudice and discovered that they were electable even in districts with very small Jewish votes.

Jewish demographics and organizational skill, however, only begin the story. There has been since the end of World War II consistent popular support for the existence and security of a Jewish state. In 1945, 76 percent of those Americans who said they had been following events in the Middle East favored permitting Jews to settle in Palestine. Images of Israelis in popular American culture were overwhelmingly positive, even heroic (Paul Newman as a *Haganah* fighter in the 1960 movie *Exodus*), and those of Arabs were negative or overtly racist (Grose 1983; Finkelstein 1995; Shaheen 1997; Christison 1999; Rosenthal 2001). Gallup polls in 1967 reported 59 percent of those following events generally sympathized with the Israelis and only 4 percent with the Arabs (Curtiss 1982: 187–8).[14] Schneider and Lipset found that 25 percent of voters supported Israel fervently enough to punish politicians who undermined the U.S.–Israeli relationship; they refer to this as the only "veto group" in the American electorate relating to the Middle East (Novik 1986: 8).

These phenomena – identification with Israelis, antipathy toward Arabs and predisposition to accept arguments favoring Israel – were reinforced by pro-Israel advocates, but were not caused by advocacy. There was a "presumed congruence of values between the two nations," based upon a perceived sharing of pioneering spirit, democratic institutions and ideals of individualism and freedom (Quandt 1977: 16). This "culture-bound, color-conscious world view that still positions nations and peoples in a hierarchy" limited what Americans would easily accept as true (Hunt 1987: 177). Affinity was reinforced by Christian, particularly evangelical, identification with the Zion of the Bible and by feelings of moral responsibility for victims of the Holocaust; repugnance for Arabs was reinforced with each terrorist act attributed to Arabs.

Even when Israeli policy seemed at odds with American interests, there was no public support for responses that would risk Israel's security; however, there was also little support for defense of Israel with American forces. Persistent if diffuse and conditional public support of Israel predisposed elected officials to look favorably on assistance for Israel, and created presumptions against presidential initiatives that were arguably threatening or unfriendly to Israel. This "permissive consensus" (Orren 1988: 33) was more constraining in the case of Israel than in other cases because there was no countervailing set of interests with similarly consistent public support (Quandt 1973: 269, 282). Support of Israel would garner approval from the general public and from the very active Jewish community; there was no organized support for Arab, or anti-Zionist, positions that could reward or punish votes.[15]

The effects of events, 1967–1977

The Six Day War: the new image and centrality of Israel

The Six Day War in June 1967 galvanized and unified the American Jewish community. Reform Judaism, which had been anti-Zionist, declared its solidarity with Israel that year (Waxman 1996: 381). Intense shock and fear for the tiny state facing seemingly overwhelming Arab forces were overtaken by pride at the ferocious effectiveness of the Israeli Defense Forces (IDF). The war demonstrated Israel's substantial military supremacy, but the lessons "learned" were that Israel might be destroyed at any moment, that no one cared about Jews and that Jews should care only for themselves (Goldberg 1996: 137). Donations to the United Jewish Appeal (UJA) shot up, as did contributions to AIPAC. It had been said that politics was the secular religion of American Jews; it was now said that a Jewish leader could be forgiven for lax religious observance, but not for insufficient enthusiasm for Israel. Enthusiasm was more prevalent than discernment; most American Jews did not know that Begin and Peres were in different parties, much less that they were arch-enemies (Novick 2000: 149).

Studies suggested, however, that what had changed was the basis for Jewish community leadership, not the opinions or priorities of the community. Sociologist Marshall Sklare's 1965 studies of Jewish religious and social patterns had found deep concern for Israel's welfare, but supporting Israel came in fourteenth out of 22 factors in defining oneself as a Jew, far behind "living a moral and ethical life" and supporting humanitarian causes. Surprisingly, those rankings did not change appreciably in a 1968 study (Goldberg 1996: 147–8). However, three minorities within the Jewish community for whom militant defense of Israel was central were allowed to take over public leadership of the community and to speak for it on issues affecting Israel: the Orthodox (or religious Zionists), secular nationalist Zionists and neoconservatives. Neoconservatives will be treated separately; the other two types of "New Jew" deserve mention here.

Traditional Orthodoxy was anti-Zionist; belief that men could re-establish Israel by their own works was heresy. In the 1920s, the chief rabbi of Palestine, Rabbi Abraham Isaac Hacohen Kook, began to teach that God must have sent secular Zionists to carry out His work. Much of American Orthodoxy came to accept those teachings after the seemingly miraculous 1967 victories.

Strong support of Israel became essential to leadership of a major Jewish organization, and those who thought it permissible to question Israeli policy were replaced by those who did not. The period from 1967 until the election of Menachem Begin in 1977 is called the "Golden Age" of the "Mobilized Model" of American Zionism, when it was easy to raise money and lobby on behalf of Israel. Zionist leaders were happy to send money in return for recognition ("status awards") and to stay away from policy (Cohen and Liebman 2000: 6). Some saw the war as the crucial element in a "folk theology," involving redemption of the Jews after the Holocaust. The war thus helped bridge the historical antipathy between secular and Orthodox Jews (Novick 2000: 148–50).

The 1967 war also changed the way Israel was perceived by non-Jewish political actors. Geostrategists could now argue that Israel was a regional military power and a worthy potential ally. When in September 1970 Israel agreed (subject to detailed assurances) to assist Arab Jordan against Syrian incursions, her role as reliable strategic American partner was sealed, at least in the mind of the author of the Nixon Doctrine. Military aid then flowed freely. Conversely, social liberals and anti-war activists from the Vietnam era soon found themselves at odds with their old Jewish colleagues. Israel was now a regional military hegemon and an occupying power. Some saw the Palestinians as victims of denied human rights and colonialism. Efforts at interfaith dialogue faltered as traditional Protestant churches and the Catholic Church passed resolutions on Palestinian issues that were seen as anti-Israeli by Jews. Relations with Black leaders became increasingly difficult over the next several years, primarily because of Black nationalism and quotas, but also because some Black leaders identified publicly with the Palestinian cause.

Redoubled anxiety and effort in 1973

The surprise war of 1973 caused American Jews great anxiety. Israel might not have survived without massive assistance from the United States. There was widespread belief that President Nixon, or Henry Kissinger, delayed needed aid in furtherance of strategic goals. Popular support of Israel was still strong, but the energy crisis sensitized Americans to political demands by moderate Arabs, which meant that the Palestinian issue was for the first time on the American policy agenda in a meaningful way. The war and the feared unreliability of American support drove many further toward a survivalist, particularist view of Israel.

AIPAC was in a difficult position. The Israeli government had asked the lobby to hold back, perhaps because it was overly optimistic early in the war, or perhaps because of a Kissinger request as part of his management of the relationship with Israel. When it became clear that the IDF was in trouble, AIPAC suddenly had to demand an immediate and massive airlift. Si Kenen believed that deference to the Israeli government had harmed AIPAC's credibility (Goldberg 1990: 48). Thereafter, the presumption would be to fight for all aid that could be had, allowing Israel to compromise from a position of congressional strength.

The changing role of the Holocaust

American Jews initially avoided reference to the Nazi holocaust. They focused on the courage of Jews in the Warsaw Uprising, exploits of Jewish American veterans and domestic success stories. They shunned depictions of Jews as suffering victims. In 1946, 1947 and 1948, NCRAC (encompassing all major Jewish organizations) unanimously rejected a proposed Holocaust memorial in New York as contrary to Jewish interests by portraying Jews as weak and defenseless (Novick 2000: 123). Jewish leaders saw any emphasis on the Holocaust as impeding American Jewish assimilation and access to power: harping on the subject complicated American policy toward post-war Germany and risked association with leftists and communists (Finkelstein 2001: 13–15).

Perceptions and uses of the Holocaust changed in the 1960s. The capture of Adolph Eichmann, and his trial in Israel in 1961, accelerated reconsideration of the lessons of the Holocaust that began with the 1960 publication of Shirer's *Rise and Fall of the Third Reich* and the first showing of the film *Exodus*, in which Arabs are depicted as agents and allies of the Nazis. Hannah Arendt's commentary on the Eichmann trial and Hochhuth's play *The Deputy* helped establish the idea of a separate "Holocaust" with only Jewish victims. Many argue that the 1967 war revived memories of Nazi-era isolation and vulnerability, and the unexpected 1973 war meant that the Holocaust symbolized the Jews' plight (Novick 2000: 149–51). Although American Jews no longer faced barriers in education, employment or politics, and discrimination was generally denounced, most Jews reported a dread of the inevitability of anti-Semitism (Liebman and Cohen 1990: 40–8).

However, fear of a "second Holocaust" was not the only explanation for the concurrent growth of pro-Israel advocacy by the American Jewish community and what Norman Finkelstein calls Holocaust "ideology." Israel was now a regional military power and a potential American strategic asset, meaning advocacy of a strengthened alliance was congruent with Cold War American policy and bore less risk of allegations of dual loyalty. Two core Holocaust dogmas were developed: that the Nazi holocaust was a categorically unique historical event and that the Holocaust marked the climax of irrational, eternal and murderous Gentile hatred of Jews (Finkelstein 2001: 41–2). These propositions were dubious, conflicted with each other and were not found in serious Holocaust scholarship, but they provided powerful political tools: (1) outspoken support for Israel could be juxtaposed with the cravenness of Americans, including Jews, during the Holocaust; (2) in the context of American society's "identity politics" and "culture of victimization," the "lessons of the Holocaust" provided both a powerful ethnic identity and compensable victimhood; (3) if the Jews' suffering was unique, the Jewish state's entitlement was pre-eminent and Israel's legitimacy was beyond question; (4) if the existential threat was eternal, Israel must be granted license to measure the threats and choose the means to counter them – this implied immunity from criticism.

By 1981, the Holocaust was routinely used to engender feelings of guilt, sympathy and support of Israel, to raise money and to deflect criticism of Israel and of Jews. The federal government provided space on the National Mall and funding for a U.S. Holocaust Museum, in part as atonement for purported American complicity in the Holocaust, while the Congress resisted entreaties from American Blacks and Natives for memorials of those who had suffered at American hands. Curricula of Holocaust studies were established at numerous universities and in public school systems. The uniqueness of the Nazi holocaust was defended against comparison with the killing of Roma by the Nazis, or Armenians by the Turks, or any other genocide. Arabs were portrayed in films as active collaborators with the Nazis and enablers of the Holocaust; in the four-volume *Encyclopaedia of the Holocaust,* the article on the Mufti of Jerusalem was longer than any but that on Hitler himself (Novick 2000: 158).

Those speaking for the Jewish community were becoming much less fearful of publicly flexing political muscle. American Jews who had known neither the tragedy of the Holocaust nor the limiting effects of anti-Semitism in their own lives were coming into leadership. They understood the power of the Holocaust ideology in framing – and terminating – debate, and were not afraid to use it, in the face of Israel's obvious and growing regional hegemony and their own success and prominence. During the 1981 AWACS fight, AIPAC would send a copy of the novel based on the television series *Holocaust* to every member of Congress, to remind them of the moral debt owed Israel.

Begin and the Revisionist Likud

In June 1977, Israelis elected their first government not led by the Labor Party. Menachem Begin, the new prime minister, had been a leader of the

Irgun, the military arm of the Revisionist Party of Vladimir Jabotinsky. The Irgun had used terrorist methods against the British Mandate. It had refused to obey David Ben-Gurion's provisional government or to integrate into Haganah forces until the Haganah sunk an Irgun arms ship, the *Altalena*, and put down the armed revolt that followed. Begin's Herut Party, successor to the Revisionist Party, advocated the establishment of biblical *Eretz Y'Israel*. It merged with the Liberal Party in 1965 to form Gahal, which was brought into the unity war government in 1967, only to leave the government in protest over the 1969 Rogers Plan, the 1970 ceasefire and the implications of territorial compromise.[16] Just after the 1973 war and before the December 1973 elections, Gahal had merged with minor parties including the *Eretz Y'Israel* movement to form Likud. The merged parties grew in strength until they took a plurality of the votes in the 1977 election.

Begin had long been a political pariah – Ben-Gurion called him a "fascist" and excluded Herut from coalitions – and was viewed with alarm by many American Jewish leaders. When Begin visited the United States in 1948, Albert Einstein and Hannah Arendt joined others denouncing his "Fascist" and "Nazi" tactics. Nahum Goldmann reportedly persuaded Dean Acheson that the best argument for recognizing the Ben-Gurion-led government of Israel was that it would block Begin's ambitions (Tivnan 1987: 107).

Rabbi Arthur Schindler met with Begin after his election and stated that the American Jewish community would support any incumbent Israeli government. That was a major gift to Begin, since Schindler was chair of the Presidents Conference and head of the Reform movement. Nahum Goldmann thereupon urged President Carter to "break the lobby," arguing that its support of the Begin government was a major obstacle to peace in the Middle East (Tivnan 1987: 120, 121).

Yet it is not true that Begin's election was a shock to American Jewry as a whole. Most American Jews knew little about Begin. Most defended Begin reflexively as a product of Israeli democracy, particularly after he was attacked in *Time* magazine as a "terrorist" whose name "rhymes with Fagin." Many persuaded themselves that Begin's positions on territorial compromise were tactical, that he would negotiate hard but rationally and that "he was really not the anti-Arab ideologue that he seemed to be" (Hertzberg 2002: 400). As Schindler saw it, there was little choice: support of Israel was critical, Carter was suspect and it was "impossible to say, 'Begin's terrible, but we want you [the American government] to support the State of Israel anyway'" (Tivnan 1987: 110).

Rabbi Hertzberg, president of the AJCongress since 1972, was one of few American leaders who had maintained a friendship with Begin. The new national security adviser, Zbigniew Brzezinski, asked Hertzberg to go to Jerusalem to tell Begin that the U.S. would generously support Israel's security, but "could not be pushed into supporting an expansionist, nationalist, and ultimately religio-mystical Jewish ideology to allow Israel to retain the Occupied Territories" (Hertzberg 2002: 398). Hertzberg did as he was asked, and thus ended the friendship. Begin told Hertzberg heatedly that he had been elected to maintain sovereignty over the land, and would explain his ideology to Carter (ibid.: 399). ⌐

Hertzberg believed that while many American Jewish leaders swallowed their doubts and publicly supported Begin's government in order to preserve their "dinnerability," (Marcus 1990: 548) others had long been hardliners, as frustrated as Begin had been during many years of Labor governments (Hertzberg 2002: 390–1). The election of a Revisionist Zionist began to expose differences in beliefs among American Jews, and between American Jews and Israelis.

Hardliners, dissenters and the Jewish omerta

Even before Begin's election, cracks began to appear in the façade of unanimous American Jewish support for Israel. Several considerations muted concerns about lack of progress in the peace process: (1) the 1967 Arab declaration that there would be no recognition of Israel, no negotiations and no peace; (2) Israel's claim that secret intelligence justified their positions; (3) Begin's insistence that only Israel could determine its security needs; (4) fear of providing aid and comfort to Israel's enemies; (5) concern about the true intentions of Nixon and Kissinger, or Carter and Brzezinski and (6) the willingness of Begin to relinquish the Sinai in return for peace with Egypt. Offsetting considerations were Israeli intelligence blunders before the 1973 war, and Begin's fights with Carter after Camp David about settlements. In spite of repeated calls for unity and discipline,[17] disparate views began to coalesce into new organizations.

The history of one such organization, Breira, is instructive. Breira was founded in 1973 by veterans of the Vietnam War protest movement and Jewish counterculture, "to legitimize public dissent within the American Jewish community" concerning issues including Israel's policy toward the peace process (Rosenthal 2001: 36). It had connections to the Israeli peace movement, and attracted Jewish intellectuals and Reform rabbis, many from Hillel Foundations on college campuses.[18] Breira called for negotiations with Palestinians, but only under conditions Israel said it favored: Israeli security and amendment of the PLO charter. It deviated from Israeli policy by saying that a settlement would require a Palestinian state, and in favoring contact with Palestinians. Its call for public debate guaranteed it a short and stormy life.

Rabbi Schindler initially defended Breira's right to dissent, and his Central Conference of American Rabbis (Reform) passed a resolution in June 1975 calling for open debate. Prime Minister Rabin, however, called three American-born Israeli academics in for a two-hour conference about what could be done about Breira (Tivnan 1987: 94). In October 1976, Jews including two Breira members met with two PLO members. That generated a front-page article in the *New York Times* on the "split" among "American Jewish leaders" (Rosenthal 2001: 37). The reaction was ferocious. Americans for a Safe Israel (ASFI), a group founded in 1971 to advocate against Israeli territorial concessions, published a pamphlet accusing Breira of "facilitating Israel's destruction" and suggesting the organization rename itself "Jews for Fatah." Pieces in *American Zionist, Midstream, Jewish Week, Commentary* and *The Village Voice* followed, several drawing on the AFSI pamphlet. ZOA and ADL pressured B'nai B'rith to prevent its affiliated Hillel Foundation rabbis from associating with Breira. Israeli consuls in New York, Boston and Philadelphia called Breira leaders and warned them against giving "aid and comfort to the enemy" (Wertheimer 1996: 405). Within a year, Breira held its first and only policy conference, at which Jewish Defense League toughs broke in and assaulted attendees, and Breira was gone (Rosenthal 2001: 39). Rabin told American Jewish leaders, "There is no Breira" (Wertheimer 1996: 405–6).

The history of Breira is instructive precisely because this small organization was neither particularly radical nor any credible threat to Israel. If its policy suggestions had been followed, Israel would have negotiated only under terms it had largely defined. The academics who met with Rabin were understandably astonished that he would spend time worrying about it. The point, however, was clear: American Jews were expected, by Israel and the American Zionist establishment, to follow the Israeli government line and to leave advocacy to authorized representatives. Those who deviated, particularly if they competed with AIPAC or consulted with Palestinians, would be branded as traitors or fools and cast out. There was a further point, pertaining to growing organizational rivalries: those who most aggressively enforced loyalty to Israel could claim the mantle of leadership in the new secular religion.

ASFI claimed that mantle in the Breira episode, boasting that it had destroyed the apostate organization. ASFI was a membership organization engaged in publishing and media monitoring activities. Its founders were strong anti-communists, Jabotinsky Zionists and supporters of Herut and the settler movement. AFSI sought to expose "enemies" of Israel, particularly within Jewish organizations (O'Brien 1986: 253–5).

In the late 1970s, the Jewish Institute for National Security Affairs (JINSA) was formed. JINSA began as a group of pro-Israel military analysts who believed that to be stable, support for Israel must be based upon strategic value to the United States, rather than on moral or political grounds.

JINSA exemplified the "networking" and "revolving door" phenomena prevalent in pro-Israel efforts. Michael Ledeen, an early executive director, had worked for Alexander Haig in the Nixon administration and later held positions in State, Defense and NSC under Reagan. Stephen Bryen, another executive director, had been on staff at the Senate Foreign Relations Committee, working closely with AIPAC. While still on the JINSA board, he became deputy to Richard Perle, then assistant secretary of defense. Howard Teicher, a JINSA member, served in Reagan's NSC in Middle East Affairs and Political–Military Affairs. The printed announcement of JINSA's formation was signed by, *inter alia*, David Bar Elan of the Israeli Jonathan Institute on terrorism, Rita Hauser, chair of AJC's foreign affairs committee, Max Kampelman, former aide to Senator Humphrey, ambassador and head U.S. negotiator on nuclear and space arms, Norman Podhoretz, editor of *Commentary*, and Eugene V. Rostow, former undersecretary of state, dean of Yale Law School (where he defended the legality of Jewish settlements) and co-founder of the Committee on the Present Danger (of which Ronald Reagan, Richard Allen, William Casey and Richard Perle were members). Advisers to JINSA's *Newsletter* included Si Kenen, Representative Jack Kemp, many retired generals and admirals and former presidents of ZOA. JINSA brought together military experts, legislators and administration officials to discuss one topic: how strengthening U.S. ties to Israel served American strategic goals (O'Brien 1986: 203–6; Christison 1999: 200–2).

The Center for International Security was founded by Dr. Joseph Churba, a former consulting partner of Rabbi Meir Kahane, founder of the radical Jewish Defense League and later of the outlawed Kach Party in Israel. Churba had been an adviser to Major General George F. Keegan, head of Air Force intelligence, who served on Churba's board (O'Brien 1986: 206). Keegan testified against the 1981 AWACS sale. Churba argued that a militarily dominant and unfettered Israel was vital to American interests (Churba 1977; Churba 1980: Churba 1984). He probably drafted a 1979 campaign piece in the *Washington Post* in which Ronald Reagan made the case for strategic reliance on Israel (Quandt 1988: 361, n. 5).

Thus, a network of advocates and experts was available to help a president or to work against him, depending upon the degree to which the administration's policies supported Israel.

Israelis and American politics

Initially, the State of Israel dealt directly with both the White House and Congress. Abba Eban and Teddy Kollek then sought interlocutors and fundraisers, and helped to establish AIPAC and the Presidents Conference to institutionalize channels of information and influence. Which of these methods – direct contact, individual emissaries or institutional representation – was used in a particular instance depended upon who had access to the targeted American official and the personal preferences and philosophy of the Israeli official.

Direct contact

Yitzhak Rabin began six years as ambassador to the United States in 1968 as the hero of the Six Day War. He had credibility and access. "He made it absolutely clear that he regarded Israel's relations with the United States as those of one state to another and that he wanted nothing to do with the American Jewish lobby ... He was not interested in hearing any advice or in sharing any information" (Hertzberg 2002: 387). Rabin said he "honored" the tradition of communicating through American Jewish leaders, but "tried to change it without offending [their] sensibilities" (Rabin 1996: 229). How far he fell short of his goal of not offending sensibilities may be gauged by the tone of Hertzberg's description.[19]

Rabin preferred dealing only with the administration.[20] Tom Dine says that Rabin, whose principal contact was Henry Kissinger, was a "monarchist" who believed with Kissinger that the legislature was secondary. He considered AIPAC a threat to his properly conducting Israel's affairs (Dine interview).

Labor premiers generally were received warmly at the White House. Prime Minister Eshkol, Ambassador Harmon and President Johnson were close personally, as were Prime Minister Meir, Ambassador Rabin and President Nixon. The exception was Rabin and Carter; Carter reacted badly to Rabin's stiff manner and his coolness to Carter's peace process ideas. Shimon Peres had many close friendships with American officials. This recurring phenomenon was in part the result of personal chemistry, but also because Labor governments were not ideologically committed to policies at odds with White House initiatives.[21]

Not having expended the time and effort necessary to organize congressional support, Labor leaders did not have it when they needed it. That became particularly evident when the opposition was not Arabs, but the Likud and its friends.

The individual interlocutor

Presidents typically have Jewish friends and supporters who can discuss Israel with the president.[22] The most significant of these individual emissaries was undoubtedly Max M. Fisher.

Fisher, a Detroit businessman, was the long-time general chair of the UJA, raising funds to support immigration to Israel. He dealt with the Jewish Agency and the Israeli government constantly, and knew every important Israeli official. He had raised money for and advised Republican candidates for president since the 1950s. In 1965, a failing Dwight Eisenhower told Fisher that he regretted his decisions in the 1956 Suez crisis, and said, "Max, if I'd had a Jewish adviser working for me, I doubt I would have … forced the Israelis back." This was Fisher's "epiphany," and he determined to play the role Eisenhower had described (Golden 1992: xix). Richard Nixon later said that a supporter with no selfish interest "like Max," can "have a substantial influence on a close decision" and can "change the president's mind" (ibid.: xx).

Thereafter, when Prime Minister Meir could not get a commitment from Nixon on military aircraft, Fisher obtained the commitment. When the Rogers Plan was announced, Meir arranged intelligence briefings for Fisher concerning impacts on Israeli security. Nixon privately authorized Fisher to tell Meir that he would never impose the Rogers Plan (Melman and Raviv 1994: 150–1). After long talks with Rabin in 1975, Fisher briefed President Ford and Secretary Kissinger on security reasons for Israel not to relinquish Sinai passes (ibid.: 168). Ford did not relent, but no one else would likely have been given 35 minutes of Ford's time to argue against Kissinger.

Fisher had access in Reagan's, and to some extent in the first Bush, administration. As a conservative Republican supporter and Jewish leader, Max Fisher was invited to any White House function involving issues relating to Israel, and brought groups of prominent, mostly Republican Jews to White House and State Department briefings. By the late 1980s, the role of the individual interlocutor diminished as the roles of the lobby and the Congress grew dominant. However, when an Israeli premier needed a message carried faithfully to the president by an interlocutor with independent credibility, someone like Max Fisher was invaluable.

Working the lobby

Menachem Begin knew that most American Jewish leaders publicly supported his government for fear that public criticism would help the enemies of Israel, and in hopes that he would moderate his views, and not because they concurred in his political program. They had never acknowledged him or invited him to address them, and were still talking to the Labor leaders they were comfortable with; many viewed him as an aberration (Tivnan 1987: 113).

But relations with President Carter were going to be difficult, as he knew from Hertzberg's message from Brzezinski. American supporters of Revisionist Zionism had no organizational power base. He understood the importance of the early public support of Alexander Schindler, on behalf of the Presidents Conference and liberal Reform Jewry. Even as he rejected Brzezinski's message, Begin invited Hertzberg to travel back to the United States on his plane. He wanted the symbolic power of pictures of the iconoclastic moderate leader of Conservative Judaism at his side. Hertzberg, also aware of the symbolism, turned him down (Hertzberg 2002: 399–400).

Begin set about shaping American organizations to his needs. He sent Shmuel Katz, a former propaganda chief for the Irgun, and Eliahu Ben-Elissar, a Herut deputy, to the United States to work with American media and politicians (Tivnan 1987: 113). He went over the heads of organizational leaders, undertaking a speaking tour during his first visit as prime minister in July 1977. Unlike the unemotional Rabin, he was a fiery speaker, using Holocaust metaphors for the Arab threat to Israel. He avoided preaching the necessity of *aliyah*. He appealed to businessmen with promises of a more entrepreneurial economy and he claimed to be ready to go to Geneva for negotiations with the Arab states. Unlike Labor, Begin was forthright in taking sides against the Soviet Union, and stressed the importance of Israel's potential contribution, including shared intelligence. It also helped that he was, unlike the largely secular and Socialist Laborites who preceded him, religious. Many leaders of major American Jewish organizations were rabbis (ibid.: 118–19).

Begin controlled access to himself, other officials and information, to induce discipline by rewarding those who were more compliant. NCRAC, which had formed an Israel task force to engage in dialogue with CRCs nationwide about Israel's positions, told Begin of the unease it found in April 1978. It was thereafter progressively cut out of contact with the Israeli government; it dissolved its task force and became irrelevant to policy on Israel. Begin dealt instead with the Presidents Conference and especially with AIPAC, rewarding loyalty and effectiveness with access and the power that came with it (Goldberg 1996: 212–13).

Conclusion

The American Jewish community was historically socially liberal, Zionist only in the sense of supporting a Jewish state for others and politically adept but cautious. Jewish leaders stressed tolerance and equal opportunity and avoided identification with issues that would differentiate or draw attention to Jews. Beginning in 1967, American Jewish identity and political activity was increasingly defined by Israel and the Holocaust, for several reasons: (1) perceived danger to the Jewish state; (2) diminished fear of domestic persecution; (3) domestic ethnic identity politics, which defined classes of victims to be favored; (4) the willingness of most American Jews to allow the most strident advocates of Israel to serve as their spokesmen; and (5) Israel's demonstrated military competence, which made Cold War alliance with Israel facially credible. The resulting advocacy on behalf of the Jewish community was somewhat schizophrenic, arguing at once that Israel was a strong, reliable democratic strategic asset, but also a symbol and example of eternal Jewish victimhood and therefore beyond criticism and deserving of help.

Menachem Begin personified a Manichean Revisionist Zionism quite at odds with traditional American Judaism, but most American Jews either did not understand that, or were afraid to split the community and endanger Israel by publicly objecting to his policies. Further, Begin came to power when advocacy of Israel, and of the victimhood of Jews, had become essential to leadership of the community, and he reinforced that trend by giving access and sanction only to those whose advocacy was unconditional.

AIPAC had evolved from an effective one-man congressional lobby tied to major Jewish organizations, into a professional and largely independent operation. It spoke with authority for the pro-Israel community and increasingly established and enforced the policy dialogue that pertained to Israel in Congress. Its policy of seeking the maximum possible economic and military assistance and the greatest possible freedom of political action for Israel had since 1977 enabled the Revisionist policies of the Likud. As of 1981, no effective opposition to AIPAC existed, either in the Jewish community or in Congress.

3 Pro-Israel policy networks and the congressional playing field

Introduction

The election of Ronald Reagan in 1980 marked an historic shift in governing assumptions. Reagan was the first president who combined social and fiscal conservatism, ardent anti-communism and identification with the Christian Right. It was not clear that Reagan had a mandate matching his beliefs. Americans had in part simply turned from Jimmy Carter, who spoke of a "malaise" in America, to Ronald Reagan, whose optimism and assertive patriotism made them feel better about themselves and their prospects. Nevertheless, because Reagan was president the assumptions and language of governing, and the avenues of access to the White House, were markedly different than previously. These changes were important in determining who could speak effectively for Israel and what arguments would now be persuasive.

This chapter will evaluate the connections among, and the relative impacts of, elements of the conservative political movement and other potential participants in policy networks relevant to Israel. It will also analyse the reasons Congress's role was increasingly important in the years studied.

The ascendancy of conservative beliefs

Most forms of American "conservatism" are non-Burkean, emphasizing responsible freedom and modes of change rather than institutions. American conservatism includes the Founding Fathers' Lockean liberalism and free market capitalism, a form of economic organization that destroys in order to create. Reagan asserted, "Today's conservative is, of course, the true liberal," but "today's so-called liberal" had "affixed the title conservative on those who opposed his affinity for centralized authority" (undated letter to Father Liederbach, in Skinner *et al.* 2003: 272).

Reagan combined political leadership of the Western conservative movement with rhetorical leadership of neoconservatives. Western conservatives were typically small-town Republicans who called their beliefs "basic

American values" – by which they meant something close to libertarianism – free market economics, strengthened defense and essentialist anti-communism.[1] They became a distinct movement in the years after World War II. Ronald Reagan inherited leadership of the movement from Senator Barry Goldwater after a speech laying out the ideological basis of the movement late in Goldwater's failed 1964 presidential campaign.[2] Most, though not all, were from western states: Goldwater, Reagan and long-time Reagan aides Edwin Meese, William Clark and Lyn Nofziger were leading examples.[3] They were somewhat populist, anti-intellectual and disdainful of stereotypical "Wasp" pragmatist/mechanist eastern Republicans, who were thought to have accepted too much government and compromised dangerously with communists. The westerners were strange bedfellows with the largely eastern, urban, Democratic and highly intellectual neoconservatives, converging primarily on essentialist anti-communism and skepticism about overarching government solutions.

Polls showed that from 1976, the American public and its opinion leaders began to shed the aversion to overseas commitments associated with the "Vietnam syndrome," and became concerned that the United States was falling behind the Soviet Union in power and respect.[4] These trends surged with the taking of American hostages in Iran in November 1979 and the Soviet invasion of Afghanistan the next month. Supporters of increased defense spending built from 12 percent in 1974 to 49 percent in 1980, peaking at 61 percent in 1981 before falling back thereafter (Novik 1986: 15). President Reagan could claim that he had a mandate for a more assertive policy against the Soviets and an accelerated defense build-up, although polls also showed that the public was risk averse: it wanted the president to have the wherewithal credibly to stake out tough positions, but gave no prior consent to any particular intervention involving American troops, including Arab invasion of Israel (Reilly 1979; Reilly 1983). General support of Israel, and preference for Israel in any fight with its Arab neighbors, remained high, but did not include support for use of American forces (Holsti 1996: 94).

A study by Holsti and Rosenau analyzed connections between domestic and foreign policy views of elites in the 1980s. It found that, measured by positions on issues, "liberals" outnumbered "conservatives" on domestic issues, and "accommodationists" outnumbered "hardliners" on foreign policy issues, by substantial margins. However, "hardliners" in foreign policy were overwhelmingly conservative on social and economic issues and were Republicans by an 8:1 margin (Holsti and Rosenau 1999).

These findings begin to suggest the difficulties, and the opportunities, introduced for domestic supporters of Israel by the 1980 election results. The strongest supporters of Ronald Reagan, and many of his closest advisers and appointees, were defense hawks and strong supporters of Israel, and in these positions they were joined by a majority of the public, at least on a conditional basis. They were also economic conservatives, believing in smaller government and less regulation, and usually social conservatives as well. On these matters, ranging from tax cuts that would starve the government to abortion and prayer in the schools, much of the public was unconvinced, and the great majority of the traditional core of support for Israel, organized American Jewry, was in strong opposition. However, the neoconservatives and AIPAC were poised with arguments playing to the core beliefs of the new president, unburdened by issues on which they would oppose him.

The influence of neoconservatives

"Neoconservatism" is a very odd term for the collection of views held by those associated with it. Irving Kristol, the "intellectual godfather" of neoconservatism, describes those associated with the term as "a rather heterogeneous group. What is true is that we all came out of the same pot, which is the New York socialist milieu" (Goldberg 1996: 159). Most but not all were Jewish, if nonobservant. Some were Catholic elite intellectuals. Most were of Eastern European stock, bearing old grudges against Russia and newer ones against the Soviet Union. Many had been active in the civil rights movement. The intellectual processes that had led them away from socialism varied. Kristol turned from liberalism in the 1950s to become a polemical critic of domestic liberal causes and a fervent anti-communist, defending American power and interventions. Kristol co-founded the first neoconservative journal, *The Public Interest*, in 1965 as a non-sectarian publication. Norman Podhoretz, long-time editor of *Commentary*, broke from the civil rights movement in the early 1960s and increasingly attacked the lack of principled rigor he perceived in the liberalism of that decade (Dorrien 1993).

Events in 1967 – the Six Day War and the New York City teachers' strike[5] – energized neoconservatives. Most neoconservatives had not been Zionists before 1967 (Hertzberg 1984: 153). But now events were confirming their somewhat Manichean views: the Soviets instigated the war against Israel, oppressed their Jewish citizens and were the principal source of danger in a dangerous world; and Third World radicalism (including American Black Nationalism) constituted an attack on democratic values.[6] Podhoretz, never lacking for self-confidence and published but not controlled by the AJC, began to be accepted by many in the American political elite as a spokesman for American Jews. Now the loudest and angriest Jewish public voices were all demanding unconditional support of Israel: the Orthodox, the secular Zionists and neoconservatives. Given the *frisson* of fear and uncertainty that the 1967 war sent through the community, the "survivalist" form of Judaism, privileging defense of the Jewish people and their state and hostility to their enemies, began to supplant "universalist" or traditional American Judaism and its values of tolerance and social justice, at least in the audible public discourse. The neoconservatives were both agents and beneficiaries of that trend.

Neoconservatives were influential far out of proportion to their modest numbers. In addition to *Commentary* and *The National Interest*, they established several other high quality journals and regularly appeared in leading policy journals they did not edit. They controlled or strongly influenced many policy centers, including the Manhattan Institute and the American Enterprise Institute, which in turn had substantial influence on formulation of policy. In the 1970s, they fought what they called "the culture of appeasement" through organizations such as the Committee on the Present Danger, which attacked Carter's "human rights moralism" and asserted that the United States was losing the Cold War (Dorrien 1993: 10). Ronald Reagan belonged to the Committee, as did several of his later appointees.[7] That membership, and the fact that Reagan regularly read *Commentary*, are two of many measures of the close fit between the neoconservative agenda and Reagan's.

Neoconservatives, almost all still associated with the Democratic Party in 1972, were repulsed by the anti-war and liberal views of presidential candidate George McGovern, and tried to purge the party of McGovern's influence. The candidacy of Ronald Reagan saw the conversion of many neoconservatives to Republican registration; his election saw the appointment of many of them to federal office.[8] However, repeated predictions that the movement would lead to massive defections of Jews to the Republican Party were not borne out. Although Reagan would receive 39 percent of the Jewish vote in 1980, more than any Republican since Eisenhower, it was still less than a majority. Defections from Carter went to independent John Anderson, who received 15 percent of the vote. In 1984, Reagan received 33 percent of the Jewish vote (Goldberg 1996: 34).

The Christian Right

The role of religion

In the late 1980s, seven of ten Americans claimed a religious affiliation, and two-thirds reported that they had more confidence in their church or synagogue than in other institutions (Fabian 1988: 50). "Values" issues permeate American politics, from abortion and welfare to weapons policy and foreign aid.

Of those Americans who claim affiliation, the vast majority are Christians who think of Israel (or Palestine) as the Holy Land. Many conflate modern Israel with the land of David and accept that Jews (Israelis) are the chosen people of God and entitled to sovereignty over the land. A large majority of Protestants recall the Bible verses from their Sunday School lessons that suggest a religious duty to defend the Jews' right to the Holy Land, which predisposes them to the arguments of Zionists (Anderson 2005).[9] This phenomenon, together with feelings of empathy or guilt because of the Holocaust and admiration for Israelis as soldiers, democrats and pioneers, go far to explain persistently high levels of diffuse public support for Israel. Polling tells politicians that support of Israel is popular, but these beliefs are part of the make-up of most elected officials as well.

Changes in the composition and alignments of Christian groups

Pro-Zionist Christian groups were important supporters of a Jewish commonwealth in Palestine. The American Palestine Committee, revitalized in 1941 by senators Wagner (D, NY) and McNary (R, OR), included prominent clergy, 200 congressmen, 68 senators and three cabinet members. That committee merged with the Christian Council on Palestine, a clerical group including Reinhold Niebuhr and Paul Tillich, to form the American Christian Palestine Committee. By 1945, Congress supported a resolution by senators Wagner and Taft, members of the merged committee, supporting a Jewish commonwealth (Glick 1982: 67–8).

For evangelical Protestants,[10] especially those called variously dispensationalists, millennialists or Christian Zionists, support of Israel is required by God. Dispensationalists believe that seven eras, or dispensations, are identified in the Bible as tests of man's obedience to revelation. The last dispensation is to be Armageddon, an unavoidable military clash on the plains north of Jerusalem. Believers will be "raptured," or lifted up to watch the battle beside Jesus. This cannot happen, however, until Jews re-establish biblical Israel and rebuild the temple in Jerusalem. Thus, support of Israeli efforts to retain Judea and Samaria, or even parts of Jordan, Lebanon and Syria, or to replace the Al-Aqsa mosque with a temple, is thought to be obligatory (Halsell 1989; Merkley 2001: 195–218). The obligation does not depend on the legality or morality of Israeli actions at any given time.[11]

For traditional Protestant theologians such as Tillich and Niebuhr, and for Catholics, support for Israel was a matter of justice and Christian values, and therefore was conditional (Orr 1973). Israeli violations of legal or ethical norms could affect that support. The 1967 war caused traditional churches to rethink support of Israel. Traditional denominations belong to the National Council of Churches (NCC) and the World Council of Churches (WCC); evangelical denominations do not. Many member churches of the NCC and WCC had sent missionaries to the Middle East in the nineteenth and early twentieth centuries, and tended to identify with Arabs both as oppressed peoples and as populations where proselytizing had been more successful than among Jews. Within days of the Six Day War, the WCC reported that while it recognized Israel's importance to the security of the Jews, it also recognized the resulting "suffering and injustice" to Arab peoples (Merkley 2001: 195). By 1983, both the NCC and WCC were on record in favor of a Palestinian state (ibid.: 196–7; Halsell 1989: 153).

The Six Day War galvanized American dispensationalists. In 1964, Rev. Jerry Falwell had said he could do nothing but preach the gospel, even to fight communism; in 1967, he declared that the war was won only with "the intervention of God Almighty," and became an active Christian Zionist (Halsell 1989: 72–3). Falwell was one of several prominent televangelists with audiences in the millions of people who regularly equated opposition to Israel to opposition to God.[12]

Not all evangelical Christians were dispensationalists and not all members of dispensationalist congregations acted politically based upon teachings relating to Israel. However, evangelical churches were growing while other Protestant churches were shrinking; most televangelists were dispensationalist; and dispensationalist ministers were among the most politically active religious leaders. By one account, liberal Protestants were 9 percent of the population in the late 1980s, while conservative or evangelical Protestants were 15 percent (Fabian 1988: 51).[13] A Yankelovich poll in 1984 found that 39 percent of Americans believed that the Bible said the Earth would be destroyed in a nuclear Armageddon (Halsell 1989: 10).

In 1979, Rev. Falwell founded the Moral Majority, an organization dedicated to political realization of his evangelical vision. For the most part, the agenda was a domestic one, but Falwell also preached support of Israel: "Whoever stands against Israel stands against God" (Martin 1999: 72). It was widely expected that the Moral Majority would be a major political force, given its exposure through hundreds of television stations, thousands of radio stations and tens of thousands of evangelical ministers. However, it folded in 1986, having achieved little. More sophisticated political operations succeeded it: Ralph Reed's Christian Coalition, Frank Dobson's Focus on the Family, Gary Bauer's Family Research Council.

It is difficult to identify instances when evangelical organizations made a critical difference on a policy regarding Israel. Tom Dine of AIPAC has said that the Christian Right was a "political resource" (Goldberg 1990: 25). Dine's legislative director, Douglas Bloomfield, says that there was no relationship between AIPAC and the Christian Right when he started work there in 1980.[14] He also says that the Moral Majority did not have the influence they expected within the Reagan White House, and that in Congress, "we could get their prayers but not their votes" (Bloomfield interview). There were two major problems: the Christian Right opposed foreign aid, and would not go to Congress to fight for it; and working with them offended AIPAC's traditional base, because they opposed liberal Jewish positions on social issues, and because they opposed the peace process (ibid.). Rabbi Schindler said that the Christian Right aimed at the extinction of Judaism, and that they could not make a pact with the devil (Cohen 1996: 329). Ardent Zionists like ADL's Nathan Perlmutter responded that the only relevant anti-Semitism was anti-Zionism (Perlmutter and Perlmutter 1982: 175), and neoconservatives like Irving Kristol argued that theology should not prevent acceptance of political support (Cohen 1996: 328).

The influence of the Christian Right on individual politicians was more significant than their organizational power. Jessie Helms, the ultra-conservative Republican Senator from South Carolina said after the 1982

Israeli invasion of Lebanon that relations with Israel should be "shut down," in spite of "the lobby that's so powerful in this day" (Halsell 1989: 165). By 1984, Helms was among Israel's most strident advocates, supporting aid and urging Reagan to support Israel's retention of the Occupied Territories. Helms's state had a large evangelical population, and he had publicly supported Falwell. His reversal also came after Senator Percy, whom Helms succeeded as chair of the Senate Foreign Relations Committee, was defeated for re-election with the help of AIPAC and the Moral Majority. Finally, Senator Helms was strongly anti-communist and supported increased defense spending, making him a natural ally of JINSA and neoconservatives.

To the extent that public officials or their constituencies were receptive to dispensationalist teachings, the predisposition to favor Israel's argument in a dispute was strengthened and maximalist Revisionist positions were justified. When terrorist acts were attributed to Muslims, the predisposition was further reinforced; many evangelicals agree that "much of the Muslim world is implicitly antagonistic to the West" (Smith 2000: 120). Certainly, if the Christian Right had aligned with traditional Christian churches the politics would have been much harder for the lobby.

The Likud and the Christian Right

Dispensationalist doctrine is that Armageddon will destroy all but a handful of Jews, those who convert to Christianity. Thus, support of the territorial ambitions of Revisionist Zionists is a step toward destruction or conversion of all Jews. Told this, Prime Minister Begin is reported to have said, "I tell you, if the Christian Fundamentalists support us in Congress today, I will support them when the Messiah comes tomorrow" (Ball and Ball 1992: 203). Israelis could not see why American Jews would take seriously the beliefs of Christian Zionists (Bloomfield interview).

Begin was suspicious of Christian proselytizing (Melman and Raviv 1994: 361). However, he saw the advantage of alliance with the fastest-growing and most politically active Christian denominations. There was no evident disadvantage to doing so, as traditional churches had sharply curbed their support of Israeli policies and were less fervent and active in pursuing their political agenda. Israel paid for visits to Israel by Falwell in 1978 and 1979. In 1979 Falwell went at Begin's request to the illegal Elon Moreh settlement, already a provocation to Carter, and said that America must protect Israel or cease to be important to God (Halsell 1989: 74). In 1980, Begin awarded Falwell the Jabotinsky Medal for his steadfast support. Thereafter, Falwell spoke out on the 1981 Osirak raid and the 1982 Beirut camp massacres, exonerating Israel of any wrongdoing (Novik 1986: 87). During the 1980s, a senior Israeli diplomat was detailed to liaise with the Christian Right (Bloomfield interview).

There were economic reasons for Likud ties to the Christian Right. Evangelical ministers led large groups of pilgrims to Israel. Religious tourism became important to the Israeli economy; in times of turmoil some American Jews canceled their visits but Christian pilgrims did not (Bloomfield interview). Also, American dispensationalists were important financial supporters of land purchases and settlement expansion in Judea and Samaria (Halsell 1989: 170–2).

The Congress

The impact of post-Vietnam, post-Watergate reforms

Vietnam and Watergate sent shock waves through American society that, when they reached Congress, transformed it.[15] Congress reorganized to deal with foreign and security affairs, and was resolved to use its powers, notably the appropriations power, to condition or direct the conduct of foreign policy.

The large freshman class of 1974 insisted on reform and immediate involvement. In the House, 75 freshmen Democrats overthrew the seniority system, undermined the committee system and organized caucuses to formulate amendments not sanctioned by their leaders (Abshire and Nurnberger 1981: 85–100). This Balkanization meant that, to be effective, a lobby could no longer deal only with committee chairs, or expect acquiescence in legislation prepared by committee "experts" when bills were voted upon (Cohen 1981). Most lobbies did not have the capacity to organize contacts with most or all members, track their positions and supporters, and respond quickly to their requests. AIPAC had developed that capability under Amitay and further expanded it under Dine.

Control of information had been a major weapon of the executive branch in blunting congressional efforts at oversight and policy-making. In the 1970s Congress strengthened the Congressional Research Service and the General Accounting Office, created the Congressional Budget Office (1974) and the Office of Technology Assessment (1972), and added substantially to committee and personal staffs.[16] Expertise allowed members to question administration assertions and to defend legislative initiatives. Ironically, it also meant that members were deluged with more information than they could digest, requiring them – and particularly senators, with broader responsibilities – to cede increasing amounts of power to staff.

Congressional attempts to hem in presidential prerogatives escalated during the Nixon administration from nonbinding resolutions, to legislation requiring notification of executive agreements and troop deployments, cut-offs of aid by country and "legislative vetoes" (Jordan and Taylor 1984: 114–19). One of the most important veto provisions was the Nelson–Bingham Bill of 1974.[17] In 1973, Senator Nelson, an ardent supporter of Israel, opposed Nixon's intended sale of F-4 Phantoms to Saudi Arabia, and won a floor amendment that would have allowed one house of the Congress to veto arms sales. It was dropped in conference committee for fear a presidential veto would disrupt arms deliveries to Israel during the Yom Kippur War. Rewritten to require a majority vote of both houses, it was taken up again the next year and passed (Franck and Weisbrand 1979: 98–9; Novik 1986: 41).[18]

☒Committees: the distillation process ⚡

While the power of committee chairs was eroded after 1974, chairmen and their staffs were still the most important decision makers. For pro-Israel advocates, that meant committees dealing with foreign affairs and armed services, and relevant subcommittees on appropriations, foreign trade and intelligence. The most critical document was the "chairman's mark," language proposed by the chair of the committee of first referral, since it was easier to defend that language through the committee hearings and floor action than to amend it (Bloomfield interview). Party caucus chairs lost the power to force committee assignments; increasingly, relevant committees had disproportionate numbers of Jewish members (Wolfinger 1988: 10–11). There was no political advantage for most members for work on foreign relations; foreign aid was increasingly unpopular with the general public. Supporters of Israel also targeted campaigns of members of key committees, so that service on such a committee by a less than fervent supporter of Israel won no credit in the home district, and guaranteed funding of his opponent in the next election.[19] Policy toward Israel became "much more of a domestic issue" (van Dusen interview).

Committee members who were pro-Israel hired personal and committee staff who shared their views. Nearly all AIPAC staff had worked on the relevant committees or for their ranking members. Staff were critical, as they "draft[ed] the legislation, prepare[d] the amendments, organize[d] the hearings, [wrote] the reports, and plan[ned] the strategy" for the committee agenda (Bloomfield 1983: 22).

PACs: empowerment by reform

The 1974 campaign finance reform law limited individual contributions to political campaigns to $1,000 per primary, runoff or general election. Rita Hauser, chair of AJC's foreign affairs committee, thought the new law "eliminated the strongest weapon the Jewish community exercised in influencing the selection of nominees in both parties" (Tivnan 1987: 85). She was wrong. The law permitted the formation of "political action committees," or PACs. PACs were funnels: each person (and spouse, and child) could give $5,000 each year to the PAC; each PAC could give $5,000 to a candidate.[20] There was no limit to the number of PACs that could be formed or contributed to; a coordinated effort could pour unlimited funds into a campaign. There was no requirement that a PAC, or its contributors, be located in a candidate's jurisdiction; funds could be coordinated nationwide to impact campaigns where there were few Jewish, or pro-Israel, voters. The first pro-Israel PAC was formed in 1976; by the 1978 election season there were three, and by 1980, ten PACs made 208 contributions to 107 congressional candidates totalling $414,000 (Curtiss 1990: 15–16, 27).

AIPAC is not a PAC, and is legally prohibited from contributing to political campaigns. However, its Executive Committee members headed every pro-Israel Jewish organization in America, and its individual members were the pro-Israel activists in each community. They all received information from AIPAC on the positions taken by every member of Congress. Many PACs were established by AIPAC officers over the years 1978–1988.

A. F. K. Organski compared senators' voting records between 1970 and 1982 on issues favorable to Israel with their campaign contributions from Jewish voters, and found a strong correlation (Organski 1990). He argued, however, that rather than demonstrating the persuasive power of money, the correlation reflected financial support of those who were already strong supporters of Israel. Some strong supporters of Israel were not among those who received the most money. Moreover, Organski's study predates the explosive growth of PACs, and overlooks the effects of coordinated targeting. Some incumbent supporters did not need help. Senator McGovern was targeted by Amitay before the PAC era, but his Jewish contributions dried up. Pro-Israel groups used PACs to pool their efforts to help old friends, and to generate new friends by helping defeat their enemies. AIPAC's effectiveness was greater in using these tools than that of trade associations or unions because it focused on one issue, and faced no organized opposition. All it needed was a few prominent object lessons.

Where the course of least resistance led

The strong predilection of the large majority of congressmen and senators was to support Israel's security. The effect of the lobby's network of allies in key committees and their staffs was that legislation relating to Israel was usually more favorable to Israel than last year's, and more favorable than the administration's proposal. Members knew their votes and statements would be monitored and reported to an energized community of voters that would vote on a single issue. The effect of stories like that of Senator McGovern was to build conviction that the pro-Israel community could decide a close election, and that no opposing bloc could reward or punish votes. The only opposition was often the president when he wanted to limit or condition aid, sell arms to Arab states or promote a peace process on terms Israel opposed (Dine interview). Even when the risk to Israel seemed small, voting against an aid increase or for an Arab arms sale required explaining why the member did not accept the Israeli government's judgment, knowing that Israel's supporters would not be mollified. The politically and psychically easiest course was usually to support the AIPAC position.

Support for pro-Israel measures in the first half of the 1970s averaged "upwards of 80 percent of the votes in both houses" (Feuerwerger 1979: 11). In the period 1970–1977, Congress increased administration requests for economic aid to Israel by an average of 30 percent, and military aid by 3 percent (ibid.: 28–30). There was a ratcheting effect: voting for less aid than the previous year was not seriously considered. In 1972, economic aid was a grant of $50 million; for each of the three fiscal years 1978–1980, it was $785 million, $525 million of that in grants; for fiscal 1981, it was $764 million, all grants. Military aid fluctuated more widely, spiking substantially just after the 1973 war and again in 1976 and 1979, but for fiscal 1977, 1978 and 1980 it was $500 million each in loans and grants, and in 1981 the grants were increased to $900 million (Mark 2002). Most of the loans were later forgiven, and the annual appropriations act always provided that grant aid would exceed amounts Israel owed on prior loans.

Administrations generally shared the view that support of Israel was justified both morally and strategically. Henry Kissinger believed that making Israel militarily unassailable would force Arab states who were Soviet clients to deal with Israel and with the United States. In the course of the disengagement negotiations he guaranteed future levels of American support. President Carter substantially raised the floors on support to Israel as part of the Camp David assurances. However, when Kissinger and Ford proposed to "reassess" the relationship and slow aid in the pipeline, the reaction from Israel's friends in Congress was swift and humiliating. Carter managed to sell aircraft to Saudi Arabia and Egypt, but only after a bitter and damaging fight and substantially enhanced deliveries to Israel. Because aid and arms sales were the principal recurring elements of American policy in the Middle East, and because they were subject to congressional control, Congress had power to prevent consideration of any policy that diluted or conditioned support of Israel.

Former senator J. William Fulbright, long-time chair of Senate Foreign Relations until defeated in 1974, believed that "[t]he lobby can just about tell the President what to do when it comes to Israel. Its influence in Congress is pervasive and, I think, profoundly harmful – to us and ultimately to Israel itself" (Fulbright 1989: 183).[21] Senator Charles McC. Mathias, Jr. believed that members responded to the lobby "for reasons not always related either to personal conviction or careful reflection on the national interest." He knew of few members who did not "believe deeply and strongly that support of Israel is both a moral duty and a national interest of the United States," but "congressional conviction has been measurably reinforced by the knowledge that political sanctions will be applied to any who fail to deliver" (Mathias 1981: 993). He believed that the lobby's effectiveness was not always matched by wisdom: the Jackson–Vanik amendment had in his view harmed Soviet Jews and America's interest in détente (ibid.: 995–6).

Opinions differed as to whether the national interest was being served. What seemed clear was that by 1981, Congress was habituated to high levels of economic and political support for Israel, and only at considerable political cost to the president and to members of Congress who supported him could a different course be chosen.

Policy networks and Reagan

For purposes of his domestic economic agenda and core policies of his national security agenda, Ronald Reagan initially had a reasonably potent network of support. Western conservatives had taken over leadership of the Republican Party, and Republicans now effectively controlled both houses of Congress.[22] Conservative and neoconservative policy institutes and publicists and the business community supported Reagan's tax cuts, social program reductions and defense build-up. The American public was prepared to try this combination of changes. The result was a "truly remarkable rookie year" (O'Neill 1987: 408): Reagan's massive tax cuts were passed by the August congressional recess, and the first of several intended defense increases and domestic programs cuts were approved.

As to Middle East policy, there was an existing policy network that would support strong, unconditional and regionally exclusive support of Israel; to the extent Reagan's policy deviated from that standard, the same network – including many who supported Reagan generally, and including officers of his government – would work against him. The network included the traditional Jewish organizations and organized labor, normally liberal in agenda and Democratic in leanings, but also AIPAC, dedicated entirely to support of Israel. It included the government of Israel, a direct actor in the domestic politics of the United States. It included a sub-network of members and staff in Congress, well-placed to shape and shepherd legislation pertaining to Israel. Finally it included groups who supported Reagan's election, but on the understanding that the fervor of his support of Israel matched theirs: neoconservatives, members of policy institutes such as JINSA and CIS, and the Christian Right. Unlike other coalitions,[23] the pro-Israel network did not give Reagan a honeymoon.

Supporters of "balanced" policies, including restraints on Israel and arms sales to moderate Arab states, existed, but were weak reeds. They included business entities with economic interests in the policies, Arab-American organizations and representatives of Arab governments.

Reagan had established ties with business leaders as spokesman for General Electric for eight years and as governor of California. His program of slashed taxes, defense spending and less regulation was strongly supported by businessmen. They lobbied congressmen; their PACs gave to supporters of the president's economic and defense programs. However, American business generally shied away from foreign policy, fearing backlash from those with whom they did, or hoped to do, business. Reticence was particularly obvious with respect to the Middle East, as to which domestic passions ran high. Many companies doing business in the Middle East, including Bechtel and the oil companies, had been burned by congressional scrutiny and ADL lawsuits concerning compliance with the Arab boycott of companies doing business in Israel (Spiegel 1986: 222, 310). Morris Amitay said that the business community's absence from Middle East lobbying left the field to AIPAC (Tivnan 1987: 194). The oil companies in particular typically lobbied only on economic issues: taxes and depletion allowances (Bloomfield interview).

Arab-Americans were nearly as numerous as Jewish Americans, but where the Jewish community had greatly disproportionate impact on the political process, the Arab-American community had much less than proportionate impact. In fact, the first question was whether there was a community. Arab-Americans tended to fragment along the lines of rivalries in the Arab world. Lebanese-Americans were for many years the most active group, organizing and leading the principal Arab-American organizations. However, many were Christian, which at least until the mid-1980s meant they shared Lebanese Maronite willingness to associate with Israel against their Sunni rivals in Lebanon, Shiites in southern Lebanon and the Ba'athist regime in Damascus. Tom Dine found Lebanese Americans a "disorganized group" (Dine interview). Arab-Americans had no tradition of political participation and no organizational cohesion; they were not a political factor.

Arab governments similarly constituted no countervailing force to that of Likud-led Israeli governments. With few exceptions, Arab ambassadors were ineffective, making no effort to learn the American culture and political system (Handyside interview).[24] There was neither outreach to nor mobilization of the Arab-American community. When heads of state or of government visited, their only targets were the president and his chief aides; their presumption, consistent with their experience at home but repeatedly disproved in Washington, was that the American administration could deliver whatever it promised. Arabs typically saw no need to engage the American public. Senator James Abourezk, one of very few Arab-Americans elected to office, suggested to a Kuwaiti official in 1976 that they should explain their positions to the American people. The Kuwaiti indignantly said, "Why should we tell the Americans anything, because we have the truth" (Curtiss 1982: 141). Frederick Dutton experienced similar attitudes over three decades of representing Saudi Arabia in Washington (Dutton interview). Arab regimes were inevitably going to have difficult public relations challenges, because of their opposition to the Camp David peace process, their relationships with the PLO and their rivalries among themselves.

Any president's relationship with the Jewish community is important to understanding his Middle East policy. During the Reagan years, the Christian Right became increasingly visible in American politics, and Reagan was the first president to be associated with that movement. Neither group was a steady part of Reagan's policy network in the first term.

The Christian Right, particularly dispensationalists, initially seemed a natural ally on Middle East policy for Reagan. Like neoconservatives, they saw Israel's conflicts with its neighbors in Manichean terms; Israel's territory was God-given, and one could not seek détente with the devil or with his minions, the leaders of Magog (the Soviet Union). Ties between Reagan and the Christian Right were less than they appeared, however. Most of the Moral Majority's energies went into social issues such as abortion and prayer in the schools, issues to which Reagan gave rhetorical support but little energy. The one time the White House intervened during the first term to help the Christian Right, it became a major political fiasco.[25] The president's political advisers also resented assertions of the Christian Right that its efforts had elected Reagan (Cannon 1982: 315).

Further, the strongest supporters of Israel, American Jews, were very uncomfortable with the "Christianizing" domestic agenda of the Christian Right. AIPAC's efforts to liaise with the Christian Right illuminate the two ways in which Christian zionists were relevant during the Reagan administration: (1) they were trusted conduits of information to a growing segment of the public that otherwise had minimal interest in foreign affairs; and (2) they could be counted on for visible support in Washington and conservative media when issues came to a boil. The cumulative effect of the education effort was undoubtedly significant in these years; less clear is whether the Christian Right created single-issue voters.

Reagan's relations with the American Jewish community were unusual, especially for a Republican president. Among many Jewish friends in California were several who were active in national Jewish organizations and in his campaigns; some chaired or co-chaired campaign organizations and introduced him to leaders elsewhere. Known for very strong support of Israel, he received approximately 39 percent of the Jewish vote in 1980, the highest for a Republican since Eisenhower's first race. But he did not have strong ties to national Jewish organizations, which with the exception of AIPAC were still committed to the entire liberal Jewish agenda and put off by Reagan's domestic agenda and Christian Right supporters. In 1981, Jacob ("Jack") Stein, a former chair of the Presidents Conference, agreed to serve as "Special Adviser to the White House for Jewish Affairs" in the Office of Public Liaison. Stein left within months after the AWACS vote in October 1981, and was not replaced until 1983. There was friction between the White House and established national Jewish organizations as to who was entitled to select spokesmen for the community to the White House. White House staff would brief those committed to the president; the chair of the Presidents Conference would insist that it was the authentic representative of the community.

Until Tom Dine's accession in 1980, AIPAC's activities were limited to Washington, and almost entirely to the Congress. It had a national network of supporters, but their activities were limited to fundraising, contacting members of Congress and distributing information, almost entirely within the Jewish community. Ronald Reagan had no personal experience with AIPAC until he ran for president, and that contact amounted to passing the litmus test on Israel. His campaign statements and a 1979 opinion piece in the *Washington Post* passed that test. Awaiting him in his first year as president, as his first major contested foreign policy issue, was the fight with AIPAC and Israel over AWACS.

The difference of AIPAC

Like other pro-Israel organizations, AIPAC had been associated principally with Democrats. Most of its professional staff, including Amitay, Dine and Bloomfield, were former aides to liberal Democrats. However, it had always sought bipartisan sponsorship for any legislative initiative. With the election of Ronald Reagan, its unique advantage over other pro-Israel groups was that it dealt only with policy on Israel. It could join neoconservatives and defense hawks in arguing for a strategic view that encompassed defense build-ups and strengthened ties with Israel, without opposing the president on any of his fiscal and social programs. It could liaise with the Christian Right without opposing them on their domestic program. And it could continue to be the Washington voice of the broader, largely liberal, Jewish community on Israel. Thus, the moderate Democrat Tom Dine took over at a perfect time to test his theories.

4 Ronald Reagan

Beliefs and policies

Introduction

Ronald Reagan was the first president who combined conservatism, ardent anti-communism, identification with the Christian right and seemingly unqualified support of Israel as moral obligee, cultural sibling and sole reliable American security partner in the Middle East. He was seen as highly ideological, and he was, in the sense that he was driven by a Manichean idealism; but he borrowed his beliefs from several strains of American conservatism, and his pragmatism and flexibility disappointed ideological purists. His support of Israel was based less on neoconservatism, Christian Zionism or geopolitical calculation than it was on emotional affinity.

Reagan had great skill in communicating a set of principles and in persuading others to trust his choice of policies to fit those principles. He lacked interest in governing, including such basic executive functions as choosing staff, deciding disputes among principal advisers and overseeing implementation of policy. His non-involvement in governance meant that policy could be coherently pursued only when relevant cabinet officers were unanimous or when one officer had achieved effective control over an area of policy. No member of the original national security team gained such control over policy toward Israel. Only George Shultz, Reagan's second secretary of state, achieved the trust of the president and pre-eminence among cabinet officers in setting policy toward Israel, subject to limits set by the president and by domestic politics.

Reagan did not recognize contradictions inherent in his stated beliefs as applied to Israel. Israel could play at most a limited role against the Soviet Union, but repeatedly acted in ways that aligned the United States against Soviet clients under circumstances of Israel's choosing. Revisionist Zionist policies were congruent with the neoconservative and Dispensationalist Christian beliefs of some supporters, but often inconsistent with practical arrangements with friendly Arab regimes required to project American power and protect American interests. These unperceived conflicts, exacerbated by Reagan's lack of interest in detail and his reluctance to confront trusted aides or allies, proved a formula for confusion.

The principled and causal beliefs of Ronald Reagan

A tapestry of ideologies

Ronald Reagan drew on several streams of American-style conservative thought in formulating declaratory policy. One of the challenges in understanding him is discerning where his rhetoric overstated his commitment or outran his understanding, and where he simply changed his mind based upon new (or newly recognized) facts.

It was as leader of the Western conservative movement that Reagan had challenged President Ford, leader of the traditional, pragmatist/mechanist wing of the Republican Party in 1976, largely on issues of détente and big government. But he was also accepted as a neoconservative; he had turned from the Democratic Party and organized labor to a strident anti-communism based on his view of morality, and supported Israel on both moral and strategic grounds. Reagan also seemed to believe in "intuition, psychic phenomena and fate," and "was fascinated by the biblical story of Armageddon" (Cannon 1991: 34).

Foreign and security policy

As to foreign policy, Reagan "came into office with a point of view rather than a set of policies – a view that was anti-Soviet, pro-Israel and largely supportive of the Atlantic Alliance" (Cannon 1982: 400).[1] A long-serving American ambassador to Israel described him as Manichean and essentialist: "A deeply convinced ideological warrior against world communism, totally suspicious of Soviet intentions, Reagan was the United States' first true ideological president. He saw the world struggle in stark terms: good versus evil, democracy versus dictatorship, allies and friends versus enemies" (Lewis 1988: 227). During the 1980 campaign, he defined security policy entirely in terms of defeating the Soviet Union: "Let's not delude ourselves. The Soviet Union underlies all the unrest that is going on. If they weren't engaged in this game of dominoes, there wouldn't be any hot spots in the world" (*WSJ* 3 Jun. 1980: 1). As candidate and as first-term president, he seemed to question the wisdom of *contact* with the Soviet Union, seeing relations based on hopes for mutual benefit as fraught with danger. Nine days into his presidency, he said that the Soviets had as their "only morality," to do "what will further their cause," reserving the "right to commit any crime, to lie, to cheat" and any dealings with them had to be structured accordingly (PC 29 Jan. 1981 in DoS Bull Mar. 1981: 12). He invited Jeane Kirkpatrick to advise him on foreign policy based on her article arguing for support of authoritarian (but pro-Western) regimes against the Soviets (Kirkpatrick 1979). The implication, which became explicit policy, was that friends in the great East–West battle would be supported regardless of other concerns (like human rights or standards of governance), and those aligned with the Soviets would be opposed, again regardless of other considerations. Condoleezza Rice observed that the "biggest flaw" in this Reagan doctrine was that "it globalize[d] and bilateralize[d] conflicts whose dynamics [were] complicated by regional and indigenous politics" (Rice 1990: 77). Reagan had no appreciation of regional complexities, i.e. the enduring ethnic, religious and political rivalries in Lebanon. In February 1980, he said, "I can't see why they're fighting. After all, they're all Lebanese" (Spiegel 1986: 400).

Reagan's anti-communism was acquired during six years as president of the Screen Actors Guild, 1946–1952; Edwin Meese reported that he had carried a weapon for self-defense against communists (Lagon 1994: 95).[2] During his years as spokesman and motivational speaker for General Electric Corporation, he developed "The Speech," which was the basis for the October 1964 Goldwater campaign speech and many he gave as president. The readings which provided grist for The Speech importantly included *National Review*, the conservative journal edited by his friend William F. Buckley, Jr. and *Commentary*, the AJC journal dominated by Norman Podhoretz. Both journals were fervently anti-communist. Buckley argued that "statism" in the West advanced the socialist cause; Podhoretz promoted Israel as the sole reliable American surrogate in the Middle East against the Soviet and Islamist terrorist threats. *Commentary*'s neoconservative attacks on pragmatist approaches to the Soviet Union were particularly useful to Reagan in 1976, running against the détente policies of fellow Republicans Ford and Kissinger (Bell 1989).

Israel's privileged place

Ronald Reagan was perhaps the first president since Theodore Roosevelt with numerous Jewish friendships predating his political life. Hollywood was a "small community led by Jews" (Goldberg 1996: 214). Reagan had been deeply affected by films of Nazi death camps, and believed that America owed a moral debt to Israel (Lewis 1988: 227; Shultz interview). "I've believed many things in my life, but no conviction I've ever held has been stronger than my belief that the United States must ensure the survival of Israel" (Reagan 1990: 410). An FBI dossier portrays him as an emotional foe of anti-Semitism who denounced persecution of Jews in radio broadcasts, and nearly fought a party guest who said that Jews profiteered from the war (Cannon 1991: 391).

Reagan had had no comparable exposure to Arabs or Palestinians. His world view included what Spiegel gingerly refers to as a "de-emphasis on the Third World as an object of U.S. concern" (Spiegel 1986: 399). Reagan constantly watched movies, and internalized much that he saw; perhaps reflecting the way in which Hollywood portrayed Arabs,[3] he tended to see them as unsophisticated, unreasonable and unworthy of trust or concern, especially as compared with familiar, friendly, sophisticated, pro-Western, democratic Israelis.

Reagan, normally a politician who exuded empathy, was asked soon after taking office whether he had any sympathy or moral feeling toward Palestinians and their aspirations. He responded by condemning Palestinians who denied Israel's right to exist, and the PLO as terrorists and illegitimate spokesmen (Docs & Stmts 79–82: 228).[4] Reagan spoke of possible "religious war" resulting from "the Muslims returning to the idea that the way to heaven was to lose your life fighting the Christians or the Jews" (Gerges 1999: 59). Until his September 1982 "Fresh Start" initiative, he spoke of Palestinians only as refugees. He even asserted that Jordan should take responsibility for 80 percent of Palestinians, proportionate to the British division of mandatory Palestine (*NYT* 10 May 1980: 10). In his 1990 memoirs, after years of dealing with issues of Palestinian refugees in Lebanon and elsewhere, he said he understood the Palestinians' sense of loss regarding "land they considered *their* homeland"; but he attributed "Palestinian terror," to which the courageous and "tiny new country" of Israel was subjected, to ancient hatreds (Reagan 1990: 407–8). There is no evidence that he ever credited a contemporary pattern of Israeli behavior as one cause of Palestinian antipathy, or identified with Palestinian national aspirations as he did those of Israelis.

Some Arab regimes and the PLO were supported by the Soviet Union. That meant that Reagan was open to arguments of neoconservatives and AIPAC that Israel was America's only trustworthy regional ally. In addition, Reagan came to office identifying terrorism as a principal policy concern.[5] The administration linked Islam with radical extremism, with terror and with the Soviet Union. Defense Secretary Weinberger described Shiites as the "most fanatical and the most basically anti-Western sect," who did not "place any great value on human life" (Gerges 1999: 69). Secretary of State Shultz equated Islamic fundamentalism with radical extremism, and saw Islamist terror as backed by the Soviets against Western democracies (Shultz 1986). It was taken as axiomatic that the Soviet Union used surrogates to undermine the West, and that among the surrogates were radical nationalist movements and state sponsors of terrorism.

Reagan's division of the world into pro-Western friends and pro-Soviet enemies is consistent with the Armageddon story as interpreted by Dispensationalist evangelicals; it is not clear how much such beliefs influenced Reagan. While governor of California, he evidently argued that the prophesies of Ezekiel and Revelations, which he could quote at length, were to be taken literally, meaning that Emperor Haile Selassie of Ethiopia would inevitably fall to a communist insurgency (Halsell 1989: 43–7). Reagan invited only evangelical ministers to official and political events, and regularly addressed televangelist conventions. Halsell asserts that he invited Jerry Falwell to attend NSC nuclear war planning sessions, and invited Hal Lindsey (author of *The Late Great Planet Earth*, the 1970 book predicting nuclear holocaust based upon Ezekiel) to brief Pentagon planners (ibid.: 47).

Dispensationalists teach that support of Israel's efforts to control all of

King David's territory and rebuild the temple in Jerusalem is God's will. However, they also teach that attempting to prevent nuclear war on the plain of Megiddo is heresy.[6] Literal belief of that teaching does not square with Reagan's willingness to negotiate an end to nuclear weapons with First Secretary Gorbachev, the leader of the evil "Magog" of the prophesies. Reagan gave only rhetorical support to the evangelicals' domestic agenda; his fixation on Armageddon may have reflected his love of a dramatic story, an attempt to bond with the fastest-growing segment of religious America or his beliefs.

However, there is evidence the prophesies retained force for him. In 1983, he wrote friends that current events tracked those prophesied to precede Armageddon (letter to Hannafords 2 Oct. 1983 in Skinner *et al.* 2003: 278). In 1984, Reagan told Tom Dine that current events convinced him that Armageddon might be near (Blitzer 1985: 239–40). In the second 1984 presidential debate, he acknowledged "philosophical discussions" on the issue, but since no one knew when it might come, he would not say America "must plan according to Armageddon" (Cannon 1991: 289). National Security Adviser McFarlane believed that the Armageddon prophesy explained Reagan's support of the Strategic Defense Initiative; he believed that as a heroic figure, he could protect America from the general conflagration (ibid.: 290). Reagan also responded to Defense Secretary Frank Carlucci's arguments in favor of traditional nuclear deterrence by relating the Armageddon story (ibid.: 291).[7]

Whatever the relative strength of these influences, Israel had a very privileged place in Ronald Reagan's thinking. In his 1979 opinion piece, probably written by Joseph Churba, candidate Reagan said that

> our own position would be weaker without the political and military assets Israel provides … The fall of Iran has increased Israel's value as perhaps the only remaining strategic asset in the region on which the United States can truly rely … Israel's strength derives from the reality that her affinity with the West is not dependent on the survival of an autocratic or capricious ruler. Israel has the democratic will, national cohesion, technological capacity and military fiber to stand forth as America's trusted ally.
>
> (Reagan 1979)

He argued further that Israel's dominance of critical zones of access and transit restricted Soviet options and that anything done to weaken Israel, including support of a Palestinian state or inadequate American aid, violated American national interests.[8] Nowhere in this piece on American Middle East policy is there reference to the Camp David process or to the stalled autonomy talks. Palestinians are referred to only as a threat to Israel.

Statements to Jewish leaders during the campaign echoed the themes in the 1979 article, and hinted at Reagan's mix of neoconservatism and expectations based on prophesy: "Israel is the only stable democracy we can rely on in a spot where Armageddon could come ...We must prevent the Soviet Union from penetrating the Middle East ... If Israel was not there, the United States would have to be there" (Safire 1980).[9]

Some obvious questions were never addressed by Reagan during the campaign, or for that matter during his presidency: against whom could Israel defend American interests? Against the Soviet Union, the most Israel could do was to provide intelligence, limited facilities and monitoring of the eastern Mediterranean. Israeli defense of American interests in the Gulf against supposed surrogates of the Soviet Union, themselves all Arab or Muslim or both, was unacceptable to Gulf Arabs. And were Israel's strength and stubborn independence a source of stability in the region and protection for U.S. interests? The closest the superpowers came to conflict in the Middle East were occasions when Israel fought its neighbors, often against American advice; during Reagan's presidency, that was a "war of choice" in Lebanon.

Ronald Reagan's leadership attributes

Ronald Reagan was consistently engaged as president only in two ways: in the conceptualizing of policy, consistent with his fundamental beliefs, and in the "performance" aspects of the office. He was perhaps the most masterful "performer" the office has ever seen; when adequately briefed, he could win support, or at least acquiescence, from millions on television or from leaders brought to the Oval Office. But he had little curiosity about the facts relevant to policy, and little understanding of the consequences of conflicts among key aides. When his first-term White House "Troika" of James Baker (chief of staff), Michael Deaver (deputy chief of staff) and Edwin Meese (counselor) served him well, he was protected from many of the effects of such deficits. Reagan's strong predisposition to favor Israel, his aversion to confrontation and his disinterest in detail made unconditional support of Israel the default position of his administration.

His disinterest in policy detail was infamous.[10] This freed him to ignore the impediments that facts often presented,[11] but tripped him when he was badly served by aides.[12] He was accustomed to following a detailed working schedule. He was "produced" for public events by Michael Deaver and Communications Director David Gergen to ensure a tightly controlled message. He was scripted for meetings with anyone aside from White House staff and Cabinet. Reagan read his remarks from note cards, even in meetings with domestic political leaders, and always had others explain legislative proposals (O'Neill 1987: 431–2).[13] The schedules, and the contents of the note cards, were determined by aides; Reagan's assumption was that his staff would tell him anything he needed to know.

Ronald Reagan "delegated" more broadly than any president since Franklin Roosevelt. Unlike Roosevelt, however, Reagan often did not understand what it was that he had delegated; he provided no detailed guidance or performance standards and generally took no initiative to test results. Donald Regan reported that he never met with Reagan between being asked to serve as Treasury secretary and the inauguration, never saw the president alone and never had any policy discussions with Reagan during his four years as secretary. The president "was content to exercise the symbolic powers of his office," leaving key officers to "fly ... by the seat of [their] pants" (Regan 1988: 142–3). Reagan was often silent throughout important meetings.[14] Because he was often "either ambiguous about or indifferent to follow-up concerning statements he had made in the Oval Office ... those present could each take their own interpretations of events back to their own agencies, and in some cases to the press, and tell different stories as to what happened" (Kemp 1999: 169). Kemp attributes the administration's problems "on arms control, relations in the Middle East, and, most tellingly, the Iran-Contra affair" on confusion about what, if anything, was decided at Oval Office meetings (ibid.). Richard Perle agreed: "It never ceased to amaze me how inconclusive meetings at the highest level were. They were almost never decisive" (Cannon 1991: 339).

Reagan's disinterest in governing extended to key appointments and the organization of the White House. Reagan had promised Alexander Haig that he would be the single formulator of and spokesman for Reagan's foreign policy (the "vicar," as Haig said), and the national security adviser would "fill a staff role for the President" (Haig confirmation testimony in DoS Bull Feb. 1981: E; PC 28 Jan. 1981 in DoS Bull Feb. 1981: H). Haig attempted to formalize that guidance in a draft National Security Decision Directive; Edwin Meese simply kept it and may never have shown it to the president. Haig was stunned, but could never solve the problem of getting around Meese (Haig 1984: 76). Meese, with no experience in foreign or security policy and no formal responsibility for it, arrogated to himself the oversight of all policy matters, foreign and domestic. National Security Adviser Richard Allen had cramped basement quarters and reported to Meese instead of to the president. Meese largely supplanted the role that Reagan had said he wanted for the NSC with a non-statutory National Security Planning Group (NSPG), made up of the president, vice-president, secretaries of state and defense, and the Troika, with Allen acting only as scribe. This NSPG was supplemented by interdepartmental committees, each chaired by the cabinet member with the most at stake. That tended to substitute top-down direction for interdepartmental coordination and option generation. Allen generally saw the president only at larger meetings. One looks in vain for evidence that this system was Reagan's choice.

Reagan's near obliviousness to staffing and organizational decisions allowed tensions between Western/neoconservative aides and pragmatists to erupt into open competition for policy supremacy. There was an "inner circle" of those who strongly identified with Reagan and his beliefs, made up of Meese, CIA Director William Casey, U.N. Ambassador Jeane Kirkpatrick and Deputy Secretary of State (and then National Security Adviser)

William Clark.[15] They agreed as to the external rivals (the Soviet Union and all allied with it), domestic opponents (traditional centrist Republicans and liberal Democrats), and factional rivals within the administration (pragmatists Baker, Deaver, Baker deputy Richard Darman, Haig and ultimately, Shultz). These "Reaganauts" fought to control access to Reagan and his message; in the first term, they usually prevailed. In interviews, all agreed on the importance of there being a self-conscious group enforcing the Reagan vision (Lagon 1994: 105). The White House speech-writers were strong supporters of the policy views shared by the Western conservatives and neoconservatives,[16] as were several officials at the defense department and in the NSC staff.[17]

When policy fights concerned Israel, the division was between those who counseled heavy strategic reliance on Israel and those who accepted a commitment to ensure Israel's security but who were dubious of its value in the East–West conflict. CIA Director Casey, U.N. Ambassador Kirkpatrick and National Security Adviser Allen all supported the conclusions of a 1981 Rand Corporation report (later published as an AIPAC monograph) recommending reliance on Israel to the exclusion of Saudi Arabia and Jordan (Puschel 1992: 47). Others holding similar views included Paul Wolfowitz (director of planning at State),[18] Harvey Sicherman (speech-writer at State) and three founding members of JINSA.[19] Those counseling caution in relying on Israel included Secretary of Defense Caspar Weinberger, many within the permanent bureaucracy at both State and Defense, and uniformed officers.

In part, Reagan's distancing himself from details of governance reflected his extreme discomfort with confrontation with or among aides. In California, he had relied heavily on two small circles of confidantes, one of cabinet members and a second "kitchen cabinet" of wealthy, conservative friends. Reagan welcomed diverse ideas, even debate, but could not tolerate contentiousness; the California system lent itself to civil discussion. In Washington it was not possible to replicate the California system; Reagan expected his cabinet to present him with a consensus recommendation, presumably through the Troika. This meant that (1) major policy issues stewed in the cabinet cauldron indefinitely and (2) the opponent of an initiative or policy change was greatly advantaged, since it was easier to prevent change than to accomplish it.[20] In disputes between Weinberger and Shultz, these traits favored Shultz in supporting Israel, which Weinberger opposed; but they favored Weinberger in blocking force deployments which Shultz and McFarlane supported.

Presidential decisions were shaped by the options chosen and presented to the president by the Troika (plus "Judge" William Clark, when he became national security adviser) (Kessel 1984). Even on very major issues, the president was given a memorandum of one to two pages; he discussed the issue informally and then announced his decision. The process did not include discussions in Cabinet, in the NSC or with individual cabinet members. Even the question of when the 1982 Middle East peace plan should be unveiled was determined by this process, although it was Shultz's initiative (ibid.: 254). None of the four had had any previous experience in foreign policy (except for Clark's year at State); none had close ties with American Jews (Spiegel 1986: 405). According to Deaver: "If a suggestion trigger[ed] one of Reagan's stereotypes, that determine[ed] his position. If the subject [was] novel, then the president may well be guided by political considerations" (Kessel 1984: 256).

Where Reagan was strong, he was very strong. While he did not want his "boys" to fight in the Cabinet, he could overrule a consensus recommendation when that appeared necessary to uphold his principles (or stereotypes). He was at sea, and largely silent, when the decision did not clearly implicate his principles and did not call for him to perform; but he was both decisive and persuasive when he was convinced of his course and "on stage." As we will see in the AWACS battle, he could be both tough and charming in swaying even senior politicians publicly committed to oppose the president's position. His public persona was his most valuable asset; as they came to know him as president, Americans seemed not to mind that he was vague on details and sometimes inconsistent in policy pronouncements. His self-deprecating humor and cheerful confidence in a strong, principled, honorable America made the majority of Americans feel good about him and themselves. They simply forgave him his faults. People wanted to trust, and to help, Ronald Reagan, and when he was adequately briefed he could call on that wellspring of good will to move many of the undecided, and some of the weakly opposed, into his column on an issue. It seems unlikely that any other president of recent decades could have survived the Iran-Contra scandal, and left office again carrying the warm good wishes of the great majority of the public. However, in the area of foreign affairs his skills were used more often to dig himself out of public relations holes than to overcome obstacles to policy initiatives.

Elliott Abrams[21] may have put the best positive gloss on Reagan's leadership attributes when he said that Reagan was "a terrific president but not a terrific prime minister"; he was better as "symbolic leader of the people … than … manager of the government's institutions" (Abrams 1993: 96).

President Reagan's national security "team"

Both of President Reagan's secretaries of state were conservative pragmatists; both were accused of disloyalty to the true Reagan faith by Western conservatives and neoconservatives.[22] Reagan had intended to downgrade the position of national security adviser; with the highly ideological and ineffective Richard Allen, he succeeded too well. His replacement, William Clark, knew the president's mind much better than he knew national security issues. They were the first of six persons to hold the position; not until the last two years did Frank Carlucci and then Colin Powell combine the experience and judgment needed to make independent assessments of policy options, with the interpersonal skills required to achieve coherent and timely decisions. Again, both were pragmatists.[23] A president with the requisite interest and skills might have (1) chosen a team which minimized philosophical and interpersonal conflicts or (2) imposed discipline so that differences could inform the president without creating confusion about what the policy was. Reagan did neither.

The secretaries of State

Alexander Meigs Haig, Jr.

General Alexander Haig had served as deputy to Henry Kissinger on Nixon's NSC, and as Nixon's last chief of staff. Nixon recommended Haig to Reagan, praising his toughness and knowledge; Nixon warned against appointing George Shultz as lacking adequate understanding of international relations (Cannon 1991: 73, 79).

Reagan's inner circle did not trust Haig, because of his identification with pragmatists Nixon and Kissinger, and because of his suspected presidential ambitions. Five of them summoned Haig to a pre-appointment interrogation; Haig thought it "ludicrous and naïve" to inquire about his political aspirations (ibid.: 194). This inauspicious beginning – mistrust, met with contempt – was a true augury. Haig found "the White House ... as mysterious as a ghost ship," where it was impossible to know which of the crew – Meese or Baker, or someone else – was at the helm (Haig 1984: 85).[24] Within two months, Haig was being asked about his conflicts with the White House ("Meet the Press" 29 Mar. 1981 in DoS Bull May 1981: 4, 5).

Alexander Haig was an unconditional supporter of Israel. Yitzhak Shamir said that Haig "made no pretence of neutrality where the Middle East was concerned," seeing Israel as a "natural partner" against terrorism, and hopefully against Soviet aggression (Shamir 1994: 117). In his first news conference, Haig denied any "sense of urgency" about the Israeli–Egyptian peace talks (PC 28 Jan. 1981, DoS Bull Feb. 1981: K).[25] It is unclear whether that was in order to avoid pressing Israel for concessions, or for other reasons.[26] In early testimony, he strongly endorsed support of Israel's military capability, so that it could "play a major role in countering the more serious threats involving the Soviet Union" (SFRC Hrg 19 Mar. 1981 in DoS Bull Apr. 1981: B).

Haig believed that friendly states in the region were more anxious about Soviet moves in Afghanistan, South Yemen and elsewhere than they were about regional rivalries, and would work with the United States in deflecting or defeating Soviet incursions. This was Haig's "consensus of strategic concerns" in the Middle East: a series of strategic dyads to face a perceived common foe. "Strategic consensus" was not an attempt to recreate the failed

Baghdad Pact, as some charged. However, no Arab state would agree to an Israeli role in defense of the region, even if less than the Shah's former role; and Israel would never agree to the enhancement of Arab defense capability, even if ostensibly aimed at the Soviets and their surrogates.

Haig felt himself "mortally handicapped by lack of access to President Reagan" (Haig 1984: 356), and he was; but he was disinclined to involve Reagan in developing policy options,[27] and he insulted the gatekeepers. Haig had destroyed any chance at rapport with the president by the time the burden of discord he represented became too heavy. When Reagan "accepted" a resignation Haig had threatened but never formally tendered, the justifications were legion.[28]

George P. Shultz

George Shultz replaced Haig in June 1982, in the midst of the Israeli siege of Beirut. He had been an economist, business school dean, president of Bechtel Corporation, and secretary of labor, director of the Office of Management and Budget and secretary of the treasury in the Nixon administration. As Nixon had said, he lacked foreign policy experience, but had had substantial experience with international economic business issues, especially in the Middle East. He was pragmatic, tenacious, used to tough negotiations and difficult people, and experienced in Washington's intramural policy fights. He sometimes was described as "Buddha-like," because he could sit listening placidly for long periods, but he had a volcanic temper. He saw himself as an implementer, negotiator and mediator, but he was forced to formulate policy in the Reagan administration. His policy decisions were strongly influenced by his reactions to the people with whom he was dealing.[29] That trait led him at times to stake out a very personal agenda over the nearly unanimous advice of those with relevant expertise.[30] He had a moralistic streak, which among other things fueled his reaction to terrorism.

George Shultz was not a Reagan insider, but was much better acquainted with Reagan and his confidantes than Haig had been. He had worked with Secretary of Defense Weinberger in the Nixon administration and at Bechtel, where Weinberger was general counsel; and had worked with several others in the administration. He had advised the Reagan campaign on economic issues, and had stayed in touch with key members of the Reagan team, including William Clark. He thought that Reagan got "to the essence of the problems pretty well," unlike some who got immersed in detail and lost the main track (Cannon 1991: 134). His instinct was to take the president's stories as keys to Reagan's understanding of the world, and to involve him as deeply as possible in working out the main themes of policy.[31] He worked methodically at breaking through the insiders' lines of defense; in this he was welcomed as a counterweight to Clark and Weinberger by Baker and Bush, the administration's pragmatists. Michael Deaver was a key ally in the White House, arranging for lengthy weekly lunches with the president (ibid.: 309).[32]

Within perhaps a year, Shultz was undisputed leader of the pragmatists within the administration, and hence the target of neoconservatives. Shultz came to distrust intelligence from William Casey's CIA, where there was a tendency to run a separate policy agenda.[33] He won and lost battles with Secretary Weinberger over commitment of forces in Lebanon, policy on terrorism and arms sales to Arab regimes. The Shultz–Weinberger relationship was described as "poisonous," deeply affecting working relationships among their aides (Abrams 1993: 114). Reagan was aware of some coolness between them (Reagan 1990: 511). In order to maintain harmony, Reagan often sought to shape policies to mollify one or the other of them (Cannon 1991: 403). By 1987, Shultz was essentially in full command of foreign policy, Casey was dead and Carlucci (a pragmatist who had previously worked for Shultz) replaced first Poindexter as National Security Adviser and then Weinberger as Secretary of Defense.

Shultz was at first feared by the Israelis as much as Haig had been loved. Yitzhak Shamir, then foreign minister, said the appointment was "viewed with nothing less than alarm" (Shamir 1994: 118). Shultz had co-authored a book with his new deputy secretary, Kenneth Dam, severely criticizing the Jackson–Vanik Amendment (Schultz and Dam 1977: 145–7). It was said that the only policy disagreement between Reagan and Shultz during the campaign was over Reagan's unconditional support of Israel (*NYT* 26 Jun. 1982: 1).[34] Bechtel had undertaken many major construction jobs in Saudi Arabia and the Gulf; as president of Bechtel, Shultz had made sure that all senators were aware of the company's support for the 1981 AWACS sale to Saudi Arabia (Brownstein and Easton 1983: 728). The early evidence was that Shultz would be "even-handed" in his approach to Israel and its neighbors, including Palestinians. In the strange patois of American Middle East policy, being "balanced" or "even-handed" is code to Israel's friends for "untrustworthy" and "biased against Israel," if not anti-Semitic. Just before Haig's resignation, Shultz had called Clark to express concerns about the Israeli invasion and the "destruction of Beirut" (Shultz 1993: 3, 5).

At his confirmation hearings, Shultz said "The crisis in Lebanon makes painfully clear a central reality of the Middle East: The legitimate needs and problems of the Palestinian people must be addressed and resolved, urgently and in all their dimensions." While American commitment to Israel's security remained complete, "a comprehensive peace acceptable to all the parties involved ... is the only sure guarantee of true and durable security." That required "an agreement that will satisfy the vital security interests of Israel and the political aspirations of the Palestinians," as well as the interests of others in the region (Shultz 1993: 19). Asked by Senator Rudy Boschwitz, a staunch supporter of Israel, if the security of Israel was the cornerstone of U.S. policy, Shultz agreed, but said, "It is not military strength that we want; it is peace that we want" (ibid.: 21).

Shultz immediately formed a "Middle East group" made up of government officials and civilian experts to advise him on policy, and a departmental group to develop secretly a comprehensive approach to resolving the Israeli–Arab–Palestinian conflict. One of his early decisions, however, was to reject the advice of the composite panel, which was to tie the Lebanon crisis to broader issues of West Bank and Gaza (Shultz 1993: 50). Doing so would have involved having the PLO meet the terms of the 1975 Kissinger letter, and then including them in negotiations on the issues laid out in the Camp David Framework for Peace. Not for the last time, Shultz declined to entertain a way forward that would involve dealing with the PLO.

In February 1983, Israeli Defense Minister Moshe Arens said that the "frustration and impatience and anger" in the U.S.–Israel relationship was perhaps the worst ever (*NYT* 20 Feb. 1983: 1). Fifteen months later, Arens said the relationship was "probably better" than "ever before" (*NYT* 31 May 1984: A4). In between, all of the players in the Middle East, but particularly Israel, had repeatedly frustrated and angered Shultz and the president and defeated their initiatives. Nevertheless, American policy was continuously adjusted to accommodate and strengthen Israel. By 1986, Tom Dine could quote Shultz as saying that he intended to institutionalize strategic cooperation arrangements so that a less sympathetic secretary of state "will not be able to overcome the bureaucratic relationship between Israel and the U.S. that we have established" (Dine 1986: 139).

Early national security advisers

Richard V. Allen

Richard Allen's essentialist views on the Soviet Union were laid out in a 1967 book identifying Moscow's "strategic purpose" as "the isolation, encirclement, weakening and final destruction of the free world and its way of life" (quoted in Novik 1985: 21). Allen wrote a forward to Joseph Churba's 1980 book, calling Churba's argument "indispensable" (Churba 1980: x). He thus endorsed Churba's extreme pro-Israel advocacy, in which Israel was an implicit asset whose value was enhanced by independence of action, and who must never be limited in any way. Allen's staff were chosen in part through connections with AIPAC; no one not "compatible with the dominant pro-Israeli mindset" would have been considered (Tanter 1999: 45, 101–2).

Allen did not have relationships with Reagan or the Troika that assured access to the president, and lacked interpersonal skills that might have achieved access. Elliott Abrams thought it "clear that Alexander Haig regarded … Allen as someone who was there to be destroyed" (Abrams 1993: 115). The NSC staff had little role in interagency coordination and suffered low morale (Kemp 1999: 160).[35] Allen was, unsurprisingly, the author of no significant policy initiatives.

William P. Clark

The role of the NSC and its staff changed "overnight" with the arrival of Clark, who took the position on condition he have direct access to the president (ibid.). Like Meese, Clark was sure he knew what the president wanted, but unlike Meese he was a forceful and efficient administrator. Clark briefed the president, vice-president and Troika every morning, usually with relevant staff members; this not only increased Reagan's timely exposure to information, it exponentially increased access of largely neoconservative NSC staff to White House policy makers. Middle East issues were regularly elevated to the White House; NSC staff now had the lead in interoffice coordination and in preparing for visits by heads of state, so that now "the NSC staff had considerable influence on Middle East matters" (Kemp 1988: 16).

William Clark saw his job as converting Reagan's philosophy into policy.[36] To that end, he urged Reagan to accept Haig's resignation, and later prevailed over Shultz in having Robert McFarlane replace Philip Habib as special envoy in the Middle East (Destler *et al.* 1984: 231, 257–8).[37] Clark's efficiency and access made him effective when he took a position; his loyalty, lack of relevant background and Western conservative views meant that he both reflected and reinforced predispositions of the president.

Conclusion

Ronald Reagan's mix of neoconservative, Western conservative and religious beliefs yielded two presumptions in foreign affairs: (1) the Soviet Union and its surrogates were behind all mischief in the world, and all danger to the United States; and (2) relations with all other countries must be defined principally in terms of the competition with the Soviet Union. He identified Israel as the sole capable and reliable Middle East ally of the West in the struggle with Moscow, without working through what that meant. In addition, Reagan felt a strong moral debt to Israel, and may have believed that God intended Israel to recover its biblical lands. Stated very broadly, policies derived from these beliefs – strengthened defense, more aggressive opposition to Soviet expansionist moves and support of Israel – were supported by all relevant officers of the new administration.

The administration's attempt to apply this single policy template to each set of bilateral relations in the Middle East would reveal flaws inherent in the underlying assumptions. Israel would use American economic and military support not in the service of anti-communism, but to achieve security in the context of Revisionist Zionist goals. That meant acting against its Arab adversaries; in 1981 Israel struck Iraq's nuclear reactor, Syrian strategic positions in Lebanon and Palestinian leaders wherever it found them. Israel's policies in the Occupied Territories were inconsistent with the American interpretation of UNSCR 242, and with needed security accommodations with moderate, anti-Soviet Arab regimes.

As attempts to implement the declaratory policy of the new administration disclosed its inherent conflicts, divisions within the administration became clear. In most cases a pattern was discernable: the Western conservatives against the pragmatists, with neoconservatives at lower levels urging fidelity to declared principle, and those outside the government making up the very vocal chorus. By making gatekeepers of Meese and later Clark, Reagan gave Western conservatives the enormous advantages of access and the last (and sometimes only) word. But he chose pragmatists as his secretaries of state, and came to rely increasingly on Shultz. By the end of his first term, the Troika was gone; by the end of his second term, the national security team was made up of pragmatists.

Reagan's stunning achievement in enacting massive tax reductions and major increases in the defense budget in his first year demonstrated his remarkable ability, given favorable political circumstances, to translate his core principled and causal beliefs into national policy. As to those issues, he had long practiced his arguments, and all of his strengths could be brought to bear: strong general convictions, tactical flexibility, good negotiating skills and the public image of an active, confident leader (Greenstein 2000: 151). On domestic issues he also had a talented team to whom he could delegate substantial responsibility. When it came to foreign affairs, his strengths, and his principal officers, did not serve him as well. His reliance on narrative and analogy rather than detail and deductive logic made him vulnerable to arguments long on drama and emotion and short on facts (George and Stern 1998: 224). Because he was passive in acquiring information and did not push to generate or reshape policy options, his commitments were based on prior convictions rather than on events, and sometimes contradicted each other (ibid.; Neustadt 1990: 278). His principal advisers on foreign affairs were not a cohesive team, and had substantial unaddressed conflicts on key issues. When it came to Israel, Reagan's effectiveness in choosing a coherent course and embedding his ideas institutionally was limited by two factors: (1) his core beliefs led in different directions and (2) when his principles led him in any direction but unqualified support for Israel, some of his most ardent supporters would lead the political fight against him, both inside and outside the administration.

Reagan had not confronted the contradictions created by his beliefs by the time of the AWACS fight in 1981, and was faced with the first major foreign policy dispute of his administration before he was ready for engagement.

5 The AWACS sale
Testing beliefs and political capabilities

Introduction

President Reagan's first major foreign policy decision was to concur in a tentative decision by President Carter to sell a package of advanced arms to Saudi Arabia. The issue intruded itself on a White House that was organized to deal with domestic issues. The president had not recognized the inherent conflicts between his publicly expressed strategic reliance upon Israel and the practical imperatives that flowed from commitments to curb Soviet expansionism and guarantee access to Gulf oil. Reagan ultimately was able to avoid a congressional veto of the proposed sale. However, his inability to explain policy choices in terms of his proclaimed beliefs, exacerbated by disorder in his national security team, meant that Reagan had to rely heavily upon arguments centered on the need to avoid damage to presidential authority.

AIPAC was the undisputed leader of a unanimous pro-Israel community opposing the sale. While it used a range of ideological and practical arguments and political leverage, everything AIPAC did was driven by core principled and causal beliefs concerning Israel and its Arab adversaries. The terms on which the campaign was fought, and the political costs as perceived by the administration, strengthened AIPAC and accelerated the process of embedding a presumption that the administration would support Israel's view of regional security issues.

The case for AWACS

President Carter had tentatively decided to sell Saudi Arabia enhancements to Saudi F-15 fighter-bombers to increase their range and lethality, and a system of aerial surveillance and command/control capability, probably the E-3A Airborne Warning and Control System (AWACS).[1] The reasons to do so were: (1) the vital oil facilities of the Gulf had to be defended against attack by the Soviet Union, its proxies or Iran; (2) the sale would entail facilities and thickened security cooperation upon which the United States could rely in planning for force projections in the region; and (3) it was hoped that a strengthened relationship with the Saudis, and through them other moderate Arab regimes, would improve cooperation in the peace process and on regional security issues. The case for weapons systems and infrastructure to defend the oil facilities was crystal clear, but the case for Saudi ownership required understanding of Saudi strategic and political issues and a degree of trust in the monarchy and its stability, and ran counter to core beliefs embedded in congressional presumptions concerning policy toward Israel.

A short history of weapons sales to Saudi Arabia[2]

Between 1950 and 1973, the United States sold Saudi Arabia approximately $2.3 billion in weapons, equipment and related services. A 1974 Defense Department study of Saudi air defense capabilities resulted in a massive Saudi build-up, particularly of infrastructure. As of 30 June 1980, Saudi Arabia had purchased $34.4 billion in defense-related goods and services, of which $25.5 billion was for services (SFRC Staff Report: 2). Saudi Arabia paid in advance, and less than one-third of goods and services contracted for in the period 1950–1980 had been delivered by mid-1981. "If Saudi Arabia had not mortgaged its security to preserving its ties with the United States, it had certainly come close" (Cordesman 1984: 252).

A major recommendation of the 1974 survey was to replace obsolescent British aircraft with advanced fighters capable of responding to perceived threats, principally from Iraq. The administration proposed a sale of arms to Israel, Egypt and Saudi Arabia including 62 F-15s for Saudi Arabia. This "packaging" of sales helped overcome congressional resistance, as did sharp deterioration of regional security conditions, including a Soviet coup in Afghanistan and Soviet-backed Ethiopian victories over Somalia and Eritrea.

Nevertheless, congressional opposition was fierce. Arguments against the sale presaged those made in 1981 against the AWACS sale: (1) the F-15 provided the Saudis, and therefore all Arabs, with enhanced capability to strike Israel; (2) requests for surveillance, radar and command and control capabilities would inevitably follow, further destabilizing the Arab–Israeli military balance; (3) enhanced capabilities made Saudi involvement in any future Arab–Israeli war more likely, complicating Israel's defense planning and making pre-emptive strikes more likely; (4) Saudi Arabia should accept United States protection; and (5) Saudi technological capabilities would be exceeded by the sale, requiring increasing numbers of U.S. personnel.

Ultimately the Senate narrowly defeated a resolution of disapproval, based on sweeteners to the Israelis[3] and assurances from senior administration officials. Defense Secretary Brown assured Congress that the U.S. would not increase the F-15s' range or ground attack capability. Assistant Defense Secretary Bennett testified that Saudi Arabia was "not scheduled to get the AIM 9-L all-aspect Sidewinder missile," and that the sale would "not lead to the sale of ... E-3A (AWACS)." These assurances would haunt Reagan administration officials when they argued for the sale of each of the mentioned capabilities in 1981.

After the 1978 sale, Saudi interest in F-15 enhancements and AWACS intensified as threats to the kingdom increased. By June 1978, South Yemen had shifted into the Soviet camp, and the conflict with North Yemen intensified and threatened to spill over into Saudi Arabia; South Yemen was probably militarily superior to Saudi Arabia. Relations with Iraq improved, but Libya and Ethiopia, both supported by the Soviet Union, were increasingly hostile. There was an expanding Soviet role in Afghanistan. By January 1979, the Shah was driven from power and American arms in the hands of the ayatollahs became threats to nearby Saudi oil facilities. In early 1979, North Yemen began playing the West against the Soviets for arms. Saudi Arabia asked for, and obtained, deployment of two U.S. AWACS to Saudi Arabia in March and April 1979; senior Saudi officials who flew in those aircraft learned their capabilities in tracking and intercepting multiple airborne attacks, and requested a feasibility study. Finally, in September 1980, the war between Iran and Iraq began, and their attacks on each other's oil fields demonstrated the extreme vulnerability of the Saudi facilities. At Saudi request, the United States operated four AWACS out of Saudi bases beginning 1 October 1980.

The Saudis requested sale of F-15 enhancements and AWACS in February 1980. They were told that AWACS presented significant problems, but that the United States was prepared to conduct a study without prejudice to any decision. Saudi officials nevertheless told American reporters they had a commitment for sale of AWACS (SFRC Staff Rept: 4). U.S. Air Force officials believed AWACS was required for adequate defense of the airfields, and presented no significant threat to Israel; they may have given the impression that the sale was inevitable. Saudis saw the sale as a commercial transaction and a test of the security relationship; they could not fathom why two presidents could not sell five planes to a friendly country with a critical need to defend a major part of the world's oil supply.

The Defense Department study was ordered in July and completed in December. It showed that even with 48 ground radars, the Saudis could not identify low-flying attack aircraft until they were 20–30 miles from the border. Saudi oil facilities were concentrated on the coast facing Iran; without more warning, the Saudi Air Force could not intercept attacking aircraft, even with fully enhanced F-15s.

The Carter administration announced in June 1980 that it was considering a Saudi request for F-15 enhancements and aerial reconnaissance and command systems. On 8 July 68 senators warned Carter that such a sale would breach the 1978 assurances and would be disapproved by Congress (Tivnan 1987: 138–9). The letter, which had been coordinated by AIPAC, signaled a bloody fight in a presidential election year. Thirteen days before the election, in an effort to staunch the loss of Jewish support, Carter said that his administration would "not agree to provide offensive capabilities for the planes that might be used against Israel" (CRS, Saudi Arabia and the U.S.: 63). The Jewish community believed Carter was abandoning the sale, although "offensive capabilities" could have meant only bomb racks. Israel's Ambassador Evron would later claim that the "only target" of the weapons "would be Israel" (Tivnan 1987: 138), even as Israelis were claiming that their bombing raid on the Iraqi nuclear reactor at Osirak was a "defensive" action. As always, the battle was to make definitions accord with beliefs.

On 26 February 1981, Undersecretary of State James Buckley told the Senate Foreign Relations Committee in closed session that the Reagan administration had agreed to sell AIM-9L missiles and conformal fuel tanks, had reached agreement in principle to sell an airborne surveillance system and had held for further study the sale of ground-attack bomb racks. On 6 March, the administration made those decisions public, and on 21 April announced that the package would include AWACS.

The decision confronting Reagan

Ronald Reagan said that he agreed to the sale as a gesture of even-handedness and to strengthen ties to Saudi Arabia, and because he was told the sale would not materially change the balance in the Arab–Israeli conflict (Reagan 1990: 410). Consistently, he omitted reference to the crucial role the Saudis were expected to play in administration plans for an integrated regional security infrastructure. Yet that need drove the Defense Department's negotiations with the Saudis. It was the challenge Carter had been struggling with: obtaining a reliable platform from which to project American power.

After the Soviet invasion of Afghanistan, the Carter Doctrine had committed the United States to repel any attempt to gain control of the Persian Gulf, using military force if necessary. Secretary Brown testified in February 1980 that "what is at stake in the Persian Gulf is the economic and political well-being of the United States and its allies" (Record 1981: 1). The administration attempted to reconfigure existing resources to permit effective deployments to the Gulf, creating a Rapid Deployment Joint Task Force (RDJTF).

Defending the Gulf, however, required basing rights that were proximate and secure, which was difficult because of local political impediments. The Sultan of Oman, the most cooperative Gulf ruler, had threatened to deny use of Omani facilities in the Iran hostage rescue attempt. Bases in Berbera and Mombassa were nearly 2,000 miles from the Gulf; Diego Garcia was as distant as Nuremberg, Germany. Saudi Arabia was the key to defense of the Gulf, because of its oil facilities, central location and terrain. The RDJTF commander told the Senate Armed Services Committee that:

> if the United States is to deploy meaningful combat power to that part of the world under any scenario ... it is absolutely essential that we have

free and willing – and I emphasize those two words, free and willing – access to Saudi land bases, Saudi ports, Saudi host nation support, and a considerable labor pool from the Saudis.

(Gen. P. X. Kelley, SASC Hrgs: 38–9)

The Saudis publicly condemned the Carter Doctrine but welcomed it in private, so long as U.S. forces were "over the horizon" and did not require visible Saudi cooperation (Kupchan 1987: 131). A permanent American military presence on Saudi soil would create real risks for the Saudi royal family, both internally and from the wider Arab world. The American-sponsored Camp David process had in Arab eyes ignored the Palestinians and separated Egypt from its Arab family. America was seen as enabling Israeli oppression of Palestinians. Arab regimes played the Palestinian issue cynically for local and regional audiences, but it constituted a real constraint on Arab cooperation with the United States.

Other reasons for Saudi reticence were: (1) lingering anti-colonialism; (2) concern that the United States would seize the oil fields;[4] (3) U.S. ties to Israeli intelligence services;[5] (4) doubts about American reliability and capability, based on weak American support of the Shah, the Soviet invasion of Afghanistan and the failed 1979 Iran hostage rescue attempt; and (5) concern that pro-Israel political actors could prevent America arming an Arab country.

Saudi officials told senators that while the Soviet Union might be the principal source of threats to them, the Arab–Israeli conflict created opportunities for the Soviets (Baker Rept: 10). They insisted on ownership of the arms systems to avoid compromising their sovereignty or making obvious their dependence on the United States.

Israel was the optimal regional partner for the United States, if measured only by military competence. Neoconservatives argued for strengthening Israel and not Arabs. Paul Wolfowitz, director of Haig's planning staff, had advocated reliance on Israel for RDF basing in the Carter administration (Kupchan 1987: 136 n. 34). Secretary Haig also favored relying on Israel to the extent feasible (ibid.: 154). Regional political realities, however, made Israel impossible as a partner in defending the oil fields, and there is no evidence that the idea was ever seriously considered.

The vulnerability of Gulf oil facilities and the absence of dependable basing were urgent problems. The planned Reagan defense build-up would not add significant new capabilities for several years, and would not solve the basing problem. The proposed AWACS package offered major advantages over any other action that could be implemented in the short term: (1) the Saudis could defend against an initial attack and provide cover for American reinforcements; (2) Saudi overbuilding of facilities, parts inventory and other infrastructure would accommodate approximately 140 American F-15s in crises (SFRC Staff Rept: 17; Weinberger testimony in SASC Hrgs: 4); (3) American training of Saudi personnel and maintenance of the AWACS would mean that the Saudis were fully integrated with American systems and dependent on continuing American good will;[6] (4) the risk of AWACS technology compromise was thought to be manageable;[7] and (5) Saudi Arabia would pay the system's cost, nominally $8.5 billion but probably $15–20 billion or more over ten years, in cash. Funding alternatives were few, given Reagan's massive tax cuts and defense build-up. In addition, it was hoped that Saudi Arabia would sponsor a security network among Gulf Arab states. The Gulf Cooperation Council, founded in 1980 to deal with economic issues, began faltering steps toward security cooperation after Iran attacked Kuwaiti oil facilities.

The administration tended to assume that Saudi eagerness for the sale signified agreement on the primacy of the Soviet threat. Kupchan calls this inability to recognize alternative grounds for tactical agreement "perceptual imperialism" (Kupchan 1987: 217). It could more accurately be called "blinders of belief." Senior officials, particularly President Reagan and Secretary Weinberger, overpromised Saudi cooperation, underestimated the salience of Palestinian issues and did not see that Saudis, like Israelis, focused primarily on their position vis-à-vis other regional states.

Reagan's decision to sell the AWACS package to Saudi Arabia was inconsistent with the pure "strategic asset" commitment to Israel that his campaign rhetoric promised. But Reagan meant what he said about Israel's security: the United States would insure that Israel had a "qualitative edge" over any conceivable combination of regional adversaries. Reagan refused to use security assistance as leverage against Israel. That resulted in independent Israeli capabilities adequate for security challenges as seen by *Israel*, not conditioned on Israeli cooperation in the peace process, or in any other way. Israel was thus in a position to reject any American initiative that depended upon congressional approval, including arms sales to Arab states. This was an unintended and surprising result from Reagan's perspective. He fully expected that Israel and her supporters would take him at his word when he pledged the complete security of Israel, and that they would then cooperate in his overriding foreign policy goal, the rollback of Soviet influence. He was shocked and hurt when they doubted him.[8]

The opposition: beliefs and practical politics

It was an article of faith in the American Jewish community that Saudi Arabia was an enemy of Israel, and no true friend of the United States. Saudi Arabia had aligned against Israel in every Arab–Israeli war, they funded the PLO,[9] they rejected the Camp David peace process,[10] and some Saudi princes called for *jihad* against Israel or called Israel their greatest enemy. Sophisticated weapons systems could erode Israel's qualitative edge or even encourage the Arabs again to attack Israel. There was also fear that President Reagan was abandoning his commitment to the security of Israel, and would (like the French and British) sell the Saudis whatever they wanted. These fears were real, if not always justified, and they energized the community against this sale.

Those knowledgeable about the equipment and regional strategic realities did not fear that Saudi Arabia, alone or in combination with others, would pose a military threat to Israel as a result of this sale. Their concern was rather about political and institutional impacts, particularly if the administration paid a small political price. The logic supporting the 1978 sale, as had been predicted, supported this sale as well, making it increasingly difficult to distinguish and oppose future sales. An Israeli general said the problem was not with the pending sale, but with the one after it (SFRC Staff Rept: 32).

More ominously, the sale could evidence a shift in the principled and causal beliefs undergirding policy. Israel the exclusive trusted ally and moral sibling could become one among several friends in the region whose needs would be addressed in relative terms. The lobby's goal was not just to stop this sale, but to expose the "errors of Arabism" and demonstrate that American interests "were better served through a policy more sensitive to Israel's concerns" (Goldberg 1990: 71–2). Israel had earned trust and support; Arabs had not. Arming Arabs was dangerous to Israel, and that should be decisive.

It was also necessary to set the terms of engagement with the new administration. Tom Dine wanted an early show of strength so daunting that the proposal would be withdrawn, thus avoiding an open fight with a potentially very supportive administration. Bloomfield's dictum was, "The best vote is the vote avoided" (Bloomfield interview). Public confrontation, if successful, could force concessions in future battles; but it also put friends in Congress and the administration in awkward positions, and risked making enemies. Dine says he had not wanted any "blood on the walls. That was an unnecessary fight. But they had not paid any attention" (Dine interview).[11] If necessary, however, he was prepared to test the strength of his organization and his theories of congressional control of foreign policy. If AIPAC succeeded, it would be in a position to negotiate with the administration over its entire Middle East policy, since the policy depended almost entirely on arms sales and aid, matters which could be controlled by Congress.

The Israeli government worried about what the sale presaged for its relationship with Reagan, and the precedential effect of abrogating assurances made only three years earlier. Together, U.S.–Saudi security cooperation, Western dependence on Gulf oil and Saudi investment could seriously erode presumptions favoring Israel. Foreign Minister Shamir told Reagan in late February that Israel adamantly opposed augmenting offensive capabilities of any Arab state (Haig 1984: 176).

However, there were also reasons to accommodate Reagan. Notwithstanding hostile rhetoric from some members of the Saudi royal family, Israeli leaders did not attribute to all Saudis the implacable hostility of some, or aggregate Arab capabilities as a single hostile force. The Mossad worked with Saudi security and intelligence officials to weaken radical and fundamentalist forces in the region (Melman and Raviv 1994: 191).[12] Israelis also knew that the sale was part of Reagan's global effort against Soviet expansionism, an effort with which at least the Likud wanted to be associated; and that Reagan was personally committed to the security of Israel. Finally, their military planners were unconcerned about the effect of the sale on their margin of superiority.[13]

Foreign Minister Shamir tentatively agreed with Secretary Haig in late February or early March to mute Israeli opposition to the sale of F-15 enhancements, and some (as yet unspecified) aerial surveillance system. Israel would again accept compensation, including 15 F-15s, $600 million in concessionary loans, permission to export the Kfir fighter to Latin America and political concessions (Haig 1984: 177; Blitzer 1985: 139). However, someone then leaked to the Israeli press that AWACS would be part of the Saudi package, with what Haig calls "grossly exaggerated" descriptions of AWACS' capabilities. In the run-up to an Israeli election, this generated accusations by the Labor Party that Begin was acquiescing in risks to Israel (Blitzer 1985: 136; Melman and Raviv 1994: 193). When anonymous sources then said that the Saudis would buy five AWACS and up to seven KC-135 in-flight refuelling tankers (*NYT* 26 Feb. 1981: A1, 15 Mar. 1981: A9, 17 Mar. 1981: A6), and those reports were not repudiated, the Israeli government announced that it would oppose the sale in its entirety.

The Israeli ambassador and military attaché in Washington, Ephraim Evron and General Menachem Meron, felt so strongly that it was unwise and futile to oppose Reagan that they flew to Jerusalem to make that case. Begin said that the sale would be opposed on principle (Melman and Raviv 1994: 193). Presumably the principle involved was the exclusivity of Israel's security relationship with the United States. That principle, however, would have prevented Shamir negotiating with Haig for compensation. There were practical fiscal and military concerns. Israel's economy was already under great strain; it could not afford an arms race with oil-rich Arabs. The IDF would have to devise tactics and divert resources to deal with AWACS, and Israeli capacity for pre-emptive action would be eroded. However, fiscal impacts were matters for negotiation with Washington; military impacts had been discounted by military planners and could be mitigated by restrictions on the Saudis and American largesse. What was left was politics.

The American lobby had pressed Begin not to compromise. Tom Dine, other leaders of AIPAC and the Presidents Conference, and congressional supporters told Begin that any softening of Israel's opposition to the sale would "pull the rug out from under the feet" of those who had already publicly opposed the sale as a threat to Israel's security (Blitzer 1985: 139–40).

By taking a hard line very early, and obtaining public commitments by members of Congress, AIPAC had made it difficult for an Israeli prime minister to do other than oppose the sale. Shai Feldman argues that AIPAC takes hard line positions to obtain the most American politics will allow, from which Israel can choose to compromise, and to facilitate fundraising (Feldman 1988: 77–8). Dine denies fundraising as a motivation, but otherwise agrees (Dine interview). However, after Israel's American supporters had strongly opposed the sale, many against their own (Republican) president, compromise would have been costly to Begin in both countries.

Begin's opposition on principle was, however, not made operational. AIPAC's Doug Bloomfield describes the Israeli government as "neutral" on AWACS. He personally sought Begin's cooperation in blocking the sale, telling him, "We're not asking you to do anything ... Just tell your people [to give us] technical information [when we ask for it], that's all." Begin so instructed Ambassador Evron in Bloomfield's presence, but Evron then actively impeded cooperation (Bloomfield interview). Bloomfield attributes Evron's intransigence to his distrust of AIPAC, which he saw more as competitor than ally. Evron may also have sought to distance himself from a decision he thought wrong.

AIPAC and Israel would both publicly oppose the AWACS sale. However, this was more an AIPAC fight to embed beliefs and establish power relationships than it was an Israeli effort to ensure its security.

How the battle was fought, and why that mattered as much as the outcome

The lobby: beliefs and advocacy

AIPAC heard about the proposed sale before Reagan's inauguration (Tivnan 1987: 139). Officials opposed to arms sales regularly alerted AIPAC in hopes of killing them. Anthony Cordesman alleges that "several members of [the NSC] staff who opposed the sale ... privately briefed the Congress" (Cordesman 1984: 331). Congressional staff may have been AIPAC's source. AIPAC began distributing materials against the sale in December. It mobilized CRCs around the country, and letters and wires to the White House and Congress began arriving soon after the first of the year.

By late February, Senator Edward Kennedy had warned against the sale (*Facts on File* 19 Feb. 1981: 122); a majority of the Senate Foreign Relations Committee had sent the president a letter protesting violation of the Carter assurances; and Dine had warned Edwin Meese against a fight with the Jewish community. This all *predated* the administration's first *closed* briefing of the Senate Foreign Relations Committee. In March and April, AIPAC organized "colloquies," scripted sessions in each house committing members against the sale. The Senate colloquy on 24 March included speeches by 11 Republicans and ten Democrats, a clear signal of trouble (Cong Record 24 Mar. 1981: S2532–50; CRS, Congress & Foreign Policy 1981: 29).

Dine and Reagan had very different expectations of Congress. Reagan had reason to believe that the Senate would accede. He was highly popular; this was his first major foreign policy decision; and Senate leaders were in his

political debt. Twelve new Republican senators, swept into office with
Reagan, had allowed the Republicans to organize the Senate for the first
time since 1954; it was not in their interest to weaken the president. Dine
did have concerns: several pro-Israel senators had lost in 1980,[14] and the
National Conservative Political Action Committee (NCPAC) was targeting
remaining liberal allies (Dine 1984: 130–1). However, the relevant committees, and especially their chairs, were pro-Israel, and pro-Israel Democratic
staff were being augmented by neoconservative staff. On most issues, Congress was in closer ideological harmony with Reagan's views than had been
the case for presidents Nixon, Ford or Carter (Destler 1982: 67). However,
members of Congress had largely accepted that the appropriate, and politically safe, default position was to support Israel.

Thus, it was a senior Republican senator, Robert Packwood, who organized a letter to the president from a majority of the Senate opposing the sale,
and co-sponsored the resolution of disapproval. Packwood chaired the
Republican Senate Campaign Committee, responsible for raising money to
elect Republican senators. A confrontation with the Jewish community
would not just imperil financial support, it would mobilize active opposition (Bloomfield interview). Packwood's co-sponsor on the resolution,
Senator Alan Cranston, was chair of the Democratic Senate Campaign
Committee.

Dine approached Senate Majority Leader Howard Baker in early April to
urge either withdrawal of the sale, or a delay in its formal submission
(Tivnan 1987: 148–9). Baker knew that the sale would fail if voted upon
then; he urged the White House to delay submission, and organized a delegation to the Middle East to investigate the proposed sale. On his return,
Baker recommended delaying consideration of the sale until after the 30
June Israeli election.

Once it was clear that the administration intended to fight for the entire
package, AIPAC coordinated efforts with the Presidents Conference, while
resisting shared control. AIPAC sought to have each member of Congress
contacted by constituents who had supported them for election, and to have
letters sent to the White House by those who had contacts there. Presidents
Conference chair Howard Squadron sent the first of many letters on 10
March; it was to James Baker with a "Dear Jim" cover letter and copies to
Meese and Haig (RRPL, David Gergen Files, AWACS 1981, OA 10520).[15]
Baker showed the letter to Reagan and instructed his deputy Richard
Darman to draft a response. The draft was edited by Elizabeth Dole (head of
Public Liaison), her assistant Red Cavaney and Richard Allen; copies were
sent to Meese and Baker. Such senior staffing of correspondence was extra-
ordinary. The resulting letter from Reagan, however, was anodyne, mention-
ing his commitment to Israel's security and his hope for Saudi cooperation
in the peace process. The White House was not prepared to defend the sale.

Most White House responses were to Jewish leaders with prior relationships with the president or key aides. Two groups of Jewish leaders, one

headed by Max Fisher and one by George Klein of New York, received regular briefings and meetings with the president. However, no one could get the White House to take seriously the possibility that they could lose.

It was always clear that the sale would be disapproved by the House of Representatives, still controlled by Democrats and more thoroughly pro-Israel. By 5 August, when Reagan finally sent a letter to congressional leaders asking them not to prejudge the issue, a majority of senators had signed Packwood's letter of opposition (DoS Bull Oct. 1981: 52).[16]

AIPAC's nominal allies outside the Jewish community helped little. Organized labor was solidly against the sale, but its influence was mostly in the House, where help was not needed.[17] Christian opponents of the sale included liberals who opposed arms sales; it was an ineffective effort.[18] Key evangelical leaders assured Reagan that they would not oppose him publicly, perhaps in the vain hope of active presidential help on their domestic agenda; those included Rev. Jerry Falwell, Rev. James Robison, Ed McAteer of the Religious Roundtable and Paul Weyrich, a political adviser to much of the Christian Right (Blackwell Memorandum 11 Sep. 1981 in RRPL, FO 003–02 04119655). Robison assured Reagan that there were "no biblical problems with the sale" and offered his help (RRPL, FO 003–02 043035).

Prime Minister Begin increased the rancor surrounding the sale during his September visit. Reagan wrote in his diary that Begin "mellowed" on AWACS after Reagan's explanation, but "almost immediately after he left the White House, Begin went to Capitol Hill and began to lobby very hard against me, the administration, and the AWACS sale – after he had told me he wouldn't do that." Reagan seemed naïve about Israel's role in Congress, and about Begin's lawyerly parsing of commitments: "I didn't like having representatives of a foreign country – *any* foreign country – trying to interfere in what I regarded as our domestic political process and the setting of our foreign policy." He told the State Department to warn Begin he was "jeopardizing the close relationship of our countries unless he backed off." He "felt [Begin had] broken his word and I was angry about it" (Reagan 1990: 415).[19] Reagan ordered Haig fly to New York to confront Begin. Haig, and Ambassador Lewis, accepted Begin's denial that he had lobbied improperly (Haig 1984: 188). Haig and Lewis, both very protective of their relationships with Israeli leaders, may have been the wrong people to send. Senator Charles Percy, host of Begin's meeting with legislators, says that he tried bluntly and repeatedly to turn the conversation, but Begin persisted in lengthy denunciations of arming Israel's enemies (Percy interview, Frontline Diplomacy).

AIPAC had to rely on its own resources and the network of national and community-based Jewish organizations. Nevertheless, the lobby very nearly defeated a popular president on his first, and a critical, foreign policy issue.

At May hearings, Tom Dine laid out AIPAC's arguments: (1) regional consensus against the Soviet threat was desirable, but not if it required "over-reliance on unstable Arab regimes"; (2) Israel was a uniquely reliable democratic ally with shared ethical values and a willingness to undertake great risks for peace, and should be a full (exclusive) military and intelligence partner; (3) the sale would start an arms race and cause greater strains on the Israeli economy;[20] (4) F-15 enhancements, useless against the real threat to the Saudi regime (internal instability) or against the Soviet Union, were designed for use *only* against Israel, violated U.S. commitments and would destabilize the region by enabling coordinated Arab offensives; (5) lax Saudi security risked compromise of classified technology;[21] (6) involvement of American personnel for years after the sale would make U.S. entanglement in regional conflict more likely (HApp Hrgs, Part 3: 322–5, 339–49).

Dine made several dubious assertions, including that Saudi Arabia led the rejectionist states and was becoming a front-line state militarily against Israel (ibid.: 318, 324–5). That seemed especially far-fetched after Prince Fahd announced his August 1981 plan. Unlike those representing Arab-Americans, Dine was never asked to justify his statements.[22] Statements that AWACS would expose every Israeli defense system while flying safely within Saudi airspace, and would permit coordination of an all-Arab air attack, were just wrong:[23] (1) the Saudis would have to abandon their oil facilities and deploy AWACS where Israel could easily detect and destroy it; (2) such deployment would end U.S. support, making the system unusable within days; (3) ground movements under about 100 miles per hour, and aircraft movement in valleys, would never be detectable; and (4) the information collected could not be timely communicated to other Arab forces because of incompatibilities with Soviet-supplied equipment.[24] These facts supported the Israeli military consensus that the sale presented no serious threat. But the administration's delay in making its case was costly, as many members relied upon the alleged threat to Israel in committing against the sale.

AIPAC's advocacy was not driven by dubious technical arguments, but by core beliefs. Only Israel could be trusted; Arabs were dedicated to the destruction of the Jewish state. It followed that no Arab state should be sold sophisticated arms systems until it had negotiated peace with Israel. Arabs, including Saudis, were aligned against the West.[25] Israel had fought the Arabs three times, and as moral obligee and strategic partner of the United States should not be asked to take *any* additional risks. To emphasize America's moral obligation, each senator was given a copy of the novel *Holocaust* (Tivnan 1987: 158).

Some members parsed the arguments carefully. Representative Lee Hamilton, then chair of the relevant subcommittee of House Foreign Relations, rejected the argument that the sale represented a threat to Israel, but opposed it based on the risk of technology compromise and the need for greater Saudi participation in the peace process. He thought Israel's opposition was driven by anxiety about the primacy of Israel's relationship with the United States (HFAC Report: 9–11). Senator Grassley, who based early opposition on the threat to Israel, later said, "I was deceived by anti-

AWACS people" (RRPL, Box 90083, 21 Sep. 1981 and 19 Oct. 1981 Post Brief Assessments). He voted for the sale. Most who opposed the sale chose among AIPAC's arguments without challenging the more sweeping characterizations. A very few confessed that they would have voted for the sale, but were unwilling to pay the political price of opposing the lobby.[26] AIPAC sought to build a majority by adding to its core supporters those who could be convinced by non-ideological arguments and those who could be frightened by political muscle.

The Reagan administration's campaign

The administration contained natural coalitions for and against the AWACS sale. Western conservatives (Meese, Clark and Weinberger) focused on the global mission of fighting Soviet expansionism; lacking an overriding commitment to Israel, they favored the sale. Also favoring the sale were regionalists ("Arabists") and those with particular stakes in the sales, including corporations who built the systems or who did business with the Saudis. Opponents were largely neoconservatives and others who saw Israel as the sole reliable regional ally, and were willing to work actively against the sale. The 1 April NSC decision adding AWACS to the package was to be made public on 21 April; it promptly leaked, and opponents organized over 100 statements of outraged opposition on the House floor on 7 April.

The administration made many mistakes: they did not explain how the sale was consistent with commitments to Israel, allowing opponents to charge inconstancy and incoherence. They underestimated the extent to which the Arab–Israeli conflict inhibited Arab cooperation, and the ways in which Arab positions on the peace process would be used by opponents. The wrong team was chosen: Secretary Haig had formal authority for arms sales and understood the region's complexities, but was neither trusted nor enthusiastic about the sale. Those relied upon, Richard Allen and Caspar Weinberger, had neither Haig's knowledge nor the Troika's political skills. Defense Department officials were allowed to negotiate details of the sale before anyone had identified opponents' arguments and possible responses thereto; changes that could have been made quietly in March could not be made under public pressure in September. The Troika, fixated on the economic program, prohibited detailed briefing or responses to questions for over four months after the sale was announced, allowing AIPAC to obtain public commitments from senators based upon uncorrected facts and unrebutted arguments. But the economic program was tied up in the Democratic House, where AWACS was conceded as lost. There was no justification for ignoring senators, among whom the battle was to be fought (Destler 1982: 72).

Secretary Haig exemplifies the disorder. He says he knew nothing about selling AWACS prior to press reports in March; the Pentagon's terms "surprised [him] greatly" and wrecked his "carefully wrought, though still tentative, understanding" with Foreign Minister Shamir (Haig 1984: 178). He would have us believe that he discussed an aerial surveillance system with Shamir, unaware that both Saudi Arabia and the Defense Department strongly preferred AWACS. He clearly was not authorized to rule AWACS out. His report is thus suspect, but at a minimum shows his dysfunctional relationship with Weinberger and the Troika. By 1 April, when the NSC recommended the AWACS sale, Haig's relationship with the Troika had further deteriorated because of his handling of the attempted assassination of Reagan. Haig wanted to split AWACS into a separate sale, which implies willingness to see AWACS defeated. Haig doubted the administration could win a fight with the "formidable [pro-Israel] lobby" (Haig 1984: 178). He was required to testify in favor of the sale in September and October, but his testimony reads more like that of a disgruntled and defensive soldier following orders than that of a convinced advocate.

The Troika was repeatedly urged not to abandon the field to opponents. On 22 April, David Gergen presented to James Baker the consensus of Richard Allen, Lyn Nofziger (political affairs), Larry Speakes (acting press secretary) and others that the White House should lay out the basic facts and arguments to force opponents and the press to deal with them. Gergen recommended a dozen steps to do that (RRPL, David Gergen Files, OA 10520, AWACS 1981). Baker in marginal notes authorized only background briefings for selected print press and internal coordination, and directed that Gergen not "spend chips we don't want to spend now."

Baker even rejected recommendations to telephone Jewish supporters. Less than three weeks later, Allen wrote that he had been unaware the Presidents Conference was to receive an AWACS briefing on 27 May (RRPL, Marginal note in FO 003–02 026470). Thus, Baker's directions were ignored; Jewish leaders were briefed while congressional leaders were not; and the putative leader of the AWACS campaign, Richard Allen, was uninformed.

On 24 April, Senator Levin wrote the president raising questions about manning, command arrangements, control of data and other sensitive subjects (RRPL, FO 003–02 025362). Levin's letter was triggered by more press leaks. These matters had not been negotiated with Saudi Arabia nor vetted through the administration's coordinating group, just being formed. The NSC's Geoffrey Kemp advised against any detailed response, "since we don't have all the answers at this time!" (RRPL, FO 003–02 025362, 28 Apr. 1981 memo). Allen's 6 May reply provided no substantive information (RRPL, FO 003–02 025362). Until September, Republican senators' inquiries received uninformative replies; most from House members and Democrats went unanswered.[27]

Haig set out the administration's strategic thinking in Senate hearings in March and May without, however, addressing particulars of the pending sale. He testified that Soviet encirclement of the Gulf, the fall of the Shah, regional doubts about the reliability of the United States and "less than satisfactory" relations with Saudi Arabia were "the underlying motivations" of the F-15 proposal (SApp Hrgs: 25–6). His testimony was elliptical, vague and self-serving.[28] He could not respond to pointed questions, based upon AIPAC's briefings, about the threat to Israel, reasons for Saudi ownership and technology compromise. Unsurprisingly, he changed no minds.

A sub-cabinet "Coordinating Group for Certain Mideast Initiatives" was established under the NSPG to advise on the sale. The Coordinating Group established working groups for dealing with Congress, the Saudis and technical aspects. The congressional working group was limited to "short-term initiatives with Congress designed to prevent premature adverse commitments by legislators" (RRPL, Gergen Files, OA 10520, AWACS 1981, Kimmitt Memo 29 Apr. 1981). NSC staff believed that "the less said now the better." Information concerning Saudi assurances and issues of Israeli security was deleted from draft talking points for cabinet members and from draft replies to inquiries (RRPL, FO 003–02 023836 and 026470, Allen Memos 11 May 1981). Similar guidance was repeated in June.

On 13 June, President Reagan told senior officers the Saudi sale was "of vital importance to the national security of the United States" and therefore "a matter of highest priority for this Administration." Richard Allen was to chair the coordinating group, reporting to the president through the Legislative Strategy Group, co-chaired by Baker and Meese (RRPL, FO 003–02 02972055). Two-and-one-half months after approving the sale, Reagan had named a group to defend it, but had still not grappled with any of the contentious issues, and had given oversight to a non-statutory group of domestic issue specialists.

Six weeks later, Allen forwarded a Haig memorandum laying out the consequences of defeat.[29] Allen said there was a strong program to win Senate approval, but that they would "need your help at the appropriate time." Reagan wrote in the margin, "I'll help – I agree with every word in the memo. RR" (RRPL, FO 003–12 03308255, Allen Memo 30 Jul. 1981). On 5 August, after passage of his tax and budget bills, the president sent a letter to the leadership of the Congress, urging only that they not prejudge the proposal.

The White House delayed engagement partly in hopes of a different Israeli government after 30 June Israeli elections. When that did not happen, the White House again delayed until after Begin's September visit. The president sent Jack Stein to Israel to ask Begin to mute opposition to the sale. Begin assured Stein that "he would not interfere in the Executive-Legislative process" (RRPL, OA 5456, Dole files, Stein memo 3 Sep. 1981).

Reagan apparently intended that Begin be warned that "strategic cooperation" with the U.S. depended on acquiescence in the AWACS sale, but no one told Begin that (*NYT* 19 Oct. 1981: A1, A8).[30] When Defense officials then referenced a linkage, Begin derided the reports as uninformed. Haig reportedly wrote Begin on 10 July linking acquiescence on AWACS with resumption of F-16 deliveries (Cordesman 1984: 332). If so, the implied threat failed; a September attempt to link strategic cooperation and AWACS would likely have failed as well.

The administration's first defense of the sale was in closed congressional sessions the week after Begin's visit. By that time, the count in the Senate was running strongly against the sale. It was clear that the organization and methods thought sufficient to the task in April would lose the battle in October. Beginning the second week of September, the White House began to engage.

The president's most significant allies on AWACS normally did not engage in foreign policy lobbying: Saudi Arabia and corporate America.

The Saudi team was led by Prince Bandar bin Sultan, son of Saudi Defense Minister Prince Sultan. He was an American-trained fighter pilot with excellent connections in the American government.[31] He supervised three experienced lobbyists as registered agents: Frederick Dutton, Stephen N. Conner and J. Crawford Cook. The Saudi effort was high energy but low profile. Bandar coordinated the efforts of the White House and Majority Leader Howard Baker in the Senate. He said that he would answer questions if a senator asked, but that "[w]e are not fighting this battle, the president is" (*WSJ* 22 Oct. 1981: 1). Dutton was not allowed to lobby the Congress, which he later admitted sounded "nonsensical" (Emerson 1985: 188). The Saudis wanted to test the strength of the administration's commitment, but in any event aggressive lobbying would invite characterization by AIPAC as Arabs buying American support at the expense of Israel.

Confidential reports to Bandar from Robert Kimmitt of the NSC staff evidence some tension. Kimmitt urged execution of a proposed General Security of Information Agreement to deal with Senate concerns, and accommodation of Senator Glenn's proposal for joint command arrangements. More pointedly, Kimmitt noted: "Public pronouncements by Saudi officials that 'Israel is the real enemy' are particularly unhelpful" (RRPL, Box 90090, Memo 23 Sep. 1981).

The unusual level of corporate lobbying on the sale undoubtedly resulted in part from pressure by Saudi officials.[32] The Business Roundtable in Washington was led by Richard Hunt, an officer of NL Industries, an oil industry equipment manufacturer. The American Businessmen's Group in Riyadh was led by Northrop Corporation officials, and included most of the largest financial, oil, arms and construction companies. These groups coordinated efforts to utilize pre-existing relationships with senators. That meant heavy pressure on senators from Connecticut, where UTC and several other defense companies were located, and on Senator Jepsen of Iowa, pressed hard by farm equipment manufacturers, farm co-operatives and defense contractors. Jepsen stridently opposed the sale at the June 1981 AIPAC policy conference as threatening Israel and jeopardizing U.S. technology (Tivnan 1987: 159). He attributed his last-minute conversion to "highly classified" information that "lessened his concerns" (*NYT* 28 Oct. 1981: A14), but home-state corporate pressure undoubtedly played a role.

Elizabeth Dole asked six representatives of the Business Roundtable to direct an AWACS steering committee, and promised the "full resources of the Administration," including detailed technical briefings and an AWACS tour (RRPL, Dole Files, Box 4, AWACS, Cavaney Memo 23 Sep. 1981). By early October, companies had urged subsidiaries, suppliers and customers to contact their senators. UTC sent 10,200 mailgrams to customers; 60 percent of them contacted members of Congress (RRPL, Dole Files, Box 4, AWACS, Burgess Memo 6 Oct. 1981).

Nicholas Laham contends that business community involvement was "practically nonexistent" (Laham 2002: 61–2). Haig asserts that commercial considerations "played a persuasive role in [the administration's] deliberations" (Haig 1984: 178). Others contend that big business pushed the sale through (Perlmutter 1983; see also Spiegel 1984: 114). Compared to most instances where security policy (rather than trade negotiations or tax laws) impacted business interests, corporate America played an unusually active role. However, most corporate advertising campaigns and lobbying presentations were cast in terms of protecting American security interests and achieving peace in the region.[33] The evidence supports only a conclusion that corporate efforts made some senators more amenable to presidential persuasion.

When it finally engaged, the administration had cogent rebuttals to AIPAC's assertions concerning military threats to Israel and the risk of technology compromise, but made a weak strategic case for the sale. The Saudis would not allow the details of their security cooperation to be made public, so that key arguments for the sale were unavailable.[34] There was no permanent or effective constituency for improved relations with Arab regimes. Reagan would never publicly say that Israel was not America's sole regional strategic ally, although that was the implication of the sale. Overcoming institutionalized beliefs concerning Israel and its Arab neighbors while carrying those burdens was an enormous challenge, particularly in the few weeks the administration gave itself.

Having already gone through long negotiations they considered disrespectful of their sovereignty, capabilities and intentions, the Saudis rejected pleas to add more confidence-building measures. Senator Glenn, whose expertise in military affairs was highly respected, held out for joint crewing. A senatorial delegation to Saudi Arabia was suggested in September, and was rebuffed. Haig, ever tactful, blasted "**** senators making foreign policy" and then broached the same ideas with the Saudis, compounding the political problem (Destler 1982: 73–4).[35]

Efforts the Saudis did make were vigorously attacked by Israel and AIPAC. President Reagan cautiously welcomed Crown Prince Fahd's October 1981 plan to resolve the Palestinian–Israeli dispute, although it diverged from the Camp David formulation. It was immediately rejected by Israel, and referred to by Begin as "the Saudi annihilation plan" (Speech 1 Nov. 1981 in Docs & Stmts 79–82: 53). AIPAC used every sign of Saudi hostility to Israel, support of the PLO or cooperation with Soviet clients, to devalue the idea of Saudi moderation. The Saudis would not make concessions on Palestinian issues as an additional price for a cash arms purchase. By overflying Saudi Arabia in U.S.-supplied F-16s to attack the Osirak reactor in June, Israel demonstrated the primacy of the Arab–Israeli conflict. Public debate over the sale thus dramatized and exacerbated the conflict between Israel and its neighbors.

The initial AWACS team was dysfunctional. A supporter of the sale said that Allen had a talent for "p****** people off on the Hill," and that he, Haig and Ikle were all uncomfortable advocates (Tivnan 1987: 141–2). A key House staffer says that Haig's "heart was not in it" (van Dusen interview). David Gergen had to script responses to inquiries about tangled lines of responsibility (RRPL, Gergen files, OA 10520, AWACS 1981, Gergen Memo 28 Sep. 1981). By mid-September direction was assumed by Baker and Darman.

On 1 October, President Reagan announced formal submission of the sale to the Congress. In the scripted part of the news conference, he stressed the goal of constructive relationships leading to regional peace (PC 1 Oct. 1981 in DoS Bull Nov. 1981: 16). However, Reagan then showed his pique at Begin, saying, "It is not the business of other nations to make foreign policy. An objective assessment of U.S. national interests must favor the proposed sale." He was immediately asked if he was warning Israel to "keep its hands off ... national security matters in the Middle East." Reagan denied meaning the statement "in any deprecating way," but then said that "other countries must not get a perception that we are being influenced one way or the other with regard to foreign policy" (ibid.).[36] Responding to a question about the risk of technology compromise in light of the fall of the Shah, Reagan added to his woes by stating flatly that "Saudi Arabia, we will not permit to be an Iran." His warning against foreign-inspired influence inflamed and frightened American Jews, who heard suggestions of dual loyalty; his statement that the United States would not "permit" Saudi Arabia to be another Iran, intended as an assurance of American steadfastness, instead intensified fears of intervention in Gulf affairs.

The Jewish community's reaction to Reagan's remarks put the White House on the defensive immediately. Some Jewish leaders expressed anger and distress to friends within the administration.[37] Key Jewish supporters of the president wrote him personally.[38] Al Spiegel, Reagan's long-time friend and supporter, was promptly accorded a personal meeting with Reagan to discuss "ways to minimize any lasting adverse effects" on the relationship with the Jewish community (RRPL, CFOA 740 043566, Dole Memo 9 Oct. 1981).

The 1 October testimony of secretaries Haig and Weinberger had no effect (RRPL, CFOA 740 043554, Turner Memo 1 Oct. 1981). Senators sought to revise the sale. Senators Nunn and Warner proposed to apply new restrictions on all sales of AWACS. Senators Mattingly and Quayle requested the president certify that various conditions had been met (RRPL, Box 90090, Mattingly/Quayle draft 14 Oct. 1981). The challenge was to satisfy senators that their concerns had been met, without re-opening negotiations with the adamant Saudis (RRPL, FO 003–02 04210755, Darman Memo 5 Oct. 1981).

Reagan found himself in one of the most difficult political positions imaginable: needing to reverse public commitments of several senators, but unable to give them justifications that were credible with their constituents or consistent with Reagan's stated principles. He succeeded by using a combination of techniques that had little to do with the substance of the arguments: very intense personal lobbying by the president, particularly of Republican senators; stressing that the president would be crippled in his conduct of national security policy if his promise was dishonored by Congress; and deft use of a draft presidential letter of assurances.

The letter of assurances was an ingenious device. All wavering senators were invited to suggest language that the president might incorporate in assurances he would give the Congress. However, the letter remained under the control of James Baker and his deputy Richard Darman and was released only on the day of the Senate vote, when it was too late to quibble with the language. It covered subjects on which Saudi Arabia would not give written assurances, such as the duration of American participation, but went very little beyond what Reagan had already said. By allowing senators to claim they had fought for and received assurances on issues that had motivated earlier opposition, "the letter gave 'em a legitimate out, an excuse" (Baker, in Smith 1988: 221). However, even the letter's broad assurances gave ammunition to opponents of later sales. Release of the aircraft required presidential certification that the sale "enhance[d] the atmosphere and prospects for progress toward peace," and that "significant progress toward [the peaceful resolution of disputes in the region] ha[d] been accomplished with the substantial assistance of Saudi Arabia" (Letter of 28 Oct. 1981 in Docs & Stmts 79–82: 254). Any such certification invited argument.

The president met with senators individually and in groups. Each meeting was separately scripted based on briefing team reports. Talking points in September had stressed defense of the oil fields, the need to encourage Saudi participation in the peace process and the lack of threat to Israel (RRPL, Box 91402, Allen Memo 12 Sep. 1981). October talking points added two arguments: that the Senate had approved the sale of advanced aircraft in 1978, when the threat to Saudi oil fields was less, and that detailed provisions had been negotiated with the Saudis to meet senators' concerns. Also added was a statement of resolve and implied threat: "I intend to win this battle, and am prepared to use all the means available to me to do so"[39] (RRPL, FO 003–02 0454555, Talking Points, n.d.).

Between 1 October and 28 October, Reagan held 47 meetings with individual senators, one with senators Mattingly and Quayle, and one with all Republican senators. Republicans with substantial Jewish constituencies were very skittish. Senator D'Amato of New York would not support the sale, but would help with others and would vote last (RRPL, FO 003–02 046044, RR notes on Friedersdorf Memo 26 Oct. 1981). Senator Hawkins of Florida asked that senators from states with substantial Jewish populations be "immuned" (*sic*) (RRPL, FO 003–02 046050, Friedersdorf Memo 23 Oct. 1981). Of senators from New York, Florida, California and Illinois, only senators Hayakawa of California and Percy of Illinois voted for the sale.

Reagan was sometimes urged to have Richard Allen describe the "new developments" in agreements with the Saudis (RRPL, CFOA 740 043554, Friedersdorf Memo 1 Oct. 1981). The pattern of redactions suggests that the Saudis had given assurances on several sensitive points, probably including crewing and deployment controls (e.g., RRPL, Box 90090, Kimmit Memo 16 Oct. 1981). The president held the senators to strict confidence. The continued classification of this information after a quarter century evidences the sensitivity of Saudi Arabia's security relationship with the United States.

On 5 October, 16 former senior officials subscribed to a statement of support of the sale.[40] The statement gave no detailed defense of the sale, emphasizing only the damage that a veto would do to the president's credibility (*WP* 6 Oct. 1981: A1). This was apparently all that could be agreed. Henry Kissinger argued in an opinion piece that substantial doubts about the sale were outweighed by the "grave, perhaps irretrievable" damage to "the president's authority in international affairs" (ibid.: A21).

Former presidents Ford, Carter and Nixon also publicly supported the sale. Nixon warned in a *New York Times* piece that American Jews would "become their own worst enemies" if they undermined this most pro-Israel president, and that a defeat would be attributed to Israel and part of the American Jewish community (RRPL, Box 91402, Allen Memo 3 Oct. 1981). Allen told Reagan that the "splendid piece" was "exactly what we had hoped [Nixon] would do," but that was Allen's tin ear for political music. The Nixon article was taken as evidence that supporters of the sale thought of Jews as somehow less than full American citizens.

The first visible shift of momentum in the president's favor did not occur until 15 October, when the Senate Armed Service Committee voted out a favorable report. Reagan lost the vote in the Foreign Relations Committee, but only eight to nine. Reagan met again with several key senators in the last two days before the vote, and senators Grassley, Schmitt, Zorinsky and Jepsen reversed their previous opposition.[41] That was the margin of victory; Senator Exon switched only on the day of the vote.

The final vote was 52 to 48 against the resolution of disapproval, thereby allowing the sale.

The long-term importance of the AWACS vote

If Reagan had lost the AWACS vote, the effects both domestically and abroad would have been dramatic. Domestically, it would have seemed to many that AIPAC controlled American policy in the Middle East. That would not have been entirely true, since many senators had opposed the sale on grounds that did not reflect AIPAC's core beliefs: opposition to arms proliferation, concern about technology compromise, insistence on more overt Saudi cooperation or fear that the Saudi monarchy was as unstable as the Shah had been. However, as the most visible and effective force against the sale, AIPAC would have received the credit and the blame for defeating Reagan's first foreign policy initiative. Regional policies that depended upon security cooperation with Saudi Arabia, or indeed any state aside from Israel, would necessarily have been radically curtailed or abandoned; that would have required a complete recalibration of policies on oil security, power projection and the peace process.

It is possible that, as Nixon had suggested, there would have been a backlash against Israel, AIPAC and the Jewish community. Private polling as of 30 September indicated that 82 percent of the American people supported Reagan in attempting to strengthen the relationship with Saudi Arabia; that included a majority of every ethnic group. After being presented with the president's arguments for the sale, 64 percent supported the sale and only 33 percent opposed it, although Jews still opposed the sale 63 to 37 (RRPL, Dole files, AWACS, Box 4, Smith & Harroff Confidential Poll 30 Sep. 1981). A Cambridge poll in mid-September had similar results (Cordesman 1984: 333). However, opponents relied on other polling showing a plurality or majority opposed to the sale, and the great majority of those who would act politically based on the sale opposed it. Fear of backlash caused anxiety among many who lobbied for the wider Jewish agenda; that ultimately motivated Senator Cohen to vote for the sale.

In the Middle East, a congressional veto would have bolstered those who argued the United States was untrustworthy and committed to total Israeli hegemony. If Saudi Arabia had purchased the British Nimrod surveillance system and French fighter-bombers, they would have come without the restrictions favoring Israel that AWACS carried. Security cooperation among Saudi Arabia, other Gulf states and the United States would have been crippled; American influence over Saudi policies would have been diminished. Members of the Saudi royal family leaning toward accommodation with radical Arab movements would have been strengthened, as would the movements themselves. In Israel, where both Labor and Likud had opposed the sale, the reality of greater influence over, and dependence on, the relationship with America would have had unpredictable effects. Prime Minister Begin might have been further encouraged to pursue the pure Revisionist vision; his opponents might have either been silenced or energized to avoid the poisonous effects of regional hegemony and national dependence. As Henry Kissinger argued, whatever one thought of the sale as proposed, its defeat would make any American policy initiative in the region problematic if not impossible.

Winning the vote, however, did not avoid all of these adverse results. The president had relied heavily on non-substantive arguments – the need for Republican solidarity, the harm done the presidency by a defeat – and did not establish a strategic vision based on core beliefs that would serve him in future policy battles. Many senators who voted for the sale did so in spite of believing that it was unwise policy.[42] Members of Congress came out of the battle with heightened respect for, or dread of, AIPAC. The White House was anxious to make amends with the Jewish community, who had fought out of conviction and were now nursing what they thought were wounds of renewed prejudice.

Further, the victory did not accomplish intended policy goals, with the exception of enhanced ability to defend the oil facilities. The Saudis were smarting over assertions that the monarchy was unstable and untrustworthy, and that they should adopt American (and Israeli) views on the peace process as a condition of security cooperation. They were unlikely to take public positions in line with the opponents' demands. A senior Saudi official told Fred Dutton, "If we have to be in the papers and have all these bloody show-downs ... we just don't want to buy in the U.S." (Dutton interview). Reagan's relations with Prime Minister Begin were seriously damaged by mutual accusations of betrayal. Israelis were alarmed by evidence of Saudi influence, evidenced by Reagan's qualified support for Crown Prince Fahd's eight-point plan. "Strategic consensus" was moribund after Haig's eye-opening Middle East tour in April, but the AWACS battle closed the casket lid on the concept.

Within the administration, the political team had again proven its competency, but the national security team had not. Within two months, Richard Allen was on his way out of office. Within eight months, Secretary of State Haig would follow. Allen's handling of the AWACS issue was apparently a significant part of what made him vulnerable. While Haig's problems were numerous, AWACS demonstrated that he was neither trusted in the White House nor effective with Congress. The most telling point is that none of the policy or political problems the sale presented had been identified, much less provided for, before the administration publicly committed itself to the sale.

AIPAC had a clear set of beliefs by which to measure policy affecting Israel, and had lost narrowly while never deviating from those beliefs. They, and much of the Jewish community, were willing to measure Middle East policy, and candidates for office, by the degree of security and freedom of action afforded Israel.

President Reagan and his principal advisers had demonstrated the costs of a confused or conflicting set of beliefs, and the absence of convinced advocates. Reagan's private reconciliation of his conflicting beliefs was suggested by his decision to sell AWACS, his comments about Israeli interference in American security policy, and his intended message to Begin linking security cooperation to AWACS: he would guarantee Israel's security, but not rely on Israel for America's.

The presidential letter of assurances suggested how much more Reagan and his aides had to learn about the battle of beliefs. In it, Regan promised to release AWACS aircraft only if, *inter alia*, Saudi Arabia made substantial contributions toward regional peace. To most Americans, "peace process" meant Camp David, land-for-peace and Palestinian rights; to Menachem Begin and Yitzhak Shamir, Camp David required nothing of Israel but to negotiate based upon Israel's security needs. President Reagan believed, with reason, that the Saudis had contributed to regional peace. Israel, and her true believers, did not think that any Arab regime could contribute to peace until it accepted a framework that reflected Revisionist beliefs. What Reagan had not focused on, nor yet engaged in, was the battle to tie beliefs to lexicons and presumptions and in turn to policy.

6   The metamorphosis of the lobby, 1981–1988

Strength and division

Introduction

The AWACS fight demonstrated that the lobby could fight hard and publicly with a popular president on a crucial issue, lose, and yet emerge with
greater power and respect in the issue community, Congress, and even the
administration it had nearly embarrassed. AWACS had been "the bench
mark. We lost the vote but won the issue" (Dine, in Tivnan 1987: 163).
Tom Dine would use this momentum, and lessons learned, to institutionalize policies favoring Israel, by building a national membership independent
of other organizations, undertaking executive branch lobbying, building an
in-house think tank to promote strategic reliance on Israel, establishing pro-
Israel political action committees (PACs) and coordinating political contributions, and accelerating programs to identify and train local leaders and
political candidates.

AIPAC was remarkably successful in achieving these goals over the
ensuing seven years. Not all of their success was their own doing; exogenous
events, including terrorist acts, helped their cause. However, AIPAC was
widely and correctly given substantial credit for the increased difficulty of
selling arms to Arab regimes, and the tendency in the administration to
accede to Israel's position on security issues in the Middle East.

AIPAC's metamorphosis also had effects which were less foreseeable and
more divisive. Organizing to lobby the executive branch, in years when a
conservative Republican administration was in power and Revisionist
Zionist premiers led Israel, privileged the views of neoconservatives and
hardliners within the activist community and led to positions and relationships that dismayed friends in the wider Jewish community.[1] Building a
larger organization with ambitions to develop strategic policy led AIPAC to
the right in two ways: those hired to develop policy arguments appealing to
hawks and neoconservatives displaced historically Democratic and liberal
AIPAC staff; and the resulting growth of AIPAC's budget meant increasing
reliance upon wealthy conservative contributors, who then took over governance of the organization.

There was a shift of influence within AIPAC toward those who supported

Revisionist Zionist positions. The Revisionist vision of security involved a larger Israel dealing with Arabs through power, rather than through territorial compromise or negotiated security arrangements. The majority of the Jewish community supported Israel in the belief that it was a liberal democracy, the embodiment of Jewish ethical principles (as understood in America) and a seeker after peace. For many, the 1980s were years of confusion and anguish.

The transformation of AIPAC

Reorganization

Immediately after the AWACS vote on 28 October, it was clear that AIPAC had garnered respect for a hard-fought campaign. Administration officials and Republican leaders in Congress were anxious to work with them.[2] However, Tom Dine saw his first task as analyzing why they had lost. He sat with maps of congressional districts and a box of colored pencils, and he color coded states by their votes on the sale and then by district and political party (Dine interview).[3] The maps exposed weakness. States where Jewish communities had political strength had been taken for granted, but others had been written off. The 1980 census documented a demographic trend that made that practice costly, as population shifts to the south and west required reallocation of congressional seats to areas lacking Jewish organizational strength. By 1984, 25 percent of House members would come from Texas, Florida and California. Dine resolved to go, not where the Jews were, but where the votes were.

Dine set out to establish a regional support system. Working with AIPAC Executive Committee members, he set up offices in San Francisco, Austin and Miami (Dine interview). Local pro-Israel activists were identified to organize contact teams for each member of Congress – people who had known and worked with members, but had not lobbied them on Israel for AIPAC. Over the next two years, Dine built a network of AIPAC members who were regularly informed on issues and had access to members of Congress. That greatly increased the congressional base from which AIPAC's Washington staff worked (Bloomfield interview).[4] It also recruited a much larger, and younger, corps of activists who provided information about local politicians and could be groomed for political office. Being a local leader of AIPAC was increasingly a badge of distinction within the Jewish community.

Dine had sent out a very effective mass mailing on 6 October 1981. It described Saudi Arabia as Israel's "declared enemy" and part of the "Arab treachery" of 1973, and asked respondents to help by signing memoranda for delivery to senators and sending contributions which would make them members of AIPAC (RRPL, Dole Files, Box 4, AWACS File, AIPAC Alert 6 Oct. 1981). A total of 400,000 Alerts were mailed; 10,000 new AIPAC members resulted (Blitzer 1985: 123). A February 1982 Alert quoted praise for AIPAC from press and politicians, and claimed credit for the level of aid to Israel: "On a budget of just $1.8 million, AIPAC successfully lobbied Congress in 1981 for $2.2 *BILLION* in foreign aid. *This means that every membership gift of $35 to AIPAC resulted indirectly in $42,777 of U.S. AID TO ISRAEL!*" (O'Brien 1986: 172) (emphasis in original). This mailing also produced thousands of new members; the technique was repeated regularly thereafter, especially during periods of crisis in U.S.–Israeli relations.

AIPAC members regularly received issue briefs, requests to contact elected officials, invitations to briefings and training sessions, and solicitations for funds. Between 1978 and 1987, membership grew from 9,000 to over 55,000 (Smith 1988: 217). AIPAC sought to mobilize, educate and direct supporters, but not to ask for advice. AIPAC had always been a tight professional organization, and would maintain control of policy.

AIPAC held annual Washington policy conferences with multiple purposes: (1) briefing on current issues and policy goals for the coming year; (2) having administration officials and legislators address the conference (inviting competition for the strongest support); (3) giving members the opportunity to lobby personally; (4) holding workshops on lobbying techniques; and (5) building members' loyalty and their stature at home. Over 1,200 members attended the 1983 conference, which featured a workshop on fundraising and media relations led by senior officials from both major national parties. It was addressed by two senators and seven representatives; 15 senators and 37 representatives attended the banquet (O'Brien 1986: 170). Those figures grew steadily.

Dine decided to lobby the executive branch after seeing during the AWACS battle that the job was not being done. The Presidents Conference was not focused exclusively on Israel, and did not have professional staff in Washington. Its access to the Reagan White House was uneven. Jack Stein, the White House liaison with the Jewish community, was a past chair of the Conference, but left within a few months after the AWACS vote, and was not replaced for over six months. In addition, Dine sensed that the Reagan administration was anxious to avoid another public fight with AIPAC, and that the president was sensitized to perceptions that he was reneging on campaign commitments and was indifferent to disrespect for the community. There was an opportunity, then, to use AIPAC's new stature and momentum to build relationships that might allow AIPAC to negotiate issues with the administration before they could become public fights.

Dine believed that effectively lobbying senior administration officials required an in-house capability to produce high-quality policy studies. In mid-1982, he hired Steven J. Rosen, a former political science professor, to fill a new position of director of research and information. Rosen was associate director of the National Security Studies Program at Rand Corporation, where he had just authored a study for the Pentagon arguing that the United States had unwisely excluded Israel from strategic planning for the

Gulf and the eastern Mediterranean, appeasing rejectionist Arab opinion at the expense of the objective American national interest. The Rand study was published as *The Strategic Value of Israel*, the first in a series of "AIPAC Papers on U.S.–Israel Relations," in October 1982 (Rosen 1982).[5] It provided an academician's aggressive espousal of policies based upon AIPAC's core beliefs, with the added lustre of having first been a government-ordered study by the nation's premier national security policy institute. Dine hired Martin Indyk, an Australian academic, as Rosen's deputy.[6] Rosen and Indyk believed that more could be accomplished dealing with the "proactive" executive than with the "reactive" Congress.[7]

Over the next seven years, Rosen wrote or edited 16 studies in the "AIPAC Papers" series and innumerable other papers. Most AIPAC Papers were detailed arguments for strategic cooperation by integration of naval and air force operations, reciprocal defense materiel procurement and other means. There were also studies of a free trade area, moving the American embassy to Jerusalem, and the Arab–Israeli military balance.

Three studies went directly to defining what principled and causal beliefs toward Israel and the Arabs should be, and how to expose and discredit those who disagreed (Goott and Rosen 1983; Kessler and Schwaber 1984; Rosen and Abramowitz 1984). *The Campaign to Discredit Israel* replaced an annual photocopied "Who's Who" of "anti-Israel organizations and personalities" said to be engaged in an "energetic campaign ... to undermine the moral and strategic ties between the two countries" (Dine, in Goott and Rosen 1983: v). Goott describes a coordinated effort to undermine Israel's image as a democracy (by focusing on human rights), to question her reliability and to redefine the national interest to favor Arabs. The rest of the pamphlet is a directory of participants in this purported campaign, ranging from Arab-American associations and Arab studies centers to registered agents of Saudi Arabia (Messrs. Dutton, Connor and Cook) to scholars (Professor Noam Chomsky, Director Michael Hudson of Georgetown's Center for Contemporary Arab Studies, Professor Walid Khalidi, Professor Edward Said, Professor Hisham Sharabi) to former officials (Senator James Abourezk, Undersecretary of State George Ball, former ambassadors Andrew Killgore and John West). There was in fact no coordinated "campaign" to discredit Israel; efforts to explain Arab perspectives on the conflict with Israel were generally ineffective and disjointed.

The 1983 study was followed by *The AIPAC College Guide: Exposing the Anti-Israel Campaign on Campus* (Kessler and Schwaber 1984). The *Guide* defined enemies of Israel as those espousing competing beliefs concerning Israel's ethical identity and strategic role: Israel as oppressor, strategic burden and Goliath. Readers were urged to expose the "extremism," "anti-Americanism" and "sensationalism" of the opponents, and to stress that opponents sought to destroy Israel, the only Middle East democracy.

The *Guide* was part of an expanded AIPAC Political Leadership Development Program, an effort begun in 1979 to monitor and influence discussion of the Middle East on 350 college campuses. Many of the participants later served in congressional staffs, presidential campaigns and the White House and executive departments. Some would have done so anyway; politics, however, is largely a process of networking and building common understandings, and the campus program integrated young leaders with AIPAC. Training materials were detailed primers in advocacy, political networking and suppression of competing advocates' efforts.[8] The program's leader, Jonathan Kessler, saw the program as "the final component of a political revolution which took place in stages after the Holocaust, the 6-day war, the Yom Kippur War, and the AWACS battle of 1981" (Melman and Raviv 1994: 312). He sought to set the terms of debate for the long term. The focus was not on the current aid bill or peace plan; it was on convincing future leaders that Israel was America's cultural and moral sibling and strategic partner against the great threats to the West – and that Arabs were none of those things. Support for Israel would then be their default position on any policy issue in the Middle East.

By 1987, AIPAC's staff had grown from 25 to 85 persons (Smith 1988: 217). Its budget grew from $1.8 million to $15 million by 1988. However, the congressional lobbying staff, which had been four in 1980, grew only to five (Bloomfield interview). The rest of the new money paid for the research department, the costs of building and educating a large national membership, and fundraising.

The relationship between AIPAC and its financial supporters changed. Many wealthy supporters of Israel also supported Reagan's economic programs, and were happy to help AIPAC build strong relationships with the administration. Being successful people, however, they wanted, and were accorded, titles and the promise of access to senior officials, even briefings at the White House. Doug Bloomfield says that the small contributions AIPAC got by on earlier came without strings, allowing a small, professional organization to concentrate on the congressional lobbying it did best. Large contributions, however, "come with ropes," and Bloomfield spent increasing amounts of time briefing the new "owners," and scrambling to explain or correct statements they made (Bloomfield interview).

Morris Amitay, Dine's predecessor, said executive lobbying was "utterly stupid – an oxymoron!" Constituents could ask for a vote and offer a congressman political and financial support in return.

> [T]hese congressmen or senators … don't know that much about [the issues], and basically have to vote "yes" or "no" or to sign a letter.… But in the White House or at State, they can't be bamboozled or co-opted. And they're negotiating things that involve Israel's security.
>
> (Melman and Raviv 1994: 322)

Amitay's caustic comments capture the gulf between "old AIPAC," an autonomous professional staff of former congressional aides, and "new

AIPAC," neoconservative academics overseen by a board of conservative wealthy Jewish leaders fascinated with policy-making.

AIPAC's executive lobbying aggravated liberal friends in Congress and the Jewish community by identifying AIPAC with conservative administrations in the United States and Israel. However, Democratic members of Congress and candidates for the presidency continued to outbid one another in their support of Israel. It is difficult to perceive what was given up in terms of effectiveness, at least during the Reagan administration.

Political coordination

Because it dedicates a substantial amount of its resources to lobbying, AIPAC is prohibited by law from contributing to, or directing contributions to, political candidates. Its coordinating role in rewarding and punishing candidates has always been denied, even as the results of that effort were trumpeted. After the AWACS vote, AIPAC's blessing or curse grew in importance. Many candidates solicited AIPAC's help in ways that ranged from position papers to advice on staff hiring decisions. Several members who had voted against AIPAC were targeted for defeat.

In the 1980 election cycle, there had been ten pro-Israel PACs. In the 1982 cycle there were 40, and contributions rose from $414,400 to $2,027,200. In the 1984 cycle, there were 81 PACs contributing nearly $3.8 million. In the 1986 cycle, the numbers grew to 94 PACs and at least $4.6 million (Curtiss 1990: 37, 56, 75).[9] The absolute numbers are not that impressive; pro-Israel PAC giving in the 1984 cycle was only about 4 percent of total PAC giving (*WSJ* 26 Feb. 1985: 1). However, it was $1,000,000 more than that of the single largest PAC, the 110,000 member Realtors PAC (ibid.). More importantly, the effectiveness of pro-Israeli PACs was multiplied: (1) they focused on close races involving key supporters and opponents, or where the incumbent held a key committee position; (2) they focused on the Senate, where most foreign policy issues were determined; and (3) unlike almost any other issue area, there was no meaningful opposition. Commercial entities with interests in the Middle East had no discernible pattern of organizing on that basis. Arab-American groups had only one PAC until the 1988 cycle, when they had three, giving a total of $38,370 (Curtiss 1990: 127–8).

Studies of the impact of single-issue organizations on campaigns have focused on PACs because they are required to file reports with the Federal Election Commission, and are therefore easier to track than coordinated individual contributions. However, PACs may have been responsible for only a fraction of coordinated giving by pro-Israel activists. One experienced observer, a former State Department official, senior member of the Senate Foreign Relations staff and lobbyist, estimates that well over half of all non-PAC "out of district" campaign contributions are from pro-Israel advocates (interview of "A").[10] Such money can be critical, particularly in tight races and poorer districts. While PACs had significant impact, they were limited to $5,000 per candidate per campaign; large amounts of money were possible, but only by setting up and coordinating numerous PACs. Individual contributions were limited to $2,000 per contributor per campaign, but that meant that a family of four could contribute $8,000 in the primary and $8,000 in the general election to each of an unlimited number of candidates.

Candidates had many reasons to believe that coordinated giving based on policy toward Israel was critically important. Defeated incumbents were widely quoted saying so.[11] After Senator Percy was defeated in 1984, the term "Percy factor" entered the political lexicon (*IHT* 8 Aug. 1986: 5). The "power of the lobby" in political campaigns was widely covered in the press; the *Wall Street Journal* ran front-page summaries of the lobby's impact after each election, and the *Washington Post* and *New York Times* ran multi-page stories several times during the 1980s. Patterns of contributions became difficult for campaign professionals to miss. In the 1984 election, of $1.82 million given to Senate candidates by pro-Israeli PACs, 44 percent went to opponents of five Republican senators who had voted for the AWACS sale (*WSJ* 26 Feb. 1985: 1).[12]

Connections between AIPAC and PACs were obvious. Former AIPAC executive director Morris Amitay formed WashPAC; WashPAC gave to Senator Percy's opponents in both primary and general elections, and Percy complained to the Federal Election Commission that Amitay also directed an illegal campaign that spent $1.1 million against him.[13] The largest pro-Israel PAC, NatPAC, was managed by Richard Altman, former AIPAC political director. PACs were formed by former AIPAC presidents Robert Asher and Larry Weinberg. The *Wall Street Journal* reported that at least 51 of 80 pro-Israel PACs in 1987 were operated by AIPAC officials (*WSJ* 24 Jun. 1987: 1). Essentially all pro-Israel activists, and therefore all managers of pro-Israel PACs, were members of AIPAC and received AIPAC's detailed analysis of the voting patterns and position statements on candidates.

Dine took credit for what the "Jewish community" had done, and welcomed candidates' inquiries about support. In April 1984, Dine said that 87 congressional candidates from both parties had sought AIPAC's help since 1982 (*WP* 10 Apr. 1984: A17). Just after the 1984 election, Dine told the Council of Jewish Federations that the three essentials of a political race were: "Early money, middle money and late money." He claimed that Jewish giving had been "essential" to defeating Senator Percy, swayed several other races, and produced the most "pro-Israel" Congress in history (*WSJ* 26 Feb. 1985: 1).

Perception was not necessarily reality. AIPAC supported candidates who lost; each "success" had multiple explanations; and legislators who served on foreign affairs committees (as had Percy and Findley) were always vulnerable, because many constituents saw them as less productive on local issues. Percy had narrowly avoided defeat in 1978, and was also targeted by the National Conservative PAC. However, his share of the Jewish vote went from 70 percent in 1978 to 35 percent in 1984. The resulting perception was crucial.

Dine denied illegally directing contributions.[14] However, in November 1988 a 30 September 1986 memorandum from AIPAC deputy political director Elizabeth Schrayer to an assistant was reproduced in the *Washington Post*. In it, Schrayer gave instructions for calls to specific PACs urging specific contributions to named candidates (*WP* 14 Nov. 1988: A1).[15] Managers of the PACs denied taking direction from AIPAC. AIPAC declined comment (*JP* 15 Nov. 1988: 12). At a minimum, the memorandum showed that AIPAC monitored giving patterns and sought to influence them.

AIPAC regularly rated candidates on the basis of support for Israel.[16] In 1987, Dine named 19 senators, including six Republicans, as "friends of Israel" who should be supported for re-election in 1988 (*NYT* 7 Jul. 1987: A8). In the same speech, Dine reported that in the 1985–1986 campaign season, "AIPAC lay leaders and staff met with every senator up for re-election except one, plus 49 Senate challengers and 205 House challengers, including every new freshman member."

Presidential candidates also courted AIPAC. By July 1987, 16 months before the 1988 election, nearly all presidential candidates had been interviewed by AIPAC and given a briefing book. Some, Dine said, asked how they thought a planned speech "would play in the Jewish community," and some asked AIPAC's reaction to prospective aides (*NYT* 6 Jul. 1987: A1).

Asking for a lobby's support does not prove subservience to the lobby; politicians routinely seek support from disparate groups. Most interest groups understand that officeholders balance opposing interests in legislation, and cannot support them each time.[17] AIPAC was different. It would track, publicize and punish every deviation from its positions, and no opposing group could compensate. Asking AIPAC for support implied a promise of fealty.

AIPAC had always been assiduously bipartisan, although its staunchest support had come from liberal Democrats. As AIPAC changed, it and the PACs which followed its lead were increasingly identified with Republican candidates. In 1984, Democratic candidates received 79 percent of pro-Israel PACs' contributions (*WSJ* 26 Feb. 1985: 1). But in 1985, Republicans received 55 percent of that funding. The leading recipient was Senator Robert Kasten, a social conservative who took positions opposed by the majority of Jews on prayer in schools, civil rights, and abortion (*HChron* 6 Nov. 1985: 32). Two Jewish Democratic congressmen were strongly warned not to run against incumbent senators Bob Dole and Bob Packwood. Another strong supporter of Israel was discouraged from running against Senator D'Amato in New York (ibid.). All three incumbents were Republicans who had been helpful to AIPAC. Packwood had led the fight against the president on AWACS.

In May 1988, Tom Dine essentially endorsed Vice-President Bush over the presumptive Democratic presidential candidate, Governor Dukakis of Massachusetts, while acknowledging that Dukakis had been "very close to the pro-Israel/Jewish community in Boston." Dine touted Bush's pledge "to stay on the Reagan–Bush course ... the last eight years have been one hell of a course" (*WP* 29 May 1988: 12). AIPAC was facing the first change of administration since it had invested heavily in executive branch influence; it was now awkwardly sorting out how best to protect its investment.

By 1988, neoconservative and pro-Likud beliefs had not just defined policy at AIPAC, they had remade the organization. Conservative officers had initially wanted to fire all staff identified with Democrats, which would have included Dine and Bloomfield. Bloomfield, the legislative director, was perceived by the pro-Likud members of the board and staff as a dove, an opponent of executive lobbying and a liberal (Bloomfield interview). On 12 December, 1988, Bloomfield was ordered to resign[18] (*WSJ* 20 Dec. 1988: 1; *WP* 21 Dec. 1988: A9). In the summer of 1988, editors of *The Near East Report* refused an order from AIPAC chair Robert Asher and president Edward Levy to print a statement by Max Fisher from the Republican Convention, urging Jews to support Republicans. By December, AIPAC officers had forced the resignations of the editorial board (ibid.).

AIPAC's relationship with the government of Israel

AIPAC's mission was to build ever-stronger ties between the United States and Israel, if necessary to the exclusion of other relationships in the Middle East. Often, that entailed pressing the Congress and the president to accede to Israel's requests – for more aid or arms, or better terms, or curtailed arms sales to Arabs, or particular approaches to the peace process. Frequently, AIPAC had to explain Israeli actions that came as unpleasant surprises. At times, AIPAC undertook initiatives that had not been cleared with the Israeli government, or made statements that varied, even if only briefly, from the public Israeli position. That happened: (1) when AIPAC believed that more could be obtained from the Congress or the administration than Israel had asked; (2) when supporters in Congress insisted on taking actions without prodding by AIPAC; or (3) when it seemed necessary to the lobby's credibility to state an independent position.

Dine describes AIPAC's relationship with the government of Israel as comparable to that of an American ambassador, trying to explain each side to the other. He means to emphasize that he was not acting as an Israeli. The relationship is certainly more complex than that, however. When asked who AIPAC's constituency is, Dine names three American groups: founding Jewish organizations, politically active leadership Jews and non-Jewish supporters of Israel, many of them Dispensationalist Christians (Dine interview). That response omits the government of Israel and the broader American Jewish community; yet policy could not be set nor long pursued without considering the beliefs, policies and reactions of leaders of those entities as well as those of executive and legislative leaders. Persistent conundrums resulted for AIPAC: (1) it could not separate itself from Israeli government positions forcefully or often, or it would lose critical access to the government of Israel and support among Israel's fiercest American supporters; (2) it could not wed itself to every position of the government of Israel without raising issues of "dual loyalty" or even of being an unregistered foreign agent; and (3) if it supported Israeli policies seen by most American Jews and American officials as antithetical to their values, it risked its credibility and political effectiveness. When he could, Dine focused on giving the Israeli government maximum freedom of action and said as little as possible about policies that were awkward to explain.

Because "the greatest growth in American Jewish political activism came during the Likud's stewardship ... many new leaders were trained, educated and indoctrinated with Likud policy" (Bloomfield, in Melman and Raviv 1994: 323). During the period of a National Unity Government in Israel (1984–1988), Labor leader Shimon Peres was unable to call on support from AIPAC, regardless of whether he was premier or foreign minister (Goldberg 1996: 216–18).

Tom Dine says that AIPAC's identification with the Likud was "much, much overrated" (Dine interview). Dine did not personally support the Revisionist agenda. However, he concedes that at least one Executive Committee member, Jonathan Mitchell, raised money for the Likud; and he told a Jewish leader who raised money for left-of-center Israeli parties that he should stop.[19] AIPAC staff members, particularly Steve Rosen, were increasingly identified with the Likud. In 1984, Rosen treated two dovish members of the Israeli Knesset dismissively when they tried to explain their views; Rosen favored not just aggressive settlement but annexation of the West Bank (Tivnan 1987: 207–8).[20] Israeli cabinet member Yossi Sarid said AIPAC pressured sponsors to cancel his speaking engagements; "AIPAC thought that my calls for an Israeli–Palestinian reconciliation should not be expressed on American soil" (Melman and Raviv 1994: 327).

Many events during the period 1981–1988 tested AIPAC's ability to balance its core mission against the demands of its several constituencies.[21] Two will be discussed here: (1) President Reagan's 1 September 1982 plan for re-framing the peace process; and (2) the interrelated 1984 fights in Congress over moving the United States embassy to Jerusalem and sales of Stinger missiles to Jordan.

Fresh Start: Between Reagan and Begin

Reagan's "Fresh Start Initiative" of September 1982 went beyond the Camp David Accords by anticipating what the negotiations should lead to.[22] Specifically, the proposal called for self-government by Palestinians in association with Jordan as a preferred goal, and a freeze on Israeli settlements in the Territories (DoS Bull, Sep. 1982: 23–5).

Prime Minister Begin had not been consulted, and was infuriated by the slight as well as by the substance of the proposal.[23] He obtained a cabinet communiqué rejecting the plan as violating the Camp David Accords and inviting an armed Palestinian state, led by the PLO and allied with the Soviet Union (Nakhleh and Wright 1983: App. B, 137–40). Having negotiated over every word at Camp David, Begin believed that Israel had given all it was obligated to give when it returned the Sinai in April 1982; questions of final borders, Palestinian rights, the status of Jerusalem, *inter alia*, were subject to perpetual negotiation.

Most American supporters of Israel appreciated Reagan's commitment to Israel's security, but rejected any suggestion that Israel should make concessions before there were genuine negotiating partners. Core supporters of Israel in the House thought Reagan undercut Camp David and pushed Israel too hard, but did not reject the initiative. Senate leaders gave the initiative bipartisan support (*WP* 2 Sep. 1982: A14).

For AIPAC, this was treacherous ground. Dine wanted to support the president where possible, as part of the effort to build influence with the administration. Further, while the proposal suggested end results, it did not mandate them, and the suggestions accorded with the view of most American Jews that Israel had agreed to trade land for peace. However, Israel's strongest American supporters agreed with Begin.

Immediately following Reagan's speech, Tom Dine told reporters that AIPAC was pleased with the president's commitment to Israel's security and his rejection of a Palestinian state, but opposed any attempt to dictate the outcome before negotiations (*WP* 2 Sep. 1982: A14). Five days later, he told a reporter that "there were many constructive points" to the plan, that it had "been very well received by the American population" and that he assumed that members of Congress would "receive it in the same way." As to what the plan could deliver, the "ball [was] in Jordan's court" (*NYT* 3 Sep. 1982: A1).

Dine was thinking strategically. Doug Bloomfield had drafted an AIPAC response in Dine's absence, saying that the plan should be the basis for further discussion. The point was to avoid rejection of the president and put the onus on King Hussein, and on the Arabs from whom Hussein would need acquiescence. Bloomfield had called Benjamin Netanyahu, then Deputy Chief of Mission at the Israeli embassy, to ask what the embassy was recommending. Netanyahu agreed completely with AIPAC's approach.[24] Netanyahu called Ambassador Arens, who was with Prime Minister Begin in Israel; Arens took the argument to Begin, but Begin rejected the advice (Bloomfield interview).[25] By the time of the Gwertzman interview, the Israeli government had vehemently rejected Reagan's plan.

Tom Dine faced harsh criticism from within the pro-Israel community. His president, Larry Weinberg, was particularly incensed.[26] Within days after the story appeared, however, the camp massacres at Sabra and Shatila delivered a major blow to the image of Begin's government. Dine believes that his earlier statement, conditionally supporting the president and maintaining some separation from Israel, gave AIPAC "enormous credibility" (Dine interview).

However, AIPAC cannot long oppose the Israeli government. On 4 February 1983, AIPAC arranged for senior aides of approximately 50 senators and representatives to be briefed for two hours by an Israeli specialist on Lebanon, to explain that Israel might have to keep troops in Lebanon for five to ten years (Evans and Novak 1983). Whatever the security justification for such a lengthy occupation, it would be fatal to the Reagan initiative. King Hussein was known to believe that the Reagan administration's ability to end the Israeli occupation of Lebanon was a test of the feasibility of Reagan's vision for the West Bank. Secretary Shultz had enabled either Israel or Syria to block negotiations under Reagan's proposal, by making negotiations contingent on having all foreign troops out of Lebanon (see, Quandt 1984: 241–2). By sponsoring an Israeli briefing on the need for a lengthy occupation, AIPAC signaled that it was back on message – the Begin government's message.[27]

Moving the embassy or stopping the missile sale

In March 1984, resolutions requiring that the American Embassy in Israel be moved to Jerusalem were introduced by Representative Lantos and Senator Moynihan without prior consultation with AIPAC. By 1 April they had 38 Senate sponsors and 215 House sponsors. The issue became a test of fidelity to Israel in the Democratic presidential primary in New York; former vice-president Walter Mondale (advised by Morris Amitay) accused Senator Gary Hart of inconstancy on the issue. Senator Hart responded with an AIPAC statement that he had been "consistent" in supporting Israel (*NYT* 24 Mar. 1984: 8).

The congressional initiative was awkward for AIPAC. The embassy move was one of five announced 1984 AIPAC policy goals. Yet it did not want a bill that dictated to the president, and the government of Israel was not pushing the issue.[28] Shamir needed Reagan's help, given Israel's dire economic straits and pending arms sales to Saudi Arabia and Jordan, and had no intention of negotiating the status of Jerusalem in any event. The initiative carried considerable baggage: (1) an embassy move was contrary to the policy of every president since 1967 that the city's status was to be negotiated;[29] (2) the legislation was of dubious constitutionality, since the president had substantial authority over diplomatic relations under Article II, Section 2; and (3) Arabs would react strongly, fearing abandonment of Resolutions 242 and 338 and recognition of the third holiest site in Islam as Israel's capital. Secretary Shultz made these points strongly (*NYT* 11 Mar. 1984: 1). The president called the initiative "unwise" and signaled a possible veto (*WSJ* 27 Mar. 1984: 1; *NYT* 1 Apr. 1984: E5).

Nevertheless, the bill's sponsors pushed for hearings. AIPAC had to support bills sponsored by its most fervent supporters. As Dine said later, "What else could we do?" (Tivnan 1987: 197).

However, Dine believed he could use the issue as leverage on a primary goal of AIPAC's and Israel's – stopping a proposed sale of 1,600 Stinger missiles to Jordan. In March, AIPAC had succeeded in amending a pending aid bill to prohibit sales to Jordan unless the president certified Jordan's commitment to recognition of Israel and direct peace talks with Israel. The sale was in such serious trouble that President Reagan made a remarkable speech to the Young Leadership Conference of UJA, pleading for under-standing of his need to support moderate Arab leaders (Speech 13 Mar. 1984 in DoS Bull, May 1984: 6–8). Reagan did not reveal that to encourage King Hussein to agree to negotiations under his initiative, he had made several commitments, including selling Jordan arms.

Hussein had waited until after the 1982 mid-term elections for Reagan to submit the arms proposal to Congress. Now, 18 months later, the president was pleading for Jewish understanding. The next day, the king said, "The U.S. is not free to move except within the limits of what AIPAC, the Zion-ists and the State of Israel determine for it," and had lost "credibility" as a mediator (*NYT* 15 Mar. 1984: A1, A10).

The king's outburst strengthened opposition to the Stinger sale. Dine used this development to leverage negotiations with Undersecretary of State Lawrence Eagleburger for cancellation of the Stinger sales in exchange for AIPAC's killing the embassy move bill. When the administration did cancel the sale, AIPAC knew about it 12 hours before Assistant Secretary of State Murphy, the official with responsibility for U.S. Middle East policy (*NYT* 22 Mar. 1984: A8). The embassy move bill was "killed" by substituting a nonbinding resolution for it (*NYT* 3 Oct. 1984: A12).

The episode illuminates AIPAC's relationship with Israel: (1) AIPAC set policy goals based upon what it thought feasible and useful in keeping sup-porters engaged, and not necessarily what Israel wanted; (2) once an AIPAC policy goal was publicly set, it was difficult to prevent supporters from pur-suing it, even when Israel and AIPAC found that awkward; and (3) AIPAC had achieved the remarkable status of being the entity with which the administration had to negotiate issues pending in Congress relating to Israel.

AIPAC and Likud-led governments of Israel generally agreed strongly on the policy goals to be sought, but the belief systems from which the policy goals were derived overlapped incompletely. Some key AIPAC staff, notably Steve Rosen, and some officers, shared Revisionist beliefs; others, including Bloomfield and Dine, did not, and looked for ways to support Israel that were consistent with their beliefs. By 1988, the ideological distance between AIPAC and Revisionist Zionism had narrowed significantly.

AIPAC's relationship with the American Jewish community

By the 1980s, American Jews had an identity crisis. It had long been accepted in the Jewish community that an open, compassionate and tolerant society, one that protected freedom of expression and religion and welcomed diversity, would be the best guarantee of safety for American Jews. Jewish leaders fought for civil rights as an expression of that conviction. The subsidence of feelings of oppression or exclusion combined with secularization and intermarriage to generate anxiety among Jewish leaders about the loss of a separate Jewish identity. Jewish identity and leadership were increasingly measured by support of Israel. Most American Jews had felt they could take pride in the Jewish state, and contribute to its security through financial and political support, without compromising their beliefs. So long as the founding myths of Israel were undisturbed, governments of Israel were led by social democrats, and Israelis were seen as cultural siblings and allies against the West's enemies, no cognitive dissonance was generated by defining oneself as an American Jew, a liberal and a strong supporter of the government of Israel.

In 1977, most American Jews were relatively oblivious to the differences in policy that Likud leadership meant. Beginning in 1981, the differences became increasingly plain. The June 1981 Osirak raid using American-supplied F-16s caused minimal concern because President Reagan seemed to accept it.[30] The July raid on an apartment complex in Beirut which killed hundreds of civilians, however, began a pattern of actions against Palestinians which caused anguish for many American and Israeli Jews.[31] In December 1981, Begin's government annexed the Golan in defiance of American policy that it was territory subject to negotiation; when Reagan then suspended the Memorandum of Agreement signed weeks before, Begin gave Ambassador Lewis a furious 50-minute tongue-lashing. Begin's diatribe, which he released to the press before Ambassador Lewis could report it to Washington, included the statement that American Jewry would support Begin as was their duty, and would not be frightened by suggestions of anti-Semitism in the Reagan administration (Isaacson 1982).[32] The following June, Israel invaded Lebanon, used anti-personnel cluster bombs and indiscriminate shelling in civilian areas,[33] and repeatedly violated assurances to the United States about its intentions. Distress became horror and revulsion at Israel's complicity in massacres of over 700 Palestinian civilians in the Sabra and Shatila refugee camps in September.

These events did much to break the self-imposed *omerta* of liberal American Jews. For a time at least many liberals found it very difficult to reconcile support of Israel's government, as contrasted with support of Israel's existence, with American Jewish values or with American interests. Rabbi Arthur Hertzberg, descended from six generations of rabbis, former chair of the AJCongress and lifelong Zionist, called for the resignations of Begin and Defense Minister Sharon in the *New York Times* (reprinted in Hertzberg 1992b: 24–5). Howard Squadron and Rabbi Alexander Schindler, past chairs of the Presidents Conference, called for an independent commission to investigate the massacres, and Schindler, once arguably Begin's most important American Jewish supporter, told Begin personally that he must fire Sharon (Tivnan 1987: 174). Schindler said Prime Minister Sharett once noted that American Jews had been milked like cows for moral and financial support and treated with contempt. "But we've crossed a watershed now, and our open criticism will continue and increase" (Cohen 1988: 99). A Gallup Poll had reported in mid-1981 that 53 percent of American Jews felt that Begin's policies were hurting support for Israel in the United States;[34] after the camp massacres, 78 percent felt that way (Rosenthal 2001: 59, 73).

Many American Jews were realizing for the first time that there were two very different Zionisms competing for control in Israel.[35] The Mamlakhtuit Zionism of Jewish ingathering, integration and state-building, identified with secular Labor leaders, had been somewhat mythologized, but meshed easily with the views of an American Jewish liberal. The Zionism of Jewish separateness espoused by the Likud and the religious parties seemed a witch's brew of political reaction and religious fanaticism; the deep-seated hatred of Arabs evident among Sephardim who supported the Likud added to liberals' sense of alienation. Milton Viorst wrote in dismay that Zionism had "become identified with territorial expansion, with religious zealotry, with military oppression, with political intolerance," and that Israel after 1967 "appeared to have wandered into a moral desert" (Viorst 1987: 2).[36] In contrast, Norman Podhoretz defended the Lebanon invasion in neoconservative terms, as defeating Soviet proxies with American arms; those who maligned Israel's morality were applying a dual standard and were anti-Semitic (Podhoretz 1982). Podhoretz later called on American Jews to avoid "dual loyalty ... between Israel and liberalism," and to support Israel against calls for compromise, which would threaten its existence (Podhoretz 1989: 18). Irving Kristol argued that liberalism had abandoned American Jews, leaving them in the ancient condition of being politically homeless; conservatives and Evangelical Christians were now their natural allies, however uncomfortable that made them (Kristol 1984).[37]

However, a preponderance of American Jews continued to see themselves as liberals and egalitarian democrats. In April 1988, a *Los Angeles Times* poll found that four of five American Jews said that being Jewish was very important to them. Asked to rank the characteristic most important to Jewish identity, 50 percent said "commitment to social equality," while only 17 percent cited support for Israel (*LAT* 12 Apr. 1988: 1).[38] Three months after the first Intifada began, two-thirds of American Jews favored accommodation with the Palestinians. Real danger to Israel was considered a matter of the gravest personal importance to American Jews (Cohen 1996). However, many were alienated by Israeli use of force seemingly beyond any requirement for security, and were repelled by actions and policies that seemed inconsistent with their moral principles.

Jewish dissent did not generally create real impediments for AIPAC. Tom Dine said that AIPAC took positions only where there was broad consensus, such as aid; on matters such as the Likud settlements policy, where "the constituency [was] in fact deeply divided," he claimed that the organization took no position (Melman and Raviv 1994: 327). Sometimes, AIPAC had no choice but to join the general outcry against Israel's actions. That was the case with regard to Jonathan Pollard, an American Jew who stole thousands of classified documents for Israeli intelligence; Israel had stupidly made dual loyalty a credible concern. It was also the case when Yitzhak Shamir, attempting to form a government in 1988, agreed to amend the law to constrict Jewish identity to that defined by Orthodox clerics.[39] That would have denied the Jewishness of most American Jews, who were Conservative, Reform or unaffiliated. These incidents outraged and humiliated American Jews and diminished Shamir's government in their eyes, but did not perceptibly affect AIPAC's ability to preserve Israel's independence of action by enhancing economic and military aid and denying arms to Arabs. On those issues, AIPAC's restructured organization was increasingly successful, both in the Congress and in the administration.

AIPAC was also usually able to mute public criticism of Israel related to the peace process and Palestinian rights. Polls showed that pluralities of American Jews conditionally favored a Palestinian state and talks with the PLO by the early 1980s, contrary to the position of Likud governments (Brettschneider 1996: 29).[40] Tom Dine claimed that intra-communal debate was necessary and healthy; rather than calling for ostracism of dissenters, he denied there was dissent (Goldberg 1990: 20, 22). Open dissension was in fact dealt with vigorously. In major part, this worked because those supporting the Likud's policies were those who had the deepest connections with Israel and increasingly dominated organized Jewish life, while opponents, though larger in number, were not engaged.[41]

The Palestinian Intifada, which began in December 1987, tested the control exercised by AIPAC and conservative activists. The media barraged the American public with stories of Israeli soldiers forcibly suppressing protests by rock-throwing Palestinian youth.[42] Defense Minister Rabin referred to "break[ing] their bones" in an Israeli television interview, which was taken as a recommendation if not an order to the IDF (Schiff and Ya'ari 1990: 150).[43] American sympathy for Israel had been based in part on the horror of the Holocaust; after Lebanon, and particularly with the onset of the Intifada, some began to see Palestinians as a people oppressed by a hegemon.[44] Israelis of the peace movement argued that silence on the part of American Jews amounted to massive intervention in Israeli politics, on the wrong side (Gruen 1990: 221).

In September 1987, after Shamir refused a peace conference on the future of the Territories, the AJCongress issued a statement: occupation could "in the long run only corrupt the values which are associated with the Jewish state" (Rosenthal 2001: 94). Shamir called the Congress's statement an attempt to circumvent Israeli democracy,[45] but Shimon Peres praised the statement and urged American Jews to call for a peace conference. Other major organizations did not then follow the Congress's lead, but after the

Intifada began the head of B'nai B'rith blamed the occupation for the rioting, and Alexander Schindler said that the "status quo ... is a time bomb ticking away at Israel's vital center." The Conference chair, Morris Abram, initially blamed the PLO for the uprising and worked to convince the State Department of Israel's restraint. However, at a conference in Jerusalem called by Shamir, even Abram endorsed Secretary Shultz's call for a peace conference, saying "the status quo is not indefinitely acceptable to American Jews" (ibid.: 96–7, 101).[46]

American Jewish reaction to Israel's policies briefly seemed a real threat to AIPAC's control of the policy dialogue. Thirty senators, including most of Israel's strongest supporters, signed a letter criticizing Shamir's resistance to Shultz's peace efforts and expressing dismay at his rejection of territorial concessions (*JPS* XVII, 4 (summer 1988): 189–90).[47] Senator Levin, one of the authors, had rejected entreaties by Dine to delete references to "land for peace" from the letter (Cohen 1988: 103). By October, AIPAC's defense of Israeli policies had resulted in a joint letter from AJC, AJCongress and ADL to AIPAC, stating that AIPAC was out of step "with the consensus of the organized Jewish community," demanding that AIPAC coordinate lobbying with them, and announcing the formation of a joint committee to deal with political issues (*NYT* 18 Oct. 1988: A1). The letter was a shot across the bow, but nothing more. Dine promised better coordination, but that would have required prior consultation, open debate, slower response times and ultimately diluted positions and loss of independence. The deputy chief of mission at the Israeli Embassy, clearly aware of the implications of a split, said that "a united community is a strong community," and it was best to have a united voice (ibid.). Tom Dine now dismisses the incident as reflecting "sibling rivalry" (Dine interview). The "joint political committee" never operated, and AIPAC remained the leader on policy toward Israel.

Effectively advocating the views of liberal American Jews would have required replicating AIPAC, an organization dedicated to lobbying and sustained by a national network. AIPAC would not change, at least while conservatives governed in the United States and the Likud led Israel. As anguished as much of organized Jewry was over Israeli policies, there was never the kind of sustained will needed to build such an alternative organization in the face of predictable attacks.[48]

As advocacy for Israel became central to Jewish identity in America, criticisms of Israeli policies were increasingly cast as attacks on all Jews. A conscious effort to redefine "anti-Semitism" as dissent from Israeli policies may have started with a book by two ADL leaders (Forster and Epstein 1974). In his December 1981 tirade to Ambassador Lewis, Begin said that American Jews would not be deterred from their duty to support Israel by "anti-Semitic propaganda," meaning criticism of his government (Isaacson 1982). Nathan and Ruth Ann Perlmutter defined "the new anti-Semitism" entirely in terms of attitudes toward Israel (Perlmutter and Perlmutter 1982: 175). Norman Podhoretz expressly labeled those "vilifying" Israel over its actions in Lebanon and other policies anti-Semites, whether they were Jews or Gentiles (Podhoretz 1983). The tactic worked: a former State Department official and senior SFRC staff member confirms that opposition to Israeli policy became equated with anti-Semitism, and that being publicly labeled an anti-Semite was seen as career-ending (interview of "A").

A major impediment to structuring negotiations with the Palestinians had always been reaction to the PLO, seen by supporters of Israel as terrorists bent on the destruction of Israel and by conservatives and neoconservatives as clients of Moscow. The letter negotiated by Henry Kissinger in 1975, promising not to "recognize or negotiate with" the PLO until it met stated conditions, had been a remarkable act by a superpower, denying itself power to conduct diplomacy as it chose. By its terms, however, the letter did not forbid meetings with Palestinians, whatever their political connections. Arrangements for peace talks necessitated talking to Palestinians associated with the PLO, given Palestinian political realities. But at AIPAC's urging, Congress had made the terms of the letter binding, and had added a requirement that the PLO renounce terrorism. AIPAC and its friends in Congress then enforced the complete "shunning" of anyone even indirectly associated with the PLO. United Nations Ambassador Andrew Young was forced to resign after attempting to hide the fact that he had met with Palestinians. Secretary Shultz met with two American academics who were members of the Palestine National Council in March 1988;[49] he promptly received a letter from 24 senators urging him not to have "other" meetings with the PLO, as it set "a dangerous precedent" (Shultz 1993: 1029–30). Whenever meetings did occur, they were freighted with fear of being "outed" by the ever-vigilant lobby and its friends in Congress.

By 1988, dealing with the PLO risked political leprosy. It therefore was a stunning demonstration of the extent to which Shamir's policies had alienated and mobilized major elements of the Jewish community that Jewish leaders nevertheless undertook to negotiate recognition of the PLO. Rita Hauser, an AJC leader and Republican insider,[50] headed a delegation of five prominent Jews to Stockholm. They met with a PLO delegation, including Arafat, on 6 and 7 December 1988 and then announced that the PLO was sincere about peace and that the United States should end the ban on contact (*NYT* 8 Dec. 1988: A1). That day, Yasser Arafat made the first of a series of statements attempting to satisfy the law; by 14 December, he had satisfied Secretary Shultz that his conditions were met, and the White House announced the beginning of official contacts with the PLO (DoS Bull Feb. 1989: 51–3). The reaction of the Jewish community was surprisingly mild. Some called the delegation "renegades" or expressed skepticism about relying on an Arafat statement. Many, however, undoubtedly agreed with Alexander Schindler that it was a "step in the right direction and merits further study and consideration" (*NYT* 8 Dec. 1988: 11).

Conclusion

AIPAC had transformed itself in the aftermath of the AWACS fight. It had developed an independent network of activists, and had instituted systems to identify and train the next generation of pro-Israel leaders. It had greatly strengthened its reputation for delivering significant support or opposition to political candidates based entirely on their support of Israel.

AIPAC had also aligned itself with the beliefs of American neoconservatives and Israeli Revisionists.[51] That made it easier to argue for support of Israel to an administration fixated on the Soviet Union and Islamist terrorism; to maintain access and influence with the government of Israel; and to raise money and support from the most focused and dedicated supporters of Israel.

However, a large majority of American Jews did not share these beliefs, and were repeatedly alienated by the actions of Revisionist Israeli governments. Their disillusionment with official Israel did not lessen their attachment to and identification with Israel; even among unaffiliated Jews, that remained strong. As to matters clearly important to Israel's security under any set of beliefs, Americans, including the entire Jewish population, insisted on an overwhelming margin of safety. However, when Israel pursued policies that were consistent with Revisionist views of security – or destiny, or right, or power – but were inconsistent with concepts of compromise, human rights and morality held by the majority of American Jews, and unnecessary to their concept of security, a rupture was inevitable.

Pro-Israeli politics in the United States had become divisive, reflecting divergent ethical views of what Israel was and should be, and increasingly dissonant sets of principled and causal beliefs concerning Israel's role in American foreign and national security policy.

7 Reagan after AWACS

Policy as the product of unexamined beliefs and political constraint

Introduction

The Reagan administration avoided a major political defeat on the AWACS sale. However, it did so without having formulated, much less persuasively explained, a strategic framework encompassing both sales of advanced arms to Arab regimes and reliance on Israel as America's key strategic ally. The reasons for disconnects between public rhetoric and policy decisions, and between Israel's putative and real roles, were straightforward: reliance on Israel as a proxy or a platform in pursuit of American strategic interests was usually not feasible and sometimes counterproductive; and Israel used American aid and political support in pursuit of its own, sometimes quite different, beliefs.

Reagan's policy choices indicated that Israel was not the strategic partner described in his speeches. By the end of his administration, however, the relationship with Israel increasingly resembled the model preferred by Israel. Aid to Israel substantially increased and was converted to grants, and Israel was given trade, military procurement and manufacturing concessions unequaled even by NATO allies. Presumptions favoring Israel were embedded in law, bureaucratic structure and political relationships. "Strategic cooperation" in November 1981 was an "agreement to agree" applicable only in case of direct Soviet intervention. After 1983 it acquired a depth, complexity and permanence which allowed Israeli planners to count on massive reserves for their own purposes and forced Israel's adversaries to see Israel as America's invincible partner. Israel achieved virtual impunity.

There were several explanations for this result. (1) The pro-Israel lobby had gained strength. After AWACS, Congress would generally not limit aid to Israel or grant the president the authority to sell arms to Arab states except as Israel and AIPAC agreed, and sometimes not even then. Efforts to build security relationships in the Gulf, and to structure a peace process that relied heavily upon King Hussein, had to be curtailed or abandoned. (2) Ronald Reagan never lost his belief in the "special relationship," and would not overtly pressure Israel to cooperate. (3) Shultz became the vicar that Alexander Haig had aspired to be. His problem-solving approach to foreign policy, and his bureaucratic skills, moralism and strong personal reactions to leaders with whom he dealt, all shaped policy toward Israel. Shultz saw Israel as a key ally against terrorism, which he identified with Islamists, the PLO and ultimately the Soviet Union. The presumptions Shultz helped to embed would persist long after he left office.

Damage control with the Jewish community

Even before the AWACS vote, the White House was flooded with warnings about growing damage to the administration's relationship with the Jewish community. Jewish supporters conditioned their support on Reagan's campaign commitments to treat Israel as a strategic ally. Many were angry about perceived tolerance of contempt toward them. Hopes for a "permanent Republican majority" in Congress were threatened; that had been the unmistakable message when Senator Packwood led the battle against his party's president. An alienated Jewish community would also make cooperation on domestic issues difficult, particularly in the House. To the Troika, the stakes seemed very high.

Elizabeth Dole, under Ed Meese's direction, urgently addressed the problem. Meese met with George Klein's group a week after the AWACS vote.[1] Dole met on 10 November with Zionist leaders, including the president of ZOA and the national director of ADL. She reported "great anger at all levels of the American Jewish community toward the President and the Administration, *not over AWACS*, but over events leading up to and following the vote" (RRPL, OA 5456, Dole Files, Dole Memo to Meese 11 Nov. 1981, italics added). They sensed that Reagan had "written off Jews," the evidence for which was: (1) Nixon's op-ed, not repudiated by Reagan and seen as an attack on the loyalty of Jews; (2) perceived tolerance of anti-Semitism by staff; (3) Reagan's favorable comments about the Fahd Peace Plan; (4) failure to appoint an emissary dedicated to the Camp David process; and (5) inadequate early coordination with the community. The group opined that "neither the President nor the GOP could get five percent of today's Jewish vote." Their numerous recommendations sought control of the policy agenda by requiring early and authoritative consultations. Dole received similar messages in meetings with Orthodox leaders and former officials.

The president had earlier agreed with Al Spiegel[2] to meet with AIPAC leaders to discuss Israel's security and relations with the Jewish community (RRPL, Dole Files OA 5456, Weinberg letter 27 Oct. 1981). On November 19, Reagan hosted separate meetings in the White House with his Jewish supporters and with leaders of major Jewish organizations. Elizabeth Dole stated the purpose of the meetings as "To bridge the chasm of misunderstanding that has developed between the Administration and the American Jewish community" (RRPL, Dole Files OA 5456, Memo 19 Nov. 1981). Reagan was scripted to speak about anti-Semitism, exclusion of the PLO from any peace process and the "strategic partnership with Israel." Defense Minister Sharon was expected on 30 November, when the pending Memorandum of Understanding would be signed. The president was to say that the meetings with Sharon would "transform our strategic *dialogue* into *actual strategic cooperation*" (ibid., emphasis in original). That was inaccurate. Secretary Weinberger insisted not only that the MoU be stripped of all commitment by the United States, but also that Sharon be deprived of any public signing or press coverage, precisely because of concern that Sharon would make the agreement sound like a mutual defense pact.

High-level emissaries including Meese and Weinberger were sent to Jewish organizations over the next several months. Still, in mid-March 1982, George Klein wrote the White House that "[r]elations between the Administration and the American Jewish community are at a dangerously low state," and detailed the potentially disastrous effects in upcoming elections.[3] He recommended either a designated liaison with complete access to the Troika and Cabinet, or an advisory committee with regular access to the president (RRPL, Dole Files OA 5456, Memo 15 Mar. 1982). Klein's proposals were not adopted, but the White House thereafter demonstrated that it had been sensitized and conditioned by the AWACS experience.

Battles in Congress

Aid to Israel

By December 1982, Israel had demonstrated how difficult it could be to have the Jewish state as an ally. Secretary Haig had welcomed Sharon's Big Pines plan to destroy PLO forces. Few were prepared for what followed, however, and Secretary Shultz signaled beginning with his confirmation testimony that the siege of an Arab capital was unacceptable. Begin and Sharon then repeatedly deceived Reagan and American officials about IDF operations and Israeli objectives; the IDF used American-supplied anti-personnel cluster bombs (CBUs) in civilian areas; and after the United States assured Palestinians that Israel would safeguard refugee camps, Israeli commanders stood by while their Phalangist allies massacred hundreds in the camps.[4] The president reacted so strongly to nightly pictures of civilian suffering that he told Begin it resembled a Holocaust, knowing that the term would evoke explosive anger in Begin (Reagan 1990: 428). Begin also had roughly rejected Reagan's Fresh Start initiative, which George Shultz believed to be the most feasible route to peace. Ambassador Lewis pointedly advised Begin to postpone a visit planned for early 1983 (Quandt 1988: 236).

Then Congress took up foreign aid appropriations in December 1982. The administration had requested $785 million in ESF (economic) aid for Israel and $1.7 billion in FMF (military) aid and credits, for an unprecedented total of $2.485 billion. The proposal increased military aid by $300 million, the amount previously agreed as compensation for AWACS, but as loans. The economic aid proposal was recast to make one-third loan rather than grant. The request increased aid substantially, but on less favorable terms. President Reagan and Secretary Shultz repeatedly denied conditioning aid levels on Israeli cooperation (RR PC 11 Nov. 1982 in DoS Bull Jan. 1983: 31; GS PC 18 Nov. 1982 in AFP 82: 774).[5] However, they also did not want to reward intransigence, and when Congress began adding money they explained their opposition in a series of personal meetings with congressional leaders (*WP* 25 Dec. 1982: A1).

The Israeli government feared Reagan might reduce aid in proportion to Israeli spending on settlements, to induce the settlement freeze called for in Reagan's initiative (Ben-Zvi 1984: 51–2). AIPAC believed the administration intended leverage both on pullout from Lebanon and the Reagan initiative (Bloomfield, in Silverman 1996: 210). It also feared the precedent of an appropriation less than authorizing committees had specified. AIPAC argued that Israel needed additional aid to maintain its edge after AWACS. Supporters had expected the agreed $300 million in added military aid to be grants.

The congressional mood was to compensate Israel, and the pro-Israel community, for hard feelings generated by AWACS. Many had been angered by Israel's arrogance, and stunned by the camp massacres. However, massive Israeli protests over the massacres and appointment of the Kahan Commission had reassured them that Israel was after all an ethical democracy with which Americans could identify. The November 1982 mid-term election had elected supporters and defeated opponents. Unlike the AWACS fight, where the choice was between supporting the president and important business interests and supporting Israel, now there was no reward for voting against aid, and no credible threat of punishment for supporting it. The votes were assured for substantial aid increases in the December appropriations hearings.[6]

Somehow, that surprised the administration. Shultz and Reagan only learned of an effort to add $250 million in FMF in early December. Shultz was amazed: "This in the face of Israel's invasion of Lebanon, its use of cluster bombs, and its complicity in the Sabra and Shatila massacres!" (Shultz 1993: 112). Even today, Shultz says the request "astonished" him (Shultz interview). Shultz sent Congress a letter warning against appearing "to endorse and reward Israel's policies" (Shultz 1993: 112).[7]

However, "the Congress increased grant aid by $510 million above what the administration recommended, providing the most favorable aid package Israel had ever received" (Bloomfield 1983: 17). Shultz says, "it went through like we weren't even there"[8] (Shultz interview). One might have thought that the lessons were that the administration needed to enunciate clearly a strategic framework for the Middle East and coordinate better with Congress. But that is not what George Shultz learned:

> that sent me a message that it's a good idea to try to work with the
> Israelis and try to get something established that they would agree to

and we would agree to on the budget; otherwise when it gets into Congress it's totally out of control.

(Ibid.)

This bowing to perceived necessity may have reflected advice from senior department officials that continued confrontation with Israel would be ineffectual or even politically fatal (Quandt 2001: 258–9; Neff 1995: 122). Whatever the explanation, there were immediate consequences. In February 1983, Shultz appointed a "blue ribbon" panel to advise on foreign aid. Of 42 members, all were members of relevant congressional committees or former aid administrators, except for one lobbyist – Tom Dine of AIPAC (Findley 1985: 30). This constituted recognition that the entire aid program was a train pulled by the Israeli engine. Beginning in 1984, the State Department testified annually that Israel had agreed to the aid proposal (Murphy test, HApp 15 Mar. 1984 in DoS Bull May 1984: 67; SFRC 21 Mar. 1985 in DoS Bull May 1985: 75). In 1984, aid was for the first time converted to all grants; the 1985 proposal increased ESF by $1.44 billion to underwrite Israeli economic and fiscal reform. A 1988 Memorandum of Agreement institutionalized, in the Joint Security Assistance Planning Group, the process by which the two governments "agree upon proposed levels of security assistance" (MoA 21 Apr. 1988 Art. III.B, App. 2 in Puschel 1992: 182).

The evidence strongly suggests a judgment that aid to Israel could not be controlled; it could only be negotiated with AIPAC and Israel. The corollaries were: (1) since Israel was going to receive aid on increasingly favorable terms, the administration might as well take domestic political credit for that and try to use associated goodwill as a basis for Israeli cooperation in American initiatives; and (2) if Israel still would not cooperate, there were few if any tools available.

Arms to Jordan and the peace process

The Reagan–Shultz approach to the peace process required Jordan's active participation. Reagan had promised to use "the full panoply of U.S. influence" to deny the PLO, considered a terrorist organization, any "voice or role" in future negotiations (Segev 1997: 41), and forbade contact with anyone associated with the PLO. King Hussein combined good relations with the United States and Israel with deep involvement in Palestinian issues. Reagan looked to Hussein to lead a delegation including representatives of the Territories.[9] Announcing the "Fresh Start" initiative, Reagan said that "self-government by the Palestinians of the West Bank and Gaza in association with Jordan offers the best chance for a durable, just and lasting peace" (Speech 1 Sep. 1982 in DoS Bull Sep. 1982: 25).

To take on the proffered role, Hussein needed substantial support. Jordan was a weak state, dependent on relationships with Iraq, Syria and Saudi Arabia. Egypt, the natural leader of the Arab world, had been suspended from the Arab League, and President Sadat assassinated because of his negotiations with Israel. Shultz knew that Hussein's role would require a "general consensus on the part of the Arab leaders," and he assumed the king would take the views of the PLO into account (Interview 5 Sep. 1982 in DoS Bull Oct. 1982: 12). The Arab League maintained their designation of the PLO as sole legitimate representative of the Palestinian people, and Arafat would not consent to a negotiating team that did not guarantee him a veto. Syria, Iraq and the Soviet Union would use their influence over PLO factions to discourage Arafat's cooperation; Syria would threaten Jordan militarily. At a minimum, Hussein needed reliable political and security support from the United States. Reagan reportedly sent Hussein two letters (*NYT* 30 Jan. 1983: A1). One committed the U.S. to seek a settlement freeze if Jordan offered to join peace talks; Jordan would have no further obligation if the U.S. failed. It also promised an "American draft" agreement, and sales of advanced F-16 aircraft. A second letter made a "personal commitment" by Reagan to talks consistent with "land for peace."(*WSJ* 14 Apr. 1983: 1)[10] In the end, Reagan could deliver none of what he promised.

Jordan had for many years carried on quiet diplomacy with Israel. In September 1970, at U.S. request, Israel had been ready to counter Syrian tanks as Hussein drove the PLO out of Jordan; in 1973, unlike 1967, Jordan did not join the Arab coalition against Israel. While Jordan's forces were considered highly professional they posed no serious threat to Israel.[11] Nevertheless, Israel had consistently and usually successfully worked to block arms sales to Jordan. In 1982, Foreign Minister Shamir explicitly raised the spectre of AWACS, and said that sale of sophisticated weapons to any Arab country was a "serious danger" to Israel, which they would "do anything in [their] power to frustrate" (*WP* 13 Feb. 1982: A27).

Israel and AIPAC opposed all arms sales to Arabs as a corollary of their core beliefs, but also for practical reasons: (1) it avoided the "slippery slope," the need to distinguish sales that added significantly to Israel's risk; (2) it gave repeated opportunities to reinforce congressional beliefs about Arabs and Israelis, and to practice blocking sales;[12] (3) militancy helped AIPAC's morale and fundraising; and (4) it disrupted efforts to build strategic relationships between the United States and Arab states, which could dilute Israel's influence in unpredictable ways.

Reagan's Fresh Start initiative gave Begin and AIPAC new reasons to block sales to Jordan: to show that Reagan's support was not reliable and to disable Hussein as a credible interlocutor. When Reagan told Begin that security cooperation with Jordan could encourage "more Egypts," Begin "angrily said that was impossible, no other Arab state would do what Egypt had done and recognize Israel" (Reagan 1990: 424).[13] In fact, the Fahd Plan and the Fez communiqué implicitly recognized Israel, as had Hussein; and the Saudis promised to support any agreement to which Palestinians and Jordan could agree. But if the king could be backed off, Israel could again avoid a showdown at the negotiating table. That was the result Tom Dine had anticipated when he conditionally supported Fresh Start.

This dynamic played out over several years. Hussein said in April 1983 that he could not obtain PLO clearance and could not join the initiative (Shultz 1993: 435). He then signaled renewed willingness to attempt the mission, and Reagan assured him of support. The 1984 effort to sell Stingers to Jordan came to the dramatic end described in the preceding chapter. Hussein nevertheless pursued negotiations with Arafat, concluding an agreement in February 1985 on a common approach, and in August met secretly with then Prime Minister Peres to identify acceptable Palestinian delegates. In the end, these and later efforts failed, for reasons that included the inability of either Arafat or Peres to achieve necessary support from splintered political constituencies. In the summer of 1988, the king severed ties with the West Bank, cutting off aid which paid local administrators and ending West Bank representation in Jordan's parliament.

The administration increasingly saw unconditioned aid to Israel as sacrosanct, but aid to Jordan as requiring prior concessions by Hussein. George Shultz repeatedly asserted that Israel would not refuse to negotiate if a credible Arab partner were found, but would not consider using aid to pressure Israel, even to gain acceptance of his plan as a starting point. When King Hussein sought the legitimacy afforded by an international conference, the administration demanded that he publicly declare that he was willing to negotiate directly with Israel, and that Jordan was not in a state of belligerency with Israel. The king was clearly willing to negotiate, and had privately said that there was no state of belligerency. The problem was rather that he was being asked to make a series of public concessions when Israel was not, and when the promised support of the United States was suspect.

Shultz took Hussain's failure fully to meet those demands as evidence of his lack of commitment (Shultz 1993: 445, 451).[14] President Reagan doubted that Arab leaders "were as serious about supporting our peace efforts in the Middle East as ... [Hussein and Fahd] said they were" (Reagan 1990: 463). It is difficult to credit those statements. Hussein critically needed to find a stable resolution of the Palestinian issues, because Palestinians were more than half of the population of Jordan. Radicalization of the Palestinian population in the region, or implementation of the Likud maxim that "Jordan is the Palestinian state," could bring his monarchy down. Revisionist Zionists, on the other hand, would tolerate violence and friction with the United States, rather than accept negotiations that could lead to a Palestinian state in part of *Eretz Y'Israel*.

Arms sales constituted the acid test for the administration, because Jordan had legitimate security needs related to the peace process, a long-standing security relationship with the United States and pressing need for tangible American support. The administration understood the stakes but vacillated in the face of congressional hostility. In May 1985, Reagan again promised the king personally that he would press for the sales (*WP* 7 Aug.

1986: A1). Seventy senators introduced a resolution opposing arms to Jordan until it entered peace talks with Israel; Shultz said that was "sticking a finger in the eye" of Hussein just as he signaled readiness for serious negotiations (*LAT* 5 Jun. 1985: 9). In September, Reagan told Congress that sale of over $1.5 billion in arms to Jordan was "essential" because "It convey[ed] ... a powerful message of political support for King Hussein's efforts" in the peace process and met Jordan's largest military need, air defense against external attack. It was "an absolute necessity" to achieving peace (Stmt 27 Sep. 1985 in DoS Bull Dec. 1985: 62). On the same day, the king told the United Nations that Jordan was "prepared to negotiate, under appropriate auspices, with the government of Israel, promptly and directly" (*WSJ* 30 Sep. 1985: 1). Nevertheless, congressional opposition hardened.

In October, Shultz testified that Reagan had promised Hussein that he "could count on us for the economic and security assistance Jordan would need to address the risks it was taking." The sale was "an absolute necessity" in the peace process (Test 10 Oct. 1985 in DoS Bull Dec. 1985: 64; *LAT* 10 Oct. 1985: 2). Shultz did not disclose that Reagan had already told Hussein on 12 June that congressional opposition might require use of Reagan's waiver authority, or that Shultz had opposed the sale as unachievable (Shultz 1993: 451). The Congress promptly barred arms sales to Jordan for six months unless Jordan and Israel began "direct and meaningful peace negotiations," and Reagan acquiesced (Stmt 25 Nov. 1985 in DoS Bull Feb. 1986: 89).[15]

"Direct and meaningful" negotiations would require Israel's agreement. Hussein would have had to meet Israel's demands: no international conference, even as powerless convener; Israeli veto over Palestinian representatives; and no consideration of Palestinian rights beyond the Likud's reading of Camp David. As AIPAC knew, however anxious Hussein was to enter negotiations, he could not cede so much to Israel. Israel would have maintained its positions in any event, but forcing Hussein to back away allowed Israel to argue that the onus for the failure of Fresh Start was on the Arabs, as Dine had anticipated.

Secretary Murphy described Regan's concession as a "compromise" to avoid disrupting the peace process (Test HFAC 28 Jan. 1986 in DoS Bull Mar. 1986: 40). He knew better.[16] The administration had several contentious matters pending before Congress, and backed away from a fight.[17]

Hussein again alienated Congress, calling the requirement of "meaningful" negotiations "blackmail" (*WP* 7 Aug. 1986: A1). Later, clearly humiliated, he said the action signaled "almost the termination of our relations with the U.S.A." (*LAT* 2 Apr. 1986: 13). He also looked briefly to the Soviet Union for arms, and met for the first time in years with Syria's Assad; those actions further minimized any chance of arms sales and set back American relations with Jordan.

Arms to Gulf Arabs

After AWACS, Congress repeatedly blocked sales to Saudi Arabia. In 1984 Reagan used his waiver authority for the first time to sell tanker aircraft and Stinger missiles to Saudi Arabia because of the "immediate danger" posed by the Iranian build-up (Armacost test, SApp 5 Jun. 1984 in DoS Bull Jul. 1984: 81–2).[18] In 1985 he deferred all sales to Middle East states for nine months, ostensibly to conduct a study, but really because of stiffening congressional resistance. Prince Bandar sensibly obtained political insurance: a letter stating Reagan's understanding that the monarchy would shop elsewhere (Ball and Ball 1992: 273). Soon, the monarchy bought over $12 billion worth of fighter-bombers from the United Kingdom, with no basing restrictions protecting Israel (DoS stmt 11 Mar. 1986 in DoS Bull May 1986: 77; Murphy test HFAC 22 Apr. 1986 in DoS Bull Jun. 1986: 72). British sales alone probably totaled $30 billion over the next several years.[19]

After negotiating with AIPAC, the administration stripped proposed sales of everything opposed by AIPAC except missiles (*WP* 7 Aug. 1986: A1). Israel, and then AIPAC, thereafter signaled that they would not actively oppose the missiles. Nevertheless, the House voted 356 to 72, and the Senate 73 to 22, to block the sales. Congress was on automatic pilot, enforcing policy that conformed to beliefs AIPAC had advocated. The administration was now sufficiently embarrassed to make a stand. Reagan vetoed the resolution of disapproval, and was sustained in the Senate by a single vote – but only after further stripping the sale to one-tenth of the original value.[20] Several senators changed votes only because of concern about damage to the presidency if he could not obtain even 34 votes for such a minor sale (*WSJ* 6 Jun. 1986: 1). Five years after AWACS, President Reagan would have lost that larger and more sensitive sale; even with Israel and AIPAC on the sidelines, their beliefs now controlled outcomes.

In 1986 and 1987, Iran-Contra severely damaged the administration's credibility. The Tower Commission described the Reagan national security team as chaotic and unsupervised (Tower *et al.* 1987: Part IV).[21] The sales to Iran, and attendant deception, disarray and incoherence, alarmed Arab leaders looking to the United States for security cooperation. To reassure them and to claim a semblance of consistency, Reagan began in January 1987 to propose substantial additional sales to Saudi Arabia, Egypt, Bahrain, Kuwait and Jordan.

Because it had not established coherent beliefs or integrated policies, the administration started from a weak position. AIPAC was aggressive: Saudis had not assisted when the USS Stark was attacked by Iraq;[22] Saudis would not defend the Kuwait re-flagging effort; and proposed sales were payoffs for $32 million in Saudi contributions to the Nicaraguan Contras. AIPAC signaled they would not oppose limited sales proposed in January, but opposed later-announced Maverick missile sales "really actively" (*WP* 30 Jan. 1987:

A30, 2 Jun. 1987: A11, 11 Jun. 1987: A30). Having rushed to announce sales of Mavericks, Reagan then rushed to pull them, blaming Congress for "exactly the wrong signal" to "our staunchest ally in the Gulf" (Stmt 11 Jun. 1987 in DoS Bull Aug. 1987: 80). Even replacement Saudi F-15s were held.[23] Given the administration's disarray, opponents had little difficulty in defeating yet another sale.

In 1988, George Shultz essentially admitted that a pending sale to Kuwait had been negotiated with AIPAC before it was announced (Interview 31 Jul. 1988 in DoS Bull Sep. 1988: 2). The administration could sell arms to Arabs, but only sporadically and in diminished amounts. Arab partners could not expect reliability when considering how far to risk identification with American initiatives. Most importantly, AIPAC had achieved control of the political meaning of arms sales, as against a president who was usually the master of political symbolism. AIPAC's opposition to sales to Arabs usually had little to do with any immediate risk to Israel's security; it was, rather, for the purpose of reinforcing beliefs about Israel and Arabs that justified a persistent hardening of support for Israel.

Ronald Reagan wanted strengthened ties and friendship with moderate Arab countries, believing that "their cooperation would help produce a lasting solution" to regional problems, but each time he "was thwarted by the friends of Israel in Congress" (Reagan 1990: 705; also 463, 493). Thwarting the president may have made Israel less secure: American influence on moderate Arab regimes, and its ability to impose measures protective of Israel, were reduced or lost.

The growing role of George Shultz

George Shultz had strong views on Soviet communism and on terrorism, but brought a mediator's problem-solving mentality to most issues. He thought of himself as a manager, not a conceptualizer: "A tremendous amount of policy comes about through the way whatever little things you do all day long add up, or if they don't add up" (*WP* 3 Feb. 1986: A1). He spoke hundreds of thousands of words about Israel and Middle East conflicts but, like a mediator, largely offered suggestions and cajoled the parties to find their own solutions. Aside from those he saw as terrorists, he expected leaders to be rational and to do what was in the obvious interest of their people. He became frustrated when they seemed not to do so. Lacking a comprehensive understanding of regional politics, however, he often failed to understand the strategic perspectives of key leaders, including Assad and Begin. That led him to make the kind of mistakes mediators make when they misunderstand the parties' goals. Excluding Assad killed any chance of implementing a treaty involving Lebanon; delaying efforts on the Fresh Start initiative until the Lebanon issues were resolved allowed Begin (and then Shamir) to delay indefinitely any serious discussion of Reagan's plan.

George Shultz increasingly identified with Israel. Aside from terrorism, to which we turn next, two reasons for this affinity stand out from inter-viewing him: Shultz liked and admired key Israeli leaders; and Israeli eco-nomic problems presented a challenge that he could manage more confidently than he could the endemic regional conflicts.

Four Israeli officials had particular impact: Arens, Shamir, Peres and Netanyahu. It was critical that Moshe Arens, whom Shultz had grown to trust in Washington, replaced Ariel Sharon as defense minister. Shultz was accustomed to stubborn negotiators, and did not hold stubbornness against them so long as it was principled. Sharon had lied repeatedly to Shultz's close friend Phil Habib, and to Reagan; Shultz thought of Arens as the tough, direct, MIT-trained engineer that he was (Shultz 1993: 49). Shamir repeatedly rejected and undermined Shultz's ideas for the peace process. Nevertheless, Shultz respected his open, blunt manner. He volunteers that what "made [him] feel good about his relationship with the Israeli leaders" was an unexpected expression of trust by Shamir. Discussing the possibility of using a Reagan–Gorbachev summit for meetings with Hussein, Shamir said, "Well, Mr. Secretary, you know our hopes, and you know our fears. We trust you. Go ahead" (Shultz interview). Shamir's "trust" extended no further than attending the summit; he maintained rigid positions on Pales-tinian representation and final status issues.[24] As Shamir notes, Hussein's basis for declining, that Shamir would never "accept any Israeli withdrawal ... was true." Shultz told Shamir, nonetheless, that Reagan greatly appreci-ated his "flexibility" (Shamir 1994: 173–4).

Shultz takes great pride in the economic partnership that he formed with Shimon Peres during his 1984–1986 premiership. Shultz had repeatedly told Israelis "they were headed for a catastrophe," ignoring their economy in favor of security issues. Peres was more forthcoming on the peace process and worked well with American counterparts.[25] The administration wanted him, and Labor, to succeed.[26] He asked Shultz for help. Shultz says, "So I got heavily involved in their economy, and I think helped them engineer a miraculous soft landing, from an inflation that was totally out of control" (Shultz interview). The help was massive: (1) supplemental aid of $1.4 billion, conditioned on fiscal reforms; (2) the first American Free Trade Agreement; (3) conversion of all aid to grants; and (4) dozens of initiatives to ease defense burdens, by declaring Israel a Major Non-NATO Ally, arranging co-production agreements, committing to substantial purchases of Israeli equipment and pouring $2 billion into the ill-fated LAVI project.[27] Shultz also asked Max Fisher to organize "Project Independence" to open up the statist Israeli economy and attract inward investment, but Fisher was thwarted by the Israeli bureaucracy (ibid.).

Economic reform was achievable with American aid; the peace process was "intractable" (ibid.). Donald Rumsfeld, who briefly served as special negotiator for Shultz, told him, "'Just and lasting peace,' you're out of your mind. There's never going to be a just and lasting peace in that area" (ibid.). Shultz would never concede the impossibility of peace. However, Shultz undoubtedly understood by 1988 that a Shamir government was never going to negotiate sovereignty over any part of *Eretz Y'Israel*; he hoped only that continued visible effort would keep the lid on the intifada by maintaining some hope in the Territories (Shultz 1993: 1031). He says ruefully that even his efforts to sustain a "quality of life" program for the Palestinians "didn't get very far. The Israelis wouldn't let it work" (Shultz interview). Shultz retained compassion for Palestinians, and understood the advantages for American interests if a credible peace process could be brokered. He was willing to invest his credibility in the barely conceivable rather than passively awaiting success, but would not blame Israelis for failure when Palestinians chose leaders associated with terrorists and supported by radical Arabs and the Soviets.

By the end of 1986 if not before, George Shultz was pre-eminent among foreign policy advisers. Judge Clark had left the White House in November 1983; the Troika had been allowed to disperse at the end of the first term, stripping Reagan of their political acumen. Admiral Poindexter, Reagan's fourth national security adviser, was fired in November 1986 and faced felony charges stemming from Iran-Contra. He was replaced by Frank Carlucci, Shultz's former deputy at the Office of Management and Budget; Carlucci went on to replace Weinberger as secretary of defense in November 1987. Although Shultz threatened to resign several times, over issues ranging from polygraph testing of senior staff to turf battles with the NSC and CIA and Iran-Contra, Reagan both trusted his secretary of state and could not afford his resignation. He was the administration's exemplar of steady calm and good judgment, unscorched by the Iran-Contra firestorm. His judgments about Israel and the peace process progressively prevailed; increasingly, the result was to support Israel whenever there were alternative courses.

Terrorism and recalculating the strategic value of Israel

Terrorism through Cold War and Israeli lenses

The Reagan administration saw terrorism through the prism of the Cold War, and terrorists as agents of states that were clients of, if not controlled by, the Soviet Union.[28] The Soviet role was indirect and difficult to prove. The Soviets had armed Syria and Libya, and supported PLO factions and insurgencies linked to terrorists, but did not control Qaddafi or Assad, much less the Iranian ayatollahs. A declassified 1985 State Department briefing paper found no hard evidence of direct Soviet connections to terrorist groups; "ideologically and historically, the USSR has been uncomfortable with the instability generated by terrorism," particularly Muslim terrorism against Soviet citizens (Briefing Paper, "Terrorism," 16 Oct. 1985 in DoS FOIA). Nevertheless, the administration often asserted that the Soviet Union supported such groups "to weaken liberal democracy and undermine world stability" (e.g. Shultz speech 4 Jun. 1984 in DoS Bull Aug. 1984: 33).[29]

In 1983–1986, terrorists killed and held hostage hundreds of Americans, Frenchmen and others, acts of terrorism forced the United States to abandon an ill-conceived military insertion into Lebanon and hostage-taking led to the Iranian arms misadventure. The administration's rhetoric promising crushing responses to terror was seldom fulfilled, for reasons of wise restraint and cabinet paralysis: available intelligence and the tactical situation seldom allowed a forceful response, and Secretary Weinberger seldom lost an argument when he counseled inaction. Counter-terrorism official Robert Oakley said that Reagan's policy on terrorism had been "more popular at home, and more successful abroad, than any other single policy" (Oakley 1987).[30] Popularity at home was enhanced because: (1) Reagan aimed rare but spectacular strikes at America's most notorious adversaries (Qaddafi, Abu Abbas) and (2) policy increasingly converged with the beliefs of Israel's supporters, and was coordinated with Israel.

In 1983, Syria allowed Iranian Republican Guards to infiltrate southern Lebanon, where they blew up the American Embassy, killing 67, including 17 Americans; the French Embassy was bombed the same day. In October, Iranians killed 241 Marines with a truck bomb at the Beirut airport. There were over 600 reported incidents of terrorism in 1984, up from 500 the year before, and 11 American deaths; 1985 saw more attacks and over 16 deaths (Briefing Paper, "Terrorism," 16 Oct. 1985 in DoS FOIA). The president of the American University of Beirut was taken hostage in 1982; in 1984 and 1985, two university officials and the associated press chief in Beirut, Terry Anderson, among others, were taken. TWA Flight 847 from Athens to Rome was hijacked with 153 passengers, mostly American; an American sailor, Robert Stethem, was shot in Beirut. In October 1985 the cruise ship *Achille Lauro* was seized by a Palestinian group headed by Abu Abbas, a member of the PLO EC, and Leon Klinghoffer, a disabled American Jew, was murdered. Terrorism was used by insurgencies in Latin America, Pakistan, Spain and Ireland, but American understanding of terrorism was shaped by experience with Palestinians and Iranians in the Middle East.

It was thus natural, if not entirely logical, that the administration would draw closer to Israel. Reagan and Shultz saw Israel as their embattled ally and expert on terrorism. Israel had fought terrorists for years, and had a reputation for tough and effective security and the best intelligence in the Middle East. The perception was that groups that attacked Israel were groups that also attacked the United States.[31]

Beliefs about Israel skewed what was perceived as terrorism. The truck bombing of the Marine barracks was inevitably called terrorism. However, the Beirut airport had been in a war zone for 16 months, and American forces had begun acting not as peacekeepers, but as participants in a war begun by Israel. Palestinians attacking Israeli armor near Beirut were called terrorists by an American officer in the multinational force (Christison 1999:

7). Thus, Israel had a right to attack Palestinians, but retaliation, at least if by irregular forces, was terrorism. When Israel bombed PLO facilities in Tunis in October 1985, in retaliation for the deaths of three Israelis in Cyprus, they killed 30–60 people and injured a like number, including civilians and Tunisian security forces (NYT 2 Oct. 1985: A1(two articles)). President Bourguiba had admitted the PLO to Tunisia at Ambassador Habib's request after other Arab leaders refused. Tunisia's ambassador to France called the raid "state terrorism." The White House described the attack as "a legitimate response" to "terrorist attacks," and President Reagan added, "I've always had a great faith in [Israel's] intelligence abilities" (ibid.). Unlike the Osirak raid in 1981, the Tunis raid was openly approved. Further, it became a template for at least one case of American retaliation: the 1986 bombing of Colonel Qaddafi's family compound.

George Shultz and terrorism

George Shultz reacted to terrorism with ferocity unmatched even by President Reagan. In part, that was the product of three traits: (1) he was a highly moral if not moralistic person, and the taking of innocent life for political purposes generated real anger; (2) he was more willing to use force, and to act on incomplete information, than were others including Secretary Weinberger and Vice-President Bush; and (3) he always saw issues in terms of the people involved. In looking for allies and methods to defeat terrorism, he increasingly looked to Israel. Shultz's positions were critical, because he combined implacable persistence with canny bureaucratic skills, and by the middle of Reagan's second term he was the pre-eminent national security leader.

The 1983 Beirut Embassy bombings occurred as Shultz was completing negotiations on a treaty between Israel and Lebanon. Israel was attempting to install a Christian Lebanese government which would favor Israel over Syria; Assad responded by allowing Iranian fighters to infiltrate Lebanon. Among the 17 Americans killed was Robert Ames, the CIA's leading Lebanon expert and Shultz's mentor on Levantine politics. This was also the embassy out of which his personal friend Phil Habib was working. Within months it was clear that President Assad could and would block the treaty in which Shultz had invested his personal credibility. These events triggered great anger and resolve in George Shultz.

The October 1983 Marine barracks bombing was a policy disaster for the administration. There had been no policy independent of Israel's, and no consensus on the mission of the deployment (Ball 1984; Quandt 1984; Kemp 1988). When the IDF unilaterally decamped from high ground ringing the airport, the Marines served little purpose except as targets. Shultz had lost "his" Marines,[32] for no reason he could credibly defend. After asserting that the United States would not be forced out by terrorists, President Reagan pulled the Marines offshore.

Shultz linked the failure of his personal diplomacy to state-sponsored terrorism. To him it was clear that terrorism policies were not "sufficient or effective" (Shultz 1993: 644). He convened an all-day seminar on 24 March 1984 to frame terrorism initiatives. He and fellow former Marine Robert McFarlane pushed NSDD 138, signed by President Reagan 3 April, establishing principles of pre-emptive and retaliatory strikes against terrorists. Soon thereafter, he began a series of speeches arguing that "passive-defensive" policies should be replaced with pre-emptive, preventive action to the extent consistent with law (Speech 25 Oct. 1984 in DoS Bull Dec. 1984: 12–17).[33] He found skepticism in his own government. Vice-President Bush questioned pre-emptive action as administration policy; after some confusion, the White House said that Shultz's 25 October speech "was administration policy from top to bottom" (Shultz 1993: 649). Shultz thought that Secretary Weinberger "escalated and codified" the debate by proposing six prerequisites to the use of force; Shultz saw such caution as perhaps reasonable for conventional warfare, but as "inaction bordering on paralysis" when dealing with terrorism (ibid.: 650).

Shultz increasingly looked to Israel for intelligence, tactics and international support, and to the American Jewish community for domestic political support. Shultz told the Netanyahu family's Jonathan Institute[34] that terrorism was allied with totalitarianism against freedom and democracy, that the PLO and Libya aided Soviet efforts in Central America by arming and training communists there and that "terrorists who assault Israel are also the enemies of the United States" (Speech 24 Jun. 1984 in DoS Bull Aug. 1984: 31–4).

Shultz made his alignment with Israel even clearer in a speech at New York's Park Avenue Synagogue. While noting that moderate Arabs were also targets of terrorism,[35] he asserted that the principal goal of Middle East terrorists was to destroy the peace process by dissuading the United States from insuring Israel's security. He praised Israel for avoiding the "moral confusion," self-condemnation and retreat evident in America; "no nation has made a greater contribution to our understanding of the problem and the best ways to confront it ... The rest of us would do well to follow Israel's example" (Speech 25 Oct. 1984 in DoS Bull Dec. 1984: 12–17).

Terrorism became a major theme of the administration's public statements, and Jewish groups provided the favored fora.[36] By early 1986, the Shultz approach to terrorism, including reliance on Israeli intelligence and methods, became operational. When TWA 847 was hijacked in June 1985, Shultz coordinated with Bibi Netanyahu, then ambassador to the United Nations, rather than Prime Minister Peres, to urge a hard line on prisoner releases. Netanyahu endorsed Shultz's approach through secure channels (Shultz 1993: 657).[37] In the *Achille Lauro* hijacking, Shultz relied upon Israeli intelligence in supporting the interception and forced landing of the charter carrying the hijackers (ibid.: 669–75).[38] Netanyahu called Shultz to congratulate him. The following April, when intelligence supported a conclusion that Qaddafi had authorized the bombing of a Berlin nightclub, killing American servicemen, Shultz urged and Reagan authorized bombing Libyan security facilities and Qaddafi's residential compound. The raid predictably killed persons innocent of involvement in the terrorist incident to which it responded. That prospect would have prevented lethal action in peacetime prior to 1983. There had been a recalibration of beliefs, and operational guidelines, closer to those of Israel.[39]

Shultz's speech to the Jonathan Institute became a chapter in Netanyahu's book, *Terrorism: How the West Can Win* (Shultz 1986).[40] The book was intended to define more credible and durable strategic roles for Israel. Participants attributed the rise of terrorism to a network of totalitarian states and oil money of which the PLO was the hub. Moynihan, Ledeen, Arens and Kirkpatrick emphasized links among terrorism, totalitarianism and the Soviet Union;[41] others, including Netanyahu, Elie Kedourie and Bernard Lewis, argued that Islamic societies naturally condoned or encouraged terrorism against the West. Netanyahu made the case for Israel's role: "Middle East radicals did not develop their hatred of the West because of Israel; they hated Israel from its inception *because it is an organic part of the West*" (Netanyahu 1986: 62–3; emphasis in original).

Shultz did not speak of Arabs or Palestinians in blanket terms, and did not expressly adopt the arguments of others at the symposium. However, it is clear from the powerful official American participation and the general convergence of views that the core beliefs espoused at the conference had been accepted in advance: terrorism was a menace that linked anti-Western radical states, the Soviet Union, and amoral insurgencies; terrorism in the Middle East was identified with Arab nationalism and Islamist extremism; and Israel was a bastion of Western values and America's key ally against terrorism.

The default option as policy

Unconditional and exclusive support for Israel became America's default Middle East policy during the Reagan administration; justifications for that result reflected the beliefs of their advocates. At least five rationales were offered. None justified massive aid regardless of Israeli policy.

First, Shultz believed with Reagan that the original and fundamental basis of support was moral; he told the Council of Jewish Federations that Jewish traditions were a major source of Western civilization and values, and told Jewish leaders at Yeshiva University that Israel was a model of how to balance justice against security (Speech 19 Nov. 1983 in DoS Bull Jan. 1984: 32–5; Speech 9 Dec. 1984 in DoS Bull Jan. 1985: 1–3). There was truth to these assertions, but it was a selective and partial truth, and glossed over Israeli policies, enabled by American aid, that were inconsistent with an image of Israel as moral exemplar. Shultz's department reported annually on patterns of human rights abuses by Israeli forces and acts of Jewish terrorism in the Occupied Territories.[42] The United States repeatedly voted for Security Council resolutions deploring or condemning Israeli violations of international norms;[43] that was not true of other key allies. More to the strategic point, moral considerations justified willingness to defend Israel, but not unconditional economic, military and political support, particularly when that course empowered Israel to undercut American policies.

Second was Israel's putative role as an ally against the Soviet Union. Ronald Reagan was elected claiming a unified strategic view, focused on interdicting and rolling back the Soviet Union. The administration struggled to fit two other policies within that simple template: strong support of Israel and guaranteed access to Gulf oil. Those within the administration who were willing to rely explicitly on Israel's capabilities against Soviet inroads never prevailed. Blaming the Soviet Union for a problem even when the Soviets were not the principal concern was sometimes useful.[44] Shultz saw, however, that lack of progress on the peace process was a "source of radicalism" which the Soviet Union could exploit (Speech 10 Dec. 1985 in DoS Bull Feb. 1986: 24–6).[45] The official administration estimate was that threats to American interests would most likely come from intra-regional conflicts which gave openings to the Soviets (see CRS, Are We Committed?). Saudi Arabia was demonstrably more at risk from Iran than from the Soviet Union; Israel could not defend the oil fields against either.

Israeli enthusiasm for a role against the Soviet Union was also in doubt: Labor Party leaders said the November 1981 MoU was no help against Arabs and jeopardized Soviet Jews; Yitzhak Rabin said that "America's part in the Strategic Cooperation Agreement is not worth the paper it is written on" (Puschel 1992: 50). The MoU was suspended over annexation of the Golan, an issue with the potential to cause conflict with a Soviet client. Yet Rabin favored the 1983 MoU, and signed the 1988 agreements as defense minister. What had changed was not Israel's attitude about its role against the Soviet Union, but its relationship with the United States. When the 1983 agreement was signed, Reagan said that the JPMG (Joint Political Military Group) would "give priority attention" to the Soviet threat. Shamir, however, ignored the Soviets, describing the purpose as being "to strengthen Israel and deter threats to the region" (PC 29 Nov. 1983 in AFP 83: 721–2). As Shamir undoubtedly knew, McFarlane had persuaded Reagan to adopt the NSC's draft of NSDD 111, which relied heavily on a strong Israel as the cornerstone of American Middle East policy.[46] The directive transferred control of the JPMG from Defense to State, facilitating Shultz's effort to create an "interlocking web of institutional interests [favoring Israel] across the spectrum of Washington's bureaucracy" (Puschel 1992: 77).[47] A "senior administration official" (unquestionably Shultz) had been asked by Jewish journalists whether Israel would be able to use pre-positioned American equipment whenever needed; he responded that Israel having "an effective military advantage in the region" was "sort of the point of all of these things" (PC 19 Nov. 1983 in AFP 83: 720). Whatever the

Cold War rhetoric, Israel was interested in capabilities against confrontation states, and the administration quietly signaled that it had no objection.

A third justification, remarkably, was to dissuade Israel and its supporters from effectively opposing initiatives with Arab states. Judge Clark, advising Reagan on what became NSDD 99 ("U.S. Security Strategy for the Near East and South Asia") said,

> Simply put, a clear expression of U.S. resolve to defend the core security interests of Israel will make it much more difficult for Israel to question our reliability as we undertake to cooperate [sic] and equip moderate Arab states with similar stakes in a strategic relationship with the U.S.
>
> (RRPL, Exec Sec NSC, Box 91290,
> Memorandum 11 Jul. 1983, NSDD 99 [2 of 3])

Two years after AWACS, this privileged hope over experience and failed spectacularly.

Fourth, President Reagan and Secretary Shultz believed that Israel would compromise on land and Palestinian issues only when certain of its security.[48] The evidence never supported their hope. Israel reacted to uncertainty about American support by aggressively striking out to secure objectives before the United States acted firmly – their "first mover" advantage. A related phenomenon was U.S. fear of Israel's unpredictability if pressured – their "wild man" advantage. Dr. Kissinger, who had dealt with nuclear-armed Israel during its most anxious moments in 1973, advised in November 1982 to show Israel "compassion … maybe even affection, rather than unremitting pressure," which could "harass [Israel] into emotional and psychic collapse" (*Econ* 13 Nov. 1982: 30). However, he also counseled that Israeli politicians could make concessions "only when it is absolutely clear that America cannot be persuaded to an alternative; therefore it is imperative for the United States to … persevere [in a clearly stated position] in the face of [Israeli] opposition" (ibid.: 33). Reagan and Shultz never shared this insight. As Israel was unconditionally gifted with overwhelming military superiority, Revisionist Zionists could see no reason to reconsider their intended ownership of Judea and Samaria.

The fifth basis for strengthened ties with Israel was the partnership against terrorism. Israel was an excellent partner against terrorism, but with a major caveat that was not consistently observed. As with Soviet communism, Israel used the administration's fixation on terrorism for its own purposes.[49] Israel defined terrorism in terms of its adversaries and their methods, in order to nominate Israel as the only fit regional partner, and to permanently bar the PLO (and thus almost all Palestinian leaders) from any peace process. Israel's instrumental view of terrorism is shown by the Iran arms sales. Iran had done more damage to American interests than any other state sponsor of terrorism, starting with the embassy hostages and continuing in Lebanon and the Gulf. Yet Israel, for its own purposes, inveigled naïve operatives of the Reagan CIA and NSC into providing arms to, as it turned out, the radical ayatollahs in charge of the Islamic Republic. Shultz recognized that Israel's interests in Iran differed from America's, and that Israel would take American involvement as a green light for further deals (Shultz 1993: 795, 812, 814).[50] Believing that the Israelis had "suckered" the administration, he distanced himself (Cannon 1991: 681, 685). However, during the same period he pushed to make ties between Israel and the United States irreversible. Shultz had largely adopted the principled and causal beliefs of Israel and AIPAC; like a sibling he forgave them their mistakes.

Each time Israel or AIPAC caused strains in the relationship with Reagan and Shultz, they found that the strains did not have lasting costs. To the contrary, it was as if the administration felt it had to compensate Israel. They had learned that open disagreement with Israel produced two undesirable political results: (1) it generated strong domestic pressure to mend the relationship and (2) it allowed Begin, and then Shamir, to consolidate political support in Israel by resisting American pressure in a crisis – even one produced by Likud policies (Ben-Zvi 1984: 46–7). The administration felt it could not condition aid to Israel on policy cooperation, but also that it could not prevent Congress from conditioning support of key Arab partners in very awkward ways, or blocking that support entirely. In order to avoid advancing the political fortunes of the Likud, the administration had to design carrots, because it could not use sticks; hence the administration's massive assistance during the two years Peres was prime minister, and its foolish attempt to assist Yitzhak Rabin's LAVI project.

The administration's recognition of the PLO during its last full month in office was a shock to Shamir. Arafat had just been excluded from the United States as leader of a group designated a terrorist organization under a law Shultz administered. In 1987, speaking to the AIPAC policy conference, Shultz had led a "call and response" with the audience: "PLO, hell, no!" (Speech 17 May 1987 in DoS Bull Jul. 1987: 10–17). This attitude was not shared by Israelis who understood the fractured nature of the PLO and were seriously interested in negotiated peace.[51] Shamir had grown accustomed to stopping American initiatives by simply saying no, and in this case he was not consulted before the decision was announced (Schiff and Ya'ari 1990: 305). The significance of the outgoing administration's action, however, was primarily in the fact that President-elect Bush had approved it. The Reagan team allowed only mid-level contacts, and would not deal directly with Arafat or treat the PLO as a government-in-waiting.

More importantly, the strength and depth of Israel's bilateral relations with the United States were not affected. The relationship in all its complexity was now thoroughly entrenched in law and self-perpetuating bureaucratic structures and procedures.

Conclusion

Support of Israel rested on three interlocked pillars: (1) the diffuse but resilient support of the American people, based primarily on emotional, cultural and religious bonds that were shared by President Reagan and Secretary Shultz; (2) very real constraints on policy generated by congressional and electoral politics, driven by AIPAC; and (3) the operating assumption of the president and Secretary Shultz that consistent strong support of Israel could help on some critical issues, such as terrorism, and would not produce worse results on other issues than would a different policy. Arab leaders were skittish about strong visible bonds to the United States; Israelis insisted that such bonds were their due. Arabs seemed inconstant and unpredictable, and some fostered terrorism; Israel made a strong case that it was targeted as part of the West, and was America's inevitable partner against Arab machinations. The administration could not see gains from efforts it had made in opposition to Israel on the peace process, and gains in security cooperation with Arabs had come at considerable cost.

The administration had always used the language of strategic partnership in talking about Israel, and at every point of contention was called upon to act as if it were true by those who believed it. The default decision on nearly every issue after 1983 was to support, or at least to enable and not to constrain, the government of Israel. That practice did not purchase cooperation from Israel. It often made coordination of policy more difficult, particularly with Likud-led governments, because Israel was increasingly confident that all delicts would be forgiven if not rewarded. The infrastructure of support for Israel which resulted was also grossly disproportionate to the actual strategic role played by Israel in American plans, and arguably in excess of any legitimate needs of Israel after the peace treaty with Egypt. However, the policy did minimize electoral losses, avoid costly fights with Congress and maintain a policy line in the region that was consistent if not always logical or effective in serving American interests.

By the time Ronald Reagan published his memoirs in 1990, he made no mention of a strategic justification for the infrastructure of support that was embedded on his watch; support of Israel was justified entirely in terms of the moral obligation he recognized (Reagan 1990: 410).

8 George H. W. Bush, James Baker and Israel

Introduction

During the administration of George H. W. Bush, many elements of the reality and the mythology of the U.S.–Israel relationship changed: (1) the end of the Cold War eliminated a key basis for strategic cooperation with Israel; (2) the Gulf War deflated a major threat to Israel, demonstrated that ties with Israel could be a burden and encouraged Gulf states and Syria to cooperate openly in American-led peace efforts; (3) the direct control of policy-making by Bush and Secretary of State James Baker minimized the advantages of executive lobbying for AIPAC and magnified the costs of Shamir's intransigence for Israel; and (4) organized opposition to Likud policies and their moral and political implications coalesced in major Jewish organizations and in Congress. That further limited the effectiveness of AIPAC.

George Bush and James Baker would pursue policies where their calculations of interest and opportunity took them. Their foreign policy was reactive and situational. They came to office with no appetite for involvement in the Arab–Israeli conflict and no plan to confront Israel or the lobby; conversely, their disdain of ideology and inattention to domestic policy networks meant that policy choices would be relatively unaffected by neoconservatives or AIPAC. Their advisers on Middle East issues counseled detachment, to allow regional conditions necessary for a peace process to "ripen." However, major shifts in global and regional geopolitics nearly all suggested a reduced and more tethered role for Israel, and provided reason and opportunity to pursue resolution of regional conflicts. If Israel had been any other state, the suggested adjustments would have seemed unremarkable, a normalization requiring only that the client not use added aid to pursue policies deemed contrary to law and the interests of the donor. But AIPAC and Likud leaders had grown accustomed to unconditional support, and were not prepared to accept less.

Bush, Baker and Israel

Bush and Baker

George Bush and James Baker joked about lacking "the vision thing." Self-deprecating humor masked real disdain for ideologues. Bush's distrust of Soviet communism was, like all of his judgments, driven by personal experience, not ideology. His views about Israel and the Middle East also derived from experience and calculation of interest rather than from ideology or affinity.

Most Americans expected that Bush's administration would be a "third Reagan term," but the two men differed in important ways. Reagan focused on core beliefs, and had an unsurpassed ability to persuade individuals and mass audiences to trust him to choose policies consonant with those beliefs. He left, not just the details of governing, but some would say governing itself, to aides. He was emotionally committed to Israel, and could never for long withhold support. George Bush had "no political ideology ... His ideology [was] friendship" (Schweitzer and Schweitzer 2004: 279, quoting a Bush nephew). He was conservative, but in the sense of Edmund Burke, the one political thinker Bush quoted: changes in institutions or policies should be incremental; sweeping ideological commitments were dangerous.

His résumé notwithstanding, George Bush had seldom enunciated national policy. Most of his service consisted of appointive positions of short duration. He was detail oriented and involved himself personally in all aspects of any job. Having no overarching political philosophy, he could not explain policies in terms of one. He was effective in small groups, but very uncomfortable "performing." He said, "Fluency in the English language is something I'm often not accused of" (*sic*) (Greenstein 2000: 164).

The administration mirrored the president: principal officers were competent, loyal, pragmatic and non-ideological, but sometimes hobbled by the absence of a coherent set of beliefs by which to explain policies chosen by instinct and experience.[1] Bush's national security adviser, Brent Scowcroft, was one of several highly competent pragmatists who had served Ford but not Reagan. Scowcroft had no known views on the Arab–Israeli dispute (Quandt 2001: 292). He and Bush would work closely on the largest issues, particularly those of the disintegrating Soviet Union; Scowcroft would have little input on the Middle East.[2] Scowcroft lacked Richard Allen's connections with the pro-Israel lobby, and hired NSC staff who would have been "inconceivable" in the Reagan staff, because not "compatible with the dominant pro-Israeli mindset" (Tanter 1999: 101–2).

James Baker had long been George Bush's closest friend, political adviser and rival. They talked up to a dozen times a day; Bush said Baker was someone he would talk to about personally painful subjects (Dowd and Friedman 1990: 36, 58). Baker was admired for political judgment and tactical abilities in handling bureaucracies and the press, but distrusted by those with ideological agendas, because he had none.[3] One critic saw him as a "tinkerer and a deal-maker" with a limited attention span (Ajami 1996). In the Reagan White House he had finessed Ed Meese on domestic policy by controlling paper flow, but Meese, Casey and Weinberger blocked his attempt to become national security adviser because they doubted his loyalty to Reagan principles. Baker had said he did not need a vision, because Reagan had one; he was "more interested in the game than in philosophy" (Kramer 1989: 33). He describes himself as "more a man of action than of reflection" (Baker 1995: xiii). Baker avoided association with failure; any initiative was carefully analyzed for probable congressional and public reaction, and chance of success, before he allowed himself to be identified with it (Newhouse 1990: 50).[4]

Unlike Reagan and unlike his son George W. Bush, George H. W. Bush did not have strong ties to the Evangelical movement. Bush was disdainful of neoconservatives,[5] and they would have no voice in his administration. AIPAC also had little direct access or influence. Conversely, Bush and Baker expended little effort on policy networks or public education, thereby forfeiting important tools of the presidency.

Bush expected to be trusted and saw no need to explain his actions. Baker hated being thought of as a political operative, and disliked engaging with the public. He spent little effort building rapport with domestic groups, including Jewish leaders accustomed to constant attention from George Shultz. Baker did not "like meeting with anybody: Jews, Arabs, Palestinians, Japanese, foreign service officers, ambassadors ... the rest of the State Department" (Dowd and Friedman 1992, quoting a departmental official). Baker relied upon a small coterie of trusted aides, bypassing permanent staff. Because Bush had substantial expertise in national security policy and personal relationships with leaders in most countries, Bush and Baker and regional experts could operate effectively without constant input from other staff.

The advisers

On Middle East issues, Bush and Baker relied on four men: Dennis Ross, Richard Haass, Daniel Kurtzer and David Aaron Miller. All four were Jewish, but widely seen as aligned more with the Labor Party than with Likud. Shamir aides called them "self-hating Jews" or "Baker's Jew boys" (Melman and Raviv 1994: 446). Martin Peretz called them "four Jewish flunkies who write the sharp memos on how to cut Israel down to size" (Pipes and Peretz 1992: 22).

Ross had held posts in the NSC and at the State Department in the Carter and Reagan administrations.[6] In 1985, he wrote a Middle East policy paper for the Washington Institute urging "a strategy of motion while patiently awaiting real movement from the local parties" (Christison 1999: 252). He became director of Baker's Policy Planning Staff, and his closest advisor on Middle East and Soviet issues.

Richard Haass became senior director for Near East and South Asia at the NSC. In 1986, he had argued that the "basic [land for peace] paradigm is moribund," because those who would have to change core policies (the Soviets, Jordan, Syria and the PLO) were not prepared to do so. The status quo was not unstable or prejudicial to American interests, at least so long as the United States was *seen* to be working on a solution. Pressure on Israel would only embolden Israelis who rejected reliance on the United States, and discourage compromise by Arabs (Haass 1986). In 1990, Haass restated his arguments as a "ripeness" thesis: only when essential conditions were present could American involvement be productive; those conditions not being present, the United States should limit engagement and "encourage ripening" (Haass 1990).

Ross and Haass shaped a 1988 Washington Institute report, *Building for Peace*, in which they argued that quick breakthroughs would be "extremely difficult," and "to make peace in this environment will be virtually impossible" (Washington Institute 1988: xii).[7] The first American interest in the region was "survival and security of Israel, a fellow democracy and strategic ally" (ibid.: 25). Arabs and Palestinians were to blame for lack of progress in the peace process; Israel should not be pressed for concessions. The Intifada, although conceded to be a spontaneous reaction to occupation, was an entirely negative development, radicalizing Palestinians and hardening Israelis.[8] Palestinian leaders were radical and overly ambitious, intimidating the (obviously preferable) "middle class elites in the West Bank who accommodated themselves to the Israeli occupation," or were Gazan Islamists (ibid.: 15). The duties of the president were to foster Israeli confidence and flexibility by reinforcing support, and to insist that Palestinians repudiate violence, as a condition not of substantive negotiations, but of relaxed restrictions and a lengthy "ripening" process.[9] The advice of Ross and Haass fit the predilection of James Baker to leave the Israeli–Palestinian conflict alone, and defined early policy choices.

Another official who later had a very different role was John Sununu, Bush's chief of staff. Sununu used his access to Bush to present color-coded maps tracking the aggressive settlement policies of Housing Minister Sharon in the West Bank (Baker 1995: 128). That information often conflicted sharply with assurances Bush thought he had received from Shamir.

Initial attitudes toward Israel

As director of Central Intelligence, George Bush had ordered a threat assessment of the Soviet Union by outside experts that served as a bible for conservatives, including Reagan (Greenstein 2000: 162–3). Bush still described the world at his inauguration as "the familiar bipolar one of superpower rivalry, if no longer of total confrontation" (Bush and Scowcroft 1999: xiii). He did not doubt the efficacy of working with the Israelis against Soviet clients. He thus had no initial reason to lessen strategic cooperation, or to buck the lobby. However, unlike Ross and Haass, he saw Western access to Gulf oil and the sea lanes, not the security of Israel, as the fundamental regional national interests (Bush 1990: 47–9). The Arab–Israeli conflict was important primarily as it affected the East–West rivalry. Arabs were seen as either radical or moderate, based almost entirely upon their relationship to the Soviet Union (Herrmann 1994: 108–9; Hurst 1999: 30).

From service at the UN and CIA and as vice-president, George Bush knew the value of close cooperation with the Mossad and IDF. However, he also knew the concerns, and the strategic value, of moderate Arab leaders, particularly those of the Gulf states. At the United Nations, he had stated the regret of his government that Israel would not acknowledge its obligations in the Territories under the Fourth Geneva Convention, and that its "actions ... [were] contrary to the letter and spirit of this convention" (Boudreault *et al.* 1992: 126–7). The Seacat subsidiary of his Zapata oil service company had built the first offshore drilling rig for the Emir of Kuwait (Parmet 1997: 443). He knew Arab leaders well, including King Fahd, President Mubarak and King Hussein. As vice-president he became quite close to Prince Bandar (Dutton interview). He knew the economics, security requirements and personalities involved in the oil industry and regional politics as no previous president had, which made him impervious to arguments that Arabs were inherently untrustworthy or bent solely on the destruction of Israel.

AIPAC had other reasons for anxiety about George Bush. He was a leading critic of Israel's incursion into Lebanon (Cannon 1991: 396; Baker 1995: 118). Haig had accused him of frustrating the purposes of that incursion by assuring the Saudis (and thereby, Arafat) that Israel would not go into Beirut (Haig 1984: 343). According to Donald Regan's notes of a 1986 White House meeting, Bush was concerned that, having facilitated the Iranian arms debacle, Israel might try to "squeeze" the administration (Hitchens 1992: 62). The question of Bush's involvement in Iran-Contra dogged him in the 1988 campaign, and he evidently held Israel partly responsible.[10] AIPAC's grounds for concern would expand rapidly in the first year of Bush's administration.

James Baker had no experience with or strong feelings about Israel. His instincts were to see "the Arab–Israeli dispute as a pitfall to be avoided rather than an opportunity to be exploited," and to accept Nixon's advice that "the Middle East is insoluble. Stay away from it!" (Baker 1995: 115–16). However, there were vital interests in the region; it was a "perpetual tinderbox" and the relationship with Israel and "the political power of the American Jewish community" made it a "perpetual feature of domestic politics." To avoid being managed by the issues, he would seek to manage them with "a moderately activist policy in the Middle East," without believing it would significantly change the status quo (ibid.: 116). Thus he accepted the advice of Ross and Haass to be engaged, but ask little of Israel.[11] In an early meeting in the Oval Office, Baker took control of Middle

East policy, to preserve for Bush the prerogative to intervene when necessary (Dowd and Friedman 1990: 64).

Baker sought what would "succeed," meaning a process accepted by all sides rather than a particular result. In an uncharacteristically revealing early interview, he described the guile needed in Texas turkey hunts:

> The trick is in getting them where you want them, on your terms. Then *you* control the situation, not them … The important thing is knowing that it's in your hands, that you can do whatever you determine is in your interest to do."

Asked a question on the assumption he was really talking about turkeys, Baker said, "No. I mean Israel." He explained how dialogue with Arafat and divisions within Israel might be used to create options, by talking to the PLO but not to Shamir's government (Kramer 1989: 27–8). Baker refused to promise in confirmation hearings that the PLO dialogue would be terminated at the first threat or act of terrorism by a PLO faction (Baker Confirm Hrgs: 96–7, 269). In March, he testified that the United States would promote direct and meaningful negotiations between Israelis and Palestinians, and that might require involvement of the PLO (HFAC 1989: 472). These early signals of cool willingness to manipulate the parties unsettled the pro-Israel community, and generated legislation designed to end all contact with the PLO.

Early lessons from Israel and its advocates

Dennis Ross requested that Prime Minister Shamir bring to his first meeting with Bush a proposal for dealing with the Palestinian issues. Shamir's proposal was truly minimal: initial talks would depend on ending the Intifada and other conditions, but might lead to elections of Palestinian negotiators from the Territories and thence to substantive negotiations. Shamir had avoided prior vetting of the plan with his Likud ministers, but the Likud party conference later conditioned the proposal further to prevent legitimization of Palestinian leaders. On return to Israel Shamir dismissed his own plan as "idle fancy" (Schiff and Ya'ari 1990: 319). No one at the White House or State Department believed Shamir when he said he was serious about peace (Ross 2004: 64).

One month later, Baker addressed the AIPAC policy conference. He described the talks with Shamir as positive. He then called on each party to do things necessary for a peace process: Arabs to end the boycott, repudiate the General Assembly's "Zionism is racism" resolution and take steps to regularize relations; Palestinians to speak with one voice against terrorism, amend the Covenant and accept that no one would "deliver" Israel; and Israel, *inter alia*, to "lay aside, for once and for all, the unrealistic vision of a greater Israel…. Forswear annexation. Stop settlement activity" (Speech 22 May 1989, AFP 1989: 406).

The speech had broken little new ground, although the requests to Israel clearly reflected the initial experience with Shamir. Tom Dine told Baker that the speech was "perhaps the best ever" (Baker 1995: 121). However, others in the pro-Israel community quickly made clear that Baker and Bush were on probation, and statements would be parsed to an exacting standard. Shamir rejected as "useless" the suggestion of giving up greater Israel or settlement programs;[12] within two weeks, 95 senators urged Baker to be "fully supportive" of Shamir's plan (Jacobson 1991: 149–50).

By March 1990, Baker had persuaded Mubarak to present a plan based on PLO positions, and had tabled his own variation when neither side would accept the other's proposal. Shamir then refused to go forward with what Baker said was Shamir's own plan. The reasons were distrust of Bush and Baker, and domestic politics in both countries. Shamir had told the Knesset on 14 January that hundreds of thousands of prospective Soviet Jewish immigrants required "the Land of Israel and a big and strong state of Israel," and a policy of letting immigrants go where they wanted (Neff 1994: 61). The administration publicly called the statement "unhelpful," but Baker says they were "furious" (Baker 1995: 126). On 3 March, President Bush said that America firmly opposed Jewish settlements "in the West Bank or in East Jerusalem" (PC 3 Mar. 1990 in AFP 90: 567). That was longstanding American policy, but presidents had not recently included Jerusalem in a restatement of the policy.[13] Even dovish American Jews were outraged at the statement (Grossman 1992: 241). Shamir had cover for withdrawing from a process that had been excruciating. Shamir then lost a no-confidence vote on the Palestinian representation issue, but after the resulting elections was able to form a coalition of right-wing and religious parties. With that hard-line government in place and the PLO dialogue ended,[14] the Baker initiative was dead. Baker says that the experience made him "cynical" but taught him how to "refine his strategy" for later efforts (Baker 1995: 116).

Settlements, loan guarantees and Russians

The constant nettle in the bilateral relationship was the Shamir–Sharon settlement policy. Bush had long seen the settlements as obstacles to United States efforts in the Middle East, and as illegal.[15] Shamir had said, "The slogan 'territories for peace' is a hoax ... If we leave, there will almost certainly be war" (*JPS* 18: 4 (summer 1989): 177). He claimed that "security, territory and homeland are one entity," and that settlements constituted security (Quandt 2001: 309). Jewish enclaves amid Palestinian populations were in fact security burdens.[16] However, settlements in Gaza, Judea and Samaria were the fulfillment of Zionism as they understood it, concrete expressions of intent to remain forever. Shamir could not abandon that policy without losing the leadership of the Likud and his premiership.

Any process that posited Palestinians with popular support as negotiators of a political settlement was seen as leading to a Palestinian state and defeat of the Revisionist project. Israel and AIPAC waged a fierce campaign to reinstate the former policy of shunning the PLO as a terrorist organization; since any negotiator with authority to reach binding agreements would have at least tacit acquiescence of the PLO, even Faisal Husseini and Hanan Ashrawi would be tainted.[17] Shamir saw his task as winning a war of wills: if Israel could stall effective Palestinian political organization, the Territories could be populated and the Palestinians would give up.[18] He never hid this agenda, and after his 1992 defeat he was quoted as confirming that he would have drawn out autonomy negotiations for ten years, "and in the meantime we would have reached half a million people" in the West Bank (*NYT* 27 Jun. 1992: 1).

For Bush, an aggressive settlement program enabled by American funds emptied UNSCR 242 of meaning and made it impossible to persuade Arabs to participate in an American-sponsored peace process.[19] Even if the goal was a visible peace process rather than final status agreements, the first demand at almost every Arab stop on Baker's travels was a settlement freeze (Baker Test 25 Feb. 1992 in SApp/FO 1992: 25). But Sharon was proceeding as quickly as possible with homes, infrastructure and incentive programs for settlers.[20] As signals to his own base and Shamir as well as to the Arabs and the Americans, Sharon announced new settlements each time Baker was about to land in Israel; these "Baker settlements" helped Baker and Bush understand that settlements were both symbolic and real impediments to a peace process.

Gorbachev's "new thinking" meant Soviet Jewish emigration. The prospect of hundreds of thousands of immigrants provided motivation and rhetorical ammunition to all sides. Shamir insisted that all Soviet Jews must come to Israel, and that America was morally obligated to underwrite their absorption. Israel could not afford the costs of housing and employing refugees who could exceed 20 percent of the population.[21] Politically, they would solve the Likud's demographic conundrum; hence Shamir's ecstatic call for a "big Israel" in January 1990.[22] American Jews were joyous that Soviet Jews were allowed to leave. There was initial division about whether the immigrants should be allowed to choose the United States,[23] but all major Jewish organizations quickly called for massive U.S. housing loan guarantees for Israel. Most agreed with AIPAC that this was the most critical humanitarian mission for the Jewish community for decades, and leaders hoped that it would galvanize and unify the increasingly fractured community.

As vice-president, George Bush had led efforts to facilitate Soviet and Ethiopian Jews' immigration to Israel, and was committed to absorption aid. He also understood the danger to any peace process of combining a massive influx of immigrants, American aid and unconstrained settlements. Initially, Bush had told aides that he accepted that this Israeli government would not stop all settlement activity because of its ideological commitments; he simply wanted to know that the United States was not funding it (Melman and Raviv 1994: 416). At their first meeting in April 1989, Bush pressed Shamir hard on settlements, and believed Shamir promised that they would slow or stop, only to learn days later that new settlements had been announced.[24] Bush thereafter saw the issue as a test of whether Shamir was taking him seriously (Dowd and Friedman 1990: 64).

On 1 March 1990 Baker testified that, because of the fungibility of aid funds, the administration would want "some assurances that [Israel] would not be engaging in any new or additional settlement activity in the territories," before it could support an initial Israeli request for $400 million in housing loan guarantees (Test HApp/FO/Pt 3 1990: 191–3). Such assurances were never forthcoming.

Bush became convinced of the need for a firmer line. Hard feelings about Shamir spilled into public remarks and affected both the substance and the perception of policy. For example, Bush's statement in March 1990 that the U.S. firmly opposed settlements "in the West Bank or in Jerusalem" was apparently triggered by his having been told by Shamir in January that less than 1 percent of Soviet immigrants were moving to the Occupied Territories. Scowcroft had just given Bush figures showing that, including East Jerusalem, close to 10 percent of Soviet immigrants were doing so (*Newsday* 21 Mar. 1990: 3). Baker had advised not pushing Shamir on settlements before Shamir had responded to Baker's proposals, but Bush reacted to Shamir's perceived duplicity (Dowd and Frieman 1990: 63).

Shamir knew that Bush felt "deceived on matters having to do with the settlements," and wrote Bush that settlements were not an obstacle to peace; no Arab of good faith would support "the repugnant *Judenrein* ["Jew-free"] policies of the past" (Shamir 1994: 210–11). He evidently hoped Bush would adopt George Shultz's approach, lamenting the effects of settlements but saying that Jews should be able to live anywhere. However, he was claiming rights for Jews he would not grant Arabs, while demanding American guarantees that would facilitate state-sponsored settlements. The new Israeli government's guidelines, published 8 June, had committed "to strengthen settlement, to broaden and deepen it" throughout "*Eretz Y'Israel*" as a "right of the people" (*JPS* 20: 1 (autumn 1990): 172).[25]

Dennis Ross negotiated with Foreign Minister David Levy a letter of assurances, intended to remove settlements as an impediment to peace talks (Letter 2 Oct. 1990 in DoS FOIA 199104529). In it, Levy said Israeli policy was "not to direct or settle Soviet Jews beyond the green line," guaranteed that loan money would be used within the green line and promised Israel would periodically disclose the government's plans for immigrants, including incentive programs. Levy also promised his "best efforts to provide annually as complete information as possible" on governmental support for settlement activity and periodic information about government settlements. The letter was both beyond Levy's writ, and misconstrued by Baker. Ross later said their expectations for the letter were "wrong," because Shamir could not afford to reveal the extent to which funds were diverted to settlements from development in Israel, nor abide distinctions based on the Green

Line (Ross 2004: 82–3). Secretary Baker believed Levy had stated that immigrants would "not be settled beyond the Green Line," and that no incentives for settlement beyond that line were planned (PC 2 Oct. 1990 in AFP 1990: 588). The letter did not say that. The episode apparently contributed to a growing rift between Levy and Shamir (Melman and Raviv 1994: 432).[26] Levy retracted the letter on 18 October (Baker 1995: 543). When information available to the administration indicated that expenditures in the Territories had tripled, and the American Embassy reported plans to add 50,000 settlers in a year, mistrust of Shamir escalated (Melman and Raviv 1994: 415–17).

An initial $400 million guarantee package was released as part of a larger settlement with Israel during the Gulf War.[27] Finance Minister Modai had announced that, given Israel's war losses and the burden of immigrants, it would request $3 billion in direct supplemental financial aid and an additional $10 billion in loan guarantees (Baker 1995: 545). President Bush was irritated: American-led forces had defeated Israel's most potent enemy, the United States had gifted Israel with Patriot anti-missile batteries, and the compensation claims were inflated. Bush, however, agreed to $650 million in added aid and released the $400 million in guarantees, and Israel agreed to delay requesting an additional $10 billion in loan guarantees until September. The administration now anticipated what was to come. Baker sent Congress a report providing the department's best information concerning settlements and government expenditures, to be used as a baseline in considering future aid requests (Memo 6 Mar. 1991, Kelly to Baker, DoS FOIA).

The interconnected issues of settlements, loan guarantees and the peace process would be contested again in the fall of 1991. By then, the effects of major global and regional change on the U.S.–Israel relationship, and on politics in each country, would be obvious.

Extrinsic events and domestic ferment

The Cold War and the Gulf War

The end of the Cold War removed one ideological veil from Middle East politics, revealing competing nationalisms that had had little to do with Soviet communism or pan-Arabism. The Iraqi invasion of Kuwait in August 1990 accelerated the process of removing the veils of myth and realigning policies to reflect long-standing interests and new power realities.

For Israel, substantial benefits flowed from the end of the Cold War. (1) Israel's adversaries had to adjust to the fact that the only superpower was Israel's principal ally. Syria was forced to abandon its dream of strategic parity with Israel, which depended on Soviet support.[28] (2) The release of Soviet Jews was a humanitarian triumph, and promised demographic and ideological salvation for the Likud and the religious right. These advantages came with associated risks and costs. Soviet immigrants constituted a burden that required massive help from the United States; that underlined Israel's dependence and made the settlement policy vulnerable to leverage. Israel's unquestioned military supremacy depended upon strategic cooperation programs that Reagan and Shultz had institutionalized; the principal public justification for those programs was now gone. The "special relationship" based upon bonds of history, religion, culture, guilt and democratic identification remained, but the Intifada and the IDF's sometimes brutal response to it, among other things, put those bonds in question. It now seemed possible that neither the special relationship nor strategic cooperation doctrine would preserve Israel's accustomed impunity.

The end of the Cold War and the Gulf War had domestic effects that ran against Israel. The Cold War had provided American foreign policy a "missionary focus" (Spiegel 1990–1991: 21). Its end, and the Gulf War, left the public drained of enthusiasm for overseas commitments. Eastern Europe and Russia needed help transitioning from communism. There was a recession deepening in 1991, and pressure was mounting to spend on economic recovery. Senator Dole's proposal in January 1990 to divert 5 percent of aid given Israel and Egypt to emerging democracies reflected irritation with Israel, but also these other pressures. The administration felt "obliged to oppose the idea" but was not "at all unhappy" with it (Baker 1995: 126). A Jewish member of Congress said that the proposal "would pass overwhelmingly" on a secret ballot (Bernstein 1990: 30). AIPAC organized statements of opposition, but was nervous (*NER* 29 Jan. 1990: 19).

The Gulf War forced everyone in the Middle East to re-examine the reliability and utility of their relationships. The Soviet Union cooperated comprehensively in the Bush administration's policies during and after the war. Saudi Arabia moved from a limited security relationship with the United States and occasional quiet support for American diplomacy to active military alliance (at least when under direct threat) and public support for a peace process. The Saudis wanted to demonstrate that they were more effective advocates for Palestinian and other Arab causes than Saddam Hussein. Jordan paid again for its weakness: King Hussein felt constrained to give rhetorical support to the invasion of Kuwait and thereby lost credibility in Washington and the region. Having supported Saddam, Arafat and the PLO suffered catastrophic setbacks: (1) they exchanged Egypt, America's best Arab friend and intermediary in the peace process, for Iraq, America's worst Arab enemy; (2) they lost millions of dollars in patronage from Gulf states; (3) they lost thousands of high-paying jobs in the Gulf, and their remittances home; and (4) they ended any chance that Bush would engage in a potentially legitimizing dialogue with the PLO.

Israel's major gain in security came at a cost far beyond the Iraqi Scud missile attacks: (1) the war demonstrated that, so long as Gulf states cooperated, there was no need for an Israeli role in American power projections, and reason to exclude Israel;[29] (2) Saddam's use of the Palestinian cause as rallying cry, fraudulent though it was, threatened the coalition and demonstrated the power of the Arab–Israeli conflict to derail American policies;[30] and (3) together with the Intifada and Baker's frustrated 1989 peacemaking efforts, the war had changed American public perceptions of Israelis and Arabs, to Israel's detriment.

Domestic ferment

Israel's public image as America's sole dependable democratic ally against hostile ideologies was damaged, and that suggested possible policy shifts. In a 1990 CCFR survey, the American public perceived both the Soviet Union and France more favorably than Israel (Schneider 1992: 38). NBC/WBJ polls in June and September 1991 reported more Americans favoring economic aid to Poland and the Soviet Union than to Israel (*JPS* 21: 2 (spring 1992): 163). The public's assessment of who was the biggest obstacle to settlement of the Arab–Israeli dispute was moving against Israel: by September 33 percent named the Arabs, 34 percent said the Israelis and 16 percent volunteered that they were equally responsible.[31] Potentially more ominous for Shamir was a November 1991 Wilstein Institute Survey of Council of Jewish Federations Leaders. Very large majorities of these key leaders said that occupation of the Territories threatened Israel's democracy or its Jewishness; that Israel should freeze settlements for an end to the Arab boycott and Intifada violence or for American loan guarantees; that gradual emergence of a demilitarized Palestinian state was desirable; and that under the right conditions Israel should negotiate with the PLO (*JPS* 21: 2 (spring 1992): 165–6). Shamir dismissed the Wilstein Institute as controlled by "well-known left-wingers." Although the survey was commissioned by the dovish Project Nishma, those surveyed represented all major groups including AIPAC and AJC (Hertzberg 1992a: 22).[32] The one issue on which they split evenly, unsurprisingly, was whether public criticism of Israeli government policies was permissible.

Although still skittish about going public, highly informed supporters of Israel believed the Likud's policies dangerous to Israel and contrary to Jewish values. In March 1989, Shamir had held a "Prime Minister's Conference on Jewish Solidarity" in Jerusalem, transparently intended to reimpose discipline and send a message to Washington about the cost of pressuring Israel (Shamir 1994: 197). However, that same month a conference on the peace process at Columbia University demonstrated growing bonds among peace activists. Attending were two dozen Israeli activists 'including four Knesset members', six members of the PLO inner circle and leaders from the American Jewish and Arab communities (Oppenheim 1989).[33] Several Jewish leadership groups expressing similar opinions and seeking to affect policy were increasingly active.[34]

This growing phenomenon did not reflect weakening support for Israel, but rather a cracking of the *omerta* among the great majority of American Jews who rejected Revisionist beliefs about Israel. That majority had always been "conditional doves," distrustful of the PLO but supportive of compromises insuring the safety of Israelis while satisfying legitimate aspirations of Palestinians (Cohen 1989; Raab 1990).[35] They were being implored to weigh in publicly by Israeli leaders of Labor and the left and military and intelligence officers experienced with the occupation. Israeli academics and liberal Knesset members insisted that the unconditional aid for which American Jewish organizations fought constituted counterproductive interference in internal Israeli affairs (Roundtable 1991). Yehoshafat Harkabi, former head of Military Intelligence, found the Likud's belief that occupation could lead to peace "preposterous." He argued that Israeli politics were so calcified that change could only come from outsiders, including American Jews (Harkabi 1992: 11, 15, 29).

The Gulf War, with its pictures of Palestinians cheering Iraqi Scud attacks on Tel Aviv, chilled American Jews' willingness to contemplate negotiations with Palestinians or to criticize the Israeli government. Israelis who expected unswerving support from the diaspora denounced Americans who had advocated taking risks for peace (Golan 1992). Peace organizations were greatly weakened; many suspended operations (Gedal 1997: 175).

The differences between strategic cooperation and absorption aid

Responding to shifting realities, neoconservatives and others recast justifications for Israel's privileged place in American beliefs and American policy. A "Committee on U.S. Interests in the Middle East" was formed, to "reject the notion of *moral equivalency* that underlies current U.S. policy toward Israel and her Arab enemies," and to argue that morality *excluded* even-handedness, since Israel was a fellow democracy under attack (advertisement, *NYT* 26 Feb. 1992: A11; italics in original).[36] AIPAC published numerous articles and interviews arguing Israel's continuing strategic value in 1990 and 1991; one article listed 14 measures of strategic value (*NER* 29 Jan. 1990: 1). The principal argument was that Israel was a dependable ally against what Charles Krauthammer called "Global Intifada," attacks by radical Islamists throughout the "Crescent of Crisis" from Kashmir through the Caucasus, Balkans and Levant that mirrored Israel's experience in the Occupied Territories (*WP* 16 Feb. 1990: A23).[37] This line of argument had theoretical appeal but substantial real-world limitations. Further, although Manicheans like Krauthammer lumped Arabs and Islamists together as obsessed with obliterating Israel, Arab leaders had to support the reversal of the Likud's Palestinian policies even if they did not seek Israel's destruction. No one explained how Israel could suppress radical movements without further galvanizing them; the Gulf War made clear the effect of the Arab–Israeli conflict on America's freedom of policy choice. The principal attraction of the argument to neoconservatives was its major drawback to others: in the critical arenas of perception and belief, basing unconditional support of Israel on threats of "Global Intifada" would align the United States with Israel, and against Arabs and Islam.

An alternative argument was that the dissolution of the Soviet Union, the growth of radical movements and the instability of regional regimes required a strong working relationship with a stable, democratic ally of proven military ability, against *whatever* threats eventuated. The United States had failed to predict the threat-producing events of the previous two decades: the fall of the Shah, the Soviet invasion of Afghanistan and the Iraqi invasion of Kuwait (Feuerwerger 1993b: 35). Deputy Secretary Eagleburger said that strategic cooperation with Israel "serve[d] the general purpose" of planning "for any number of contingencies" (Puschel 1992: 154). Supporting arguments were: (1) growing public opposition to overseas commitments made partnership for contingencies and for research and development more attractive; (2) visible weakening of strategic cooperation would destabilize the region and undercut Israel's deterrence; and (3) Israel would only compromise for peace if securely allied with the United States. Each rationale was flawed, and each required accepting the questionable proposition that Israel would use the power given by the United States in ways that would advance American interests.

No advocate could identify a potential crisis where Israel's separate military involvement would be a boon rather than, as in the Gulf War, an impediment. Advocates used the September 1970 Jordan/PLO/Syria incident as the single example of such Israeli usefulness. Putting aside the question of whether highly conditioned Israeli willingness to assist was decisive then, Israeli adventures with American arms had more often violated the terms of transfer and greatly complicated relations with friendly Arab regimes. As for the "destabilizing signal" argument, Arab states had accepted the unshakable American commitment to Israel's survival and security, and were openly antagonistic only when American aid enabled Israel to strike or bully them. Nevertheless, the process of strengthening Israel as a free-standing military power again accelerated after the Gulf War.[38] It is hard to see how assistance limited to Israel's defense needs, rather than measured by hegemony over all Arabs, would have been destabilizing. Finally, as to the argument that only a strong Israel could "risk for peace," the problem was not lack of Israeli strength, but strength of Israeli ideology. A truly weak Israel would never risk large territorial concessions, but Israel was now led by a man who used its strength to realize Jabotinsky's vision of Zionism: "A Jewish majority in a Jewish state in the whole of the biblical Land of Israel" (Shamir 1994: 11). Shamir's arguments amounted to: "When I am weak, how can I compromise? When I am strong, why should I compromise?" (Friedman 1991)

The Cold War rationale for strategic cooperation had not been subjected to stringent analysis; it served as cover for decisions reflecting emotional ties and political costs rather than serious American strategic planning. William Quandt said the United States was "stuck with a strong, solid relationship with Israel" (Puschel 1992: 146). Everyone Puschel interviewed, including many senior Israeli and American political and military officials, believed that the fading of the Soviet threat would have no effect at all on strategic cooperation between Israel and the United States, which was based upon shared values, heritage and morality (ibid.: 155–60). Proffered replacement rationales would likewise need only surface plausibility.

There were critical differences, however, between strategic cooperation (including issues of arming Arabs) and aid for absorption of immigrants. Uncertainties about the intentions and capabilities of Israel's enemies persuaded many to err on the side of more assistance. Few were prepared to argue that close working relationships and a stronger Israel were bad policy goals, even when Israel misused the resulting power. In addition, the institutionalization of strategic cooperation had built momentum that was difficult to reverse, for classic bureaucratic reasons: (1) personal friendships and mutual admiration built since 1983; (2) protection of budgets, organizational missions and staffing built to carry out the mandated programs;[39] (3) sharing of military technology and research, which may have saved no taxpayer money, but spread and politically protected budgets and extended production runs; and (4) occasional technical or methodological breakthroughs reached in partnership, as symbols of the virtue of the growing military cultural symbiosis. The requested housing loan guarantees did not have comparable entrenched political and bureaucratic support.[40] Further, there was an inherent and obvious linkage between massive absorption aid for refugees and Likud settlement programs. The president could make loan guarantees a test of the settlement issue and thereby of the land-for-peace formula; as to those issues, pluralities in Israel and the American Jewish community opposed Shamir's policies. Even strong pro-Israel partisans admitted that the "dichotomous viewpoint" of American Jews, favoring Israel's guaranteed safety but also land-for-peace, gave the president leeway to press Israel (Eizenstat 1991: 103).

9   The loan guarantees

New equilibrium, old result

Introduction

President Bush forced Shamir to choose between aggressive settlement of the Occupied Territories and loan guarantees to fund absorption of Soviet immigrants. His insistence was both shocking and enabling. In Israel, it combined with the re-emergence of Yitzhak Rabin as a credible opposition leader to force a change of government. In the United States, Bush's seeming success and Rabin's election discredited AIPAC's leadership and forced temporary restructuring of that organization. In the broader Jewish community, the effects were mixed. The president's stand energized those who opposed the Likud's policies. In electoral politics, however, Bush's cool approach toward Israel made it easy for the Democrats to reclaim their traditional hold on the Jewish vote.

As Bush left office, the new Rabin government in Israel had been granted more in loan guarantees than it could use; other aid to Israel was stable in the face of American recession and isolationism; and the infrastructure of strategic cooperation continued to strengthen even as advocates struggled to justify it. The relationship between Israel and the United States had undergone a series of shocks. It found a new equilibrium, not very different from the old one. This chapter will examine why the changes were not greater.

Housing loan guarantees (reprise)

The administration

Perhaps the only perceptive decision Saddam Hussein made in 1990 was his effort to use the Palestinians to drive a wedge between the West and its Arab coalition partners. Saddam's gambit of announcing a *jihad* on behalf of the Palestinians ultimately failed, but it further neutralized Jordan, insured that Israel was sidelined and made the coalition harder to manage.[1] Partly to hold the coalition together, President Bush promised that after the war he would lead an effort to restart a meaningful peace process.[2]

As William Quandt has argued, there were reasons to take on the peace process other than Bush's promise: (1) to strengthen Israeli–Egyptian peace; (2) to prevent further radicalization of Israelis and Palestinians; (3) to prevent further damage to the U.S.–Israel relationship from corrosive images of occupation, annexation or expulsion of Palestinians; (4) to prevent debilitating effects of massive aid long after the "strategic asset" concept was discredited; and (5) to minimize the possibility of another regional war, this time possibly with weapons of mass destruction (Quandt 2001: 305). The opportunity was present because of changed regional power relationships (Ross 2004: 65). One should add another Gulf War lesson: threats to American interests were not predictable, but would likely require projection or credible threat of American power in a region almost entirely populated by Arabs and Muslims.[3] In most imaginable scenarios, and certainly those involving threats to oil, it would be impossible to rely upon Israel as a principal strategic ally while all neighbors but Egypt were technically and rhetorically at war with Israel. President Bush had experienced the advantages of broad cooperation, and had seen how the Arab–Israeli conflict could impede such cooperation.

Timing was critical. Bush was in a strong position of leadership in the region and wanted to keep the coalition together; at home, his popularity was at record levels. As Baker said, their "leverage [was then] infinitely more potent," but only temporarily (Baker 1995: 411). They saw Shamir's rejection of "land for peace," objectified by settlements, as their major obstacle, and believed that American sponsorship of the process was impossible if American funds facilitated settlements. Successful sponsorship of a peace conference would be an asset in the 1992 election. The opening also appealed to Bush's sense of justice. He wrote in his diary that everyone knew there would be no Middle East peace until the Palestinian question was solved; he wanted to "stand up for what is fair and right," to do what "no president [had] done since Ike," by pushing Israel to do the proper thing (Parmet 1997: 499–500).

Overruling his national security adviser,[4] the president announced his initiative in an address to Congress marking the end of the war (Speech 6 Mar. 1991 in DoS Dispatch 1991: 161). Secretary Baker began eight circuits of the Middle East the next day. Each regional party now had incentives to cooperate with, or at least not visibly impede, the American president. Baker started with the Arabs, to build pressure on Shamir (Ross 2004: 68). Shamir counted on Assad's resistance, and was shocked when Baker persuaded Assad to "leave the dead cat" of non-cooperation at Israel's door by agreeing that Syria would attend a conference. The next week, Baker persuaded Egypt and Saudi Arabia to offer an end to the Arab boycott of Israel in exchange for a settlement freeze (PC 19 Jul. 1991, PC 20 Jul. 1991 in AFP 1991: 569). Shamir rejected the offer, and said, "I don't believe in territorial compromise.... [no people would] give up the territory of their homeland" (*SFChron* 25 Jul. 1991: A12). Sharon had earlier announced 24,000 new units of housing for 88,000 settlers (Baker 1995: 547). Having rejected land for peace and a settlement freeze, Shamir on 1 August conditionally agreed to attend the conference he had rejected six weeks earlier (PC 1 Aug. 1991 in AFP 1991: 573; "Senior official" PC 1 Aug. 1991 in AFP 1991: 574).

An "administration official," probably Ross, said the parties were asked to attend the conference without a settlement freeze because (1) the United States could not provide a freeze and (2) settlements were an issue to be negotiated (PC 20 Sep. 1991 in AFP 1991: 583). The second reason was true because the first was true. Bush had asked Jack Stein to tell Shamir in July that if he did not halt settlements, "we will have major problems." Shamir said to tell Bush, "The territory belongs to Israel" (Melman and Raviv 1994: 421). [Repeatedly, Bush and Baker were asked if they expected anything from negotiations with an Israeli government committed to de facto annexation of the West Bank, and repeatedly they declined to answer or said that everything including the meaning of UNSCR 242 was subject to negotiation.]

It had been clear since Baker's 1 March 1990 testimony that the administration opposed use of U.S. funds, or Israeli funds freed by new American aid, on new settlements. The negotiated Levy letter had been intended to inhibit or stop such flow-through of U.S. money, and had failed. Baker says the "contretemps" over loan guarantees was "crucial to the quest for peace and thus to Israel's strategic interests" (Baker 1995: 541). Yet during delicate negotiations for the Madrid conference, Bush and Baker were loathe to acknowledge publicly any linkage between the requested loan guarantees and a settlement freeze. Asked directly on 1 July, President Bush said, "Well, I don't think it ought to be a *quid pro quo*," but that Israel should "keep its commitment that was given at one point not to … build further settlements" (PC 1 Jul. 1991 in AFP 1991: 613). Shamir did not believe he had given any such commitment. A Shamir adviser said they pushed for the guarantees ahead of any negotiations precisely because they knew refusing territorial concessions "could kill the chance of U.S. aid in the settling of Soviet Jews" (Kramer 1991). Baker feared a public dispute over conditions on aid would cause Shamir to disengage and call new elections (Baker 1995: 548). In the meantime, however, the Jewish community understood Bush to have promised no linkage between settlements and absorption aid.

Bush asked Shamir for an additional 120-day delay to take up Israel's guarantee request. That was ostensibly to avoid *creating* linkage between territorial issues and American funding, but realistically it was to get the peace conference underway before the inevitable fight to *use* the linkage. Shamir refused. Baker sent Dennis Ross to discuss the terrible timing with Tom Dine, but Dine did not believe the administration would fight (ibid.: 549). Bush sent his friend Gordon Zacks to tell other Jewish leaders that he would veto unconditioned guarantees and go to the public for support. They also refused to believe the president was serious (Hadar 1992b: 83).

On 6 September, Bush and Baker held a press conference to request that

Congress delay consideration of the guarantees for 120 days. While Bush favored absorption aid, he was sure the American people would "strongly support" his request to "give peace a chance" (PC 6 Sep. 1991 in FPB Sep./Oct. 1991: 64–5). On 11 September, Bush met with congressional leaders, who sympathized with the president's efforts but were afraid to support him unless he publicly committed to fight the lobby (Painton 1991).

The morning of 12 September, Bush met with AIPAC officers including President Mayer Mitchell, hoping to persuade AIPAC to call off a planned massive lobbying effort in the Capitol, and was told that "Israel's friends would embarrass him if he insisted on a vote" (Baker 1995: 551–2). He then called the press conference that was to be the watershed both of the loan guarantees issue and of the president's relationship with the American Jewish community.

President Bush reviewed the progress made toward a peace conference, and said he had asked to delay Israel's loan guarantee request because it would raise "issues so sensitive that a debate could well destroy" the chance for a conference. He underscored his support for immigrant absorption and for Israel's security, pointing out that Desert Storm had risked American lives to, *inter alia*, defeat Israel's most dangerous enemy; and that in spite of economic problems in the United States, Israel had been given "nearly $1,000 for every Israeli man, woman and child," not including the earlier $400 million in loan guarantees. He said he would veto any measure that interfered with the peace conference. Finally, he cast the issue as one of foreign policy, over which the Constitution gave him authority, and said, "Too much is at stake for domestic politics to take precedence over peace" (PC 12 Sep. 1991 in FPB Sep./Oct. 1991: 66–7).

The opening statement had been aimed at the public, who credited Bush with mastery over foreign policy but were weary of overseas commitments and unlikely to know the amount of aid Israel received. Some supporters of Israel claimed offence at references to risked American lives and per capita aid, but what really shocked them was Bush's confrontation of a united Jewish community on something they considered a humanitarian imperative. In response to questions, Bush unintentionally gave opponents ammunition. Asked why he sounded so uncompromising, he responded that he was "up against some powerful political forces," and that he had heard "there was something like a thousand lobbyists on the Hill working on the other side of the question. We've only got one lonely little guy down here doing it." He was undoubtedly irritated at having just been told by AIPAC it would embarrass him. Given Bush's self-effacing humor and his mastery of foreign affairs, it was an attempted joke, and those present laughed. Further, he quickly clarified that he was not alleging impropriety or foreign interference, and thought that everybody should fight for what they believed in as he was "beginning to do." But those who listened anxiously for allegations of dual loyalty or anti-Semitism had heard them.

Outside the Jewish community, Bush's words gave the desired signal to Congress. During the Gulf War, popular opinion had favored pressing Israel to reach a peace agreement, 63 percent to 28 percent; now, a 19 September Time/CNN poll found that Americans opposed the guarantees, 56 percent to 37 percent, with only 15 percent favoring guarantees without a settlement freeze (Hadar 1992b: 79; Painton 1991: 24). A WSJ/CBS poll found 69 percent supported the president (*WSJ* 26 Sep. 1991: A20). Congressional supporters of Israel quietly accepted the requested 120-day delay, although they still expected to authorize guarantees. The media showed a new willingness to re-examine the relationship with Israel. The *Wall Street Journal* and *New York Times*, generally supportive of Israel, ran analyses of hidden aid to Israel (*NYT* 23 Sep. 1991: A10; *WSJ* 19 Sep. 1991: A16). Karen House of the *Journal* called pushing Russian émigrés to Israel instead of competing for them an "amoral undertaking" (House 1991).

Bush had made it temporarily acceptable to treat Israel more like other states. His statements also, to his dismay, generated expressions of extreme anti-Israel sentiment verging on anti-Semitism. At the urging of Jack Stein, he exchanged published letters with Shoshona Cardin, chair of the Presidents Conference, regretting any doubts about his support for Israel or his respect for the community (Melman and Raviv 1994: 428).[5]

There is some evidence that Bush and Baker intended to pressure Shamir by demonstrating how easily Israel's image with the American people could be devalued. A State Department Inspector General's report and other information were leaked, indicating widespread Israeli violations of arms proliferation agreements, including Patriot missile technology sales to China and sales to South Africa, Chile, and Ethiopia (*NYT* 13 Mar. 1992: A12, 15 Mar. 1992: 10, 23 Mar. 1992: A7). An investigation was later closed without finding a violation or apologizing (*NYT* 3 Apr. 1992: A1). Given Baker's well-earned reputation as the administration's primary leaker, he was credited (or blamed) for the leaks.

Several indicators gave Bush confidence to confront Israel: (1) the polls; (2) broad editorial support from the nation's newspapers;[6] (3) successfully convening the Madrid conference and scheduling the first bilateral talks; (4) private encouragement from some Jewish leaders;[7] and (5) the fact that major Jewish leaders backed away from confrontation and asked him to negotiate with Shamir.[8] Beginning in mid-September, Baker made a series of proposals to Shamir and to congressional leaders. His "six-point" proposal to Israel on 16 September promised no further delays in consideration, but no support for a specific guarantee package. Israel wanted a commitment that after the delay the administration would support the full request without conditions. Bush had already explicitly ruled that out at his 12 September press conference. On 16 September, Baker said there would be no guarantees without a freeze; the next day, he refused to acknowledge linkage (Jacobson 1993: 164–5).

By late February 1992, Shamir had repeatedly rejected calls to curtail settlement,[9] and was facing likely elections. While the guarantees would be a great achievement on which to run, he could not give what Bush was asking and retain Likud leadership. The Israeli elections also made compromise unattractive to Bush. The 20 February Labor Party primary made Yitzhak Rabin party leader. Rabin was considered more electable than Shimon Peres, was known and trusted in Washington and said he favored settlements only where they enhanced security. The Israeli election would inevitably turn on settlements, security and management of the relationship with America as well as the Israeli economy. While Bush and Baker disclaimed any intent to "interfere" in Israeli politics, they certainly did not want to reward Shamir for intransigence or hurt Rabin's chances.[10]

Isolationist Patrick Buchanan had announced he would challenge Bush in the Republican primary. He railed against foreign aid, singling out the loan guarantees (Buchanan 1991).[11] Bush was confident of re-nomination, but could not afford to antagonize constituents hurt by the recession. Conditioning new aid would also wrong-foot Democrats, who intended to run against Bush on the weak economy and Bush's lack of a domestic agenda. House Majority Leader Tom Foley told a closed-door meeting of 25 pro-Israel Democrats that they could not run against Bush on domestic issues and then publicly fight him to increase foreign aid (*JP* 20 May 1992: 5A).

On 10 January, Dennis Ross wrote Baker that they must force "the Shamir government to make a basic choice between ... absorbing Soviet Jews, or continuing unchanged settlement building" (Baker 1995: 553). Baker agreed, but wanted to set up Shamir. Throughout February, he exchanged proposals with Ambassador Shoval and congressional leaders. The offers Shamir made through Shoval would have allowed settlements to grow. Baker was seeking credit for working with Congress, while making offers acceptable to Rabin but not to Shamir. Shamir helpfully rejected several proposals, including one that would have allowed completion of the approximately 9,000 units of housing under development (*NYT* 5 Feb. 1992: A1).

Senator Patrick Leahy, chair of the appropriations subcommittee, proposed to offset spending on settlements against guarantee amounts and give the president discretion after one year. AIPAC promoted this approach within the Jewish community and in Congress (*JP* 27 Feb. 1992: 2). Leahy's position – strong support of absorption aid, but unwillingness to "finance further expansion of the settlements" – carried weight because he controlled movement of the bill (Leahy 1992).

On 24 February, Baker described his position to the House committee: the full request would be supported if there was a "halt or an end to settlement activity," but only a one-time guarantee in a lesser amount if units and infrastructure then underway were completed, with a "fungibility" deduction for the cost of completion. New construction would mean no guarantees (Test 24 Feb. 1992 in HApp/FO 1992: 506–7). Baker denied accusations that this was a sanction, interference in Israeli elections or unfairly taking the Arabs' side.

Baker rejected a deal Ross negotiated with Shoval for $2 billion in guarantees, with anything further conditioned on the earlier Levy assurances. Shamir rejected a proposal agreed by Baker and Senator Leahy for a full $10 billion in guarantees, with reductions for settlement spending (Ross 2004: 84). Bush finally offered $300 million if there was no freeze and promised to veto anything more generous, to the consternation of Leahy and Jewish leaders (*JP* 19 Mar. 1992: 2).[12] The public supported his insistence on a freeze.[13] Defense Minister Arens said in Washington that Israel would "not beg, or crawl for help," and would rather abandon the request than "renounce the right of Jews to live in Judea and Samaria" (*NYT* 17 Mar. 1992: A1). The guarantees were dead, so long as the Shamir government lived.

The divided pro-Israel community

To major Jewish organizations, the guarantees represented a humanitarian commitment and an opportunity to reunify the American Jewish community. Once it was clear that there were serious prices to be paid – either fighting a popular president to fund Shamir's settlement program (and all that meant) or publicly splitting with a government of Israel – disunity became inevitable. For AIPAC, especially Steve Rosen, this was a critical test of mastery over the process and a chance to end the possibility of territorial compromise. AIPAC was confident that they could teach this administration the AWACS lesson: confronting Israel and AIPAC was too costly to contemplate. For the peace movement in both countries, this was also the moment of truth. If Shamir obtained massive new aid that allowed him to annex Judea and Samaria, the peace process as conceived up to that point was effectively over and Revisionist policies would literally be set in concrete. The majority of American Jews – the "conditional doves" – were increasingly desperate for the two governments to help refugees without enabling either side to declare victory on peace process issues.

After AWACS, AIPAC had strengthened its ability to generate constituent-based pressure and deliver votes, usually against only token opposition. However, AIPAC had also made an ideological turn toward the Likud, and was geared to influencing executive branch policy makers as much as congressional appropriators. Those changes created vulnerabilities during the fight over guarantees. Given divisions within the Jewish community and in Congress over settlements and the peace process, and the strong public position of the president, AIPAC's identification with the Likud and its lack of influence with Bush and Baker were crippling.

To avoid endorsing Shamir's aggressive settlement policies while speaking for a Jewish community largely opposed to those policies, Tom Dine had to insist that there was no connection between absorption aid and settlements. Dine said in a 9 June speech that "any attempt to imperil this vital program by linking it to the explosive ideological issue of the settlements, or the peace process" would be fought "with all our being" (Jacobson 1993: 161). He had reason for confidence. All major Jewish organizations would support absorption aid, as they had opposed AWACS. In February 1991, 1,500 supporters had descended on Capitol Hill, and $650 million for Israel was added to Bush's Desert Storm emergency appropriations bill. That bill passed the Senate 92 to eight; a proposed House amendment to reduce aid to Israel by the amount spent on settlements failed, 44 to 378 (Frankel 1995: 156).

AIPAC's aggressive advice to Shamir drowned out better advice Shamir received from his ambassador and Israel's friends in Congress. Ambassador Shoval told Israel Radio in June 1991 that Israel would have to choose between settlements and aid (*NYT* 25 Sep. 1991: A1). The Israeli Embassy's Senate liaison was Yoram Ettinger, like Shamir and Rosen an uncompromising Revisionist. Rosen derided the "defeatism" of anyone anxious about a confrontation with Bush, and convinced Ettinger they could defeat conditions on aid. Ettinger cabled Shamir that Bush had "very limited ability to dictate the agenda," and other issues would take priority (Melman and Raviv 1994: 407–8, 423–4). Those conclusions ignored warnings from, *inter alia*, Senator Leahy. Leahy had said in Israel in 1989 that the settlements constituted trouble for the relationship, and he and his staff told Ettinger in 1991 that the linkage the president saw was natural, and that he would propose offsets (ibid.: 422–3). Leahy had quickly agreed to the president's request for delay, as had Chairman Obey of the House subcommittee and Republican Senate Leader Dole (Hadar 1992b: 83). Ettinger had many other signals, but ignored them.[14]

AIPAC drafted most of the material used by all advocates of the guarantees. By the end of August, over 50,000 messages had been sent to members of Congress (Frankel 1995: 159). The core argument, that humanitarian assistance should not be used as political leverage, rang hollow. Shamir bluntly told *Maariv* in early September 1991 that "increasing immigration … goes hand in hand with a campaign of settlement" (*ChiS-T* 9 Sep. 1991: 1). For many, the leverage question was: why should refugees be hostage to political goals that impeded the peace process? Israeli opposition leaders said Shamir created the linkage (*JP* 8 Oct. 1991: 1). Israeli commentators wrote that granting the guarantees would sanction the occupation and give Shamir a great political victory (Hertzberg 1991: 24; Hadar 1992a: 6–8). A poll found that 76 percent of Israelis believed that conditioning guarantees on a settlement freeze was reasonable (Hurst 1999: 205).

AIPAC's second argument was that guarantees would cost nothing because Israel paid its debts, and would pay the subsidy cost in cash.[15] That was intended to dampen the impact of talking about $10 billion in an atmosphere hostile to aid, but the argument embroiled advocates in arguments about the true costs and Israel's creditworthiness,[16] and was off-target politically. The perceived financial cost had some resonance with the general public, but to Bush and to Congress the relevant costs were political and strategic.

Reactions to Bush's 12 September press conference both reflected the stakes and raised them. Shamir said Israel's friends would continue to press; he had told French Jews that American Jews had done "nothing" about the Holocaust, and were now very active because of bad consciences (*NYT* 16 Sep. 1991: A1). An Israeli minister called Bush an anti-Semite and a liar; he was reined in, but his accusations may well have reflected Shamir's own sentiments (ibid.; Shamir 1994: 234). In the United States, the president's remarks generated anger and anxiety. Leslie Gelb said the president had declared "political war against Israel," echoing a Shamir spokesman (Gelb 1991; *JP* 13 Sep. 1991: 1).[17] Morris Amitay said it "came as close to the line of inciting anti-Semitism as a public figure can go" (Melman and Raviv 1994: 428). Norman Podhoretz said the administration had moved from "ordinary coldness" to "outright hostility" toward Israel (Podhoretz 1992: 22). Tom Dine, evoking Japanese perfidy at Pearl Harbour, told the AIPAC policy conference that "September 12, 1991 will be a day that lives in infamy for the American Jewish community," and predicted that Jews could swing the 1992 presidential election (*NER* 13 Apr. 1992: 68). A few Jewish leaders, including Hyman Bookbinder, saw Bush's statements as a dangerous temper tantrum but thought he had a point on substance (McGrory 1991). Some of the rhetoric verged on hysteria, but it reflected soul-deep Jewish anxiety that American support of Israel was ephemeral, and that this president was capable of weighing Israel (and Jews) against other interests and abandoning them.

Shoshona Cardin, chair of the Presidents Conference, maintained that the Jewish community was united against linkage. However, divisions became blatant as preparations were made for the February NCRAC national plenum. The AJCongress had been working in Riyadh to involve Saudi Arabia more openly in the peace process. They, the Union of American Hebrew Congregations and others proposed that NCRAC call for a settlement freeze. Israeli diplomats were so concerned that they persuaded the plenum not to hold a vote. Instead, NCRAC passed a resolution urging Israel and the United States to reach an agreement, and sent a transcript of the debate to the Israeli government (Grossman 1994: 185). This result reflected division and paralysis: Abraham Foxman said it was because of "domestic concerns"; Henry Siegman said that support was difficult when Shamir valued settlements more than the guarantees (*NYT* 5 Jan. 1992: 1, 3).

President Bush was pursuing goals broadly supported by an increasingly vocal majority of American Jews, but was doing so in ways that frightened and alienated many of them. Increasingly forlorn efforts at compromise finally exploded in anger and distrust. On 6 March President Cardin and Executive Director Hoenlein had what Hoenlein called a "very intense exchange" with Baker (Grossman 1994: 186). The same day, Mayor Ed Koch of New York alleged that Baker had said of the nation's Jews, "F*** 'em, they don't vote for us anyway" (*NYPost* 6 Mar. 1992: 1). A State Department spokesman called the report "false," "outrageous" and "garbage"

(*NYT* 7 Mar. 1992: 11). However, columnist William Safire alleged that two senior officials confirmed that Baker made the quoted statement – twice (Safire 1992). Baker had put enormous effort into revitalizing the peace process, but because he and Bush had done little to build domestic policy networks, he was not defended by natural supporters within the Jewish community. When Bush or Baker appeared calculating, as in the turkey hunt story, or contemptuous as in the Koch/Safire reports, sensitized Jewish leaders responded emotionally. Peace activists felt that Bush had undercut their efforts (Oppenheim 1992). In late March, the dovish AJCongress, which only a month earlier had advocated a settlement freeze, reacted angrily to the administration's stiffening and rejected a similar proposal by their president and executive director, pending elections in Israel (Grossman 1994: 187).

New relationships

Bush and Rabin

George Bush moved quickly after the 23 June Israeli election to repair relations with Israel and revitalize the struggling peace negotiations. He sent Baker to meet with Rabin days after he took office. Rabin also had reasons to move fast. Obtaining the guarantees would demonstrate his strong relationship with the American president and ameliorate a very real financial crisis. There were also practical and political reasons to move quickly on the peace process: (1) easing tensions might permit cutting burdensome defense spending; (2) stimulating growth to address 12 percent unemployment (50 percent among new immigrants) required inward investment, which required the prospect of peace; and (3) Labor had won the new immigrant vote, 47 percent to 18 percent for Likud, but immigrants were expected to shift quickly to Likud (Feuerwerger 1993a: 182–8). The government coalition was shaky, and only dramatic progress would allow it to consolidate support. Accordingly, in his maiden speech on 2 July Rabin called for continuous negotiations to reach an autonomy agreement with Palestinians within a year (Jacobson 1994: 162). His government's policy guidelines, published 15 July, shifted priorities from settlements to development within Israel (*JPS* 22, 1 (autumn 1992): 154–9). He told Baker on 19 July that he had suspended and would cancel contracts on 7,000 units in the Territories, and would cancel the Sharon subsidies and incentives. As important as the specific changes Rabin was making was the change in the level of trust. Rabin told Baker, "We will do what we say and we will not lie to you." Baker says, "The atmospheric change was positively seismic" (Baker 1995: 556).

Based upon the Baker–Rabin talks, Rabin was invited to the president's home in Maine, an honor never accorded Shamir. There, the two leaders quickly reached agreement on outstanding issues, including a commitment by Bush to recommend authorization of $10 billion in loan guarantees (PC 11 Aug. 1992 in FPB Sep./Oct. 1992: 72). The agreements gave each leader what he believed he needed politically while allowing each to claim not to have compromised principles. However, Bush and Baker were "negotiating" with a man they trusted in the middle of a presidential campaign that was going badly. They would give Rabin everything he wanted, both because they expected him to push forcefully for agreements in the ongoing negotiations and because they could not afford any longer the soured relationship with Israel and its advocates.

The resulting authorization demonstrated implicit trust in Rabin: (1) Israel could add "strategic" settlements and settlements in Jerusalem and "thicken" existing ones, but would not add "political" settlements; (2) projects already underway, totalling some 11,000 units, could be completed;[18] (3) amounts spent on settlements would reduce aid as determined jointly; (4) the subsidy cost reimbursable by Israel was limited to 4.5 percent of the guarantees;[19] and (5) the full $10 billion over five years was authorized (Jacobson 1994: 180). There was no agreement defining "strategic" settlements, although Rabin had spoken of settlements that were defensible and allowed control of movement, primarily in the Golan and Jordan Valley. The resulting patterns would resemble the old Allon Plan, leaving two enclaves for Palestinians (Bowen 1993). Baker and Bush spoke as if settlements had been stopped, but the results on the ground depended on future, essentially unfettered, decisions by the Israeli premier.

Rabin, the diaspora and AIPAC

Rabin had always preferred direct dealings with American leaders, and valued the personal involvement and resolve of George Bush. He openly favored Bush's re-election; after he met with Bill Clinton, his aides leaked that he thought Clinton "shallow" on international affairs (Melman and Raviv 1994: 441). American Jewish leaders, largely supporting Clinton, pleaded that Rabin not undermine their attacks on Bush as anti-Israel; he warned them not to disrupt his relationship with Bush (Hadar 1993: 83).

Rabin's election vindicated Jewish leaders who had called for a settlement freeze, and was widely hailed as a harbinger of better U.S.–Israeli relations. But it also made AIPAC's identification with the ideology and leaders of the Likud a liability, and thoroughly devalued executive lobbying. Rabin knew that AIPAC had sided with Likud on issues such as an international peace conference, even when Labor held the premiership in 1984 (Rosenthal 2001: 121). He believed that information provided AIPAC in confidence concerning the 1985 Peres–Hussein London agreement had been leaked to Shamir's chief of staff, exacerbating Peres–Shamir rifts (Bloomfield interview). Immediately after Kennebunkport, Rabin met with the executive board of AIPAC, telling them, "You have failed at everything. You waged lost battles. You created too much antagonism. You did not bring Israel even

one cent." In future, diplomacy would be conducted without such interme-
diaries (*Econ* 14 Nov. 1992: 27; *JP* 21 Aug. 1992: 5A).[20] He and his aides
said that open American Jewish criticism of Israeli government policy was
unobjectionable because it was irrelevant in Israel, and that American Jews
should redirect their charity to someone who needed it more (Goldberg
1996: 347–8; Rosenthal 2001: 120–1).

The repudiation was remarkable for its force, but it reflected Mamlakhtuit Zionist views of the diaspora. Neoconservatives who had urged and
enforced the Jewish *omerta* when that favored Likud now expressly repudiated that policy and publicly attacked Rabin (Podhoretz 1993). Rabin's policies were politically risky, and more nuanced and difficult to explain than
were Revisionist policies. Because Rabin had repudiated the most effective
element of the "lobby" and had not cultivated his natural allies, AIPAC and
the Presidents Conference were for a time paralyzed. Right-wing activists
meanwhile worked hard to discredit Palestinian spokesmen, block aid to
Palestinians and undercut the peace process (Goldberg 1996: 348–9).

Bush versus Clinton

On the day he announced his presidential campaign, Bill Clinton criticized
Bush for confronting Israel to delay the guarantees (JP 4 Oct. 1991: 2). He
thereafter claimed Bush had "all but destroyed the relationship" and "broken
the taboo against overt anti-Semitism." He condemned linking guarantees
to a settlement freeze (*JP* 1 Apr. 1992: 4). However, he also called the settlements obstacles to peace, supported the Madrid process and declined to
endorse moving the embassy to Jerusalem (Grossman 1994: 188). He sought
to attract Jewish voters by appealing to their distrust of Bush on Israel,
without adopting Likud positions or committing to future decisions as
president. Although Clinton's campaign staff included former AIPAC
general counsel David Ifshin, he intended to appeal to the Jewish community based on domestic issues as much as on the relationship with Israel.

Bush's supporters argued that his policies had greatly benefited Israel,
and attributed distrust of his administration to his having a "tin ear" or
"getting the tone wrong" (Daniel Pipes, in Pipes and Peretz 1992: 15–18).
Opponents could not guarantee what Clinton would do, but argued that
Jews should not vote for national leaders who were not committed Zionists
with true affection for the Jewish state (Martin Peretz, in ibid.: 19–23).
Bush, who had received 27 percent of the Jewish vote in 1988, won 7
percent of that vote in 1992; 78 percent voted for Clinton and 16 percent
for H. Ross Perot in what had to be a protest vote (Abramson *et al.* 1991:
125; Abramson *et al.* 1995: 134). Jews made up 75 percent or more of
Clinton's margin of victory in five key states; in two, Georgia and New
Jersey, they provided multiples of his winning margins (Goldberg 1996:
32). Bush had defeated Israel's greatest enemy, supported increased aid and
engineered the direct peace talks Israel had always claimed to seek. But he

was not trusted by those who put Israel first, and not supported by those who preferred progressive domestic policies.

AIPAC

AIPAC had threatened to work against Bush, and it and affiliated PACs did so. However, AIPAC had gained much of its new organizational muscle raising money from and for conservatives and Republicans. For some time, AIPAC was disoriented and defensive about its failed aggressiveness. It engaged in internal recriminations about mismanagement of the community's key issue and AIPAC's relationship with Israel. Many of the conditions that had determined outcomes were beyond AIPAC's control, but it was natural to apportion a major part of the blame to them, given their earlier claims of power over policy and their public dressing-down by the new premier.

There followed a year of turmoil, unaccustomed clumsiness and realignment. AIPAC President David Steiner was forced to resign immediately after the election when a tape of a conversation he had had with a prospective contributor surfaced; he had claimed that a dozen AIPAC people in Clinton's campaign would get "big jobs" and influence policy (Transcript 22 Oct. 1992 in *JPS* XXII, 2 (winter 1993): 161–4; *NYT* 8 Nov. 1992: 153). Tom Dine was forced out in June 1993 after a book about Orthodox Jews quoted him saying that they were "smelly" and "low class" (*NYT* 29 Jun. 1993: A10). The Rabin government then forced the resignation of vice-president Harvey Friedman after Friedman told Deputy Foreign Minister Yossi Beilin in the presence of three congressmen that Rabin had no right to trade territory for peace and later called Beilin a "little slime ball" (Melman and Raviv 1994: 457; Rosenthal 2001: 124; *JP* 5 Jul. 1993: 14). A board member of Americans for a Safe Israel protested the firing, arguing (probably correctly) that Friedman's views reflected those of most AIPAC members (*JP* 28 Jun. 1993: 6). Beilin said AIPAC was a right-wing group, more extreme than the "moderate, liberal, pragmatic" American Jewish public, and that it did not represent the Israeli government (*JP* 5 Jul. 1993: 14).[21]

Replacing Steiner as president was Steven Grossman, a Democrat active in the Clinton campaign and "prominent supporter of territorial compromise by Israel" (Grossman 1994: 189). Grossman wrote AIPAC members of a need for "change to meet new challenges and opportunities," and pride in AIPAC's "pluralism" and passionate support of the peace process (*NER* 19 Jul. 1993: 127–8). Rabin wrote Grossman that AIPAC was an important friend of Israel, and that one of its strengths was that it represented the diversity of the American Jewish community (*NER* 26 Jul. 1993: 131). Just after the Oslo accords were signed in 1993, Grossman met with Faisal Husseini, then leading the Palestinian delegation to the peace talks. He also proposed a Jewish–Arab institute to facilitate joint business ventures (Melman and Raviv 1994: 520). To some extent, AIPAC was "coming home" to the larger Jewish community and to the Labor and Democratic parties from which it had sprung. Steve Rosen survived the culling, however, and so long as the organization retained key hardliners and funding sources tied to the Likud and settlers, it would veer to the right as political conditions permitted. But to re-establish its effectiveness AIPAC had to deal through people who had credibility with Rabin and Clinton. Its public faces and positions were chosen accordingly.

Conclusion

The loan guarantee issue to fight provided a battlefield upon which the implications of substantial geopolitical and domestic political changes for U.S.–Israeli relations.

After the Cold War, allies were expected to foster peace in their respective regions. When Israel was perceived as being the obstacle to peace, that was "very dangerous for Israel and for the role of American Jews in American society" (Samuel Lewis, *NYT* 22 Mar. 1992: 1). American Jews did not trust Bush or Baker, but most believed in the moral and political necessity of land-for-peace, and they wanted the direct negotiations that would test that paradigm. No American politician would garner wide Jewish support explicitly espousing the beliefs of Yitzhak Shamir. There was an analogue in Israeli politics: when there was no credible Arab negotiating partner, even opponents of the Revisionist project would choose leaders on the basis of security. When an American president brought Arabs to the table, and identified the settlement polices as a major obstacle, the majority who favored a political solution would insist on an Israeli government that would participate fully in negotiations.

President Bush and Secretary Baker calculated issues of leverage and timing as Shamir did, which meant high-wire acts to perform at home and abroad; they achieved significant progress, but their success was limited by their operating methods and perceived attitudes. Israel's supporters feared that the president's initiative reflected cool calculation aimed at improving relations with Arab regimes, rather than an empathetic desire to solve Israel's long-term security problems. Bush could have argued that Israel's founding rationale and the basis of American support was that it was a democratic state where a Jewish majority could thrive; Likud settlement policy led either to a binational state or to permanent occupation and civil war, results no true friend of Israel could support (Yaron Ezrahi, *NYT* 19 Sep. 1991: A1). Without a peace process, the American relationship with Israel also might not survive the corrosive effects of occupation and dependence. Such arguments would have been totally ineffective with Shamir and AIPAC. However, they would have reflected widely shared beliefs and encouraged those of like mind in Israel and in the American Jewish community. The emotional component of the relationship was critical, and was neglected. Verbal gaffes exacerbated the problem. The result was not

policy failure, but unsustainable success, as Bush and Baker got little political credit for their achievements.

Guarantees that had seemed so critical and were so politically costly were
not used to absorb refugees. The governor of the Bank of Israel said there
was little need for the initial $2 billion tranche in 1993 (Neff 1994: 67).
Through 1995, Israel had borrowed $4.8 billion of $7.3 billion available
after offsets, and spent $2 billion on infrastructure projects, $1.3 billion on
power generation and $172 million for commercial bank loans (Mark 1996:
6). Russian immigrants were outraged that they were helped so little.[22]
American Jews paid little attention; those who did, like ADL's Abraham
Foxman, thought it sad that an issue that had set the governments against
each other and American Jews against their government was "ending with
such a whimper" (Sommer 1994: 48).

The Kennebunkport agreements also had little effect on the pace of settlement construction. In 1993, President Clinton offset $437 million in set-
tlement spending against the guarantees (Nowels 1995: ii). In its first two
years, the Rabin government completed 11,500 units and planned an additional 4,000 in the West Bank and Gaza, and completed an additional
13,000 and planned an added 15,000 in East Jerusalem. Settler population
increased by 28,000 in the Territories excluding East Jerusalem, and 50,000
including East Jerusalem (Aronson 1995: 99). In July 1996 Dan Meridor,
Finance Minister in a new Likud-led government, praised Labor for having
increased Jews in Judea and Samaria by 40 percent (Aronson 1996: 128).

AIPAC had not entirely lost its ability to reward and punish: Rep. Gus
Savage, sponsor of an amendment which would have eliminated funds for
resettling Russian refugees, was successfully targeted for defeat in 1992
(Frankel 1995: 155). But AIPAC had veered far enough away from its
domestic support base that it was vulnerable when beliefs could be tested in
negotiations. For a time, it lacked credibility when it claimed to speak for
the community on matters related to the United States' relationship with
Israel.

Congressional support for aid and strategic cooperation programs,
however, was still strong, based upon established rationales and electoral
politics, and the programs now benefited from powerful bureaucratic inertia.
AIPAC's credibility problems did not jeopardize the institutionalized web
of support that AIPAC had helped build. If anything, that infrastructure
was more secure, because both the outgoing and the incoming American
administrations had faith in Rabin's intentions.

10 Conclusions

The ultimate determinant in the struggle now going on for the world will not be bombs and rockets but a test of wills and ideas – a trial of spiritual resolve: the values we hold, the beliefs we cherish and the ideals to which we are dedicated.

Ronald Reagan

What matters most about political ideas is the underlying emotions, the music to which ideas are a mere libretto, often of very inferior quality.

Sir Lewis Namier

Time is the condition to be won to defeat the enemy.

Ho Chi Minh

Overview

Our two issue studies, AWACS and the loan guarantees, demonstrated the power of the presidency when circumstance and presidential will converged; what followed each presidential victory showed how highly conditioned that power was by domestic politics. We have shown the importance of the competition of beliefs, and the "causal pathways" by which principled and causal beliefs define default positions, become embedded in political institutions and thereafter mold policy choices.

The observed trend toward increased, unconditional and exclusive American political, military and economic support of Israel was most marked during the last six years of the Reagan administration. This ratcheting occurred for broadly the reasons posited: (1) diffuse, conditional but persistent popular support of Israel grounded in affinity with Israelis as Western democrats and cultural and moral siblings; Holocaust guilt and religious doctrine; and negative beliefs concerning Arabs and Islamists; (2) acceptance of Israel as a key strategic ally against the Soviet Union and sponsors of terrorism; and (3) increasingly effective coordination of a policy network and a system of electoral punishments and rewards by the pro-Israel community, led by AIPAC. The lobby reinforced beliefs about Israel and its regional adversaries, translated those beliefs into policy presumptions and succeeded in embedding those presumptions in law, programs and institutional structures.

And yet, key assumptions implicit in the core beliefs justifying unconditional support were seriously undermined in the years we examined. The policies and actions of Likud-led governments eroded the idealized image of Israel upon which broad support was based, spurred increasingly vocal dissent within the Jewish community and blocked a peace process increasingly seen as necessary to defend American interests and to preserve Israel's identity as a Jewish state and a democracy. When the Gulf War demonstrated post-Cold War reality, it was difficult to argue that Israel was a key strategic ally against foreseeable conventional threats. Israel had a role against terrorism and radical Islamists, but that role did not require support on a scale that assured impunity to Israeli governments, and Israel's impunity provided fodder for radicals. In the course of restructuring after AWACS, AIPAC had become identified with Likud governments and policies. After 1988, it did not have the unified support of the Jewish community, nor the access to the White House that had increased its effectiveness in the Reagan years.

Both the "special relationship" and the "strategic asset" pillars of the relationship were thus weakened, as was Israel's principal domestic advocate. These dramatic changes enabled President Bush and Secretary Baker to convene direct negotiations between Israel, Palestinians and Arab regimes, and contributed to the Likud's electoral defeat. However, the effect on the embedded presumption of unconditional support for Israel was essentially limited to the period 1990–1992.

Why such limited effects? The answer has to do with the nature and implications of the "diffuse, conditional support" of Israel in the Jewish community and the wider American society. AIPAC's power was derived from and dependent upon ideological and emotional ties of the wider community with Israel. AIPAC had accomplished a great deal in reinforcing beliefs about Israel, persuading the "issue public" and officials to apply those beliefs to specific issues, maintaining discipline within the Jewish community and developing the means to reward and punish elected officials. However, while popular and Jewish support of Israel against perceived existential threats was unconditional and unanimous, support of Revisionist policies on the peace process was not. The Revisionist agenda was inconsistent with beliefs about Israel held by most Americans, including American Jews. When peace negotiations were possible, testing Israel's willingness to compromise, a substantial plurality of the Jewish community would not follow AIPAC in supporting an Israeli government that rejected land-for-peace and constraints on settlements while demanding unconditional absorption aid.

However, this concurrence of geopolitical circumstances, ideological agendas, congressional issues and personalities was unusual, and fleeting.

When an Israeli leader said he would pursue negotiations and curtail settlements, unconditional support of Israeli policy was again consistent with broadly-held principled and causal beliefs; the rifts among the pro-Israel community, Israel and AIPAC could be bridged; and the president who had helped create the new conditions, but had coolly confronted an Israeli premier, was rejected by American Jews.

Several factors had the potential to reinforce or to limit the combined power of affinity and the lobby. The most important were: (1) presidential leadership, specifically beliefs concerning Israel and the skills required to turn beliefs into operative policy and institutional change; (2) the degree of unity within the pro-Israel community, determined importantly by whether there was a perceived opportunity for political settlement with the Arabs and Israel's response to that opportunity; and (3) chance – whether presidential leadership, global and regional geopolitics, and the degree of unity within the pro-Israel community became political force vectors all pointed in the same direction.

Presidential leadership

Reagan and Shultz: the "ripeness" doctrine at home

The emotion-laden beliefs of Ronald Reagan and George Shultz about Israelis and Arabs permitted the institutionalization of comprehensive and largely unconditioned economic and military support of Israel. Even after Israel's use of American-supplied arms evoked anger and anguish, Reagan and Shultz adopted programs that increased Israel's regional military advantage. Shultz's efforts at organizing a peace process confronted obstacles thrown up by all parties; however, none were more persistent or comprehensive than those from Shamir, who would not even cooperate in efforts to improve daily life for Palestinians. Yet the administration retreated from commitments made to its proposed interlocutor, King Hussein; and it would not publicly criticize Shamir for undercutting Palestinian leaders and then claiming to have no negotiating partner.

This pattern was certainly due in part to the AWACS imbroglio and the lost December 1982 fight over supplemental aid to Israel. The administration could not frequently ask its allies in Congress to vote against the lobby, and it lost credibility and effectiveness on other issues if it did so and failed. Such barriers seemed to grow exponentially in the years after AWACS, as AIPAC increased its power to set the terms of debate, and to reward and punish at the polls. There was a natural inclination to take political credit for strong support of Israel when that seemed to be the inevitable course in any event. There also appeared to be little strategic cost to steadfast support of Israel. Whenever there was a test, Soviet arms and vacillating support suffered by comparison with American arms and steadfastness. Moderate Arab states continued to cooperate with the premier superpower on oil and sea lane access. More fundamental than these political and strategic calculations, however, was the resilient affinity of Ronald Reagan for the Israel he imagined. In his memoirs, this strong emotional tie is all that remains of Reagan's defense of Israel. Reagan's feelings both limited and swayed George Shultz. In addition, Shultz was stung by Assad, was unconvinced of the dedication of Hussein to the perilous path of peace and found in Israel a partner matching his revulsion against terrorists. The resulting warm and sturdy support for Israel was communicated regularly to the lobby and the American Jewish community, and was reciprocated.

As Ross and Haass argued, "ripeness" for a peace process depended primarily on regional actors. But it separately depended on the American president and secretary of state. So long as Reagan and Shultz defined American policy, the time would never be ripe to put sustained, meaningful pressure on Israel.

Bush I and Baker: hearts and minds on collision courses

George Bush and James Baker did not share Reagan's emotional ties with or beliefs about Israel, and dealt with Israel as one part, sometimes the most difficult part, of a regional set of policy problems. They were willing to run political risks by confronting Israel in order to capitalize on an opportunity to realign relationships in the Middle East. Their effectiveness was limited because they disregarded domestic policy networks, public relations and the emotional element of the relationship with Israel. A majority of the American Jewish community undoubtedly agreed with Yitzhak Rabin that objectively, Bush acted in Israel's best interests by pushing for direct Arab–Israeli negotiations and forcing Shamir to choose between guarantees and settlements. They saw the Madrid conference as an historic opportunity, however fraught with risk, and greeted the election of Yitzhak Rabin with relief. Those results would have been unlikely without Bush's firmness. However, American Jews did not trust George Bush or James Baker, and preferred someone emotionally committed to Israel, even Clinton's foreign policy was unformed. AIPAC encouraged rejection of Bush in 1992, but most American Jews found it an easy choice: Clinton agreed with them on social issues, and they were sure that Rabin would seek peace without a prod from an American president.

The emotional component of the relationship with Israel – empathy with Israel as with a *real* sibling, overlooking past arguments and recent behavior – was critically important to explain both presidential policy choices and the political calculus of the pro-Israel community. When the emotional bond of a president to Israel was strong, there were few if any shackles on the uses made by an Israeli prime minister of power provided by the United States. Doubt about the fealty and motives of a president influenced the pro-Israel community more powerfully than AIPAC's efforts or the community's consensus belief in land-for-peace.

Factors determining the effects of domestic politics

The difference made by partners for peace

Nearly all American policy makers accepted that as to physical security: (1) Israel should have unquestioned capability to defeat any combination of potential enemies; (2) that goal required substantial American military assistance, and economic assistance to prevent defense costs from bankrupting Israel; (3) military assistance to states not at peace with Israel could not be allowed to risk Israel's margin of superiority; and (4) Israel had to respond to threats as it saw fit, since any defeat could end its existence. Hence, much of the AWACS debate was about whether the sale threatened Israel, or could be conditioned to avoid such a threat. The IDF's lack of concern, and believable assurances by Reagan that he would never allow Israel to be put at risk, were necessary conditions to Reagan's victory.

Core issues of the Arab–Israeli conflict – occupation of the Territories, Palestinian sovereignty, the Right of Return and borders – were also security issues. However, unlike war planning, which necessarily assumed hostility between Israel and its neighbors, these issues involved defining the conditions necessary or sufficient to a future peace, and thereby defining the nature of the future State of Israel and its relationships with its neighbors. The large majority of American Jews who were "conditional doves" saw the Camp David process as necessary to their image of Israel as a democratic, broadly liberal, pragmatic and tolerant society. The particularist, illiberal Revisionist vision of Israel was inconsistent with those mainstream American Jewish values. Most American Jews increasingly saw Likud policies as threatening either a binational state or perpetual oppression of Palestinians and radicalization of Arabs, necessitating indefinite American support of an increasingly unattractive Israel.

This chasm among supporters of Israel grew wider and deeper in the years we have studied. However, it had little impact on policies supported by the pro-Israel community so long as there were no credible Arab or Palestinian partners with whom Israel could be expected to negotiate. Facing hostility and terrorism, Israel would be supported whatever the ideological ambitions of its prime minister. Opponents of "land-for-peace" knew that they had to prevent negotiators from being seen as acceptable. Thus, opposition to arms sales to Jordan in 1985 and 1986 was not based upon Jordan's military threat to Israel, but on King Hussein's unacceptability as a partner for peace. Begin's angry retort to Reagan that it was "impossible" that security cooperation with Jordan would produce another Sadat would have been odd, given Israel's history of quiet cooperation with Hussein, except that Begin could not concede the appropriateness of any Arab interlocutor. Shamir was at least as adamant; he had quit Begin's government over the agreements Begin reached with Sadat. AIPAC persuaded Congress to condition arms sales on Hussein's first entering negotiations with Israel, knowing that the terms for entering negotiations set by Shamir would likely be impossible for the king.

Similarly, Shamir and AIPAC went to great lengths to prevent legitimization of Palestinian spokesmen, not just Arafat but Faisal Husseini and West Bank mayors. George Shultz, an old labor negotiator, understood the need to identify negotiators with genuine authority from those whose rights they would be negotiating. However, Reagan's prohibition against dealings with anyone identified with Arafat, and his unwillingness to confront Shamir, made it easy for Shamir to reject proposed negotiators. Shultz opened contact with the PLO in 1988 in the vain hope that Arafat would authorize others to take on the public role of representing the Palestinians. King Hussein had walked away from the role of interlocutor and cut ties to the West Bank. Assad had humiliated Shultz, and although Gorbachev had ended his dream of strategic parity with Israel, Assad had not yet signaled willingness to cooperate in a peace process. Saudi cooperation was still in the shadows. There were no qualified negotiating partners.

One result of the manifold changes during the first two years of the Bush administration was that Israel and its allies temporarily lost the power to reject negotiating partners. That was not because Israel owed a debt of gratitude to the United States after the Gulf War; Shamir did not believe that. Rather, it was due to James Baker's persistence in forcing parties to make public choices. Baker often spoke of the "dead cat" he would leave on the door of any party who identified himself as an obstacle to convening negotiations. That homely metaphor dramatized the political cost of rejecting American efforts to give parties what they claimed they wanted – an international conference for Arabs, and direct negotiations for Israel. For Shamir, the principal cost was facing the plurality of Israeli voters who would not tolerate a government that rejected a credible opportunity to negotiate. In addition, although Shamir seemed to think he could always cow diaspora Jews, he risked open revolt in the American Jewish community and the discrediting of AIPAC and key congressional allies. Shamir signaled in advance that he did not believe in territorial compromise, and apparently intended to draw the negotiations out while filling the territories with settlers. But he would not condition *attendance* at Madrid on unfettered guarantees, because he saw that it would demonstrate too clearly his unwillingness to negotiate final status issues.

The answer to the question of whether there existed at any given time credible negotiating partners for Israel depended on the beliefs and actions of political actors in Israel, the United States, Arab regimes and Palestinian groups. So long as Shamir was prime minister, his initial answer would be no; so long as that answer was accepted by the American administration, there was no way forward. Conditions after the Gulf War created incentives for cooperation by Saudi Arabia, Syria and the Palestinians, giving at least the appearance of an opportunity for meaningful negotiations. Bush and Baker had to be willing to force Israel to make public choices. That carried more political risk than Bush and Baker recognized originally, and was not handled well as a domestic issue. Without the express threat of the "dead cat" award, however, Madrid would not have happened. In the end, the most significant consequence of the administration's persistent efforts to pre-qualify parties for a peace conference was that Israeli voters did likewise: they elected someone who believed in negotiating a political settlement with Israel's enemies.

The singularity of the loan guarantees issue

What stands out most starkly about the loan guarantee issue is the rare convergence of elements that made it a potent tool: (1) the timing boxed Shamir in, and encouraged Bush and Baker. Soviet Jews were coming, and the need for absorption aid seemed massive and immediate. The issue gelled before the president's post-war popularity fell precipitously and election year calculations intruded. Sharon was raiding the Israeli budget to build settlements as fast as he could. Fissures were showing in the American Jewish community. The American population was impatient with foreign commitments. (2) Shamir's open intransigence made the stakes clear and compromise unattractive. Bush and Baker had learned from their 1989 experiences with Shamir not to trust vague assurances. The American Jewish community unanimously supported guarantees; a plurality agreed with a strong majority in Israel that Israel should freeze settlements to obtain guarantees. Shamir would not agree, not just to a freeze, but to any compromise that impeded settlement growth. (3) This was a request for a sizable new aid program. Bush and Baker would never have considered applying conditionality to existing aid programs, worth well over $4 billion a year. (4) The security threat to Israel was markedly lower than it had been in years, with Iraq defeated, Syria and Saudi Arabia cooperating openly with the United States and the PLO greatly weakened. That meant that negotiation, and Rabin, were viable political options to Israelis.

A different set of facts could conceivably produce a similar moment of opportunity and decision. However, in the history of U.S.–Israeli relations the 1973 war and Kissinger's shuttle diplomacy, and Sadat's initiative and Camp David are perhaps the only analogues. Each required regional catalysts and strong American involvement. The loan guarantee issue provided usable political leverage only because several very unusual conditions were present. Once Rabin was prime minister, both the reason to challenge the government of Israel and the ability of an American administration to do so evaporated.

AIPAC: the limits of advocacy

AIPAC had always seen its mission as securing the safety of Israel through American economic, military and political support that was increasing, unconditional and regionally exclusive. It claimed to leave to the government of Israel the question of what policies to pursue with the resulting unencumbered support. To achieve its mission, it had to have access to and credibility with the government of Israel, but could not appear to be Israel's unregistered agent. It had to have the support, or at least acquiescence, of the broader Jewish and pro-Israel community in order to speak with authority in Congress and the White House. It did not need, and did not want, instructions from either Israel or the Jewish community, but it could not long be fundamentally at odds with either and remain effective.

The AWACS fight showed AIPAC nearing the zenith of its power as a bipartisan, professional, Congress-based lobbying operation, geared to giving the incumbent government of Israel maximum freedom of policy choice. The AWACS sale could be framed as an issue of physical security for the Jewish state, and AIPAC had the unanimous support of the pro-Israel community and at least nominal support from the Begin government.

By the time of the loan guarantee request, AIPAC had grown more muscular, but had also changed in ways that weakened it for that particular fight. Seeking to empower the incumbent Israeli government always had the potential to identify AIPAC with Israeli policies that divided its American base of support. However, AIPAC had become visibly aligned with Revisionist goals, even when Labor led Israel. The loan guarantee issue, as framed either by Shamir or by Bush, did not directly implicate the physical security of Israel. Rather, it forced choices by Israelis and Americans in accordance with their beliefs about the peace process and the basic values of the Jewish state. The access and leverage developed within the Reagan White House, which depended on the beliefs of Reagan and Shultz as much as on AIPAC's demonstrated power, were gone. AIPAC's Rosen had stiffened the resolve of an already intransigent Shamir, crippling AIPAC as a deal maker.

Two conclusions can be drawn. First, even as effective an organization as AIPAC loses credibility and power if it diverges from its broad base of support on issues important enough to energize those supporters. Like Congress and the executive branch, AIPAC had undergone a process whereby beliefs became policy and policy became institutional presumption and structure. Tom Dine's organizational changes after AWACS made AIPAC more effective and powerful in the 1980s, but they also facilitated the takeover of his board, and eventually his staff, by people who devalued bipartisanship and held Revisionist beliefs. Those who disagreed, including Doug Bloomfield and the editors of the *Near East Report*, were forced out. Openings to Palestinians or Arab interlocutors, even if authored by an Israeli prime minister, were opposed. A minority of a minority – Cohen's "amoral Zionists" – were able to embed their beliefs and largely control the positions taken by AIPAC. There was no organizational check on the trend toward the Likud and away from the more universalist values that defined Israel for the broader American Jewish community.

Second, AIPAC's power found expression in economic aid, military assistance and arms sales. Those matters were subject to direct congressional control, and even economic aid (much of it used to repay defense loans) was seen by Congress as necessary to Israel's physical security and therefore essentially untouchable. Declarative presidential policy that did not depend upon appropriations – announcing a peace plan or recognizing the PLO – was difficult for the lobby or Congress to stop. Even in such cases, however, the administration often could not move the parties toward the declared goal (such as meaningful peace talks) because it could not or would not use appropriations or conditions thereon as leverage. The guarantee issue was the rare exception.

Historical impacts of the lobby's efforts

Impacts on policy, and on results

The lobby did not determine American policy toward Israel. Israel would have been favored over Arabs in any event, both because of widely-shared affinities and Cold War calculations by presidents starting with Richard Nixon. It is thus not possible to isolate with precision the effect the lobby had on the course of policy. However, when presidential initiatives were stillborn, cut back or abandoned, the principal reason was often congressional opposition, organized and enforced by the lobby. Ronald Reagan sought strengthened security relationships with Gulf Arabs, and sought to encourage and support King Hussein in negotiating Palestinian rights. Those efforts and others were repeatedly frustrated by Congress, and it seems highly unlikely the president would have been so constrained in the absence of the efficient advocacy and electoral power of the lobby.

It is harder to know how the consequences of American policy would have changed had presidential policy initiatives not been thwarted. That is primarily because so much depended on the reactions to American policy by Israeli and Arab leaders and populations. However, some judgments are possible. Preventing increased aid in 1982 would have signaled some limits to Israeli impunity, both to Begin and to other states in the region. Arms sales to Gulf Arabs would have built stronger regional security cooperation and confidence in American assurances, though it would also have energized Islamist reaction. Reliable support of Hussein probably would not have led to the negotiations called for in the Reagan and Shultz plans, but might have kept Hussein engaged in the West Bank and available as regional conditions changed to favor negotiations.

Most importantly, if it had been possible to sustain the conditioning of new aid on a settlement freeze, as George Bush and James Baker clearly preferred, a critical precedent would have been set. That precedent would have been much more important for the political signal it represented – regionally and within Israeli politics – than for the economic impact, which as we have seen was minimal. Long before Rabin was assassinated in 1995, everyone knew that the American government was acquiescing in the use of public and private American funds in an accelerating settlement and expropriation process. For Revisionists, who never believed in a peace that included Palestinian sovereignty over part of *Eretz Y'Israel*, American silence in the face of de facto annexation of East Jerusalem and large parts of the West Bank was all they needed. Israelis who did believe in land-for-peace, but conditioned on security that was never achieved, either (1) accepted the settlements as necessary interim security measures and negotiating tactics or; (2) opposed them but were politically emasculated by Palestinian violence and American acquiescence.

Was the lobby's impact harmful?

To the extent that the lobby's efforts empowered Israeli governments to accept or reject presidential policy initiatives, was that harmful to the interests of the United States? Obviously not, if one shares the beliefs of Revisionist Zionists and American neoconservatives; perhaps so, if one rejects those beliefs. I have not attempted to delineate where rational decision making has been compromised by beliefs that deviate from reality. It has been clear throughout, however, that the factual basis of some of the lobby's asserted beliefs was at best dubious; judgments about causal relationships were at a minimum debatable; and policy presumptions based on ethnic and religious affinities conflicted with declared American – including American Jewish – values and greatly complicated dealing with Arabs. Such flaws, however, do not demonstrate that the results in terms of consensus major American interests – preventing expanded Soviet influence, assuring access to oil and seaways, avoiding major conflict or accessing markets – were worse than they would have been had presidential initiatives relating to Israel faced no domestic obstacles. During the years under study, the obvious losers in the American policy debate were Arabs, particularly Palestinians.

The Palestinians were dispossessed in 1948 and 1967, and those remaining in the Occupied Territories have been oppressed in ways which are widely seen as illegal under international law and contrary to values perennially proclaimed by American leaders. A great power pays some price in credibility when it acts, or abstains from acting, in ways that contradict its declared commitments to justice and international law; but that price is often not obvious. Palestinian issues have been cynically used by Arab leaders and aspirants to leadership, from Saddam Hussein and Hafez al-Assad to Usama bin Laden, to further their own agendas. The Palestinians have been badly led, and some have reverted to the ugliest forms of terrorism. At least so long as Israelis believed that Palestinian sovereignty meant an Arafat-led state dedicated to the Palestinian Charter's revanchist goals, they would resist American pressure and support tough pre-negotiating positions. It is thus not possible objectively to prove either that consistent American leadership would have led to successful implementation of UNSCR 242 through the Camp David process, or that the realist kinds of

American interests referred to above would thereby have been significantly better served.]

The critical, and arguably harmful, achievement of the lobby was establishing the belief in Congress, and in administration officials, that a default position of supporting Israel's government carried no cost. It has carried costs in American credibility and in lost opportunities to test possible formulae for regional peace and stability. Unconditional support of incumbent Israeli governments to the exclusion of other possible partners crippled those partners and the peace movement within Israel. A default position of guaranteeing Israel's physical security but conditioning all other support on Israel's implementation of UNSCR 242 in accordance with American interpretations would have avoided many of those costs. The possible dividends were of great potential value. The United States would have been identified with all who would make concessions for peace, rather than with Israeli actions which in fact the United States (and its citizens) often did not favor. If Israel did reach peace agreements with Syria and Palestinians, that would have removed the issues as demagogic tools for other political actors, and Israel would have gained the psychic and economic benefits of peace. The United States would have had strengthened relations with Arab leaders and their peoples, and might have been in a much better position to prevent the first Gulf War. Even if no peace agreements had been achieved, some of these benefits would have accrued.

However, supporting the incumbent Israeli government was not a default position that resulted from a calculation of strategic costs and benefits to American interests. Rather, it was perceived as producing tolerable results given the domestic political costs of doing anything else.

Epilogue

George W. Bush – the war leader and the true believers

Overview

The more some things change, the more they stay the same. Everything changed when George W. Bush ("Bush II") became president: the president's beliefs and leadership style; the geopolitical situation (especially after 11 September 2001); the relative roles of neoconservatives, Christian Zionists, AIPAC and the lobby; and the personae and programs of Israelis and Palestinians. But America's policy quickly reverted to essentially unconditional support of Israel.

As Bush took office in January 2001, he made pro-Israel advocates nervous. His only major foreign policy speech had one brief reference to Israel, listing "peace in the Middle East, based upon a secure Israel" as a goal *after* that of advancing American interests in the Gulf (Speech 19 Nov. 1999).[1] His campaign had relied substantially on support from conservative Christians, but he received better support from Muslims than from Jews, who massively supported his opponent.[2] Devout conservative Protestants and conservative internationalists predominated among his most senior advisers; Jews and neoconservatives held second-tier jobs. The initial White House liaison to the Jewish community had little experience with organized Jewry (Foltin 2004: 36). For a year, the Middle East desk at the NSC went unfilled. Like his father, he had deep ties in the oil industry. Understandably, pro-Israel advocates feared, and Arabs hoped, that he would reprise his father's cool relationship with Israel.[3]

By April 2002, Bibi Netanyahu would tell AIPAC there had never been "a greater friend of Israel in the White House," and in October 2002, Prime Minister Sharon told Bush that Israel had never had "cooperation in everything" as with the Bush II administration (*WP* 23 Apr. 2002: A11; PC 16 Oct. 2002). The NSC Middle East position was filled by Elliott Abrams, a neoconservative opponent of Oslo, to the "serious consternation" of many in the State Department (*NYT* 7 Dec. 2002: A1). Although Bush became the first president to declare a future Palestinian state as his "vision," that statement and his later "Road Map" to final status negotiations were never matched by meaningful support of moderate Palestinian leadership or by sustained opposition to Israeli policies that undercut his "vision."

Several factors led this president to essentially unconditional support of Israel. As before, it is a story of competing beliefs and the access and influence of those who held them. Bush was a neophyte in foreign policy, but in terms of relevant beliefs and presumptions, he was not a blank slate. His religious faith predisposed him to empathize with Israel, reinforced his confidence and his tendency to see major decisions in binary terms, and led him to take forceful action against identified evils. Major decisions have turned importantly on his reading of the character of leaders with whom he dealt. His narrow political base and the leadership of Congress, disproportionately evangelicals and southern conservatives, have limited what he believed feasible. He has been intent on avoiding political "mistakes" his father made. Most of his principal advisers on national security affairs were apostles of force, who were in turn advised by neoconservatives.

These beliefs, presumptions and staffing decisions meant that the terrorist attacks of 11 September 2001 gave neoconservatives a clear field to advocate for policies they had long formulated: unilateral military action against hostile regimes and support of Israel as an ally against terrorists. Bush immediately proclaimed himself a war leader against terrorist evil. Thereafter every person, state and entity was judged in light of the goals of that war. Palestinians, particularly Yasser Arafat, blundered badly by repeatedly identifying themselves with terrorists; Ariel Sharon deftly cast Israel's actions against its adversaries as part of Bush's war. As Bush lost political strength, the war on terror became his sole viable political issue, and he saw Israel as critical to that effort.

Events in the Middle East had also changed the context for presidential decisions. The Oslo peace process had led to euphoria in 1993, Rabin's assassination in 1995, a somewhat frantic push in Clinton's last year and despondency, violence and distrust as Bush took office. Palestinian living conditions had deteriorated and settlement construction accelerated, particularly under Prime Minister Barak. A second, more violent, Palestinian Intifada began in late 2000 even as negotiations continued. For the first time, the Intifada targeted civilians in Israel. Prime Minister Barak was defeated in the Israeli elections that followed, reflecting voters' unease at Barak's tactics and bitter disillusionment with the Palestinians. Advocates of the peace process had neither a credible agenda nor an audience. President Clinton publicly blamed Arafat for refusing his "generous offer" and for turning to violence. Clinton dedicated the traditional Inauguration Day morning coffee with Bush to berating Arafat (Barnes 2006: 73–5).[4] Bush was already determined to distance his foreign policy from Clinton's; this recent history, and Clinton's warnings, made involvement in a peace process highly unappealing, and helped set Bush's face against Arafat.

Significant shifts in domestic politics had also occurred. In 1994, the Republican Party swept into power in the House of Representatives, and Ralph Reed claimed that 44 of 73 freshmen had close ties to conservative Christian groups (Friedman 2005: 220). Senior leaders including majority leaders Dick Armey and Tom DeLay were passionate Christian Zionists. AIPAC was still powerful, but its strength now depended importantly on Christian Zionists.

It is a complex picture, as always, and regional events and the president's (often conditioned) response to them changed the dynamics of policy-making and the results of policies chosen. However, the sidebars on policy were produced by the relative influence of domestic groups, and the beliefs that drove them.

Culture, faith and presidential leadership

Michael Lind argues that the differences between George W. Bush's presidency and his father's owe much to the culture in which George W. Bush was raised: Protestant fundamentalism, southern militancy and commodity capitalism, a "Texas Traditionalism" reflecting the Old South (Lind 2003: 76–7). Bush has said that to understand him, you have to understand Midland, Texas (Mansfield 2004: 28). However, while that culture identifies Bush's political base, it is a less accurate predictor of his personal beliefs; like Jimmy Carter (Aronoff 2006), Bush is frank to say that his faith guides his policy decisions.

Bush turned seriously to religion and away from alcohol only at the age of 40. He explains his faith in stories about other people of faith, particularly strongly masculine preachers and political leaders (Bush 1999: 136; Mansfield 2004: 156). He is not interested in theological abstractions. Joining his wife's Methodist church meant leaving the "ritualistic" Episcopal church, he said; "I'm sure there is some kind of heavy doctrinal difference as well, which I'm not sophisticated enough to explain to you" (Mansfield 2004: 54). Many conservative southern Protestants quote stern Old Testament prophets more than the gentle teachings of Jesus; Bush's public expressions suggest what C. S. Lewis called "mere Christianity," a tolerant, non-dogmatic faith based upon acceptance of Christ and a personal experience with God. His public rhetoric is ecumenical; he speaks often of the value of faith, but against measuring policy by a particular creed. Conservative Christians protested when Bush insisted that Islam is a religion of peace, or sent non-religious White House "Christmas" cards.

Bush's choice of faith parallels other important decisions: relational, pragmatic, simplified and neither introspective nor driven by overarching theory. There is no hint of pre-millennial beliefs in Bush or in his closest advisers (Hitchens 2003: 81). Similarly, in political terms he is not a classical realist nor a neoconservative. He sees his role as "decider" and motivator, not ideologue-in-chief. He relies on intuition about other leaders, "personaliz[ing] policy decisions beyond the limits observed by most of his predecessors" (Hoagland 2006).[5] The first president with a Masters in Business Administration, he acts in many ways like a corporate CEO, albeit one with an unusually moralistic sense of duty. His faith reinforces his natural confidence. He says it "frees" him "to try to do the right thing, even though it may not poll well," and to "not worry about what comes next" (Bush 1999: 6). One of his heroes is Sam Houston, an alcoholic who was baptized in several churches and who took unpopular stands in the belief that they were morally right and would be validated by history (Kengor 2004: 47–52).[6]

Bush has denied that his decisions are dictated or blessed by God, but he told preachers in 1999 that God wanted him to be president, and that something would happen so that the country needed him (Kengor 2004: 61–2). After 9/11, he spoke of being chosen by the grace of God (Duffy 2002).[7] His candid speeches make clear that decisions are consciously guided by his understanding of God's will. Where he believes God has spoken, he does not tolerate, or even recognize, ambiguity (Brookhiser 2003: 63). As a result, he is almost impossible to turn from announced policies, and is undeterred by mounting evidence of practical impediments, or by second thoughts of subordinates.[8]

Key policy principles are derived from Bush's faith. One is his conviction that there is good and evil in the world, and that faith obligates him to fight the evil (Remarks 7 Feb. 2002; Speech 1 Jun. 2002). A second is his belief that freedom is God's gift, which the United States must deliver. At Whitehall, Bush asserted that the "deepest beliefs" of the nation shaped its foreign policy, and that the United States and the United Kingdom shared a "mission" to spread freedom (Speech 28 Jan. 2003; Speech 19 Nov. 2003). This mindset makes it critical for advocates to identify their goals and their allies with "good" and "freedom" or "democracy," and those of opponents with "evil" and oppression. In September 2006, Bush sensed a "Third Awakening" of religious devotion in the United States, coinciding with the "confrontation between good and evil" that is the war on terror (*WP* 13 Sep. 2006: A5). He is not a conservative in the traditions of either Burke or Buckley; rather than standing athwart history and shouting "Stop!" he pushes insistently for change, corresponding to perceived moral and pragmatic necessity.[9]

The conservative southern Protestant culture from which Bush comes does define his narrow political base, which he and political guru Karl Rove carefully tend.[10] When Bush ran for Congress in 1978, he lost in part because his opponent turned Christian conservatives against him.[11] In 1992, his father assigned him to deal with Rev. Pat Robertson's candidacy in the Republican primaries; Bush II persuaded influential ministers that he was one of them and that his father could be trusted (Aikman 2004: 81–2; Mansfield 2004: 82–5). Nevertheless, Bush Sr. lost, and his son is determined never to give the Christian Right reason to abandon him. In campaigns for governor and president, he and Rove assiduously courted leading Christian conservatives. His 2000 campaign speech at Bob Jones University was a signal to extreme Christian conservatives that he identified with them (Lind 2003: 8). Asked in a debate to name the philosopher who had affected him most he answered, "Christ, because he changed my heart" (*WP* 14 Dec. 1999: A1). Some saw that as political pandering, but it was undoubtedly an honest answer from a believer who had read no secular philosophy, and it seemed genuine to born-again Christians.[12]

By 2000, the Christian Right had captured the leadership of the Republican Party in many states, and the demographic and political center of the party was in the south. Bush's victory relied upon a narrower base, both geographically and ideologically, than had his father's; Bush II won with fewer votes than Al Gore because of the overweighting of rural states in the Electoral College. The most devout believers voted for Bush II, including practicing Muslims (Abramson *et al.* 2003: 80; Frum 2003: 160).[13]

Bush's staffing decisions did not match his carefully nondenominational statements about faith. Vice-President Dick Cheney, National Security Adviser Condoleezza Rice, chief speech-writer Michael Gerson, Chief of Staff Andrew Card, Chief Political Adviser Carl Rove, Attorney General John Ashcroft and other key aides shared Bush's conservative Protestant faith. Many staffers came from major Christian Right organizations.[14] Perhaps 40 percent of Executive Office staff met in Bible study groups (Aikman 2004: 139). Gerson drafted the president's most important speeches without input from cabinet members as in previous administrations (Barnes 2006: 114–16; Woodward 2003: 30). Gerson is a "neo-evangelist" with a strong belief in the moral obligation to fight evil (Goldberg 2006: 63–4).[15] Being a person who shunned "detail work," Bush was dependent on a cadre of Christian conservatives and neoconservatives for his facts.

The Neoconservative Moment

Many key second-tier advisers to Bush were neoconservatives, and their neoconservatism had become more muscular. The founding generation of "neoconservatives" had consisted of perhaps two dozen public intellectuals, for whom neoconservatism was "a mood, not an ideology" (James Q. Wilson, in Gerson 1997: 15). There was always tension between deep skepticism that man could understand life's complexity well enough to design overarching government solutions to problems, and belief that morality required forceful state action against evil. Some neoconservatives who had focused on the Soviet threat sought a "return to normalcy" after the Cold War (Kirkpatrick 1990; Halper and Clarke 2004: 76).

Neoconservative leaders in 2001 consisted of a few hundred journalists, academics, policy institute analysts and government officials. Most were unabashed advocates of American hegemony and sweeping solutions to perceived threats. They argued that "present dangers" facing America began with flagging national will to change oppressive regimes (e.g. Kagan and Kristol 2000: 3–24). Most shared a strong commitment to Israel and several key beliefs: (1) the West was threatened by Islamist terrorism and weapons of mass destruction, both linked to certain authoritarian states;[16] (2)

democratization of the Middle East was morally required and strategically necessary to "drain the swamp" of radicalized populations; (3) multinational organizations were not reliable, so that defending and spreading "universal" values fell to the United States; and (4) unchallengeable American power, and the will to use it, were essential to these purposes, necessitating large defense budgets and doctrinal development to encourage use of the resulting arsenal. Neoconservatives had become a movement centered on force projection and the Middle East.[17]

Neoconservatives had been out of government since 1993, and had had little power then. They were busy, however, building arguments and advocacy networks. Paul Wolfowitz and I. Lewis "Scooter" Libby had drafted the 1992 Defense Planning Guidance (DPG) for then-Secretary of Defense Cheney that presaged the 2002 National Security Strategy. The DPG advocated military dominance to deter competitors and pre-emptive use of force (*WP* 11 Mar. 1992: A1). In 1996, William Kristol and Robert Kagan argued for "benevolent [American] global hegemony" and an active search for foreign "monsters" who threatened American principles (Kristol and Kagan 1996: 20, 31). That same year, eight Americans including Richard Perle and Douglas Feith prepared a report that advised Prime Minister Netanyahu to make a "clean break" with the policies of Oslo by, *inter alia*, striking Syria, seeking to oust Saddam Hussein, and generating an alternative to Arafat as Palestinian leader (Perle *et al.* 1996).[18]

In 1995, William Kristol founded the *Weekly Standard*, with funding from Rupert Murdoch. It quickly became the leading neoconservative policy journal, despite small circulation and operating losses (Halper and Clarke 2004: 187). It led a sizable phalanx of conservative and neoconservative media.[19] Foundations underwrote neoconservative think tanks. Cable television talk shows led by MSNBC and Fox companies raised profiles of neoconservative intellectuals. Conservative radio talk shows dominated that medium, and neoconservatives were welcome. Neoconservatives were still a tiny fraction of the Republican Party, much less of the nation as a whole, and yet they seemed to be everywhere.

In 1997 the Project for the New American Century (PNAC) published its Statement of Principles. Claiming the Reagan mantle,[20] PNAC urged increased defense spending, confronting regimes hostile to American values and meeting threats "before they become dire" (PNAC 1997). Twenty-five founders included six who would hold senior positions in the Bush administration,[21] two leaders of the Christian Right,[22] and Steve Rosen of AIPAC. PNAC urged President Clinton to "end the threat of weapons of mass destruction" by considering "military action" to remove Saddam (PNAC 1998).[23]

In April 2002, PNAC wrote President Bush that Israel was "fighting the same war" against "international terrorism" that Bush had declared after 9/11, and that the administration should treat the Palestinian Authority (PA) exactly as it treated al-Qaeda (PNAC 2002).[24] The letter was part of a successful effort to set the presumptions and lexicon of policy after 9/11: "International terrorism" was not a tactic, but an Islamist ideology comparable to communism or Nazism regimes were allies or targets depending on their relationships with those labeled terrorists; and Israel was an ally in Bush's war against evil.[25]

Not all PNAC members were neoconservatives, but all agreed on major points of the neoconservative policy agenda. Vice-President Cheney had signed the PNAC Statement of Principles, as had Secretary of Defense Donald Rumsfeld, Deputy Secretary Paul Wolfowitz and Elliott Abrams at the NSC. Cheney's powerful staff had status equal with the president's; it included neoconservatives Scooter Libby, David Addington, Eric Edelman, John Hannah and William Luti.[26] Working for Rumsfeld and Wolfowitz were Douglas Feith, Stephen Cambone, Dov Zakheim and Peter Rodman. Richard Perle was chair and Eliot Cohen a member of the Defense Policy Board. At State were Undersecretary John Bolton and David Wurmser. Bush told the American Enterprise Institute he had "borrowed" 20 of their minds for his administration; most were also PNAC members (Halper and Clarke 2004: 105). At the time of the 9/11 attacks, the vice-president's team and the Wolfowitz team at Defense had access to the president and were certain about what to do.

After the first term, neoconservatives lost some of their access and credibility, and began to fall out with one another.[27] The Iraq war had not gone as they had confidently predicted, and democratization carried risks in countries with authoritarian traditions and powerful Islamic movements. The vice-president's chief of staff, Scooter Libby, resigned to defend against criminal charges that he leaked intelligence to discredit critics of the Iraq war. He was replaced by counsel David Addington, an equally forceful advocate. However, Bush's trusted adviser and mentor Condoleezza Rice, a more traditional and cautious internationalist, became secretary of state and began to strengthen State's role. Paul Wolfowitz had moved to the World Bank, Douglas Feith had left government and John Bolton was exiled to the United Nations he had long denigrated. Long before these personnel changes, however, Bush had adopted the policy presumptions and lexicon of the neoconservatives as his own.

The Jewish community

American Jews in 2000 were still overwhelmingly progressives and Democrats. Bush received between 12–19 percent of the Jewish vote in 2000, and perhaps 19 percent in 2004 (Abramson *et al.* 2003: 99, 105–6; Abramson *et al.* 2006: 110). Even after 9/11, a *Jewish Week* poll showed that 85 percent wanted a more active role by the United States in brokering Israeli–Palestinian peace; 73 percent held that view even if it meant disagreement with the government of Israel (Massing 2002).

In the late 1980s and 1990s, more Jewish progressives turned from domestic social justice issues to Palestinian and peace process issues. Three such efforts were the Tikkun Community, Israel Policy Forum (IPF) and Brit Tzedek. Tikkun, founded by Rabbi Michael Lerner and including leaders from several religions, claimed some 5,000 members in 2003. It set out to break "the lock of AIPAC and the pro-Sharon forces on American politics" (*WP* 3 Jun. 2003: A16). It did not succeed. IPF was founded in 1993 with money from Hollywood and media leaders. It had ties with a number of congressmen, but no formal membership, fundraising or research staff; it was no match for AIPAC. Brit Tzedek tried to organize those active in social justice issues but inactive on Israel. It had perhaps 20,000 members in 2003 (Butler 2003: 258–9). While it undoubtedly had some success in educating those already inclined to its views, it could not change many minds.

Progressive Jews found advocacy of the peace process and the rights of Palestinians "incredibly harder" after 2000, for two reasons: (1) the second Intifada involved suicide bombers killing civilians in Israel, not boys in the Territories throwing rocks at tanks; and (2) the story of Barak's "generous offer," whatever its validity, was accepted as demonstrating that Arafat, or Palestinians generally, rejected key compromises needed for any viable final deal (Braine *et al.* 2003).

By the end of 2006, however, there was some evidence of growing cohesion among progressive Jewish groups and Israeli peace activists. IPF, the Jewish Alliance for Justice and Peace and the Religious Action Center of Reform Judaism joined former representative Paul Findley's Council on the National Interest in successfully urging changes to a pending Palestinian Anti-Terrorism Act. In its original form, as sponsored by AIPAC and core supporters such as Representative Tom Lantos, the Act would have essentially prevented American contact with the Palestinian Authority until Hamas was crushed or gave up violent resistance. In the fall, George Soros and Morton Halperin, chief of U.S. policy for Soros' Open Society Institute, began discussions with IPF and others aimed at forming and funding a progressive lobby as an alternative to AIPAC (Levey 2006). Israeli peace activists were playing increasingly prominent roles. One participant in the "Soros Initiative" was New America Foundation fellow Daniel Levy, former adviser to Prime Minister Barak and chief Israeli author of the Geneva Accords. Ori Nir, formerly with *Haaretz* and the *Forward*, took over the helm of Americans for Peace Now in late 2006.

This new effort to give effective political voice to the majority of American Jews (and Israelis) may suffer the same fate as earlier "AIPAC alternatives." Soros is linked with edgy leftist groups including MoveOn.org; that could impede efforts to build a broad and sustainable coalition. However, a combination of factors – AIPAC's legal and public relations problems, the novelty of committed funding and the recent political disarray of the Christian Right – could permit an alternative lobby to gain sufficient credibility as the voice of a real majority to give congressmen political cover for opposing AIPAC.

Meanwhile, the leadership of AIPAC and the Presidents Conference still favored the historic policies of Ariel Sharon, not his policy of unilateral withdrawal from occupied territory. Steve Grossman, president of AIPAC after the schism with Rabin in 1992, obtained a unanimous vote of his board supporting the Oslo accords in 1993, but the organization would not work for Rabin's policies as it had for Shamir's. In 1995, 93 senators signed an AIPAC-drafted letter urging the American Embassy be moved to Jerusalem, regardless of the status of ongoing negotiations. Thereafter, AIPAC persuaded Senator Bob Dole, a Republican presidential hopeful, to sponsor a Jerusalem Embassy Act, which overwhelmingly passed both houses in spite of opposition by both Clinton and Rabin on grounds it would damage the peace process (Massing 2002).

After 9/11, AIPAC recast all of its goals as ways it was "supporting the president's multi-pronged war on terrorism" (*JP* 7 Oct. 2001: 4). Howard Kohr, AIPAC's executive director, expanded staff dedicated to Congress and outreach to Jewish communities and campuses.[28] AIPAC's national paid membership grew to over 100,000, and key leaders of Congress and the administration continued to attend all AIPAC policy conferences.

AIPAC's director of research and principal executive lobbyist, Steve Rosen, and an associate, Keith Weissman, were indicted in August 2005 for receiving classified information from a Defense Department analyst, and were dismissed from AIPAC (*WP* 21 Apr. 2006: A1). The ongoing prosecution chilled relationships with sources in the executive branch. It did not measurably diminish AIPAC's support in the House, then led by Christian Zionists.

The largest members of the Presidents Conference, including the Conservative and Reform rabbinates, remained overwhelmingly progressive. However, they were regularly outvoted by small conservative and Orthodox organizations, and the long-time executive director, Malcolm Hoenlein, maintained control of the process of selecting Conference presidents. Rabbi Erik Yoffie, head of the large progressive Union of American Hebrew Congregations, did not attend board meetings, saying, "We're rarely consulted on anything" (Massing 2002).

Organized Christianity

Among Christians, fundamentalists and Zionists remained minorities.[29] Liberal Christian churches found issues of Palestinian rights and the peace process agonizing, but were loath to confront their old Jewish allies from the social justice campaigns. The Presbyterian Church (USA) was alarmed about Palestinian conditions, particularly those of Arab Christians. In July 2004 the Presbyterians voted to condemn the building of the Israeli security barrier, and to consider disinvestment from companies profiting from the occupation.[30] Organized Jewry promptly made the issue a test of interest in continued interfaith dialogue. While other churches, in particular the Anglican Church, considered disinvestment, the Jewish reaction chilled the movement, especially in New York (Clarke 2005: 50). In June 2006, the Presbyterian Church (USA) recast its divestment policy as one encouraging investment in peaceful activities (Pomerance 2006).

Among Zionist evangelicals, Ralph Reed had briefly made Pat Robertson's Christian Coalition more effective politically, networking thousands of conservative ministers and distributing tens of millions of "voter information" brochures before elections. By 1995 Reed was actively building bridges with AIPAC and other Jewish pro-Israel forces; Elliott Abrams said, "We [AIPAC] need Ralph Reed" (Friedman 2005: 220). The separate power of the Christian Coalition may have peaked with the 1994 Republican victory.[31] However, the movement had captured Republican Party leadership and groomed activists for executive branch positions.

Evangelicals outnumbered Jews, perhaps 60 million to six million, and the Christian Zionists among them were the least compromising advocates of maximalist Israeli positions. Falwell, Robertson and Franklin Graham joined neoconservatives in denouncing Islam as the ideological source of violence (Aikman 2004: 165). Evangelist leaders denounced Bush's Road Map and advocacy of a Palestinian state as contrary to the Bible (*WTimes* 18 Aug. 2003: A6). Increasingly, those who led the fight in the Congress were Republican Christian Zionists.[32] Majority Leader Tom DeLay, the most powerful member of the House, pledged to the Israeli Knesset in May 2003 that support for Israel would include opposition to Bush's Road Map, which he had already called "a road map to destruction," if it compromised Israel's security (Friedman 2005: 221–2; *NYT* 25 Jul. 2003: A1). Bush had to rely heavily on DeLay in order to achieve passage of any major legislation, making confrontation with him costly.

Religious Zionists converge

Jewish and Christian Zionists built coalitions starting in the 1980s, accelerating in the 1990s, after 9/11, and again after Sharon's Operation Defensive Shield in early 2002. A former Chicago ADL official, Rabbi Yechiel Eckstein, formed the International Fellowship of Christians and Jews (IFCJ) in 1983, and the Center for Judeo-Christian Values with senators Dan Coats and Joseph Lieberman in 1995. Substantial amounts were raised for the United Jewish Appeal. In June 2002, Eckstein and Ralph Reed founded Stand with Israel, "a sort of Christian AIPAC" (Eckstein, in Friedman 2005: 221). These groups had modest separate influence on policy, but they reminded Bush and Rove what "their" people believed. In addition, they raised substantial amounts of money for Israeli causes including radical settlers. IFCJ raised $40 million in 2003, most of which was distributed in the Holy Land (Chafets 2004). A similar group, Bridges for Peace, sent over $20 million between 1997 and 2002 (*BGlobe* 21 Oct. 2002: 6B). Christian Friends of Israeli Communities, formed in 1993, had "adopted" dozens of settlements by 2003 (*JP* 20 Sep. 2002: 6B).[33]

Walter Russell Mead calls the coalition of neoconservatives, right-wing Christians and Jewish supporters of Israel "Revival Wilsonians." In place of the progressive internationalism identified with Wilson and mainline churches, Revival Wilsonians rely upon American power and are hostile to global institutions. They see a linkage between American security and the spread of American values that is "on steroids." Many Israelis believe that a Jewish state can only express Jewish ideals if it first provides security; Revival Wilsonians argue that American values can be defended and extended only by unilateral American power (Mead 2004: 88–90). Revival Wilsonians either are, or instinctively identify with, security-first Zionists.

Bush and Israel prior to 2001

Prior to being president, George W. Bush had visited only three countries: Mexico, as governor of Texas, China, where his father was envoy, and Israel. The Republican Jewish Coalition, which supported the policies of Prime Minister Netanyahu, organized a trip for Republican governors in 1998 (Aikman 2004: 122–3). In his campaign memoir, Bush describes that trip as one of Christian–Jewish–Israeli fellowship (Bush 1999: 138–9).[34] It seems, however, that Bush formed lasting impressions of both Ariel Sharon and Yasser Arafat during the trip. Sharon took Bush on a helicopter tour, impressing him with the vulnerability of Israel. Bush told Sharon that belief in the Bible meant accepting "that extraordinary things happen," referring to Israel's accomplishments. He "bond[ed] strongly" with the tough-talking soldier-farmer (Aikman 2004: 122–3). Bush also met with and thanked the IDF pilots who had carried out the 1981 raid on the Iraqi nuclear facility at Osirak. An effort was made to set up a meeting between Arafat and Bush, but Arafat declined and then claimed that Bush had refused to meet him; that was "enlightening" to Bush (Barnes 2006: 80–1).

Bush may have come to the presidency believing that defense of the Jewish state is a duty to God. However, his later support for an eventual Palestinian state confirms that he did not hold dispensationalist beliefs, nor agree with Tom DeLay and Dick Armey that "Judea and Samaria" belong to Israel (DeLay) or that "Palestinians should leave" (Armey) (Lind 2003: 148). He personally experienced his father's problems with Israel's American sup- porters. Karl Rove counseled against the domestic risks of confronting an Israeli premier or dealing with an Arafat (Sipress 2002; Christison 2004: 47). Events in the first year of his presidency would, in his mind at least, add strategic and political reasons to favor Israel.

Bush as president: good (freedom and democracy) vs. evil (terrorist states)

The contrast in George W. Bush's foreign policy before and after 11 Sep- tember 2001 is stark. He ran for president as a modest conservative internationalist: engaged in the world, but with no plan to remake it. He defined his foreign policy almost entirely as "not Clinton's." American commitments abroad would be defined by vital interests; the American military would not be nation builders.[35] His major foreign policy speech focused on Russia and China; although he spoke of opposing "evil" and encouraging democracy, he emphasized that he would not "impose our culture," and would patiently work with those who did not share American values. His only mention of Israel supported Israel's security in the context of a peace process (Speech 19 Nov. 1999). He reflected the views of his foreign-policy mentor, Condoleezza Rice, who in a *Foreign Affairs* article set out the big-power realist principles on which a Bush administration would rely. Her only reference to Israel noted the need for defense cooperation in the context of the threat from Iran (Rice 2000: 61–2).

Like Reagan in his first term, Bush intended to focus on domestic issues, including a massive tax cut and "faith-based" social programs. The administration would distance itself from the Israeli–Palestinian conflict. There seemed little prospect of progress in any conceivable peace process, and regional violence presented no perceived threat to American interests, given cooperative Gulf oil states. However, neither the Gulf Arabs nor American Jews accepted this policy of benign neglect. Saudi Crown Prince Abdullah, someone Bush respected greatly, startled him by declining an invitation to the White House due to the lack of an American policy on Palestine. When he did visit the Crawford ranch in April 2002, Abdullah brought graphic footage of Palestinian suffering and bluntly demanded to know whether Bush would act to end their humiliation by Sharon (Telhami 2004: 97; *WP* 3 Jun. 2003: A1). Bush's May speech to the American Jewish Committee was coolly received, in part because Bush promised neither engagement in the peace process – the preference of most AJC members – nor support for Sharon's policies (Frum 2003: 250–3).[36]

The administration was divided on engagement in the peace process. The report of a committee headed by former Senator George Mitchell, who had been appointed by President Clinton to investigate the Intifada, became public the day of Bush's AJC speech. Mitchell's committee found "no basis" to conclude that the PA had intentionally incited a campaign of violence, found that both sides had failed to exercise restraint and recommended a settlement freeze and resumption of negotiations (Mitchell 2001). This "balanced" set of findings was seen by Israel's advocates as false and dangerous, but encouraged Colin Powell's State Department to admonish Israel repeatedly for aggressive military retaliation, and to propose a new American initiative. From April to September 2001, the administration's statements evidenced competition between advocates centered in the Pentagon and White House and those at State.[37] Bush attempted to placate domestic constituencies and regional allies by demonstrating concern without committing to decisive action.

The peace initiative proposed by State in mid-2001 would have committed the United States to a process intended to establish a Palestinian state within three years, defended by an international force (Frum 2003: 254). Repeated instances of Palestinian violence aided efforts to derail that initiative. President Bush, noting that the parties had quietly accepted Palestinian statehood in the context of final settlement, planned to refer to a future Palestinian state in a September 2001 United Nations speech (Kessler 2004: 176). In the meantime, Bush sent CIA Director George Tenet to seek a ceasefire and security cooperation between Israel and the PA.[38] The Tenet Ceasefire Agreement and Work Plan was announced 14 June 2001.

The speeches Secretary Powell and President Bush gave after 9/11 showed how swiftly policy shifted. Bush's 10 November address to the General Assembly still spoke of a vision of "two states, Israel and Palestine." But that language now followed this: "No national aspiration, no remembered wrong can ever justify the deliberate murder of the innocent. Any government that rejects this principle, trying to pick and choose its terrorist friends, will know the consequences" (Address 10 Nov. 2001). Nine days later, Secretary Powell mentioned the two-state "vision," but promised only to send Assistant Secretary Burns to the region and to have General Anthony Zinni consult on implementing the Mitchell Report and the Tenet Work Plan (Address 19 Nov. 2001). The priorities now were security arrangements, the cessation of violence and the "us or them" choice the president demanded of the world.

Bush's reaction to the 9/11 attacks proceeded naturally from his beliefs, but used the language of the Revival Wilsonians. Terrorism was a global ideology comparable to fascism, which must be fought in a war against regimes that fostered or harbored it.[39] Many claim credit for the key element of the "Bush Doctrine," that states harboring terrorists would be treated as terrorists.[40] However, it tracked PNAC policy prescriptions: to confront militarily and pre-emptively regimes hostile to American values that had the potential to injure the United States. The global enemy was "militant Islam" or "Islamo-fascism." Targeted regimes and organizations, including Hamas and Hezbollah, were all adversaries of Israel.[41]

Yasir Arafat clinched the case against himself. In October, Popular Front for the Liberation of Palestine assassins killed a hard-line Israeli minister, Rehavam Ze'evi, and Arafat thereafter refused to surrender captured suspects (*WP* 19 Apr. 2002: A1). Bush said the "despicable act" of assassination showed "the need to fight terrorism" (Stmt 17 Oct. 2001). Bush already thought of Arafat as the man who in 1998 had lied about him and in 2000 had rejected Clinton's "generous offer" in favor of violence. In meetings three days before Bush's speech to the United Nations, Prime Minister Blair portrayed Arafat as a necessary evil, someone who had to be dealt with; Bush increasingly thought him just evil (Woodward 2003: 297). Then, in January 2002, Arafat committed a mortal political sin: he lied in writing to Bush about his responsibility for the attempted smuggling on the vessel *Karine A* of 50 tons of arms from Iran. Oslo II prohibited the arms to the PA (Kaplan 2002). Arafat had insured he would be targeted for regime change.

Ariel Sharon seized the opportunity presented by Arafat's blunders. He accused Arafat of choosing "a strategy of terrorism" (*WP* 4 Nov. 2001: B1). Sharon and Bush began to discuss the shared challenges of confronting regimes that sponsored violence against civilians, even as Sharon moved tanks into Palestinian areas of the West Bank and blustered that Israel would not be Czechoslovakia.[42] At an NSC meeting, Powell said, "Sharon's behavior ... borders on the irrational" (Woodward 2003: 203). But of course it did not if he sought maximum freedom of action in suppressing violence, discrediting Arafat and avoiding a peace process in which he did not believe. Sharon welcomed General Zinni's efforts to coordinate security arrangements, while Arafat, unable or unwilling to control the armed factions that nominally reported to him, dithered and lost whatever remaining credibility he had.[43]

Events in the remainder of 2002 demonstrated how this dynamic would play out. The upsurge in terrorist violence and retaliation culminated in a suicide attack on a Passover Seder on 27 March in Netanya that killed 29 and injured over 170. Sharon responded with Operation Defensive Shield, a massive military incursion into West Bank Palestinian towns, including Ramallah, where the IDF imprisoned Arafat in his headquarters. Bush called Sharon, not to warn about legal or moral limits on Sharon's operations, but to give political advice: Sharon was making Arafat into "a hero and martyr again" (Aikman 2004: 147).[44] Bush did publicly call for Sharon to withdraw his forces, but soon backed away from any pressure on the Israeli premier, emphasizing instead Israel's need to defend itself (Remarks 4 Apr. 2002; Remarks 6 Apr. 2002). Bush sent Secretary Powell to the region to "spend [Powell's] political capital" on a ceasefire, but would not permit any American commitment that would make a renewed peace process feasible. Powell had to ask Arab leaders to denounce Palestinian terrorism while Arab populations were watching the destruction of Palestinian homes on television. Arafat would not cooperate, perhaps judging that being a martyr was more valuable than anything Powell could in fact deliver. Powell wanted to propose an international conference and security negotiations; he was ordered not to make such commitments by Rice. He was further undercut by leaks, attributed to Cheney and Rumsfeld, that the White House would rein Powell in for favoring Arafat (Woodward 2003: 323–5).

Political pressure to support Sharon grew. The White House received over 100,000 emails generated by the Christian Right protesting Bush's criticism of Defensive Shield (Zunes 2005: 75). Majority Leader DeLay said Bush should "support Israel as they dismantle the Palestinian leadership" (*NYT* 4 Apr. 2002: A10). In May, DeLay sponsored House Resolution 392, condemning Arafat and pledging increased support to Israel because "the United States and Israel are now engaged in a common struggle against terrorism."[45] Rove told Bush that "their people" thought the Israeli–Palestinian conflict was part of Bush's war on terror (Frum 2003: 259). Republicans and conservatives did favor Israel over Palestinians by wider margins than others (Moore 2002). Other polls taken while Operation Defensive Shield was underway, however, showed that only 17 percent of Americans thought of the Israeli–Palestinian conflict as a Middle East version of the war on terror (Telhami 2004: 43). Those were not the polls Rove followed.[46]

Bush actively protected Sharon. With Israeli and American approval, Secretary-General Annan announced a commission to investigate violence in Israel and the West Bank. When Israel then refused the commission access, the Bush administration supported Israel.[47] Even as Arab television continued extensive coverage of Israeli strikes on Palestinian towns, Bush referred to Sharon as "a man of peace" (*WP* 19 Apr. 2002: A1).[48] This statement was startling even to many of Israel's supporters. For many others, it confirmed that this president so identified Israel with what he once called a "crusade" against terrorism that he would never acknowledge moral limits to what Israel did.[49]

Bush thought it more likely Sharon would engage in meaningful negotiations if the Palestinians had a new government that was freely chosen and democratic (Barnes 2006: 68–9, 86–7).[50] Sharon's intelligence chief formulated, vetted with allies and Arabs, and sold to the Bush administration a plan to disempower Arafat. Bush announced the plan on 24 June 2002 (Halevy 2006: 213–14).

On 24 June, Bush promised to support "creation of a provisional state of Palestine," but only if Palestinians would first "embrace democracy, confront corruption and firmly reject terror." He called explicitly on the Palestinian people "to elect new leaders, leaders not compromised by terror," and repeated that "nations are either with us or against us in the war on terror" (Stmt 24 Jun. 2002). This combined Sharon's long-held goal of eliminating Arafat with Natan Sharansky's policy of "democracy before negotiation."[51] The announcement undercut Palestinians working for reform and Israelis, like Shimon Peres, advocating intensive diplomacy in tandem with the use of force (*NYT* 26 Jun. 2002: A1).[52] More violence, and more targeted Israeli assassinations resulting in civilian deaths, ensued. As conditions under occupation worsened, moderate Palestinians who could do so left the Territories (*NYT* 29 Jul. 2002: A1).

Bush's intended regime change in Iraq required Bush to placate Arab leaders. He assured King Abdullah, Crown Prince Abdullah and others who were concerned that Palestinian issues would be shelved, that he would "be involved in moving the Middle East peace process forward" (Remarks 4 Jun. 2003). For several months prior to the invasion, the administration negotiated, not with Israel and the Palestinian Authority, but with the EU, Russia and the UN Secretary-General (the Quartet), producing "A Performance-Based Road Map to a Permanent Two-State Solution to the Israeli–Palestinian Conflict" (Department of State 2003).[53] The Road Map was announced on 14 March 2003, seven days before Iraq was invaded; Condoleezza Rice emphasized that the Quartet expected it would be "implemented, not renegotiated" (Al-Jazeera interview 14 Mar. 2003).

The Road Map's life was predictably short and unhappy. It described three "phases": ending violence and building Palestinian institutions; creating a Palestinian "state" with provisional borders and limited sovereignty; and final status issues. Obligations in each phase were to be "reciprocal," performed "in parallel." The Quartet undertook to facilitate each phase and to determine when obligations were met and the next phase could begin. In each phase, parties were asked to make concessions intended to build confidence, but that also ceded leverage in later, more critical phases of the process. The Palestinians were to strip Arafat of authority, not just over negotiations but over much of the PA. The Israelis were to release territory and loosen security controls concurrently with the new Palestinian prime minister's "visible efforts" (not "successful efforts") to reform the PA and control terrorist groups. Even if both sides had fully accepted the document in good faith and the Quartet had remained forcefully involved, the formula was flawed.[54] In the event, Israel heavily conditioned its nominal acceptance, Arafat probably never really accepted it and the Quartet's involvement depended upon the United States, which was otherwise occupied.

New Palestinian Prime Minister Mahmoud Abbas announced that the PA accepted the Road Map without reservations (PC 4 Jun. 2003). However, it was soon clear that Arafat would not cede Abbas needed authority. Israel's cabinet, after a stormy session, issued 14 conditions on acceptance of the plan. They included a complete absence of violence before Israel had any obligations, insistence on the United States as sole monitoring authority and rejection of references to UNSCR 1397 or to Crown Prince Abdullah's March 2002 initiative as standards (Editors 2003). Many Israeli analysts saw Sharon's conditioned acceptance as irrelevant, as his actions in the Territories created the reality (Siegman 2003). Both sides carefully avoided steps that could not be reversed, creating a cycle of stutter-steps and retreats (*NYT* 17 Aug. 2003: 43).

Since the United States had imposed the Road Map on the parties, they sought negotiations with Bush rather than each other. Within weeks, both Abbas and Sharon were in Washington requesting presidential recognition of their efforts and pressure on the other side. Abbas said that Bush's vision could not be realized "if Israel continues to grab Palestinian land" and to build "the so-called separation wall on confiscated Palestinian land," among other things (PC 25 Jul. 2003). Sharon acknowledged that it had been "relatively quiet," but attributed that to Israeli efforts, and demanded "a complete cessation of terror, violence and incitement" and "full dismantlement of terrorist organizations" prior to any political process (PC 29 Jul. 2003). Bush praised both men and told neither of them he had violated his Road Map undertakings. By September, it was clear that Arafat was blocking Abbas; in October, he resigned, blaming lack of support by the United States and Israel. It is not clear that Arafat's intransigence could have been overcome, but it would at a minimum have required sufficient Israeli and American support of Abbas to improve the lot of Palestinians. Sharon had no interest in empowering a Palestinian leader; Bush would not confront Sharon.

Soon thereafter, Sharon apparently reached two conclusions: first, that he had established his place in Bush's pantheon of allies in the war on terrorism and, second, that indefinite occupation of the territories threatened Israel's security and its future as a democratic Jewish state. Sharon's plan, to withdraw settlers unilaterally from Gaza and complete a wall enclosing Israel and West Bank settlements, was bitterly opposed by a majority of his own party. Political vulnerability at home, however, constituted leverage in seeking support from President Bush.[55] By April 2004, Sharon had achieved truly remarkable concessions from Bush. In a presidential statement and letter to Sharon, Bush said the unilateral Gaza pullout was "real progress" toward Bush's "June 24, 2002 vision"; that Israel retained its right to "take actions against terrorist organizations"; that it seemed "clear" Palestinian refugees would have to return to Palestine, not Israel; and that "in light of new realities on the ground," including "major Israeli population centers," it was "unrealistic" to expect Israel to return to the 1949 armistice lines (Presidential Stmt and Letter 14 Apr. 2004).

These statements were historic: they stated American expectations as to final status issues in ways prior administrations had avoided; they applauded unilateral actions in lieu of negotiations, contrary to the Road Map and all previous frameworks; they sanctioned, seemingly without limit, actions taken against organizations denominated terrorist; and they accepted as inevitable that settlements long called illegal would be annexed into Israel, without even reminding Israel of its obligation to freeze their expansion. Sharon was understandably ecstatic, and thereafter ignored attempts by Bush or his State Department to soften or condition some of the statements.[56] This was the greenest of lights.

Events since 2004

Events since the 2004 green light have extended earlier trends. The death of Arafat in November 2004 gave hope of a reformed PA, but Abbas still faced great difficulty in curbing corruption and enforcing the monopoly of force that any nascent state must have. He received constant demands from Sharon's government, but little meaningful help. Bush was not willing to overrule Sharon's insistence that terrorists be crushed before other issues were addressed, and efforts to direct aid to the PA were stymied in Congress. In his second inaugural, Bush formally declared democratization – "ending tyranny in our world" – to be American policy (Speech 20 Jan. 2005). Promptly put to the test, he pushed Israel to permit, if not exactly to facilitate, a Palestinian election. That election brought Hamas to power. Bush then felt enormous pressure, from his prior rhetoric and from the Congress, to strangle the Hamas-led government. Palestinian life became even less bearable. Palestinians blamed Israel and the United States rather than

Hamas, whose charter promised an end to the Jewish state. Although Hamas succeeded in damping down violence against Israelis for over a year, a resurgence of violence was inevitable.

Sharon formed a new party, Kadima, to capture the Israeli plurality supporting his planned unilateral withdrawals and shed intransigent Likud Revisionists. After Sharon's stroke removed him in January 2006, his deputy Ehud Olmert bluntly stated his plans to withdraw unilaterally from parts of the West Bank. That probably limited the margin of Kadima's victory in March elections, but made his mandate clear and defined his program to the Americans. In their first meeting, Bush may have surprised Olmert somewhat by insisting publicly that negotiations be seriously attempted, but both men knew that Hamas would not quickly renounce its charter and that Abbas had nominal negotiating authority but little ability to deliver what he negotiated. Further, Bush had been so crippled politically by the war in Iraq and his failed domestic initiatives that the war on terror was his sole remaining claim to credibility; he could not push an Israeli premier to negotiate with a government led by a designated terrorist group. Negotiations would be paid "lip service" (David Makovsky, in *NYT* 25 May 2006: A10). Once again, Israel could claim that there was no credible negotiating partner.

Events in 2006 demonstrated that Bush would not object if Israel destroyed the two movements that exposed the risks inherent in his democratization initiative: Hamas and Hezbollah. By invading Lebanon to attack Hezbollah, Olmert was fighting an "axis of evil" (Syria, Iran, Hezbollah and Hamas) on behalf of the United States as well as Israel.[57]

The midterm elections in November 2006 swept the Democrats to power in both the House and the Senate. That did not affect congressional support of Israel. Democratic National Committee chair Howard Dean and incoming House Speaker Nancy Pelosi repudiated on behalf of their party the criticism of Israel found in Jimmy Carter's new book (Carter 2006; Forward 27 Oct. 2006 in Siegel 2006). Incoming chair of the House International Relations Committee Tom Lantos, a Holocaust survivor, was a principal co-sponsor of the draconian Palestinian Anti-Terrorism Act.

Conclusion

Bush's nature and elements of his faith inclined him strongly to identify the evil-doers responsible for 9/11, declare war on them and stamp them out. That predilection was reinforced and given substance by key aides, many of whom had long been arguing for unilateral military action against Middle East regimes identified as sponsors of terrorism. War was declared on terrorism as though it were twenty-first century fascism. Regimes were required to prove themselves as allies in two ways: forceful action against terrorists and development of democratic institutions. Arafat's Palestinian Authority failed both tests; Sharon's Israel successfully claimed full marks.

The occasional vacillation in the administration's statements and policies was the product of two phenomena: the early contest to set the presumptions and lexicon of policy for a president with no foreign policy experience; and the president's felt need from time to time to placate Arab and other participants in his war on terror. The political pressure on Bush from the "true believers" – the neoconservatives, Christian Right, AIPAC and their supporters in Congress – was always strong. Christian Zionists in particular had access, credibility and key spokesmen in Congress who could generate overwhelming support for a bill or letter drafted by AIPAC. Karl Rove would monitor that fervor and warn against confronting it. For the most part, however, the president did not require pressure. While he would talk about the "vision" of a Palestinian state, and describe steps to approach that vision, he would never force an ally in the war on terror to negotiate with Palestine leadership identified with terrorism. Even when the elected president of the Palestinian Authority publicly opposed terrorism, Bush would not confront Sharon in order to empower Abbas. As Bush's credibility on all issues except fighting terrorism evaporated, he could not have explained to his base why he would second-guess Israel, a key ally in that war.

Since 11 September 2001, the beliefs of Revival Wilsonians – neoconservatives and Christian Zionists – have predominated, and have insured support of anything Israel does, so long as it is done in the name of the war on terrorism. To the extent American policies – unilateralism, the invasion of Iraq, democratization of Arab societies or support for Israeli hegemony – are seen to fail, the political dynamic will again change. Either isolationism or multinational approaches may gain strength. Support of Israel is still unlikely to flag, for several reasons: (1) support of Israel is deeply embedded in Americans' religious faith, their politics and their government institutions; (2) the international costs of this exclusive support are not yet felt, or credited, by the vast majority of Americans; and (3) facilitating regional Israeli hegemony may still appear the best, or even the only available option, so long as Israel faces armed groups (Hamas and Hezbollah) dedicated to its destruction, an unstable Iraq, and a hostile, potentially nuclear Iran. As always, facilitating Israeli hegemony runs the risk of Israeli impunity. Israeli impunity often generates crisis. American presidents generally do not confront Israeli leaders when Israel is in crisis, even if that crisis is in good part the product of Israeli and American policy.

The more things change, the more they are likely to stay the same.

Notes

1 Explaining the extra-special relationship

1 Goldstein and Keohane distinguish their argument from those based upon cognitive psychological approaches (such as those by Jervis and Lebow), which demonstrate the ways in which beliefs vary from objective reality and compromise the "rationality" of the decision maker (1993: 6–7). Similarly here, we are interested in the impacts of ideas on policy rather than their psychological explanations or their objective deficiencies.

2 One function of ideology is to deal with uncertainty resulting from "cognitive limits on rationality" (George 1987: 1). Steven Krasner argued that after 1945, the United States turned from interest-based expansionism to often ideologically driven foreign policy, "non-logical" in Pareto's terms because often based upon misperception and lacking a clear end-means calculation (Krasner 1978). David Deese argued that policy was often "nonrational," but blamed that result on "domestic preoccupations" squeezing out "external realities" (Deese 1994). The difference may be less than appears, if among the "domestic preoccupations" one counts cultural affinities and ideological commitments.

3 Martin Indyk argued that Arabists moved to think tanks and established a false "conventional wisdom" that the Palestinian problem was key to regional stability and that Israel was the impediment to peace (Indyk 1988). Malcolm Kerr argued the opposite: that selective images and distorted histories, reinforced by charged language, created a "conventional wisdom" that Palestinians had no claim to a nation and that Arabs blocked progress toward peace (Kerr 1980).

4 This process is similar to that described by Walter Carlsnaes in his synthesis of structure–agency approaches, but limited to the domestic level of the "two level game" (Carlsnaes 1992).

5 These uses of beliefs constitute part of the dynamics of the bureaucratic politics model. That model describes foreign policy as "a result of bargaining among players positioned hierarchically in the government," where "the bargaining and the results are importantly affected by a number of constraints, in particular, organizational processes and shared values" (Allison and Halperin 1972: 43). The explanatory power of the bureaucratic politics model varies with (1) the forcefulness of involvement of the president; (2) whether key stakes for the bureaucracy (budget, structure and positions) are at risk; and (3) whether the success of a policy depends upon implementation by the bureaucracy (Art 1973). This study focuses on peace process, assistance and arms sales decisions. Those decisions were made almost entirely by the president and the secretary of state, as shaped by their beliefs and perceived constraints imposed by electoral and congressional politics. The model is accordingly of limited utility.

However, bureaucratic politics will be part of the explanation for disputes among departments and resistance to implementation of policies. In addition, the model is helpful in understanding the behavior of the bureaucracy when policies have become embedded over time, and in understanding how working relationships between American officials and Israeli counterparts, which were at first resisted, become institutionalized.

6 Unless otherwise noted, the facts concerning aid and other programs are taken from Sharp 2006, Migdalovitz 2006, the USAID Greenbook (1 Mar. 2006, updated through 2004) and the CIA World Factbook (updated 2 May 2006).

Congressional materials are set out in References, alphabetically by author in the case of Congressional Research Service papers (Mark, Migdalovitz, Nowels, Sharp), and otherwise by House and Senate, chronologically within each house. They are abbreviated in text cites by reference to the committee (i.e. HFAC is House Foreign Affairs Committee) or, in the case of CRS or staff reports published as committee prints, by reference to the subject matter e.g. CRS, Are We Committed?).

7 The CIA estimates Israel's GDP at $121.2 for 2005, so that aid amounts to a little less than 2 percent of GDP, or about $407 per Israeli citizen.

8 This means approximately $595 million spent with the Israeli defense industry in 2006; this feature is seen by many analysts as "the most valuable aspect of its assistance package" (Sharp 2006: 11).

9 The United States is Israel's principal trading partner, and Israel ranks about twentieth among U.S. trading partners.

10 One effect of this technological superiority is that Israel was in 2004 the eighth largest arms supplier in the world, which from time to time has generated disputes with the U.S. over unauthorized transfer of military technology to China and other states.

11 U.S. vetoes of resolutions are collected through October 2004 in Neff (2005). Lists of all vetoes are in United Nations 2004.

12 Geographically, Israel would fit in the Defense Department's Central Command, but political realities required that all DoD coordination be through the European command structure and limited to Mediterranean operations.

13 Realists would like to ignore domestic politics in seeking to explain a state's conduct in international affairs. Kenneth Waltz claimed that failure to look first to international structural factors led to misattribution of the causes of that conduct and to an infinite proliferation of variables for explanations (Waltz 1979). But if persistent domestic effects do substantially define a policy, failure to account for them will similarly lead to a fruitless search for structural variables as explanations.

14 Stephen Krasner defined it inductively as the policy preferences of central decision makers; that had its own utility in the context of his statist analysis, but recognized that a range of policies could reflect, or approximate, the national interest so long as they were consistent with goals shared generally in the society (Krasner 1978).

15 See, Zakaria 1992. Zakaria demonstrates the necessity of separating structural causes from domestic ones if the aim is to evaluate the causation of policy outcomes; and also that the relative power of the United States can explain both "slow learning" (e.g. the agonizing domestic process of reversing Vietnam policy) and the capacity to absorb the negative impacts of misjudgments.

16 Richard Herrmann effectively demonstrated that the concept of "national interest" lacked explanatory or predictive power by describing some of the results the model yielded in the Middle East (Herrmann 1994). He described four distinct positions, based upon how three consensus objectives of U.S. policy in the region (containing Soviet influence, protecting stable access to oil and defending

Israel's security) were prioritized and accommodated. The importance of the interests was conceded by all, but the policies drawn from them depended upon what principled and causal beliefs were held by the policy maker.

17 There is considerable but incomplete convergence of "globalists" and "strategic asset" advocates, and of "regionalists" and "strategic burden" advocates. Those who support Israel out of feelings of affinity (and who may not be globalists), but fear reliance on emotion or moral duty as a basis for long-term American support, are drawn to the concept of Israel as strategic asset. Globalists who fear Israel's ability to draw the United States into conflict, including historically many Defense Department officials, favor security guarantees and conditions on support.

18 Extending that logic, some argued that settlement of the Arab–Israeli conflict, implying the trading of land for peace, should not be a policy goal of the United States (Churba 1977: 104–7).

19 Advocates of this line besides Spiegel include Geoffrey Kemp, Eugene Rostow, Joseph Churba, Richard Perle, Elliott Abrams, Martin Indyk and Robert Tucker. All of those named gathered in the Reagan administration except Spiegel and Indyk; Indyk was at AIPAC from 1982 until 1985. Perle and Abrams have held positions in the second Bush administration.

20 The Israeli Labor Party opposed the 1983 Reagan strategic cooperation agreement because it was limited to cooperation against the Soviets.

21 These included Parker Hart, George Ball, Graham Fuller, Cheryl Rubenberg and Anthony Cordesman.✗

22 Presidents favor Hamilton's view of the presidency; academics favor Jefferson's model, involving party and popular control of government. Neither favors Madison's insistence on checks and balances.

23 The title of his book, *The Other Arab–Israeli Conflict*, reflects this: "Battling for hearts and minds of the American elite has been the true subject of the Arab–Israeli war for Washington" (Spiegel 1986: 394). Spiegel admits that the administration "could not ignore the forces it had inadvertently unleashed" in the 1981 AWACS battle (ibid.: 398), that constellations within the administration favoring and opposing stronger ties with Israel shifted at least three times (in part in reaction to fights in Congress), and that the administration could not prevent Congress from increasing aid to Israel at the end of 1982, rewarding Israeli intransigence. Other Spiegel conclusions are similarly belied by the evidence. He asserts that, consistent with a misguided fixation on resolving the Arab–Israeli conflict, every administration attempts an initiative in its first term. But there would have been no 1982 Reagan initiative had Haig remained secretary of state; he excoriated the plan.

24 Reagan and Shultz had been the first to marry strategic and idealistic elements in an American policy favoring Israel. The Bush administration in contrast was holding Israel at arm's length. Spiegel was satisfied strategic arguments could be forged; he was more concerned that the "special relationship" could not survive erosion in Israel's moral image.

✳25 Morgenthau said struggles between morality and power created three types of policy; realist (thinking and acting in terms of power, exemplified by Hamilton), ideological (thinking in terms of morality and acting to maximize power, exemplified by Jefferson and John Q. Adams) and moralistic (exemplified by Wilson) (Morgenthau 1989). Hoffmann argued that "power elites" and the "people" were bound by "common beliefs and feelings" based on, *inter alia*, moral imperatives of self-determination and peaceful change and an action-based pragmatism (Hoffmann 1968). Huntington argued that the historical consensus favoring Myrdal's "American Creed" of liberal, democratic, individualistic and egalitarian values created cognitive dissonance when the values were not realized and led to moralism, cynicism, complacency and hypocrisy (Huntington 1989). Christopher Coker found exceptionalism (a complacent and superior kind of isolationism) and exemplarism (a belief in the universality of American values that can foster hypocrisy or a reactive form of pessimistic isolationism), contrasted with redemptionism (an optimistic Puritanism that combined Weberian work ethic and proselytizing) (Coker 1989). See also, Stoler 1987 (the "mission concept" as a core idea in American ideology, based less on John Winthrop's Puritan "city on a hill" than on a belief that America was the Enlightenment's "first true child").

26 The Puritans called the land "Canaan," and until 1787 Harvard undergraduates were required to learn Hebrew. John Adams wished for "the Jews again in Judea an independent nation" (Grose 1983: 4–6). Throughout American political life, parallels with biblical Israel and God's favor upon it were claimed. In many cases, the language is romantic or nationalistic overstatement, and does not reflect literal belief.

27 Kennan was particularly acid, describing democracy as a dinosaur with "a brain the size of a pin," slow to understand threats to its interests, and thrashing about blindly when aroused (Kennan 1951: 59).

28 In 1950, Gabriel Almond described American mass opinion on foreign policy issues in terms of "mood swings," with no underlying intellectual structure. He later attributed the continued high level of indifference to foreign policy to the proliferation of interest organizations, giving the attentive public informal as well as elected representation, and to a failure of "the elites responsible for the formulation and conduct of foreign policy" to inculcate public responsibility (Almond 1962: xxii–xxvi, 231–42). His studies were written before the massive growth of lobbies and policy institutes, and the ideological stridency which accompanied those trends. Almond and Walter Lippmann developed the concept of an "attentive public," between the policy elites and the mass public. A useful additional concept is that of "issue publics," attentive and knowledgeable only on specific issues (Risse-Kappen 1991: 482).

29 Holsti and Rosenau have found public opinion to be relatively stable, rational and events-driven (Holsti and Rosenau 1990, 1993). Holsti believes that the public makes sense of foreign policy by means of simple, even simplistic, heuristics such as the number of American soldiers killed (Holsti 2002: 356).

30 His studies echo the writings of V. O. Key, who wrote that the public can provide the president a "supportive consensus," a "permissive consensus" or a "consensus of decision" (Key 1961).

31 Some argue that inherent or manufactured cultural bias, inaccurate perceptions of Israelis and Arabs and their values, lead to counterproductive or even morally bankrupt policies (Ghareeb 1983; Suleiman 1995; Said 1997; Christison 1999). *But* see Gerges (1999). Certainly some prevalent images were distorted if not false. Israel was not egalitarian for non-Jews, nor liberal in the American sense; and its "anti-communism" was a product of the Soviet alignment of Arab confrontation states more than of ideology.

32 The United States is a "penetrated political system," in which nonmembers of the national society can participate directly (in conjunction with the society's members) to mobilize support for goals (Rosenau 1966: 65).

33 Opinion within the American Jewish community was divided concerning the policies of Likud-led Israeli governments, and the propriety or necessity of public dissent from those policies. An important part of the self-assigned role of the lobby was to educate, monitor and discipline the public dialogue of the Jewish community. As AIPAC consolidated its control of the message to both executive and legislative branch officials, and "turned to the right," substantial rifts occurred.

34 Quandt tracked the cycles of policy initiatives against the electoral cycle, and documented substantial correlations (Quandt 1986b). Similar observations were made by Steven Hess, Cyrus Vance and Zbigniew Brzezinski (Vance 1983; Brzezinski 1985; Hess 2002).

35 Members do, however, often attempt, with or without executive sanction, to interject themselves in these functions under the guise of information gathering or oversight activities.

36 The paper was commissioned by the *Atlantic* in 2002 but was then refused publication. An abridged version ran in the *London Review of Books* in March 2006, and Dean Walt posted the full version on his school's website the following month. A restated version, reflecting the storm of criticism that met the paper, was published four months later (Mearsheimer and Walt 2006b). A book will come out in late 2007.

37 In their attempt to undermine the moral case for supporting Israel, the authors erroneously claim that Israeli citizenship is based upon "blood kinship" (it is not, although one must be Jewish to qualify under the Law of Return for automatic citizenship and rights of Arab citizens are in practice less than those of Jewish citizens). The authors quote David Ben-Gurion as favoring forced expulsion of Arabs from territory desired for the state of Israel; on that occasion he disclaimed expulsion as policy but said that the British should not be impeded if they brought that desirable result about. On other occasions he did frankly support "compulsory transfer" (Morris 2001: 253) and he made sure that those who were expelled could not return. Arguing against Israel's strategic value, the authors claim that the United States has a terrorism problem in large part because of the alliance with Israel, in that it motivated Usama bin Laden. The evidence indicates bin Laden was moved primarily by desire to expel the United States from Saudi Arabia; Islamist terrorism has been visited on many countries who do not support Israel. They also hold Israel responsible for the American decision to invade Iraq in 2003.

38 The authors have since asserted that Israel's incursion into Lebanon in July 2006 was planned by Israel and the Bush administration long before Hezbollah abducted an IDF soldier, a charge for which they produced no evidence (Schoenfeld 2006: 34).

39 Zalman Shoval, who served as Israeli ambassador to the U.S. twice in the 1990s, has said, "Israel didn't want the war in Iraq. Israel wanted the United States to turn to Iran" (Statement at United States Institute of Peace, Washington, 13 December 2006).

40 In doing so, Dershowitz himself relied on such discredited and tendentious works as Joan Peters's *From Time Immemorial* (2002).

2 The pro-Israel community prior to 1981

1 NCRAC was renamed the National Jewish Community Relations Advisory Council (NJCRAC) in 1963 and Jewish Council for Public Affairs (JCPA) in 1998. It will be referred to as NCRAC.

2 The AJC was the only major organization dissenting.

3 Auerbach argues that "dual loyalty" issues for American Jews involve Israel and liberalism, not Israel and America; liberalism defines them as Americans and Jews, making loyalty to liberalism less conditional than loyalty to Israel (Auerbach 1996: 348).

4 Goldmann, a veteran of Zionist struggles in Europe in the 1930s and 1940s, also was president of the World Jewish Congress and other organizations.

5 This is the received version. Klutznick claims credit for the idea, and does not mention any part played by Israeli officials (Klutznick 1991: 164).

6 Kenen insisted AIPAC "was not organized by the Israeli government" (Kenen 1981: 2). In a dust jacket blurb, Eban said "AIPAC is very much the fruit of Kenen's imagination." Kenen wrote, however, that "Israelis" were "looking for a lobbyist [to obtain economic aid]" and that Eban asked him to lobby the Congress. They debated having Kenen maintain registration as an agent of Israel, but decided against it (ibid.: 67–8). Registration carries legal limitations and political stigma.

7 Morris Amitay argued that AIPAC steered the government of Israel "through the treacherous waters of American domestic politics," rather than taking direction from Israel (Goldberg 1990: 54).

8 For example, the favorable AIPAC statement about President Reagan's initiative of 1 September 1982, quickly followed by Begin's rejection. See Chapter 6.

9 Rabin referred to the letter as "our achievement" in his memoirs (Rabin 1996: 263).

10 Kennedy said, "They really beat us over the head with this goddamned letter," and suggested that thereafter they should "all … talk to each other first before any of this singular picking-off stuff" (Tivnan 1987: 89). Senator Mathias regretted pre-emption of the consultation process; Senator Culver admitted he had "caved" to pressure (Mathias 1981: 993).

11 Bloomfield and a staffer drafted a briefing paper literally overnight for delivery to every member of Congress on the threat of the Iraqi nuclear reactor, having had no advance notice of Israel's June 1981 raid on Osirak (Bloomfield interview).

12 Weinberg, a Los Angeles developer, was president from 1976 until 1983, and thereafter retained power over the officers and the executive director until the middle of the 1990s.

13 Members were offended by Amitay's intrusion into the caucus process and his drafting of resolutions and scripts for hearings (Franck and Weisbrand 1979: 190). Abraham Ribicoff, a Jewish senator and Amitay's former employer, said that AIPAC's tactics did "great disservice to the U.S., to Israel, and to the Jewish community" (Curtiss 1982: 118).

14 In 1973, Roper began a series of polls tracking sympathies with Israel and Arabs. Between 1973 and 1981, sympathy with Israel fell from 47 percent to 39 percent; sympathy with Arabs rose from 7 percent to 10 percent, with some limiting sympathy to Sadat's Egypt. The ratio of support ranged from nearly 7:1 in 1973 to a still robust 4:1 in 1981 (Curtiss 1982: 208).

15 When national interests are debatable or in conflict, politicians seek to conform to settled concepts of ideology or identity, and "cognitive limits" define policy. When such support proves not demonstrably harmful to U.S. interests (Mansour's utilitarian, or *post facto* instrumental, explanation for U.S. policy), the behavior is reinforced (Mansour 1994).

16 Begin had been in the national unity government that accepted UNSCR 242 in 1967. Begin never included any part of the West Bank ("Judea and Samaria"), in the "land" that was subject to negotiated return. The Sinai was not in Begin's "ideological map"; Judea and Samaria were (Dine interview).

17 The Presidents Conference insisted: "Dissent ought not … be made public … the result [of public dissent] is to give aid and comfort to the enemy and to weaken that Jewish unity which is essential for the security of Israel." (Presidents Conference annual report, quoted in Curtiss 1982: 119).

18 Hertzberg estimated that established Jewish organizations included only half of the Jewish population. The unaffiliated included academics and third or later generation Americans. Until the early 1970s, the unaffiliated allowed activated Jews to speak for them (Hertzberg 1984: 156–7).

19 After Hertzberg offered to help, Rabin refused invitations to occasions where

Hertzberg would be present, which Hertzberg attributes to a Sabra disdain for diaspora Jews (Hertzberg 2002: 387–8).

20 Begin dealt with legislators. Dayan was more effective; he convened a "private rump session of the Senate Foreign Relations Committee" in 1978 to block arms sales to Saudi Arabia (Franck and Weisbrand 1979: 185).

21 Real differences between Labor and Likud policies were often small; Labor's Allon Plan for the Territories was based on security rather than Revisionist ideology, but did not offer appreciably better chances of a negotiated settlement.

22 The exception was Jimmy Carter, one reason the Jewish community was nervous about him. Except for Vice-President Mondale, no pro-Israeli or Jewish staff members had important roles in foreign policy (Bard 1991: 214).

3 Pro-Israel policy networks and the congressional playing field

1 Dallin and Lapidus distinguish essentialist, mechanist and interactionist orientations to the Soviet Union (Dallin and Lapidus 1987). The essentialist was "highly deterministic," and "define[d] the Soviet system as inherently evil" (ibid.: 200). Mechanists, or pragmatist conservatives, saw the Soviet threat as geopolitical and containable. Soviet expansionism was opportunist (a more Hobbesian than Manichean view). Interactionists/globalists/American liberals saw Soviet policy as reactive/defensive, capable of learning through engagement. See also, Bell 1989: 11–13.

2 "A Time for Choosing," 27 October 1964, in Reagan 1983: 39–57.

3 Some in the administration challenge the political taxonomist. CIA Director William Casey was not a Westerner, but was a Western conservative if he fit any category.

4 Two survey series have been done periodically using standardized methodology and issue sets: the Chicago Council of Foreign Relations (CCFR) surveys, done every four years beginning in 1974, and the Foreign Policy Leadership Project (FPLP) surveys, done every four years beginning in 1976.

5 Black civil rights activists claimed that Jewish teachers and administrators were preventing local (Black) control of public schools, driving a wedge between the long-time partners.

6 Many neoconservatives insisted that they had not renounced their liberal values, but that those values – including nondiscrimination – had been perverted.

7 Eugene Rostow, a Committee co-founder, wrote in *Commentary* that failure to protect Israel "could spell the end not only of the Atlantic alliance, but of liberal civilization as we know it" (Rostow 1977: 46).

8 Reagan appointed Jeane Kirkpatrick permanent representative to the United Nations after reading her 1979 *Commentary* article. Other appointees included Norman Podhoretz's son-in-law Eliot Abrams (three posts in the State Department), Richard Perle (assistant secretary of defense), Eugene Rostow (director of Arms Control and Disarmament Agency), Kenneth Adelman (same); Max Kampelman (arms control negotiator), William Bennett (secretary of education), Richard Pipes (Soviet affairs in the NSC) and many others (Dorrien 1993: 10, 11).

9 In Genesis 12: 3, God tells Abraham, "I will bless those who bless you, and the one who curses you I will curse," and in 12: 7 says, "To your offspring I will give this land." Similar statements are found in Deuteronomy and Joshua.

10 "Evangelical" churches emphasize the authority of Scripture and teach that "salvation is achieved by personal conversion to faith in the atonement of Christ." "Fundamentalism" refers to belief in the inerrancy of the Bible, both as moral guide and history (Anderson 2005: 105).

11 "The Christian Zionist does not have to rework the ethical arithmetic all over when bad news appears ... [T]o prefer the blessing of Israel above all passing

things ... cannot, by definition, ever be incompatible with the will of God" (Merkley 2001: 218).

12 Others included Pat Robertson, Jim Bakker, Jimmy Swaggert, Kenneth Copeland, Richard De Haan and Rex Humbard.

13 A total of 24 percent self-described as moderate Protestants; 25 percent were Catholic, a recent increase resulting from Hispanic immigration (Fabian 1988).

14 Dine later hired a Christian Zionist to liaise with evangelical organizations.

15 The ability of Congress "independently to create and criticize policy" was given impetus by "the breakdown of policy consensus, the erosion of the notion of executive competence, [and] the shock of widespread illegal activities" (Haass 1979: 6).

16 Congressional staff grew from 11,700 in 1968 to nearly 20,000 in 1980; 100 senators had 7,000 aides, many of whom were "Senate Resolution 4" aides, independent of the committee chief of staff (Cohen 1981: 121; Franck and Weisbrand 1979: 231).

17 The notice requirements of the bill became Section 36(b) of the 1976 Arms Export Control Act (PL 94–329).

18 Presidents always asserted that legislative vetoes were unconstitutional. In 1986, the Supreme Court ruled that congressional reversal of presidential actions required two-thirds votes in both houses.

19 Prominent targets of AIPAC had held key assignments: Senator McGovern (chaired the Foreign Relations Subcommittee on Near East), Senator Percy (chaired Foreign Relations) and Representative Findley (ranking member of subcommittee on the Middle East). In each case, there are alternative explanations for their losses. For others, active opposition by AIPAC added to the difficulty of their campaigns and to the unattractiveness of their committee assignments.

20 The amount a PAC could give was later raised to $15,000. Each person could also give $20,000 annually to a political party, and unlimited amounts to issue campaigns so long as efforts were not coordinated with a candidate's campaign.

21 Fulbright was a registered lobbyist for Saudi Arabia and UAE (Franck and Weisbrand 1979: 181). His expertise and access, including to staff he had hired, were no match for AIPAC's network.

22 They controlled the Senate for the first time since the 1960s; with southern conservative Democrats, Republicans had a functioning majority in the House (O'Neill 1987: 408–9).

23 Speaker O'Neill was astonished that his liberal base overwhelmingly insisted that he "give the president's programs a chance" (O'Neill 1987: 412).

24 Ashraf Ghorbal, who represented Egypt during the Carter years, was an exception, as is Prince Bandar of Saudi Arabia, the dean of the Washington diplomatic corps for over a decade (Handyside interview).

25 Responding to Reagan's handwritten note, Edwin Meese directed his staff to work with the Treasury and Justice departments to seek tax exemptions for schools that discriminated on the basis of race. The resulting political furor, unforeseen by the politically blinkered Meese, was fierce. James Baker was irritated; Michael Deaver lied to cover the president. See, Brownstein and Easton 1983: 660–2.

4 Ronald Reagan: beliefs and policies

1 Unlike presidents before and since, Reagan did not publish a formal national security policy. He defended the lack of specificity by saying they knew where they were going, and that it "might be counterproductive to make a speech about it" (Kegley and Wittkopf 1982: 224).

2 There are suggestions that in this, as in many things, Reagan romanticized his involvement (Dallek 1984: 21–4). See also, Wills 1987: 231–40.

3 See, e.g. Suleiman 1988; Shaheen 1997; Christison 1999; Shaheen 2001.

4 Reagan also overturned established American policy that Israeli settlements in the Territories were illegal, because "the U.N. resolution" left the area open to all people (Docs & Stmts 79–82). It is not clear whether Reagan accepted Eugene Rostow's arguments on legality (Rostow 1979) or whether he meant that Jews should be able to live anywhere. The latter view, which ignored Israel's programs to promote Jewish settlement and its prohibition against return of Arab refugees to their homes, was later a mantra of Reagan and Shultz.

5 Secretary Haig stated in his first news conference that, given Soviet involvement, "International terrorism will take the place of human rights in our concern because it is the ultimate abuse of human rights" (PC 28 Jan. 1981 in DoS Bull Feb. 1981: J).

6 Reverend Jim Robison, whom Reagan invited to give the opening prayer at the 1984 Republican Convention, has said, "Any preaching of peace prior to [Christ's] return is heresy; it's against the word of God; it's Anti-Christ." (Halsell 1989: 16).

7 After his presidency, Reagan confirmed his understanding of the Armageddon prophesies, consistent with Lindsey's book (Cannon 1991: 288–9).

8 When Churba accused Reagan of abandoning Israel he quoted the 1979 article (Churba 1984: 28–30). Churba opposed settlement of the Arab–Israeli conflict, as territorial compromise would weaken Israel; he described the PLO as a terrorist proxy of the Soviet Union (Churba 1977: 104–7: Churba 1980: xiii). Campaign adviser Robert Tucker had also understood that the peace process would be finessed (Tucker 1981: 29, 31). Geoffrey Kemp, who took the NSC Middle East desk, voiced doubt about the wisdom of territorial compromise "just as those assets are growing in value" (Mansour 1994: 25).

9 He defended the "right of settlements in the West Bank"; said that an undivided Jerusalem meant "sovereignty for Israel" over the city; and doubted he would allow negotiation with the PLO even if they embraced UNSCR 242 (Safire 1980).

10 Richard Neustadt concluded that Reagan "combined less intellectual curiosity ... than any President since at least Calvin Coolidge ... with ... more convictions independent of events or evidence, than any President since at least Woodrow Wilson ... this peculiar combination exaggerated every risk to which a President is heir by virtue of imperfect information" (Neustadt 1990: 269–70). Other academics agreed: Reagan was "clearly the most ignorant" and "laziest" president since Hoover, although a political genius (Geir Lundestad, in Kyvig 1990: 156); a "simplistic ideologue" (James Tobin, in Mann 1990: 20).

11 E.g. the impossibility of simultaneously slashing taxes, increasing defense spending and maintaining fiscal discipline, or the scientific improbability of the Strategic Defense Initiative.

12 The worst, and nearly fatal, example of presidential non-involvement was the Iran-Contra scandal, when NSC staff ran a separate foreign policy that violated both announced policy and the law.

13 Reagan once read from the cards for the wrong meeting (O'Neill 1987: 360).

14 Geoffrey Kemp said: "This is what we couldn't understand. He'd come in ... and not say anything. Not anything" (Cannon 1991: 401).

15 Weinberger shared this group's strategic views, but dissented on the strategic value of Israel.

16 E.g. Anthony Dolan worked for Casey during the campaign and maintained ties to him at the CIA. He wrote Reagan's critical addresses to the British

parliament (6 June 1982) and to evangelicals (the "Evil Empire" speech, 8 March 1983) (Lagon 1994: 109).

17 At Defense, Undersecretary Perle, Undersecretary Ikle and Assistant Secretary Armitage; at the NSC, Constantine Menges, Donald Fortier (deputy under Poindexter) and John Lenczowski. Menges also maintained close ties to Casey (Menges 1988).

18 Wolfowitz had advocated that Carter rely on Israel for RDF bases (Kupchan 1987: 136). In 1981, he advocated telling Prime Minister Thatcher that the U.S. was prepared "to rid ourselves of the burden imposed by the myth of the Palestinian problem" (Evans and Novak 1981).

19 Michael Ledeen (positions at State, Defense and the NSC) and Howard Teicher (NSC) used Israeli connections in the Iran arms sales; Stephen Bryen was Perle's deputy.

20 Thus Meese and Clark served as "courts of appeal" for those trying to block initiatives seen as diluting Reagan's anti-communist policies (Menges 1988).

21 Abrams, the son-in-law of Norman Podhoretz and Midge Decter, served as assistant secretary of state for human rights and then for inter-American affairs.

22 Such accusations of disloyalty often served as cover for personal agendas, or exaggerated Reagan's dedication to neoconservative principles, or both. Some subjects of discord, such as Secretary Weinberger's extreme reluctance to deploy force, were institutional in origin. In some cases, including Haig, Allen and arms control director Eugene Rostow, difficult personalities exacerbated policy differences and made working relationships tortuous.

23 The one cabinet-level neoconservative was U.N. Ambassador Jeane Kirkpatrick; Haig and Shultz excluded her. Neoconservatives otherwise were limited to the third and lower levels.

24 Haig made his relationship with the Troika clear to Cannon: "Do you think I give a s*** about guerrilla warfare with a bunch of second-class hambones in the White House?" (Cannon 1991: 195). After Haig offered to "make that island [Cuba] a f***** parking lot," Deaver prevented Haig from meeting privately with the president (ibid.: 196–7).

25 Assistant Secretary Burt said the administration wanted "to handle the Arab–Israeli question … in a strategic framework that recognizes and is responsive to the greater threat of Soviet expansionism" (Testimony before HFAC subcomm 23 Mar. 1981 in DoS Bull May 1981: 66). Arab leaders told Haig during an April 1981 tour of the Middle East that cooperation against the Soviet Union was no more important than movement on Arab–Israeli issues. Haig thereafter spoke of the need to deny the Soviets opportunities by addressing the Arab–Israeli dispute (Statement before SFRC 17 Sep. 1981 in DoS Bull Oct. 1981: 13–14).

26 Possible reasons include awaiting Israeli withdrawal from the Sinai in April 1982, and giving priority to "strategic consensus" efforts. The Israelis may have feared Reagan was hoping for Israeli elections and a Labor government; Foreign Minister Shamir pressed to resume the talks (*NYT* 24 Feb. 1981: A3).

27 Meese told Shultz that Reagan would have been ready for a peace initiative in 1981, "but Al Haig kept the Middle East away from him" (Shultz 1993: 90).

28 Haig blamed conflict with Clark and Kirkpatrick over the Falklands (Haig 1984: 298). Cannon pointed to a fight with Clark over instructions to Ambassador Habib in Lebanon (Cannon 1991: 200–3). Destler said it was a fight with Clark over the Soviet pipeline and Haig's deals with European allies (Destler *et al.* 1984: 231). Quandt said it was Haig's handling of the war in Lebanon (Quandt 2001: 252).

29 Asked what sources of information were important to him in deciding how to proceed in the Middle East, Shultz begins with impressions of people: an especially gifted student who was one of the first killed as a tank commander in the

1967 war made him ponder what a remarkable country Israel was; talented Palestinian professionals who subcontracted for Bechtel taught him something about the Palestinian people; Prime Minister Shamir's willingness to trust him in attempting to put together his 1988 peace initiative touched him deeply (Shultz interview).

30 Examples include overruling his own panel of experts on whether to tie evacuation of the PLO from Beirut to engagement of the PLO in the peace process; pursuit of the Israel–Lebanon treaty of May 1983 on Israel's terms and without consulting Syria; and denying Yasser Arafat a visa to address the United Nations in 1988.

31 He told senators the president had directed him the day he was sworn in to give high priority to the Palestinian issues (GS Testimony SFRC 10 Sep. 1982 in DoS Bull Oct. 1982: 5). He and Reagan agreed that leaving the peace process until Lebanon was resolved "would leave us in a quagmire and encourage opponents of the peace process to prolong Lebanon's agony" (Shultz 1993: 38). That is however what Shultz then did.

32 White House neoconservatives resented Deaver for allowing Shultz such regular access (Menges 1988: 372). Menges even argues that LTC Oliver North and ADM John Poindexter's depredations in Iran-Contra imitated Shultz's conduct of policy-making in private meetings (ibid.: 378).

33 Casey may have inspired arms dealings with Iran by NSC staff because of legal constraints on the CIA. Shultz hotly opposed the approach to supposed Iranian "moderates." When the sales became known, Casey urged Reagan to replace Shultz with Kirkpatrick, "to assure loyalty to the president and his policies" (Anderson 1990: 351).

34 Asked if the report was true, Shultz says only that he was advising Reagan on economic issues, not foreign policy. However, he also says, "I made a big effort to try to understand President Reagan, and I agreed with him philosophically across the board. And I came to agree with him on the Middle East. We had back and forth on that." Asked if he shifted to agree with the president, he says, "Probably" (Shultz interview).

35 During 1981, 14 papers requiring presidential decisions were held by Meese (Cannon 1991: 189). Told that officials could never discern the status or location of their action items, Meese responded, "Exactly. That's the way we like it" (Destler *et al.* 1984: 227).

36 Assistant Secretary of State Chester Crocker described Clark as a "savvy political fighter" who "saw the permanent bureaucracy as thwarting the Reagan dream of leaping over intellectual constructs to a simpler time" (Lagon 1994: 107).

37 Shultz wanted pragmatist Donald Rumsfeld to replace Habib.

5 The AWACS sale: testing beliefs and political capabilities

1 The package was to include conformal fuel tanks (CFTs) to increase the F-15's range; seven tanker aircraft; an upgraded Sidewinder air-to-air missile, the AIM-9L, which allowed head-on destruction of attacking aircraft; and aerial surveillance aircraft.

2 This section is based largely upon the following: SFRC Staff Report; CRS, Congress & Foreign Policy 1981; CRS, Arms Sales Consultations; and Cordesman 1984: 193–330.

3 Carter added 15 F-15s to 25 already committed to Israel, and offered 75 attack-oriented F-16 aircraft.

4 Robert Tucker, Reagan's campaign adviser, had advocated military intervention in the Gulf to protect Western oil interests; his articles fed Saudi fears (Quandt 1981: 56, n. 15).

5 Israeli reports that the Saudi monarchy was unstable, attributed to the CIA, led Saudi Prince Turki al-Faisal to demand expulsion of CIA station chief George Cave (Cordesman 1984: 261). Opponents of the AWACS sale said the expulsion proved the Saudi monarchy was not trustworthy.

6 The first AWACS would be delivered in 1985; Americans were expected to be onboard the aircraft until at least the mid-1990s. American ground personnel would be involved throughout the program.

7 Loss of the guidance and seeking technology in the AIM-9L Sidewinder was a larger concern.

8 He wrote in his diary that he was "disturbed" by the ferocity of AWACS opponents because "it must be plain to them, they've never had a better friend of Israel in the W.H. than they have now" (Reagan 1990: 412).

9 Some thought that Saudi funding of more moderate PLO factions was useful, e.g. in persuading the PLO to join ceasefires in Lebanon (SFRC Staff Rept: 7–8; Cordesman 1984: 7, 34–5).

10 Haig acknowledged that Saudi Arabia desired comprehensive peace, and that the Fahd plan implicitly accepted Israel's existence (SApp Hrgs: 69–70; Haig interview 29 Oct. 1981 in DoS Bull Dec. 1981: 27).

11 Dine suggests that he could have made a deal for controls on the sale sufficient to allow it to pass (Dine interview). As we will see, controls added under public AIPAC pressure would have been rejected by the Saudis.

12 Israel suppressed news of Saudi cooperation in the rescue of an Israeli gunboat, for fear it would make the Saudis look moderate (*NYT* 7 Oct. 1981: A6).

13 Former Defense Minister Weizman said that unarmed AWACS aircraft were no threat to Israel and could easily be shot down (Ball and Ball 1992: 213). Deputy Defense Minister Zipori hysterically alleged the system would expose "all of Israel's secrets," but former air force commander General Binyamin Peled called the AWACS "buses" that were "practically defenseless" against Israel's air force (*NYT* 17 Mar. 1981: A6).

14 Senators Church, Javits, Stone, Bayh, Nelson, Durkin, Tallmadge and Culver had lost, many to "New Right" Republicans.

15 Reagan Presidential Library documents are cited "RRPL," with designation of the collection, box and serial number.

16 Document and transcript collections were periodically published by the Department of State until 2001 under various titles: U.S. Department of State Dispatch (cited "DoS Dispatch"), American Foreign Policy Current Documents ("AFP") and U.S. Department of State Bulletin ("DoS Bull"). Documents made public by the State Department under the Freedom of Information Act are cited "DoS FOIA" with such other identifying information as is provided with the document. Private publications include Foreign Policy Bulletin ("FPB") and the document section of each issue of *Journal of Palestine Studies* ("*JPS*"). A large and growing collection of interviews with American diplomats by the Association for Diplomatic Studies and Training is cited as "Frontline Diplomacy."

17 Organized labor may have influenced Senate Minority Leader Robert Byrd (Bloomfield interview).

18 There was a "National Christian Congress on Israel" demonstration two weeks before the Senate vote. However, it had no major evangelical participation, and negligible impact.

19 Reagan bitterly noted that after the vote Israel, "in a message apparently dictated by Begin, denounced the administration for anti-Semitism and betrayal" (Reagan 1990: 415–16).

20 Defense expenditures were 40 percent of Israel's GNP. Foreign debt of nearly $20 billion and debt service of $3.2 billion were projected for 1981, and inflation of 134 percent for 1980 (HApp Hrgs, Part 3: 329).

21 USAF pilots wrote Rep. Lantos against sale of Sidewinders, fearing technology compromise (HApp Hrgs, Part 7: 76–80).

22 David Saad of the National Association of Arab Americans (NAAA) was even challenged as to whether he could represent Arab-Americans; the chair began to cut him off after one-third of the time Dine had taken (HApp Hrgs, Part 3: 488–93). AIPAC represented power, and NAAA did not; and AIPAC had provided scripts from which to question adverse witnesses.

23 Retired General George Keegan testified AWACS was "invulnerable" in Saudi airspace, from where it could (1) detect tanks moving 25 miles per hour, hundreds of miles away; (2) detect Israeli air movements at Israel's "neck" and (3) direct attacks of Saudi F-15s (HApp Hrgs, Part 7: 20–6). No American or Israeli expert shared Keegan's judgments.

24 The numbered assertions are based on SFRC Hrgs, Part 1: 56–60 (Gen Jones); SFRC Hrgs, Part 1: 122–5 (GAO Report); SFRC Hrgs, Part 2: 53–6 (MG Secord); SFRC Hrgs, Part 1: 221–43 (Cordesman); and Cordesman 1984: 947–75, and authorities cited.

25 Senator Moynihan accused Saudi Arabia of responsibility for a statement of the nonaligned movement that "might as well have been written in Moscow," and referred to the Saudis' "implacable hostility" to the peace process (SFRC Hrgs, Part 2: 9–10).

26 The powerful chair of House Appropriations, Rep. Dan Rostenkowski, said he favored the sale but feared Jewish wrath (*WP* 25 Oct. 1981: C8). Rep. Long, co-sponsor of the resolution of disapproval in the House, said, "Long ago I decided that I'd vote for anything AIPAC wants. I didn't want them on my back" (Findley 1985: 38).

27 Senate Minority Leader Byrd's 9 April letter to Haig received no substantive response until September. Byrd appended the letter to his floor speech venting his frustration and explaining his vote against the sale (Cong Record 21 Oct. 1981: S11756–65).

28 He said Saudi Arabia had been constructive on the peace process until Camp David; history would judge whether "disruption" of Saudi cooperation was a "result of American incompetence and mismanagement of the problem," or "something deeper" (SApp Hrgs: 37).

29 Haig's memorandum is still withheld on national security grounds. Undersecretary Buckley testified that negative consequences included (1) doubts about U.S. commitments; (2) diminished Saudi participation in regional U.S. strategy; (3) less Saudi moderating influence on other Arab regimes; (4) a "major setback" to a U.S. framework against Soviet inroads; and (5) greater threats to Israel, as Saudis bought arms lacking safeguards for Israel, Arabs were more vulnerable to Soviet penetration, and the peace process suffered from loss of Saudi leverage (HFAC Markup: 43–4).

30 Begin later said that "one could surmise" there was linkage from conversations he had with Robert McFarlane (Ben-Zvi 1984: 37). White House staff recommended a public statement implying linkage between strategic cooperation and AWACS if not "strict conditionality" (RRPL, OA 11216, AWACS, Baroody Memo 15 Sep. 1981).

31 Bandar became military attaché in 1982 and was ambassador from 1983 to 2005. His vast estate abuts the Central Intelligence Agency; Dutton confirms a *Wall Street Journal* report that "when Prince Bandar calls for a Central Intelligence briefing, the analyst comes to him" (*WSJ* 22 Oct. 1981: 1; Dutton interview).

32 Dutton says he was not aware of any effort to coordinate corporate lobbying (Dutton interview). Steven Emerson says that negotiations on pending deals with American firms were suspended from 5 October until the vote (Emerson

1985: 191). Emerson, a former SFRC staffer, testified the sale was a "purely political deal without strategic or military justification" (HApp Hrgs, Part 7: 44–8; see also Emerson 1982).

33 Mobil Oil ran full-page advertisements in over two dozen periodicals stressing economic ties with Saudi Arabia and their impacts on employment and the dollar; AWACS was not mentioned.

34 Saudi cooperation extended beyond the Gulf to efforts against Soviet-backed insurgencies in Angola, Latin America and the Horn of Africa; Reagan had domestic reasons for not publicizing that.

35 Majority Leader Baker rejoined, "I don't want any **** secretary of state running the Senate" (*WSJ* 2 Oct. 1981: 1).

36 Reagan later insisted his statement was directed at all foreign governments, but it clearly was aimed at Israel and was seen that way. The *New York Daily News* headline for 2 October was typical: "BUTT OUT: Raps Jewish Anti-AWACS lobby." The *New York Times* editorialized that Reagan's remarks had "repugnant implications," seeking to blame the "Israeli lobby" for a likely defeat (*NYT* 4 Oct. 1981: E18).

37 Hyman Bookbinder wrote Jack Stein that he resented being seen as "something less than a loyal, committed American" while the Saudi royal family were encouraged actively to support the sale; he feared anti-Semites would be encouraged (RRPL, OA 5456, Letter 2 Oct. 1981).

38 Robert Asher predicted Reagan's statement would "serve to rekindle and fan the flames of anti-Semitism here" (RRPL, OA 9242, Misc Memos, Letter 5 Oct. 1981). Similar letters were sent by Kenneth Bialkin and Edward Levy.

39 The Arms Export Control Act allowed presidential waiver on certification of an emergency. Waiver authority was also arguably available under the Foreign Assistance Act and under Article II of the Constitution. Robert Kimmitt concluded that waiver was appropriate for this sale (RRPL, Box 90090, Memo 26 Oct. 1981). Reagan assured Senator Exon that he was "not considering any statutory waiver provisions regarding these sales" (RRPL, FO 003–02 043999, Letter 26 Oct. 1981). He never expressly ruled out such consideration.

40 They included former secretaries Kissinger, McNamara, Laird, Richardson and Brown; former national security advisers Gray, Bundy, Rostow, Scowcroft and Brzezinski; and former chairmen of the joint chiefs Lemnitzer, Taylor and Moorer. Former secretaries Rogers, Schlesinger and Rumsfeld signed the joint statement but did not attend the White House meeting. Several former officials would not join the statement, including former secretaries Rusk, Muskie and Vance.

41 Jepsen said "highly classified" information shared with him by Reagan persuaded him that the sale presented no credible threat to Israel (*NYT* 28 Oct. 1981: A14). His hometown paper, however, quoted a White House source as saying, "We stood him up in front of the grave and told him he could jump if he wanted to" (*DMReg* 30 Oct. 1981: 1A). The unnamed official, Ed Rollins, was called "drunk with hubris" within the White House (RRPL, Dole files, Box 4, AWACS, Blackwell Memo 2 Nov. 1981).

42 Senator Cranston said: "We have heard senator after senator explain in great and persuasive detail why they believe the AWACS package is a bad mistake. Then we have heard the big 'but.' But, they say, despite the evils of the package ... the Senate must support the Commander-in-Chief" (Cong Record 28 Oct. 1981: S12450).

6 The metamorphosis of the lobby, 1981–1988: strength and division

1 Menachem Begin or Yitzhak Shamir was prime minister in all but two years of the period 1977–1992.

2 Dine was given an appointment the day after the vote with Senate Majority Leader Baker (Tivnan 1987: 161). The following week, Assistant Secretary of State Fairbanks called Dine and Bloomfield to his office for a post-mortem. He praised their campaign, and added, "no one else could have come as close to beating a popular president on his first ... foreign policy vote as you did" (Bloomfield interview).

3 Douglas Bloomfield calls the colored pencils and maps "probably the most important thing that came out of [AWACS]" (Bloomfield interview).

4 The effort was particularly effective in the southwest. Eight of 12 senators from that region had voted for the AWACS sale. By 1985, nine of 12 opposed a proposed sale to Jordan, and seven of 12 opposed a sale to Saudi Arabia (Smith 1988: 227).

5 The study argued that Israel's strategic value derived from geostrategic location, political stability and reliability, and technological superiority; and that reliance on Israel and pre-positioned American materiel there would multiply force effectiveness, reduce costs and deliver a "swing force" usable in Europe or throughout the Middle East. "Political costs" of Arab opposition would be "containable if handled firmly"; Arabs already assumed the U.S. was in "a strategic alliance with Israel" (Rosen 1982: 12).

6 In 1985 Indyk became founding executive director of the Washington Institute for Near East Policy, a policy institute funded by AIPAC President Larry Weinberg. Indyk advised Democratic presidential campaigns in 1988 and 1992; he served in the NSC from 1993 to 1995, as U.S. ambassador to Israel in 1995–1997 and 1999–2001, and as assistant secretary of state for the Near East in 1997–1999.

7 Doug Bloomfield thought Rosen's lengthy monographs largely useless with Congress, and Rosen ignorant of the legislative process (Bloomfield interview).

8 Examples are in *JPS* XV, 1 (Fall 85): 114–17.

9 The *Wall Street Journal* found that 80 pro-Israel PACs gave over $6.9 million during the 1986 cycle (*WSJ* 24 Jun. 1987: 1). Pro-Israel PACs took names not identified with Israel and avoided publicity, making compilations approximate.

10 "A" notes that while contributors cannot be tracked by race, religion or ethnicity in FEC reports, they can be tracked by postal code. When an Alabama candidate's money comes disproportionately from Brooklyn, New York, inferences can reasonably be drawn.

11 Paul Findley, ranking Republican on the relevant HFAC subcommittee, had met with PLO leaders; he "was defeated after his politically little-known opponent received $104,325 from 31 Jewish PACs" (*WSJ* 26 Feb. 1985: 1). Both Senator Percy and his opponent, Paul Simon, believed that coordinated Jewish giving was important (ibid.). Rep. McCloskey was defeated in a 1982 Senate campaign where his criticism of Israel was an important issue. Senator Jepsen was defeated with the help of at least $110,000 from pro-Israeli PACs (Curtiss 1990: 59).

12 In 1986, Rep. Tom Daschle's successful Senate campaign against a Lebanese-American incumbent received $229,480 in pro-Israel PAC money: $91,000 was given by the PACs and their principals to the state Democratic Party (*WSJ* 24 Jun. 1987: 1). The amounts, very large for South Dakota, came almost entirely from outside the state.

13 The law allows unlimited individual spending that is independent of candidates' campaigns. The allegation was that Michael Goland had financed a media campaign against Percy for his friend Amitay. Goland was later convicted of campaign law violations in other campaigns.

14 AIPAC was an "information-gathering group ... [that] doesn't touch political money." He talked with PAC leaders, but only "as activists. I don't know them as the head of a PAC" (*WSJ* 26 Feb. 1985: 1,16).

15 A former AIPAC employee was quoted as saying that a pamphlet on how to set up a pro-Israel PAC was available in Schrayer's office. That was neither surprising nor illegal.

16 Even votes against other foreign aid by dependable supporters of Israel were treated as sins. Dine bluntly told Rep. Barney Frank that AIPAC was a "-bottom-line organization" that demanded support for the "overall foreign-aid 'pie'" to guarantee "the slice for Israel" (*NYT* 7 Jul. 1987: A8).

17 Defenses of interest-group politics assume that elected officials, confronted with conflicting constituent demands, will blunt the effects of partisan pressure through compromise (The Federalist No. 10 in Hamilton *et al.* 1937 (1787): 53–62; see also Berry 1989).

18 Bloomfield confirms that one reason he left was that AIPAC was abandoning its historically bipartisan approach and tying itself too closely to Likud policies and the Republican Party (Bloomfield interview).

19 His heated conversation with Franklin Fisher is reported in Melman and Raviv 1994: 348.

20 The Knesset members were Mordechai Virshubski, of the secular Shinui Party, and Haika Grossman, a survivor of the Warsaw Ghetto Uprising and Auschwitz.

21 Among them were the June 1981 Osirak raid, the July 1981 bombing of civilian areas in Beirut, the surprise annexation of the Golan in December 1981, Reagan's suspension of the November 1981 MoU, the invasion of Lebanon and lying about invasion goals, the camp massacres, the Pollard case, the willingness of Shamir to amend the Basic Law to "de-Judaize" all but Orthodox Jews, Israeli reactions to Reagan's 1982 plan and Shultz's 1988 initiative, and recognition of the PLO in 1988.

22 Former President Carter thought the initiative entirely consistent with Camp David, however (Shultz 1993: 98).

23 Begin told colleagues, "We have been betrayed by the Americans, the biggest betrayal since the state was established. They have stabbed us in the back" (Kimche 1991: 157). Begin accused American media and some administration officials of seeking to replace his government (*WP* 13 Sep. 1982: A24).

24 Bloomfield denies he asked Netanyahu for direction or clearance, for both legal and institutional reasons.

25 Ehud Olmert, then a junior Likud MK, advised Begin to sugar-coat any rejection. Begin responded, "No, my young friend, you don't understand. I have to be very blunt, or they won't know what I mean" (Bloomfield interview). Bloomfield believed that was both wrong and bad politics.

26 Dine told Weinberg to relax, he had only told the truth (Dine interview). Dine is still tender on the subject.

27 Dine wrote a column the following week, echoing Begin's charge that some in the administration were attempting to "force a new government on Israel" (Dine 1983).

28 Ambassador Arens wanted to push the issue. Bloomfield told Arens the U.S.–Israel relationship was based on security, survival and negotiating peace; a mandated embassy move was seen as a possible roadblock to any peace process (Bloomfield interview).

29 President Reagan's 1 September 1982 speech retained that policy.

30 At a 16 June news conference, Reagan repeated administration criticism of the raid, but then said, "Israel had reason for concern in view of the past history of Iraq, which ... does not even recognize the existence of Israel as a country ... Israel might have sincerely believed it was a defensive move" (DoS Bull Aug. 1981: 23).

31 The reaction in Israel was much stronger; hundreds of thousands mobilized to protest the camp massacres, a significant fraction of Israel's 3.5 million Jews.

32 Arthur Hertzberg believed that the outburst was a pre-emptive strike against Begin's critics, including some in the U.S.; if so, Hertzberg said, it was effective (Hertzberg 1992b: 16).

33 When *New York Times* editors deleted the word "indiscriminate" from Thomas Friedman's description of Israeli shelling of Beirut, he protested that they lacked "guts" (Findley 1985: 310). Friedman later wrote (about the IDF), "I always thought you were different. I always thought *we* were different." He said he "buried ... every illusion I ever held about the Jewish state" (Friedman 1989: 166). Friedman was attacked as a shallow liberal fraud, barely Jewish, who misunderstood Zionism and never supported Israel (see Auerbach 2001: 105–7).

34 However, an overwhelming majority still felt that America should not pressure Israel, and most said their sympathy for Israel had remained strong or increased over the preceding five years.

35 Bernard Avishai argues that Labor-Socialist Zionism never produced secular democracy; after the 1967 war and corrupt Labor governments, a Zionism that was based on nationalistic and messianic ideas endangered the democratic project (Avishai 2002).

36 Viorst later traced the history of internecine Jewish warfare, and what he saw as violent intolerance fostered by an increasingly politicized rabbinate, culminating in Rabin's murder (Viorst 2002).

37 Matti Golan vented the resentment of right-wing Israelis at the perceived hypocrisy of American Jews, supporters of Israel only when it acted in "moral" ways that did not embarrass them (Golan 1992).

38 Jewish respondents described themselves preponderantly as liberals (41 percent), rather than moderates (27 percent) or conservatives (17 percent). More had a favorable opinion of Secretary Shultz (70 percent) than Shamir (49 percent) or Peres (57 percent).

39 The issue reflected deep divisions between secular Israeli Jews and *heredi* (see Efron 2003).

40 Other polls showed majorities building to 70 percent by 1983 in favor of negotiating with the PLO, conditioned on recognition of Israel and abandonment of terror. Pluralities of over 30 percent, building to majorities, favored territorial compromise and a Palestinian state, and opposed permanent Israeli control of the Territories (Novik 1986: 75–6).

41 Cohen's AJC polls showed that nearly 61 percent of Orthodox Jews termed themselves "hawkish" on Israel, twice the percentage of Conservative Jews and three times the rate of Reform and unaffiliated Jews (Freedman 2000: 168).

42 According to Julius Berman, first Orthodox chair of the Presidents Conference, Henry Kissinger thought Israel should exclude media while it brutally and quickly put down the uprising (Berman Memo 3 Feb. 1988 in *JPS* XVII, 4 (summer 1988): 184–7).

43 A. M. Rosenthal wrote a *New York Times* editorial, "Jews Must Not Break Bones," calling for Rabin's resignation (Rosenthal 1988).

44 Begin had devalued the Holocaust when he justified the siege of Arafat in Beirut by analogy to Hitler in his bunker. After the camp massacres, the Holocaust analogy was used against Israel by David Shipler in the *New York Times* (Novick 2000: 160–2).

45 Henry Seigman, AJCongress executive director, responded that agreeing with nearly half of Israeli Jews, including the Labor Party, did not make American critics "accomplices of a 'non-Jewish, anti-Israel front,' as Mr. Shamir stated" (Speech 23 Mar. 1988, *JPS* XVII, 4 (summer 1988): 193–7, at 194–5).

46 Shamir insisted that Diaspora Jews had a "moral duty" to "support the Israeli government." It was "absolutely un-Jewish and very dangerous to join an anti-Israel front with non-Jews" (Gruen 1990: 220).

47 Shamir wrote the senators, "We were astonished by your words of criticism..."
    (*NYT* 10 Mar. 1988: A1). The next month he said that rioters would be
    "crushed like grasshoppers," and Israel began targeted assassinations (*NYT* 1
    Apr. 1988: A3; *NYT* 23 Apr. 1988: 6).
48 Henry Seigman proposed that the AJCongress work to convene a world Zionist
    Congress in Jerusalem, to "articulate a new version of Zionism that is inclusive
    and universal" (Speech 23 Mar. 1988 in *JPS* (1988) XVII, 4 (summer): 197).
    That failed, for the same reasons that an alternative to AIPAC did.
49 Both Edward Said and Ibrahim Abu-Lughod had been named "anti-Israel ...
    individuals" by AIPAC (Goott and Rosen 1983: 95, 127).
50 Hauser, an international lawyer, had served on the U.S. delegation to the UN,
    chaired AJC's foreign affairs committee, co-founded JINSA, advised the
    founders of NatPAC and directed the Speakers' Bureau for the Reagan–Bush
    campaign in 1980. She chaired the American branch of the International Center
    for Peace in the Middle East, founded by Abba Eban. She had been attacked by
    critics of Israel for abusing her position at the United Nations by organizing
    pro-Israeli efforts (Lilienthal 1983: 673).
51 Neoconservative beliefs and Revisionist Zionist beliefs often led to similar goals,
    but for different reasons. Likud premiers sought to smash the PLO and keep the
    Golan, not because the PLO and Syria were supported by the Soviet Union, but
    because they stood in the way of *Eretz Y'Israel*.

7 Reagan after AWACS: policy as the product of unexamined beliefs and political constraint

1 Klein had been co-chair of the Coalition to Elect Reagan–Bush.
2 Spiegel was a long-time supporter in California and coordinated efforts in the
   Jewish community.
3 Dole had requested an earlier letter analyzing the state of the relationship.
4 Israeli deception of Ambassador Habib and others is detailed in Boykin 2002. A
   list is at Boykin's App. B. See also, Rabinovich 1985 and Schiff and Ya'ari
   1984.
5 Delivery of CBUs was suspended and F-16s delayed, but neither measure
   affected Lebanon operations (see Reagan PC 28 Sep. 1982 in AFP 1982: 793).
6 Steven Spiegel attributes the votes to (1) The Kahan Commission's redemptive
   effect; (2) King Hussein's not committing to Fresh Start; and (3) the 1982
   defeat of several critics of Israel and election of several supporters (Spiegel 1986:
   423). The elections were important. However, the Kahan Commission only
   found IDF complicity in February 1983, Hussein accepted Fresh Start, subject
   to solving the problem of the Rabat designation of the PLO, and Israel rejected
   the plan outright.
7 Foreign Minister Shamir called Reagan's opposition "an unfriendly act" that
   "endangered the peace process" (Schulz 1993: 112).
8 This was called "surely ... the most substantial foreign policy defeat the administration has yet suffered" (Rosenfeld 1983).
9 The real options were to negotiate with the PLO, with persons reporting to the
   PLO, or with quislings, meaning that no agreement would be implemented by
   Palestinians (Wright 1983: 77). The second option was later adopted.
10 This summary is incomplete. Hussein had courage and his own motives to cooperate, but appreciated the risk; in addition to Sadat, he had seen his grandfather
   assassinated for similar reasons. He was also mercurial and, unknown even to his
   wife, was fighting cancer.
11 A 1984 American intelligence estimate concluded that "Israel will not only
   maintain its current margin of military superiority over every combination of

Arab forces, but will widen the gap during the next five years" (*WP* 7 Aug. 1986: A1).

12 Bloomfield believed that accommodating the administration in hopes of strengthened ties confused congressional "troops" and threatened discipline. Senator Packwood agreed, telling Dine, "Look, Tom, they don't do what they do because they love you, they do what they do because they fear you" (Bloomfield interview).

13 George Shultz later suggested Faisal Husseini, a Jerusalem-based Palestinian leader, as someone with whom Shamir could deal. Shamir, who had authorized contact with Husseini but then jailed him, would say only, "We have a file on him ... It's a very heavy file" (Schiff and Ya'ari 1990: 299).

14 At the White House, Hussein condemned violence and welcomed negotiations with Israel in an "environment free of belligerent and hostile acts" (Stmt 30 Sep. 1985 in DoS Bull Dec. 1985: 65).

15 Hussein said in 1985 that he could proceed without Arafat's blessing, but did not. Shultz criticized the king for hesitating, "even with the prospect of massive support from the United States" (Shultz 1993: 452). The king knew he could not rely on "massive support," and that he would pay a price assessed by Arab leaders and his own subjects.

16 He later testified that withdrawal of support from Hussein "at a delicate moment in the king's effort to move the peace process forward was especially troubling ... Opponents of the peace process are citing the withdrawal as proof that the king cannot count on the U.S. politically or militarily" (Test HFAC 22 Apr. 1986 in DoS Bull Jun. 1986: 71).

17 Ambassador Arnold Raphael:

> We [told the White House], "It is really important now that we show support for Jordan ... the best way to do it is to sell [Hussein] the arms he wants." The White House ... said, "The President has three key issues right now before him in Congress. Contra funding, the defense budget, and the M-X. They are a hell of a lot more important than worrying about whether [Hussein] gets arms"
>
> (Speech 2 Oct. 1986, Frontline Diplomacy).

18 RSAF F-15s shot down Iranian aircraft in the spring of 1984 (Murphy testimony HFAC 22 Apr. 1986 in DoS Bull Jun. 1986: 71).

19 The Saudis also purchased Chinese missiles. Israel could not complain: the missiles had been built with help from Israeli experts, using licensed U.S. technology (*WP* 23 May 1988: A1).

20 Twelve days later, Reagan certified Saudi compliance with his 1981 letter of assurances, relying on, *inter alia*, Saudi cooperation on the Iran–Iraq war, Egypt's readmission to Arab organizations, terrorism and radical movements, and the peace process (Letter 18 Jun. 1986 in DoS Bull Sep. 1986: 79–80). A congressional effort to derail AWACS deliveries failed.

21 Commission members were appalled at Reagan's lack of involvement, understanding or discipline; Senator Cohen said it was a "waste of time" to talk to him, because "with Ronald Reagan, no one is there. The sad fact is we don't have a president" (Cannon 1991: 714n).

22 Saudi pilots apparently followed operational restrictions placed on F-15s at AIPAC's insistence; AIPAC then allegedly said that the pilots refused to assist (Evans and Novak 1987).

23 Replacement F-15s were later agreed by the Senate, but without Mavericks (*WP* 9 Oct. 1987: A1).

24 Shamir's reaction to Shultz's "Interlock" initiative was that "apart from [Shultz's signature] the document does not serve the cause of peace"; he promised to resist it "with all my power" (Suleiman 1995: 185).

25 Reagan "found [Peres] more understanding than his predecessor of [Reagan's] desire to improve relations with the moderate Arabs – and more willing than many of Israel's lobbyists in this country to consider alternative ideas" (Reagan 1990: 493).

26 Preparing Reagan for Peres' last visit as premier, Poindexter and Shultz praised Peres' "visionary leadership" and "convergent views" on the peace process, and anticipated Shamir's premiership with trepidation (RRPL, Ross files, Chron files Sep. 1986(2), Shultz memo 10 Sep. 1986, Poindexter memo 12 Sep. 1986). Prior to a March 1988 Shamir visit, Shultz advised Reagan to press Shamir to respond to Shultz's initiative even though that might "precipitate early [Israeli] elections" (RRPL, Ross files, Chron files Mar. 1988, Memo 11 Mar. 1988).

27 The LAVI fighter-bomber was identified with Rabin; the administration apparently intended to assist him politically. Even with the aid it was too expensive a project for Israel (Shultz 1993: 443).

28 Secretary Haig in his first news conference volunteered that the Soviet Union extended its influence by means of "training, funding and equipping … international terrorism," and that terrorism would "take the place of human rights [as] our concern, because it is the ultimate abuse of human rights" (PC 28 Jan. 1981 in DoS Bull Feb. 1981: J).

29 Shultz told Jewish leaders that Israel had "irrefutable evidence that the Soviet Union had been arming and training the PLO and other groups" (Speech 25 Oct. 1984 in DoS Bull Dec. 1984: 13). President Reagan in a major speech on terrorism emphasized ties between the Soviet Union and state sponsors of terrorism (Speech 8 Jul. 1985 in DoS Bull Aug. 1985: 7–10).

30 His recounting of 1985–1986 counter-terrorism efforts includes no reference to the Soviet Union.

31 The perception was not entirely true. Acts of domestic terrorism in both 1985 and 1986 included several by Jewish terrorists, principally Meyer Kahane's JDL; they included the assassination of American-Arab Anti-Discrimination Committee official Alex Odeh days after the *Achille Lauro* hijacking. There were no reported acts of terror by Palestinians or Islamists. Mrs. Klinghoffer received a call from the president; Mrs. Odeh did not.

32 Shultz considered himself a life-long Marine, often wearing a Marine necktie (*WP* 4 Feb. 1986: A1).

33 State Department Legal Adviser Abraham Sofaer helped make the public case for lawful pre-emptive action (Sofaer 1986).

34 The Jonathan Institute, specializing in terrorism, was founded in honor of Benjamin Netanyahu's brother Jonathan, the IDF commander killed at Entebbe.

35 The department's counter-terrorism chief said that over 80 percent of acts by the Abu Nidal Organization were "enforcement terrorism" against Arab targets (Bremer speech 4 Feb. 1988 in DoS Bull May 1988: 61–3).

36 Reagan to UJA Young Leadership Conference 13 Mar. 1984 and B'nai B'rith 28 Aug. 1984; Deputy Secretary Dam to UJA at White House 1 Oct. 1984; Shultz at Yeshiva University 9 Dec. 1984 and AIPAC Policy Conference 21 Apr. 1985; Assistant Secretary Murphy to American-Arab Affairs Council 23 Mar. 1984; McFarlane to Hadassah 24 Aug. 1984. Director of Counter-terrorism Oakley, Ambassador Bremer, Shultz, Murphy and others testified often on terrorism before congressional committees, and most of Shultz's press conferences and interviews dealt in part with terrorism during 1984–1986.

37 Shultz considered Netanyahu "a compelling voice for a tough counterterrorist policy for the West" (Shultz 1993: 827).

38 Weinberger opposed the operation, but NSC staff and Justice supported it; Reagan was anxious to show effective action against terrorists.

39 The Church Senate Select Committee concluded in 1975 that assassination in

peacetime violated international standards and American morality, but no law was passed to prohibit it. President Ford's E.O. 11905 prohibited targeted killings, but could be overridden by presidential finding. Defense Department lawyers opined that it did not apply to commanders in wartime, and thus not to Qaddafi. The administration denied the raid was an assassination attempt.

40 Chapters were authored by Ed Meese, Ambassador Kirkpatrick, senators Laxalt, Cranston and Moynihan, FBI Director Webster and Rep. Kemp; neoconservatives (Michael Ledeen, Midge Decter, Charles Krauthammer); Israeli officials (Chief Justice Meir Shamgar, Moshe Arens, Yitzhak Rabin); and journalists and academics. Twenty-nine of 41 participants were American or Israeli.

41 Kirkpatrick had called the PLO the "deadliest enemies of peace in the area" (Kirkpatrick 1981: 16). She falsely claimed that Sadat "scorned" negotiations with the PLO; Sadat had strongly "urged the United States to establish contact with the PLO" (Haig PC 6 Aug. 1981 in DoS Bull Sep. 1981: 54).

42 See, e.g. DoS, Country Reports on Human Rights Practices for 1984 (Feb. 1985), excerpted in *JPS* XIV, 5 (spring 1985): 208–21, reporting human rights abuses by Israeli officials and terrorist acts by Jewish radicals as well as violence and terrorism by Palestinians.

43 Several called for Israeli withdrawal from Lebanon; others included No. 520 (17 Sep. 1982), condemning Israeli incursions into Beirut; No. 521 (19 Sep. 1982) condemning camp massacres (without naming Israel); No. 573 (4 Oct. 1985) condemning Israel's attack on Tunisia; and No. 590 (8 Dec. 1986) deploring IDF live fire on unarmed students at Bir Zeit University. The United States abstained on the last two; it voted alone to veto several others. Abstentions and vetoes were usually on grounds that a resolution was unbalanced or not helpful, not that Israeli actions were justified.

44 That was apparently done in dealing with the Syrian missile crisis in 1981 (Tanter 1990: 40–4). George Shultz also justified the 1983 MoU and the JPMG process as responses to Soviet build-up in Syria (PC 5 Dec. 1983 in DoS Bull Jan. 1984: 37).

45 Further, "the White House leadership believed that the Soviet Union profited whenever Israel over-reacted" (Tanter 1990: 162).

46 RRPL, Exec Sec NSC, Box 91291, 28 Oct. 1983, NSDD 111. The document is heavily redacted, but is known to have justified a shift in favor of Israel (Mansour 1994: 170). It may have reflected in part a desire to prevent repetitions of the unilateral Israeli pullout from southern Lebanon (Quandt 2001: 258).

47 This was the "institutionalization" of pro-Israel policies which Shultz promised Tom Dine in February 1986, and which he gave as the first principle of American policy in his speech to AIPAC in 1987 ("the strongest permanent link possible between the United States and Israel") (Speech 17 May 1987 in DoS Bull Jul. 1987: 9).

48 Judge Clark in his NSDD 99 memorandum to the president mentioned the Fresh Start initiative, tellingly, as an instance where "U.S. and Israeli interests do *not* coincide," and where expressions of U.S. commitment to Israel's security were therefore required (emphasis in original).

49 Shamir as LEHI militia leader had defended violence against civilians and assassinations as necessary to establish the Jewish homeland. He wrote in a 1943 LEHI publication:

> Neither Jewish ethics nor Jewish tradition can disqualify terrorism as a means of combat ... terrorism is for us a part of the political battle being conducted ... and it has a great part to play ... it proclaims our war against the occupier. Thus, and only thus, will the battle for liberation commence.
> (MER 18: 3, May–Jun. 1988: 55)

50 He trusted neither Israel nor the CIA, because each had its own agenda (Schultz 1993: 843–4).

51 Yehoshafat Harkabi, former head of Israeli military intelligence, said that Palestinians would freely choose the PLO to represent them; Israel could no more choose an Arab delegation than could the United States dictate a Soviet delegation, and "Israel's presumption" in attempting to do so was "an absurdity bound to fail" (Lenczowski 1990: 278).

8 George H. W. Bush, James Baker and Israel

1 Describing how he and Baker formulated policy, Bush said "I think a lot of things grow out my instincts, but ... he'll have ideas" (Dowd and Friedman 1990: 62).

2 He co-authored Bush's presidential memoir; they purposely omitted all reference to the Arab–Israeli conflict (Bush and Scowcroft 1999: xi).

3 A senior diplomat said Baker was nearly ideal for the job, with political savvy, a strong relationship with the president, intellect, energy and no ego problems. The missing ingredient was an "interest in policy" (Newhouse 1990: 51).

4 Baker quickly dissociated himself from Bush's choice of Senator Dan Quayle as vice-president (Schweitzer and Schweitzer 2004: 360–2).

5 Bush told Gorbachev he could ignore what Bush said in the 1988 presidential campaign to placate hardliners; Reagan was surrounded by "marginal intellectual thugs" who would seize on any evidence he was a closet liberal (Beschloss and Talbott 1993: 3–4). To Bush, campaign rhetoric was unrelated to how he made decisions in office (Schweitzer and Schweitzer 2004: 374).

6 From 1986 to 1988, he headed the Near East directorate at NSC; he was principal foreign policy adviser to Bush in the 1988 campaign.

7 The report was clearly modeled on a 1975 Brookings Report that had provided policy guidance and key appointees to the Carter administration (Brookings Institution 1975). Brookings' similar report in 1988 lost the think-tank contest for influence (Brookings Institution 1988).

8 Ross told Baker the Intifada created a "modest new dynamic that should be explored gingerly" (Baker 1995: 117).

9 Why would Israel cooperate? Because Israelis now knew "that the twenty year era of a benign occupation was over" (Washington Institute 1988: 40). So the Intifada provided incentive; but the authors do not explain why Shamir would negotiate once the Intifada was abandoned and Palestinian leaders who "accommodated themselves to the occupation" replaced those who would not.

10 The issue may have cost him the 1992 election; indictments of Weinberger and others were announced by the special prosecutor days before the election.

11 A 1989 NSC memorandum said that the U.S. was in a position to exercise leadership, but the time was not "ripe" for an American initiative, which would "harden positions" and "catalyze opposition" (Baker 1995: 117).

12 Shamir claimed that by challenging Israel's claim to the Territories Baker weakened Shamir's government and encouraged his enemies (Shamir 1994: 202–3).

13 President Carter attached a letter to the Camp David Accords, confirming U.S. policy to be that east Jerusalem was subject to the convention and settlements there were illegal (Letter, 22 Sep. 1978, App. E, Quandt 2001). The letter was not publicized, and Begin did not accede to it. Shamir rejected Begin's Camp David agreements, relying on them later only when they served his purposes.

14 Bush feared that ending the dialogue aided extremists (PC 20 Jun. 1990 in FPB Jul./Aug. 1990: 68). The PLF raid requiring the termination was probably sponsored by Iraq, to end Baker's initiative and co-opt the PLO; if so, the ploy succeeded (Quandt 1991: 56).

15 Martin Peretz quotes Senator Gramm as saying that, having known Bush for 25 years, there was nothing he was "more adamant about than [Jewish] settlements [in the Occupied Territories]" (Pipes and Peretz 1992: 20). Baker reports consensus "that there was a strong case to be made that the settlements were, in fact, illegal," but they chose not to contradict Reagan and "create domestic political problems" (Baker 1995: 121).

16 Begin said in 1977 that his West Bank policy was not for security, but Zionist doctrine (Hertzberg 1989: 9–10). Former Chief of Staff Haim Bar-Lev testified, "The Jewish settlements in the populated areas of Judea and Samaria ... are detrimental to security" (Findley 1995: 159). Likud MK Benny Begin said, "In strategic terms, the settlements ... are of no importance" (ibid.). Former defense minister Ezer Weizman said that "security" was "negotiable currency," and that many settlements were "a burden and a nuisance in military terms" (Weizman 1981: 226). A 1988 study estimated that 75–80 percent of the General Staff believed that security costs outweighed benefits (Hurst 1999: 32).

17 Knowledgeable Israelis conceded that a Palestinian delegation required PLO acquiescence (Kelly test 24 May 1990 in HFAC/ME, PLO 1990: 22–3). Shamir's refusal to consider individual Palestinians, and a minister's statement that Baker's proposal was no longer relevant, led Baker to question the good faith of Shamir's government: "When you're serious about peace, call us" (giving the White House phone number) (Test 13 Jun. 1990 in HFAC 1990: 39–40).

18 Shunning the PLO was not "a matter of doctrine," but to prevent steps toward a Palestinian state (Shamir 1994: 200). He later criticized Oslo because "the search for peace has always been a matter of who would tire of the struggle first, and blink." A bankrupt PLO would have collapsed (ibid.: 259–60).

19 Some asserted that Bush's "obsession" with settlements was a personal tic. However, King Fahd told Baker he understood America's commitment to Israel's survival, but that the settlements did not relate to survival and limited U.S. credibility as an honest broker. Baker agreed (Baker 1995: 548).

20 Peace Now estimated 13,650 new units cost $1.1 billion in 1991; opposition MKs alleged $1.5 billion was spent on 18,000 West Bank units (Smolowe 1992). Finance Minister Modai charged that Sharon disregarded the budget and gave inaccurate data (Hertzberg 1991: 24).

21 Finance Ministry estimates were that housing and other needs would cost $60 billion in 1992–1996; Israel could manage perhaps $40 billion (Frankel 1995: 158). The ministry estimated that without loan guarantees unemployment would increase from 11 percent to 16.2 percent (Smolowe 1992: 27).

22 Shamir said Arabs were panicked that the Intifada could not stop "the natural flow of the Jewish people toward its homeland," which was "what the conflict [was] all about" (Mansour 1994: 181).

23 Most American Jews favored freedom of choice. However, none protested when the Bush administration tightened visa requirements (Eagleburger Stmt 15 Sep. 1989 in AFP 1989: 212). Of Soviet Jews, 91 percent had been choosing countries other than Israel (Findley 1995: 119).

24 What Shamir apparently said was, "It [the settlements] won't be a problem" (*NYT* 25 Sep. 1991: A1). Baker read Shamir's response as a "brush-off" of the president (Baker 1995: 123).

25 Sharon said on 24 June that "due to the problems we have," Soviet immigrants would not be settled beyond the green line (Jacobson 1992: 233). That neither bound the government nor stopped settlements.

26 Levy was the only Sephardic senior minister; that community was angry about diversion of funds from the urban poor (Hadar 1992a: 10).

27 In February, Israeli opposition MKs alleged that the government planned

another 12,000 units of settler housing, expressly to "make it difficult for Israel to enter the political process" (*WP* 14 Feb. 1991: A16). Ambassador Shoval then complained of getting "the run-around," and Baker nearly had him recalled (Baker 1995: 545–6).

28 Gorbachev told Assad in Moscow in 1987 that the Soviet Union would not support "strategic parity" with Israel. Assad's joining the Gulf War coalition probably owed more to a belief that he needed U.S. leverage to recover the Golan than to rivalry with Saddam (Ross 2004: 48).

29 Israelis had believed that the war would prove the value of strategic cooperation (Melman and Raviv 1994: 382–3). However, political calculations in the White House and Haass's advice prevailed over Cheney and Wolfowitz (ibid.; Bush and Scowcroft 1999: 452).

30 As President Bush assembled his coalition in October 1990, the IDF killed 21 and injured over 150 Palestinians on the Temple Mount; they were violently protesting a radical Jewish group's attempt to lay a foundation stone for a replacement Temple. The U.S. supported UNSC resolutions condemning Israel's conduct and deploring its refusal to admit UN investigators. The Jewish community was "surprised, hurt, and furious" at Bush's lack of "understanding" of Shamir, but Bush notes that "[t]he deaths of Palestinians in Jerusalem made that difficult" (Bush and Scowcroft 1999: 379). Disclosure that Sharon funded settlers taking over a church-owned building in the Christian Quarter alarmed even AIPAC; Congress imposed a $1.8 million "fee" offsetting that funding (Puschel 1992: 110–11).

31 A plurality believed Israel should agree to exchange land in the Territories for peace; and a large majority favored granting the 120-day delay Bush had requested on Israel's request for loan guarantees.

32 Steven Cohen's 1991 AJC survey showed hardening Jewish opinion; a plurality approved settlements in the territories and a shrinking plurality favored return of some land. Some leaders regretted their candor and called the Wilstein survey an "ambush" (Melman and Raviv 1994: 432–3).

33 Moshe Amirav, the Likud central committee member fired by Shamir after negotiating with Faisal Husseini, represented the Council for Peace and Security, a group of retired IDF officers (including over half of all retired generals) who favored a two-state solution.

34 U.S. Interreligious Council for Peace (2,000 clergy of all faiths); Project Nishma (formed when four Israeli generals appealed for support of the peace process); Jewish Women Leaders Consultation on Israel (to engage Palestinian women); New Israel Fund (seeking funding for peace efforts outside CJF and UJA); and Committee for Judaism and Social Justice (intellectuals and public personalities headed by Jerome Segal, president of Jewish Peace Lobby) (Marcus 1990: 557).

35 Cohen identified minority opinions as "amoral Zionists" (Likudniks, neocons and religious Zionists published in *Commentary*), and "moralizing Universalists" (who only criticized Israel and were found in *Tikkun*) (Cohen 1989).

36 Over a third of the Committee were political appointees in the Reagan administration.

37 Right-wing Israeli commentator Daniel Doron also argued that the Arab–Israeli conflict was a "derivative conflict" and Israel a target of convenience for Arab and Islamic rage focused on the West (*WSJ-Eur* 30 Oct. 1991: 8).

38 In addition to $300 million in compensatory aid and $700 million in used equipment, joint projects were announced for the Arrow ATBM and other systems; Secretary Cheney announced stockpiling in Israel for use in any regional conflict (not just jointly-agreed undertakings); JMPG meetings were resumed; and joint exercises were expanded (Puschel 1992: 103–7). AIPAC constantly pushed for and bragged on these programs (e.g. NER 20 May 1991: 86).

39 By March 1990, DoD leaders uniformly praised the joint programs with the IDF (Puschel 1992: 107).

40 AIPAC argued that the guaranteed loans would generate sales by American vendors, but there is no evidence that meaningful bureaucratic or lobbying support resulted.

9 The loan guarantees: new equilibrium, old result

1 Saudi King Fahd needed a *fatwa* confirming that when the kingdom's survival was at stake, he could accept help from unbelievers (Friedman 1991).

2 Bush made the promise publicly to Arab-American groups in October 1990 (DoS Dispatch 1990: 130). Shamir believed Bush had also promised Arab leaders to withhold guarantees unless settlement construction was ended (Jacobson 1994: 179). Martin Indyk believed that Bush made such a promise in exchange for Arab participation at Madrid (Madison 1992: 925–6). There is no persuasive evidence that is so, and Bush denied it (PC 12 Sep. 1991 in FPB Sep./Oct. 1991: 67).

3 This is the reverse of Eagleburger's argument that the U.S. needed Israel as a partner against future unknown contingencies. Past surprises (Iran–Iraq, Afghanistan, Kuwait) had not permitted reliance on Israel, and future crises were unlikely to either.

4 Scowcroft opposed the initiative, arguing that Shamir would not talk to Palestinians (Baker 1995: 415).

5 Max Fisher, George Klein and Richard Fox wrote Bush urging the guarantees as a moral obligation. Bush wrote Klein that his commitment to Israel came "from the head as well as the heart," but that the test of a good relationship was "the ability to disagree on specifics without putting fundamentals at risk" (*JP* 29 Mar. 1992: 1).

6 Support for a delay or for an even harder line was expressed by the *New York Times*, *Washington Post*, *Wall Street Journal* and *USA Today*, among many others.

7 Rita Hauser told the president that he would get whatever conditions on guarantees he wanted, that a settlement freeze was key to viable Madrid talks and that the overwhelming majority of American Jews were opposed to the Likud settlement program (Hauser 1992).

8 Presidents Conference leaders met with White House Chief of Staff Skinner on 6 January to convey that message (Jacobson 1994: 176).

9 On 20 January he told cheering settlers that nothing could stop the building; on 26 January he said he hoped for a deal, but rejected a freeze. "Please forget about it" (Jacobson 1994: 177).

10 Baker says they never appreciated the issue's impact in the Israeli elections, although it was obvious "in hindsight" (Baker 1995: 555). Given Baker's political antennae, that is not credible. Ross confirms that Baker was "determined not to do anything that might help Shamir" (Ross 2004: 83).

11 He had claimed that the only two groups "beating the drums" for the Gulf War were "the Israeli defense industry and its amen corner in the United States" (Lipset and Raab 1995: 128).

12 On 6 February, however, Leahy had said that if Israel thought it could get guarantees without a freeze, they should "forget it" (Jacobson 1994: 178).

13 A WSJ/NBC poll showed 13 percent favored granting the guarantees, 32 percent favored a freeze as a condition of any guarantees and 49 percent opposed guarantees "under any circumstances" (*WSJ* 11 Mar. 1992: A16).

14 For example: (1) the November 1991 CJF leadership survey; (2) David Bonior's election as House majority whip over AIPAC's opposition (he opposed all aid, including to Israel) (Hadar 1992b: 86); and (3) advice from delegations of

Jewish and congressional leaders to compromise with the president (Grossman 1993: 173–4).

15 The Budgetary Enforcement Act of 1990 required appropriation of an amount estimated as the cost of subsidy, taking into account factors including the likelihood of repayment.

16 Commercial credit rating companies differed widely on Israel's creditworthiness, depending on political assumptions (Richman 1992). Baker pointed out that Israel repaid loans from the U.S. "because we appropriate the money …with which to repay ourselves" (Test 6 Feb. 1992 in HFAC, US FP 1992: 22–3). Cost estimates ranged from $50 million to $1.9 billion dollars (*NYT* 4 Sep. 1991: A3). The Congressional Budget Office and the General Accounting Office could not agree.

17 Gelb later supported Bush's "hardball" and criticized those who said Jews either supported Shamir or were self-hating, Israel-bashing Jews (*SLTrib* 2 Mar. 1992: A7).

18 Rabin said "political and financial costs of cancelling" the units were prohibitive (Baker 1995: 556).

19 The Kennebunkport agreement set the limit at 3.5 percent, but remarkably strong congressional opposition resulted in the higher figure (*JP* 13 Sep. 1992: 1).

20 Rabin later assured Jewish leaders that his criticisms were not of the community, but of "one organization" (*NYT* 8 Sep. 1992: A8).

21 Beilin later denied saying that AIPAC was a "right-wing organization" (*NER* 23 Aug. 1993: 149).

22 There were numerous suicides among Russian immigrants in Israel. Many advised relatives still in Russia against immigrating (Brinkley 1991).

Epilogue: George W. Bush – the war leader and the true believers

1 Documents from the White House of George W. Bush have been taken from the White House website, www.whitehouse.gov, and are cited by type of document (Speech, Remarks, Press Conference ("PC"), Statement ("Stmt") or Interview) and date.

2 Of 50,000 Florida Muslims, 88 percent may have voted for Bush; that would have provided the margin of victory (Mansfield 2004: 139–40). A total of 88 percent of Jews voted for Gore (Abramson *et al.* 2003: 99).✗

3 One knowledgeable observer believed that Arafat threw a tantrum to end the Taba negotiations in 2001 in the expectation that he would do better with Bush than with Clinton (Ignatius 2001).

4 Debates continue as to how generous the Barak offer was and who was responsible for the breakdown of the talks and the outbreak of violence. For dissenting views, see Ackerman (2003: 65–8) and Swisher (2004).

5 Asked about how he conducted diplomacy, Bush said that he concentrated on whether he could trust someone; having spent time with Sharon, he knew Sharon meant what he said. Bush also volunteered that he was "not very analytical" (PC 4 Jun. 2003).

6 Unlike Reagan, who thoroughly revamped his administration when it foundered on Iran-Contra, Bush expects to be vindicated by history like Truman, Churchill and Sam Houston.

7 Norman Podhoretz considered it "plausible" that Bush believed God chose him to rid the world of terror (Podhoretz 2002: 24).

8 Bush sees himself as "the calcium in the backbone" of the administration, and dislikes "hand-wringing" (Woodward 2003: 259).

9 Some speak of Bush and his foreign policy as "revolutionary": Stephen Hadley (Barnes 2006: 61); Ivo Daalder (Allen 2003).

10 Bush is uninterested in "conservative dogma," and leaves the ideologues to Rove (Barnes 2006: 29). Rove is "cerebral," while Bush doesn't like "going too deeply into homework" (Moore and Slater 2003: 106).

11 A Bush rally where beer was served was portrayed as leading youth astray (Aikman 2004: 60).

12 Two of the other five candidates in the debate (Senator Hatch and Gary Bauer) concurred with Bush's answer. In a 2001 Harris poll, Jesus Christ was the person most often named as a "hero" by Americans polled (Taylor 2001).

13 The more devout individuals were, the more likely they were to vote, and to choose Bush (Protestants with low or moderate religious commitment split 49 to 48 for Bush; those with very high commitment chose Bush 87 to 13) (Abramson *et al.* 2003: 80, 99). Muslims probably voted *against* Joe Lieberman, the Jewish Democratic candidate for vice-president.

14 Rev. Barry Lynn noted that as the Christian Coalition collapsed, its leadership moved into government (e.g. Robertson's attorneys into the Department of Justice) (Zunes 2005: 74). Gary Bauer said much of his presidential campaign staff worked in the White House (*CSci Mon* 16 Apr. 2002: 1).

15 David Frum took credit for the "axis of evil" idea in the 2002 State of the Union address, but Gerson substituted the word "evil" for "hatred" (Goldberg 2006: 60).

16 Terrorism had been the tool of secular nationalist movements in the 1960s and 1970s. Israel had supported Islamist Hamas as an alternative to Fatah because Islam was seen as a passive religion (Telhami 2004: 26–9). By the late 1990s, over half of terrorist organizations designated by the State Department were either acting in the name of Islam or were predominantly Muslim (Frum and Perle 2004: 34).

17 Thousands of pages of neoconservative writings contain scant reference to Africa, Asia or Latin America, or even Europe except with regard to problems of dealing with Europeans on Middle East issues and the use of force. Subjects not bearing on military pre-eminence, the unilateral use of force, Islam or terrorism are likewise seldom treated. See, for example, Frum and Perle 2004.

18 Feith had argued that the "land for peace" formula was foolish, as Arafat could easily end the "peace," while land could not as easily be retaken (Feith 2002).

19 Murdoch owns the Fox television and radio broadcasting operations, cable networks, over 130 newspapers (including the *New York Post*), 25 magazines and major publishing houses including HarperCollins.

20 Neoconservatives conveniently ignore the caustic criticism they heaped on Reagan when he took nuclear disarmament seriously, pressured Israel or otherwise strayed from the true faith.

21 Elliott Abrams, Dick Cheney, Zalmay Khalilzad, Scooter Libby, Donald Rumsfeld, and Paul Wolfowitz.

22 Gary Bauer and Robert Bennett.

23 Eighteen signatories included ten who would serve in the Bush administration (Elliott Abrams, Richard Armitage, John Bolton, Paula Dobriansky, Zalmay Khalilzad, Richard Perle, Peter Rodman, Donald Rumsfeld, Paul Wolfowitz and Robert Zoellick), and other neoconservatives (William Bennett, Jeffrey Bergner, Francis Fukuyama, Robert Kagan, and William Kristol).

24 Thirty-three signatories included neoconservative leaders (William Kristol, Ken Adelman, Gary Bauer, William Bennett, Reuel Marc Gerecht, Robert Kagan, Joshua Muravchik, Martin Peretz, Richard Perle, Daniel Pipes, Norman Podhoretz, and Marshall Wittman), as well as AIPAC's Steve Rosen.

25 These principles, including expressly analogizing Islamist terrorism to communism and Nazism, were restated by David Frum and Richard Perle in 2003 (Frum and Perle 2004).

26 Addington authored Bush's doctrine of unfettered executive power in wartime (Mayer 2006). Hannah was Cheney's Middle East adviser.

27 Francis Fukuyama, reacting to his colleagues' "illusions about the efficacy of American power," declared that he could no longer call himself a neoconservative, and founded a new journal, the *American Interest* (Fukuyama 2006).

28 Neoconservatives Martin Kramer and Daniel Pipes established Campus Watch, a website blacklist of academics thought to be anti-Semitic or supportive of radical Palestinian groups, shortly after 9/11 (McNeil 2002). Efforts were made to enact laws creating federal oversight of what professors said about Israel (e.g. HR 3077 in the 108th Congress).

29 A 2002 *Newsweek* poll reported that 45 percent of Americans considered the United States a "secular nation," 29 percent a "Christian nation" and 16 percent a "Biblical nation" in the Judeo-Christian tradition (Lind 2003: 108).

30 The disinvestment campaign began as a student movement at Berkeley in 2000. Abe Foxman of ADL and Harvard professor Ruth Wisse denounced it as anti-Semitic (Clarke 2005: 45–6). When Harvard faculty and students advocated disinvestment in 2002, Harvard law professor, Alan Dershowitz, and university president, Lawrence Summers, said that such advocacy was essentially anti-Semitic (ibid.: 45; Butler 2003: 249).

31 Even in Virginia, home of Falwell, Robertson, the Christian Coalition and Robertson's Liberty University, polls in the late 1990s showed that only 15 percent of voters considered the endorsement of the Coalition significant (Friedman 2005: 221).

32 Christian Zionists would carry bills or letters drafted by AIPAC. Sen. Sam Brownback (R, KS) led 87 senators in demanding various actions against the PLO (*WP* 6 Apr. 2001: A32). Sen. Chris Bond (R, MO) led 89 senators in demanding the president not restrain Israeli retaliation against Palestinians (*NYT* 17 Nov. 2001: A10). Kansas and Missouri have very small Jewish populations.

33 One Texas preacher, Rev. John Hagee, pledged $1 million in 1998 to settle Russian immigrants in the West Bank, rejecting advice that his actions contravened U.S. policy (Lind 2003: 147).

34 A fellow Christian, after holding hands with a Jew in the Sea of Galilee, sang a hymn about a coming time when "Gentile and Jew" would have "one Shepard and one fold" (Bush 1999: 139).

35 In September 1999, in a speech written by Cheney, Armitage and Rice, he promised to end "diffuse" and "endless" deployments and "reduce the tension on an overstretched military" (Speech 23 Sep. 1999; Moore and Slater 2003: 302).

36 Frum, who wrote the speech, took away other lessons: refer to faith, not to a Christian God; appoint someone to the NSC Middle East desk; and resolve the conflict between the State Department and the supporters of Israel in the White House over treatment of the PA (Frum 2003).

37 Throughout the first term, State Department moderates (William Burns at NEA and Richard Haass at Policy Planning) battled Cheney, Rumsfeld, Feith and Cheney's Middle East adviser John Hannah, with a cautious Powell seeking to preserve his credibility for the major issues. See Sipress 2002.

38 Mossad chief Efraim Halevy was surprised that Bush would plunge the CIA director into overt political and operational roles (Halevy 2006: 209–10).

39 Bush told Cheney within minutes after the second tower was hit that this was "war" (Barnes 2006: 63). His speeches that day, the next day and over the following months were filled with references to "evil" and "evildoers." In his speech to Congress he referred to terrorists as a global movement, "heirs of all the murderous ideologies of the 20th century ... they follow in the path of fascism, Nazism and totalitarianism." He demanded that every state choose to be "with us, or you are with the terrorists" (Speech 20 Sep. 2001).

40 Frum claims that he inserted the idea in every draft of the speech (Frum 2003:

142–3). Halper and Clarke report that Frum got the idea from Richard Perle (Halper and Clarke 2004: 32). Woodward reports the idea was Gerson's (Woodward 2003: 30). Hadley says the idea was entirely Bush's (Kessler 2004: 178). Barnes says Bush discussed the concept with Cheney on 12 September (Barnes 2006: 66).

41 Frum and Perle argued that the "Arab–Israeli quarrel" was a manifestation of Muslim culture; that the Palestinian cause was about revenge, not justice; that militant Islam sought global domination as had Nazis and communists; and that eradicating it was "our generation's great cause," where the only options were victory or holocaust (Frum and Perle 2004).

42 He also said, "Do not try to appease the Arabs at our expense." At Rice's suggestion, the White House press secretary called this insult "unacceptable" (Woodward 2003: 197–8).

43 Cheney was urged by Powell to meet with Arafat, and agreed to do so if it would mark the execution of a ceasefire and security agreement negotiated by Zinni. Although he had agreed to the terms, Arafat then refused the meeting (Barnes 2006: 84).

44 In 2003, Bush told a rabbi that any criticism he had of Sharon would always be made in private (Aikman 2004). Bush may have warned against killing Arafat, which Sharon had occasionally threatened.

45 HR 392 passed 352 to 21; a similar Senate resolution passed 94 to 2 (*NYT* 3 May 2002: A10).

46 Rove persuaded Bush to send Paul Wolfowitz to a pro-Israel rally, and irritated Secretary Powell by intruding himself into these issues (*NYT* 13 May 2002: A1).

47 The inquiry had been welcomed by Foreign Minister Peres; when Likud objections split the government, Bush backed away (NYT 4 May 2002: A6).

48 After Sharon's incapacitation in January 2006, Martin Indyk said Sharon "would find it ironical" to be so considered, since he "was not a man who believed much in peace" (Indyk 2006).

49 Bush never retracted the statement, but rebuked Sharon for not trying harder for peace when the Israeli threw the quote up to him in private (*WP* 3 Jun. 2003: A1).

50 Powell had told Arafat twice that continued failure to move against terrorists would mean that the United States would no longer deal with him. When he still did nothing, the 24 June speech was the result (Kessler 2004: 178–9).

51 Bush met with Sharansky soon after the 2004 election to discuss the thesis of Sharansky's book *The Case for Democracy* (*WP* 25 Nov. 2004: A27). Bush's words in the Second Inaugural and 2005 State of the Union mirrored Sharansky's (Speeches 20 Jan. 2005, 2 Feb. 2005).

52 Four former Shin Bet chiefs said in November 2003 that Israeli policy on the Intifada had gravely damaged the country, and that Israel could not reach peace while excluding Arafat (Sher 2004: 185–6).

53 Sharon was so upset at the contents of early drafts that he refused to engage the Bush administration or to allow his aides to do so. Halevy considered this a "grievous error" (Halevy 2006: 240).

54 Shibley Telhami said the Road Map's contradictions prevented implementation (Telhami 2004: 187–8).

55 Administration officials had not pushed in 2001 for a freeze on settlements as called for in the Mitchell Report because "[Sharon's] coalition government would fall" (*NYT* 17 May 2001: A3).

56 In April 2005, for example, Bush and Sharon separately stated their positions, ignoring obvious discrepancies. The Road Map requires Israel to "freeze ... all settlement activity (including natural growth of settlements)," and that is what

Bush said should happen; Sharon knew that settlement growth proceeded with government funding. Bush talked about the need for "progress" on suppressing violence and dismantling terrorist groups; Sharon said that total quiet and dismantlement of terrorist infrastructure was necessary before undertaking negotiations (PC 11 Apr. 2005).

57 Israelis "understood from President Bush that the United States would not take kindly to reopening a dialogue between Israel and Syria" (*Yediot Achronot* 5 Oct. 2006). Olmert reportedly told his cabinet that because of Bush's opposition, they could not test the invitation of Syria to unconditional talks (Statement of Daniel Levy at Foundation for Middle East Peace, Washington, 19 Dec. 2006). Bush apparently also discouraged any opening to Hamas, as weakening his war against Islamic fascism (Freedland 2006).

References

Interviews

"A", Principal of a consulting and lobbying firm in Washington, DC; former State Department official concentrating on Lebanon and the peace process and senior staff member on the United States Senate Foreign Relations Committee. Interviewed in Washington, DC on 20 February 2004.

Douglas Bloomfield, Political columnist; Legislative Director, American Israel Public Affairs Committee, 1980–1988. Interviewed in Washington, DC on 17 December 2002.

Thomas A. Dine, President, Jewish Community Federation; Executive Director, American Israel Public Affairs Committee, 1980–1993. Interviewed in Washington, DC on 14 January 2003.

Michael van Dusen, Deputy Director, Woodrow Wilson Center; Former Staff Director, Subcommittee on Europe and the Middle East, House Committee on Foreign Relations and Chief of Staff, House Committee on Foreign Relations. Interviewed in Washington, DC on 27 January 2004.

Frederick G. Dutton, registered representative of the Kingdom of Saudi Arabia in the United States, 1976–2005. Interviewed in Washington, DC on 15 January 2004.

Holsey Handyside, retired Foreign Service Officer and former Ambassador to Mauritania. Interviewed in Washington, DC on 11 August 2003.

George P. Shultz, former Secretary of State. Interviewed in San Francisco on 29 July 2003.

Presidential documents

Ronald Reagan Presidential Library documents are cited as "RRPL," with designation of the collection, box and serial number.

Documents from the White House of George W. Bush have been taken from the White House website, www.whitehouse.gov, and cited by type of document (Speech, Remarks, Press Conference ("PC"), Statement ("Stmt") or Interview) and date.

Oral history collections

Frontline Diplomacy: The U.S. Foreign Affairs Oral History Collection, by The Association for Diplomatic Studies and Training of Arlington, Virginia (cited as "Frontline Diplomacy").

Congressional materials

Mark, C., Foreign Affairs and National Defense Division, Congressional Research Service, Library of Congress (1996). *Israel: U.S. Loan Guarantees for Settling Immigrants (CRS Report 96–942F)*. Washington, DC, Library of Congress ("Mark 1996").

Mark, C., Foreign Affairs and National Defense Division, Congressional Research Service, Library of Congress (2002). *Israel: U.S. Foreign Assistance (Issue Brief 85066)*. Washington, DC, Library of Congress ("Mark 2002").

Migdalovitz, C., Foreign Affairs and National Defense Division, Congressional Research Service, Library of Congress (2006). *Israel: Background and Relations with the United States (Issue Brief 82008)*. Washington, DC, Library of Congress ("Migdalovitz 2006").

Nowels, L. Q. and C. Mark, Foreign Affairs and National Defense Division, Congressional Research Service, Library of Congress (1995). *Israel's Request for U.S. Loan Guarantees (Issue Brief 91–103)*. Washington, DC, Library of Congress ("Nowels 1995").

Sharp, J., Foreign Affairs and National Defense Division, Congressional Research Service, Library of Congress (2006). *U.S. Foreign Aid to Israel (RL 33222)*. Washington, DC, Library of Congress ("Sharp 2006").

U.S. Congress, *Congressional Record (Daily Edition)* (cited as "Cong Record," with date and page numbers preceded by "H" or "S" to designate House or Senate).

U.S. Congress, House of Representatives, Committee on Appropriations, Subcommittee on Foreign Operations and Related Agencies (1981). *Hearings: Foreign Assistance and Related Programs Appropriations for 1982, Part 3*. Washington, DC, Government Printing Office ("HApp Hrgs, Part 3").

U.S. Congress, House of Representatives, Committee on Appropriations, Subcommittee on Foreign Operations and Related Agencies (1981). *Hearings: Foreign Assistance and Related Programs Appropriations for 1982, Part 7 (Proposed Airborne Warning and Control System (AWACS), F-15 Enhancement Equipment, and Sidewinder AIM-9L Missile Sales to Saudi Arabia)*. Washington, DC, Government Printing Office ("HApp Hrgs, Part 7").

U.S. Congress, House of Representatives, Committee on Foreign Affairs, Subcommittees on International Security and Scientific Affairs and on Europe and the Middle East (1981). *Hearings and Markup: H, Con. Res 194, Proposed Sale of Airborne Warning and Control Systems (AWACS) and F-15 Enhancements to Saudi Arabia*. Washington, DC, Government Printing Office ("HFAC Markup").

U.S. Congress, House of Representatives, Committee on Foreign Affairs, Report No. 97–268 (1981). *Disapproving the Proposed Sales to Saudi Arabia of E-3A Airborne Warning and Control System (AWACS) Aircraft, Conformal Fuel Tanks for F-15 Aircraft, AIM-9L Sidewinder Missiles, and Boeing 707 Refueling Aircraft*. Washington, DC, Government Printing Office ("HFAC Report").

U.S. Congress, House of Representatives, Committee on Foreign Affairs (1981).

Report: Saudi Arabia and the United States: The New Context in an Evolving Special Relationship. Washington, DC, Government Printing Office ("CRS, Saudi Arabia & the U.S.").

U.S. Congress, House of Representatives, Committee on Foreign Affairs (1981). *Congress and Foreign Policy – 1981*. Washington, DC, Government Printing Office ("CRS, Congress & Foreign Policy 1981").

U.S. Congress, House of Representatives, Committee on Foreign Affairs (1982). *Executive-Legislative Consultation on U.S. Arms Sales (Congress and Foreign Policy Series No. 7)*. Washington, DC, Government Printing Office ("CRS, Arms Sales Consultations").

U.S. Congress, House of Representatives, Committee on Foreign Affairs, Subcommittee on Europe and the Middle East (1982). *Documents and Statements on Middle East Peace, 1979–1982*. Washington, DC, Government Printing Office ("Docs & Stmts 79–82").

U.S. Congress, House of Representatives, Committee on Appropriations, Subcommittee on Foreign Operations, Export Financing and Related Programs (1990). *Hearings, Foreign Operations, Export Financing and Related Programs Appropriations for 1991, Part 3*. Washington, DC, Government Printing Office ("HApp/FO/Pt3 1990").

U.S. Congress, House of Representatives, Committee on Foreign Affairs, Subcommittee on International Operations (1989). *Hearings and Markup, Authorizing Appropriations for Fiscal Years 1990–1991 for the Department of State, the U.S. Information Agency, The Voice of America, The Board for International Broadcasting and for Other Purposes*. Washington, DC, Government Printing Office ("HFAC 1989").

U.S. Congress, House of Representatives, Committee on Foreign Affairs (1990). *Hearing, First Post-Cold War Superpower Summit, May 1990*. Washington, DC, Government Printing Office ("HFAC 1990").

U.S. Congress, House of Representatives, Subcommittee on Europe and the Middle East Committee on Foreign Affairs (1990). *Hearing, PLO Commitments and Compliance Report*. Washington, DC, Government Printing Office ("HFAC/ME, PLO 1990").

U.S. Congress, House of Representatives, Committee on Foreign Affairs (1992). *Hearings, The Future of U.S. Foreign Policy in the Post-Cold War Era*. Washington, DC, Government Printing Office ("HFAC US FP 1992").

U.S. Congress, House of Representatives, Committee on Appropriations, Subcommittee on Foreign Operations, Export Financing, and Related Programs (1992). *Hearing, Foreign Operations, Export Financing, and Related Programs Appropriations for 1993*. Washington, DC, Government Printing Office ("HApp/FO 1992").

U.S. Congress, Joint Economic Committee (1981). *The Persian Gulf: Are We Committed? At What Cost? A dialogue with the Reagan Administration on U.S. Policy*. Washington, DC, Government Printing Office ("CRS, Are We Committed?").

U.S. Congress, Senate (1981). *A Report to the United States Senate by Senator Howard H. Baker, Jr.: A Senate Perspective on Spain and the Middle East (Document No. 97–1l)*. Washington, DC, Government Printing Office ("Baker Rept").

U.S. Congress, Senate, Committee on Appropriations, Subcommittee on Foreign Assistance and Related Programs (1981). *Hearings: Foreign Assistance and Related Programs Appropriations for Fiscal Year 1982*. Washington, DC, Government Printing Office ("SApp Hrgs").

U.S. Congress, Senate, Committee on Armed Services (1981). *Hearings: Military and*

Technical Implications of the Proposed Sale to Saudi Arabia of Airborne Warning and Control System (AWACS) and F-15 Enhancements. Washington, DC, Government Printing Office ("SASC Hrgs").

U.S. Congress, Senate, Committee on Foreign Relations (1981). *Staff Report: The Proposed AWACS/F-15 Enhancement Sale to Saudi Arabia*. Washington, DC, Government Printing Office ("SFRC Staff Rept").

U.S. Congress, Senate, Committee on Foreign Relations (1981). *Hearings: The AWACS and F-15 Enhancements Arms Sale Package to Saudi Arabia, Part 1 (October 1, 5, and 6, 1981)*. Washington, DC, Government Printing Office ("SFRC Hrgs, Part 1").

U.S. Congress, Senate, Committee on Foreign Relations (1981). *Hearings: The AWACS and F 15 Enhancements Arms Sale Package to Saudi Arabia, Part 2 (October 14 and 15, 1981)*. Washington, DC, Government Printing Office ("SFRC Hrgs, Part 2").

U.S. Congress, Senate, Committee on Foreign Relations (1981). *Report No. 97–249: Disapproving the Proposed Sales to Saudi Arabia of E-3A Airborne Warning and Control System (AWACS Aircraft, Conformal Fuel Tanks for F-15 Aircraft, AIM-9L Sidewinder Missiles, and Boeing Aerial Refuelling Aircraft)*. Washington, DC, Government Printing Office ("SFRC Rept").

U.S. Congress, Senate, Committee on Foreign Relations (1989). *Hearings, Nomination of James A. Baker III*. Washington, DC, Government Printing Office ("Baker Confirm Hrgs").

U.S. Congress, Senate, Committee on Appropriations, Subcommittee on Foreign Operations, Export Financing, and Related Programs (1992). *Hearings, Foreign Operations, Export Financing and Related Programs Appropriations for Fiscal Year 1993*. Washington, DC, Government Printing Office ("SApp/FO 1992").

Document collections

Foreign Policy Bulletin, *Foreign Policy Bulletin* ("FPB" with issue and page).

Institute for Palestine Studies, *Journal of Palestine Studies* (articles are fully cited; reprinted documents cited "*JPS*" with issue and page).

United States Department of State, *US Department of State Dispatch* ("DoS Dispatch" with year and page).

United States Department of State, *American Foreign Policy Current Documents* ("AFP" with year and page).

United States Department of State, *U.S. Department of State Bulletin* ("DoS Bull" with year and page)

United States Department of State, Freedom of Information Act Document Collection ("DoS FOIA" with identifying information as supplied on the document; some documents available online at foia.state.gov).

Newspapers and periodicals

Boston Globe ("BGlobe")
Chicago Sun-Times ("ChiS-T")
Christian Science Monitor ("CSci Mon")
Des Moines Register ("DMReg")

The Economist ("Econ")
Facts on File
Haaretz
The Harvard Crimson ("HCrim")
Houston Chronicle ("HChron")
International Herald Tribune ("IHT")
Jerusalem Post ("JP")
Journal of Palestine Studies ("JPS")
Los Angeles Times ("LAT")
Middle East Report ("MER")
Near East Report ("NER")
Newsday
New York Post ("NYPost")
New York Times ("NYT")
Saint Louis Tribune ("SLTrib")
San Francisco Chronicle ("SFChron")
Wall Street Journal ("WSJ")
Wall Street Journal – European Edition ("WSJ-Eur")
Washington Post ("WP")
Washington Times ("WTimes")
Yediot Achronot

Books and articles

Abrams, E. (1993). Reagan Leadership: Mystery Man or Ideological Guide? *Foreign Policy in the Reagan Presidency: Nine Intimate Perspectives*. K. W. Thompson, ed. Lanham, MD, University Press of America: 95–120.

Abramson, P.R., J. H. Aldrich and D. W. Rohde (1991). *Change and Continuity in the 1988 Elections*. Washington, DC, CQ Press.

Abramson, P. R., J. H. Aldrich and D. W. Rohde (1995). *Change and Continuity in the 1992 Elections* (Revd. Edn.). Washington, DC, CQ Press.

Abramson, P. R., J. H. Aldrich and D. W. Rohde (2003). *Change and Continuity in the 2000 and 2002 Elections*. Washington, DC, CQ Press.

Abramson, P. R., J. H. Aldrich and D. W. Rohde (2006). *Change and Continuity in the 2004 Elections*. Washington, DC, CQ Press.

Abshire, D. M. and R. D. Nurnberger, eds. (1981). *The Growing Power of Congress*. Beverly Hills and London, Sage.

Ackerman, S. (2003). Israel and the Media: An Acquired Taste. *Wrestling with Zion: Progressive Jewish-American Responses to the Israeli-Palestinian Conflict*. T. Kushner and A. Solomon, eds. New York, Grove Press: 61–8.

Aikman, D. (2004). *A Man of Faith: The Spiritual Journey of George W. Bush*. Nashville, TN, W Publishing Group.

Ajami, F. (1996). "Lucky Jim." *New Republic* (1 Jan.): 30–6.

Allen, M. (2003). Close Look at a Focused President. *Washington Post*. Washington, DC (27 Apr.): A4.

Allison, G. T. and M. H. Halperin (1972). Bureaucratic Politics: A Paradigm and

Some Policy Implications. *Theory and Policy in International Relations.* R. Tanter and R. Ullman, eds. Princeton, NJ, Princeton University Press: 40–79.

Almond, G. (1962). *The American People and Foreign Policy.* New York, Praeger.

Anderson, I. H. (2005). *Biblical Interpretation and Middle East Policy: The Promised Land, America, and Israel, 1917–2002.* Gainesville, FL, University Press of Florida.

Anderson, M. (1990). *Revolution: The Reagan Legacy.* Stanford, CA, Hoover Institution Press.

Aronoff, Y. (2006). "In Like a Lamb, Out Like a Lion: The Political Conversion of Jimmy Carter." *Political Science Quarterly* 121: 3 (fall): 425–50.

Aronson, G. ed. (1995). "Quarterly Update on Settlements." *Journal of Palestine Studies* XXIV: 2 (winter): 98–108.

Aronson, G. ed. (1996). "Settlement Monitor." *Journal of Palestine Studies* XXVI: 1 (autumn): 128–37.

Art, R. J. (1973). "Bureaucratic Politics and American Foreign Policy: A Critique." *Policy Sciences* 4: 4: 467–90.

Auerbach, J. S. (1996). Are We One? Menachem Begin and the Long Shadow of 1977. *Envisioning Israel: The Changing Ideals and Images of North American Jews.* A. Gal, ed. Detroit, MI, Wayne State University Press: 335–51.

Auerbach, J. S. (2001). *Are We One? Jewish Identity in the United States and Israel.* New Brunswick, NJ, Rutgers University Press.

Avishai, B. (2002). *The Tragedy of Zionism: How Its Revolutionary Past Haunts Israel's Democracy.* New York, Helios Press.

Baker, J. A., III (1995). *The Politics of Diplomacy: Revolution, War & Peace. 1989–1992.* New York, Putnam.

Ball, G. W. (1984). *Error and Betrayal in Lebanon.* Washington, DC, Foundation for Middle East Peace.

Ball, G. W. and D. B. Ball (1992). *The Passionate Attachment: America's Involvement With Israel, 1947 to Present.* New York, W. W. Norton.

Bard, M. G. (1991). *The Water's Edge and Beyond: Defining the Limits to Domestic Influence on United States Middle East Policy.* New Brunswick, NJ, Transaction Publications.

Barnes, F. (2006). *Rebel in Chief: Inside the Bold and Controversial Presidency of George W. Bush.* New York, Crown Forum. •

Bar-Siman-Tov, Y. (1998). "The United States and Israel Since 1948: A 'Special Relationship'?" *Diplomatic History* 22: 2 (spring): 231–62.

Bell, C. (1989). *The Reagan Paradox: American Foreign Policy in the 1980s.* New Brunswick, NJ, Rutgers University Press.

Ben-Zvi, A. (1984). *Alliance Politics and the Limits of Influence: The Case of the U.S. and Israel, 1975–1983.* Tel Aviv, Jaffee Center for Strategic Studies, Tel Aviv University.

Bernstein, C. (1990). "The Agony Over Israel." *Time* 135: 19 (7 May): 28–30.

Berry, J. M. (1989). *The Interest Group Society.* Reading, MA, Addison Wesley Longman.

Beschloss, M. R. and S. Talbott (1993). *At the Highest Levels: The Inside Story of the End of the Cold War.* Boston, Little Brown.

Blitzer, W. (1985). *Between Washington and Jerusalem: A Reporter's Notebook.* New York, Oxford University Press.

Bloomfield, D. M. (1983). Israel's Standing in the Congress: Will Foreign Aid Be Spared? *Israel in U.S. Foreign and Security Policies.* N. Novik, ed. Tel Aviv, The Jaffee Center for Strategic Studies, Tel Aviv University: 17–33.

Boot, M. (2006). Policy Analysis – Paranoid Style, LATimes.com (21 Apr.). Online, available at: www.latimes.com/news/opinion/commentary/la-oe-boot29Mar29,0, 7274839.column.

Boudreault, J., E. Naughton and Y. Salaam, eds. (1992). *US Official Statements – Israeli Settlements and the Fourth Geneva Convention.* Washington, DC, Institute of Palestine Studies.

Bowen, D. R. (1993). "Analysis of Loan Guarantee Terms." *Journal of Palestine Studies* XXII: 2 (winter): 161.

Boykin, J. (2002). *Cursed is the Peacemaker: The American Diplomat Versus the Israeli General, Beirut 1982.* Belmont, CA, Applegate Press.

Braine, N., S. Feuerstein, M. Freedman, I. Klepfisz, J. Koval, M. Lerner, E. Lippmann and M. Plitnick (2003). Doing Activism, Working for Peace: A Roundtable Discussion. *Wrestling with Zion: Progressive Jewish-American Responses to the Israeli-Palestinian Conflict.* T. Kushner and A. Solomon, eds. New York, Grove Press: 350–70.

Brettschneider, M. (1996). *Cornerstones of Peace: Jewish Identity Politics and Democracy Theory.* New Brunswick, NJ, Rutgers University Press.

Brinkley, J. (1991). A Price for Security. *New York Times.* New York (8 Sep.): SM 42–5, 52–4, 66.

Brom, S. (2003). The War in Iraq: An Intelligence Failure? JCSS Strategic Assessment Vol. 6 No. 3, Jaffe Center for Strategic Studies, Tel Aviv University. Online, available at: www.tau.ac.il/jcss/sa/v6n3p3.Bro.html.

Brookhiser, R. (2003). "The Mind of George W. Bush." *Atlantic Monthly* 291: 3: 55–69.

Brookings Institution (1975). *Toward Peace in the Middle East: Report of a Study Group.* Washington, DC, Brookings Institution Press.

Brookings Institution (1988). *Toward Arab–Israeli Peace: Report of a Study Group.* Washington, DC, Brookings Institution Press.

Brownstein, R. and N. Easton (1983). *Reagan's Ruling Class: Portraits of the President's Top One Hundred Officials.* New York, Pantheon.

Brzezinski, Z. (1985). *Power and Principle: Memoirs of the National Security Advisor, 1977–1981.* New York, Farrar Straus Giroux.

Buchanan, P. (1991). Loan Guarantees Not Wise for U.S. Or Israel. *Seattle Post-Intelligencer.* Seattle (18 Sep.): A11.

Bush, G. W. (1999). *A Charge to Keep.* New York, William Morrow.

Bush, G. H. W. (1990). *National Security Strategy of the United States: 1990–1991.* Washington, DC, Brassey's (U.S.).

Bush, G. H. W. and B. Scowcroft (1999). *A World Transformed.* New York, Vintage Books.

Butler, J. (2003). The Charge of Anti-Semitism: Jews, Israel, and the Risks of Public Critique. *Wrestling with Zion: Progressive Jewish–American Responses to the Israeli–Palestinian Conflict.* T. Kushner and A. Solomon, eds. New York, Grove Press: 249–65.

Cannon, L. (1982). *Reagan.* New York, G.P. Putnam's Sons.

Cannon, L. (1991). *President Reagan: The Role of a Lifetime.* New York, Simon & Schuster.

Carlsnaes, W. (1992). "The Agency-Structure Problem in Foreign Policy Analysis." *International Studies Quarterly* 36: 3: 245–70.

Carter, J. (2006). *Palestine Peace Not Apartheid.* New York, Simon & Schuster.

Central Intelligence Agency (2006). *The World Factbook: Israel.* Central Intelligence Agency. Online, available at: www.odci.gov/cia/publications/factbook/print/is/html.

Chafets, Z. (2004). A New Swing Vote Alliance of Jews and Evangelicals Could Tip the Election. *New York Daily News.* New York (17 Mar.): 33.

Chanes, J. A. (2001). Who Does What? Jewish Advocacy and Jewish "Interest." *Jews in American Politics.* L. S. Maisel and I. N. Forman, eds. Lanham, MD, Rowman & Littlefield: 99–119.

Christison, K. (1999). *Perceptions of Palestine: Their Influence on U.S. Middle East Policy.* Berkeley, CA, University of California Press.

Christison, K. (2004). "'All Those Old Issues': George W. Bush and the Palestinian-Israeli Conflict." *Journal of Palestine Studies* XXXIII: 2 (winter): 36–50.

Churba, J. (1977). *The Politics of Defeat: America's Decline in the Middle East.* New York, Cyrco Press.

Churba, J. (1980). *Retreat From Freedom.* Washington, DC, Center for International Security.

Churba, J. (1984). *The American Retreat: the Reagan Foreign and Defense Policy.* Chicago, Regnery Gateway.

Clarke, D. (2005). "Mainline Protestants Begin to Divest from Israel." *Journal of Palestine Studies* 35: 1: 44–59.

Cohen, E. (2006). Yes, It's Anti-Semitic. *Washington Post.* Washington, DC (5 Apr.): A23.

Cohen, M. P. (1988). "American Jewish Response to the Palestinian Uprising." *Journal of Palestine Studies* XVII: 4 (summer): 97–104.

Cohen, R. E. (1981). Congressional Leadership: Seeking a New Role. *The Growing Power of Congress.* D. M. Abshire and R. D. Nurnberger, eds. Beverly Hills and London, Sage Publications for CSIS.

Cohen, S. M. (1989). "Amoral Zionists, moralizing universalists, and conditional doves." *Moment* 14: 5 (Aug.): 56–7.

Cohen, S. M. (1996). Did American Jews Really Grow More Distant From Israel, 1983–1993? A Reconsideration. *Envisioning Israel: The Changing Ideals and Images of North American Jews.* A. Gal, ed. Detroit, MI, Wayne State University Press: 352–73.

Cohen, S. M. and C. S. Liebman (2000). Israel and American Jewry in the Twenty-first Century. *Beyond Survival and Philanthropy: American Jewry and Israel.* A. Gal and A. Gottschalk, eds. Cincinnati, Hebrew Union College Press: 3–24.

Coker, C. (1989). *Reflections on American Foreign Policy Since 1945.* London, Pinter.

Cordesman, A. H. (1984). *The Gulf and the Search for Strategic Stability: Saudi Arabia, the Military Balance in the Gulf, and Trends in the Arab–Israeli Military Balance.* Boulder, CO, Westview Press.

Curtiss, R. H. (1982). *A Changing Image: American Perceptions of the Arab–Israeli Dispute.* Washington, DC, American Educational Trust.

Curtiss, R. H. (1990). *Stealth PACs: How Israel's American Lobby Seeks to Control U.S. Middle East Policy.* Washington, DC, American Educational Trust.

Dallek, R. (1984). *Ronald Reagan: The Politics of Symbolism.* Cambridge, MA, Harvard University Press.

Dallin, A. and G. W. Lapidus (1987). Reagan and the Russians: American Policy Toward the Soviet Union. *Eagle Resurgent? The Reagan Era in American Foreign*

Policy. K. A. Oye, R. J. Lieber and D. Rothchild, eds. Boston and Toronto, Little, Brown: 193–254.

Deese, D. A. (1994). Making American Foreign Policy in the 1990s. *The New Politics of American Foreign Policy*. D. A. Deese, ed. New York, St. Martin's Press: 262–73.

Department of State (2003). A Performance-Based Roadmap to a Permanent Two-State Solution to the Israeli-Palestinian Conflict. U.S. Washington, DC, Department of State (30 Apr.). Online, available at: www.state.gov/r/pa/prs/ps/2003/20062.htm.

Dershowitz, A. (2006). Debunking the Newest – And Oldest – Jewish Conspiracy: A Reply to the Mearsheimer – Walt "Working Paper." Harvard University, Kennedy School of Government (Apr.). Online, available at: www.ksg.harvard.edu/research/working-papers/dershowitzreply.pdf.

Destler, I. M. (1982). Reagan, Congress, and Foreign Policy in 1981. *President and Congress: Assessing Reagan's First Year*. N. J. Ornstein, ed. Washington, DC, American Enterprise Institute: 66–88.

Destler, I. M., L. H. Gelb and A. Lake (1984). *Our Own Worst Enemy: The Unmaking of American Foreign Policy*. New York, Simon & Schuster.

Dine, T. A. (1975). A Primer for Capitol Hill. *New York Times*. New York (4 Apr.): 33.

Dine, T. A. (1983). Pressuring Israel is Dumb. *Washington Post*. Washington, DC (13 Feb.): C5.

Dine, T. A. (1984). An Alliance Strengthened in War: American Jewry and Israel. *Survey of Jewish Affairs 1982*. W. Frankel, ed. London and Toronto, Associated University Presses: 130–7.

Dine, T. A. (1986). "The Revolution in U.S.–Israel Relations, a speech to the 27th Annual AIPAC Policy Conference, 6 April 1986." *Journal of Palestine Studies* XV: 4 (summer): 134–43.

Dorrien, G. (1993). *The Neoconservative Mind: Politics, Culture and the War of Ideology*. Philadelphia, Temple University Press.

Dowd, M. and T. L. Friedman (1990). The Fabulous Bush and Baker Boys. *New York Times*. New York (6 May): SM 34–67.

Dowd, M. and T. L. Friedman (1992). Could Baker's Grip on Tiller Right Bush Campaign Drift? *New York Times*. New York (26 Mar.): 1.

Duffy, M. (2002). "Marching Along." *Time* (1 Sep.). Online, available at: www.time.com/time/covers/1101020909/abattle.html.

Editors, Haaretz (2003). Israel's Road Map Reservations. Haaretz.com (27 May). Online, available at: www.haaretz.com/hasen/pages/ShArt.jhtml?itemNo=297230.

Efron, N. J. (2003). *Real Jews: Secular vs. Ultra-Orthodox and the Struggle for Jewish Identity in Israel*. New York, Basic Books.

Eizenstat, S. E. (1991). "Loving Israel – Warts and All." *Foreign Policy* 81 (winter 1990–1991): 87–105.

Emerson, S. (1982). "The Petrodollar Connection." *New Republic* 186: 7 (17 Feb.): 18–25.

Emerson, S. (1985). *The American House of Saud: The Secret Petrodollar Connection*. New York, Franklin Watts.

Evans, P. B. (1993). Building an Integrative Approach to International and Domestic Relations. *Double-Edged Diplomacy: International Bargaining and Domestic*

Politics. P. B. Evans, H. K. Jacobson and R. D. Putnam, eds. Berkeley, University of California Press.

Evans, R. and R. Novak (1981). A Near Bankrupt Near East Policy. *Washington Post*. Washington, DC (7 Dec.): A15.

Evans, R. and R. Novak (1983). Israeli Lobby's New Offensive. *Washington Post*. Washington, DC (9 Feb.): A19.

Evans, R. and R. Novak (1987). The Sinking of a Saudi Arms Sale. *Washington Post*. Washington, DC (17 Jun.): A23.

Fabian, L. (1988). Religious America and Zion: Is God's Middle East Policy Simply Divine? *United States Middle East Policy: The Domestic Setting*. S. Feldman, ed. Jerusalem and Boulder, CO, Jerusalem Post and Westview Press: 50–5.

Feith, D. J. (2002). Land for No Peace. *The Mideast Peace Process: An Autopsy*. N. Kodozoy, ed. San Francisco, Encounter Books: 23–33.

Feldman, S. (1988). The United States as a Challenge for Israeli Policy. *United States Middle East Policy: The Domestic Setting*. S. Feldman, ed. Jerusalem and Boulder, CO. Jerusalem Post and Westview Press: 68–79.

Feuerwerger, M. C. (1979). *Congress and Israel: Foreign Aid Decision-Making in the House of Representatives, 1969–1976*. Westport, CT, Greenwood Press.

Feuerwerger, M. C. (1993a). Israel: Political Change in a Democratic State. *The Politics of Change in the Middle East*. R. B. Satloff, ed. Boulder, CO, Westview Press for The Washington Institute for Near East Policy: 173–94.

Feuerwerger, M. C. (1993b). The Post-Gulf War Middle East and U.S. National Security Strategy. *From Globalism to Regionalism: New Perspectives on U.S. Foreign and Defense Policies*. P. M. Cronin, ed. Washington, DC, National Defense University Press: 27–42.

Findley, P. (1985). *They Dare To Speak Out: People and Institutions Confront Israel's Lobby*. Westport, CT, Lawrence Hill.

Findley, P. (1995). *Deliberate Deceptions: Facing the Facts About the U.S.-Israeli Relationship*. New York, Lawrence Hill.

Finkelstein, N. G. (1995). *Image and Reality of the Israel–Palestine Conflict*. London, Verso.

Finkelstein, N. G. (2001). *The Holocaust Industry: Reflections on the Exploitation of Jewish Suffering*. London and New York, Verso.

Foltin, R. (2004). United States: National Affairs. *American Jewish Year Book 2004*. D. Singer and L. Grossman, eds. New York, American Jewish Committee.

Forman, I. N. (2001). The Politics of Minority Consciousness: The Historical Voting Behavior of American Jews. *Jews in American Politics*. L. S. Maisel and I. N. Forman, eds. Lanham, MD, Rowman & Littlefield: 141–60.

Forster, A. and B. R. Epstein (1974). *The New Anti-Semitism*. New York, McGraw Hill.

Franck, T. M. and E. Weisbrand (1979). *Foreign Policy by Congress*. New York, Oxford University Press.

Frankel, M. (1995). "The $10 Billion Dollar Question: AIPAC and Loan Guarantees to Israel." *The Fletcher Forum of World Affairs* 19: 1: 153–70.

Freedland, J. (2006). "The Enigma of Ariel Sharon." *New York Review* 53: 20 (21 Dec.): 32, 40.

Freedman, S. G. (2000). *Jew vs. Jew: The Struggle for the Soul of American Jewry*. New York, Simon & Schuster.

Friedman, M. (2005). *The Neoconservative Revolution: Jewish Intellectuals and the Shaping of Public Policy*. New York, Cambridge University Press.

Friedman, T. L. (1989). *From Beirut To Jerusalem*. New York, Giroux Farrar Strous.

Friedman, T. L. (1991). Baker Finds Doors Open, Minds Sealed. *New York Times*. New York (17 Mar.): E1.

Frum, D. (2003). *The Right Man: The Surprise Presidency of George W. Bush*. New York, Random House.

Frum, D. and R. Perle (2004). *An End To Evil: How To Win the War on Terror*. New York, Ballantine Books.

Fulbright, J. W. with S. Tillman (1989). *The Price of Empire*. London, Fourth Estate.

Fukuyama, F. (2006). After Neoconservatism. *New York Times*. New York (19 Feb.): SM62–7.

Gedal, Z. D. (1997). The American Jewish Community and United States–Israel Relations: Maintaining Influence in the Face of Increasing Pluralization, (PhD Thesis) Brandeis University.

Gelb, L. H. (1991). Bush vs. the Jews. *New York Times*. New York (15 Sep.): E17.

George, A. L. and E. Stern (1998). Presidential Management Styles and Models. *Presidential Personality and Performance*. A. L. George and J. L. George, eds. New York, New York University Press: 199–280.

George, A. L. (1987). "Ideology and International Relations: A Conceptual Analysis." *Jerusalem Journal of International Relations* 9: 1: 1–21.

Gergen, D. (2006). An Unfair Attack, USNews.com (3 Apr.). Online, available at: www.usnews.com/usnews/opinion/articles/060403/3edit.htm.

Gerges, F. A. (1999). *America and Political Islam: Clash of Cultures or Clash of Interests?* Cambridge, Cambridge University Press.

Gerson, M. (1997). *The Neoconservative Vision: From the Cold War to the Culture Wars*. Lanham, MD, Madison Books.

Ghareeb, E. ed. (1983). *Split Vision: The Portrayal of Arabs in the American Media*. Washington, DC, American-Arab Affairs Council.

Glick, E. B. (1982). *The Triangular Connection: America, Israel and American Jews*. London, Allen & Unwin.

Golan, M. (1992). *With Friends Like These: What Israelis Really Think About American Jews*. New York, Free Press.

Goldberg, D. H. (1990). *Foreign Policy and Ethnic Interest Groups: American and Canadian Jews Lobby for Israel*. New York and London, Greenwood Press.

Goldberg, J. (2006). The Believer. *New Yorker* (13 and 20 Feb.): 56–69.

Goldberg, J. J. (1996). *Jewish Power: Inside the American Jewish Establishment*. Reading, MA, Addison-Wesley.

Golden, P. (1992). *Quiet Diplomat: Max M. Fisher*. New York, London and Toronto, Cornwall Books.

Goldstein, J. and R. O. Keohane (1993). Ideas and Foreign Policy: An Analytical Framework. *Ideas and Foreign Policy: Beliefs, Institutions and Political Change*. J. Goldstein and R. O. Keohane, eds. Ithaca and London, Cornell University Press: 3–30.

Goott, A. K. and S. J. Rosen (1983). *The Campaign to Discredit Israel*. Washington, DC, AIPAC.

Graham, T. W. (1994). Public Opinion and U.S. Foreign Policy Decision Making. *The New Politics of American Foreign Policy*. D. A. Deese, ed. New York, St. Martin's Press: 190–215.

Greenberg, A. and K. D. Wald (2001). Still Liberal After All These Years? The

Contemporary Political Behavior of American Jewry. *Jews in American Politics*. L. S. Maisel and Ira N. Forman, eds. Lanham, MD, Rowman & Littlefield: 161–93.

Greenstein, F, I. (2000). *The Presidential Difference: Leadership Style From FDR to Clinton*. New York, Free Press.

Grose, P. (1983). *Israel in the Mind of America*. New York, Alfred A. Knopf.

Grossman, L. (1992). Jewish Communal Affairs. *American Jewish Yearbook 1992*. New York, The American Jewish Committee and The Jewish Publication Society: 238–60.

Grossman, L. (1993). Jewish Communal Affairs. *American Jewish Yearbook 1993*. New York, The American Jewish Committee and the Jewish Publication Society: 169–91.

Grossman, L. (1994). Jewish Communal Affairs. *American Jewish Yearbook 1994*. New York, The American Jewish Committee and The Jewish Publication Society: 184–205.

Gruen, G. E. (1990). The Not-so-Silent Partnership: Emerging Trends in American Jewish-Israeli Relations. *Israel after Begin*. G. S. Mahler, ed. Albany, SUNY Press: 209–31.

Haass, R. N. (1979). *Congressional Power: Implications for National Security Policy*. London, International Institute for Security Studies (Adelphi Paper No. 153).

Haass, R. N. (1986). "Paying Less Attention to the Middle East." *Commentary* 82: 2 (August): 22–6.

Haass, R. N. (1990). *Conflicts Unending: The US and Regional Disputes*. New Haven, CT, Yale University Press.

Hadar, L, T. (1992a). "The 'Special Relationship': Israel Decides Its Future." *Middle East Policy* 1: 1: 1–14.

Hadar, L. T. (1992b). "High Noon in Washington: The Shootout Over the Loan Guarantees." *Journal of Palestine Studies* XXI: 2 (winter): 77.

Hadar, L. T. (1993). "Thawing the American-Israeli Chill." *Journal of Palestine Studies* XXII: 2 (winter): 78–89.

Haig, A. M. Jr. (1984). *Caveat: Realism, Reagan, and Foreign Policy*. New York, Macmillan.

Halevy, E. (2006). *Man in the Shadows: Inside the Middle East Crisis with a Man Who Led the Mossad*. New York, St. Martin's Press.

Halper, S. and J. Clarke (2004). *America Alone: The Neo-Conservatives and the Global Order*. Cambridge, Cambridge University Press.

Halsell, G. (1989). *Prophecy and Politics: The Secret Alliance between Israel and the U.S. Christian Right*. Chicago, Chicago Review Press.

Hamilton, A., J. Jay and J. Madison (1937 (1787)). *The Federalist*. New York, The Modern Library.

Harkabi, Y. (1992). *The Arab–Israeli Conflict on the Threshold of Negotiations*. Princeton, NJ, Center of International Studies.

Hauser, R. E. (1992). "Interview with Rita E. Hauser." *Middle East Policy* 1: 1: 15–26.

Herrmann, R. K. (1994). U.S. Policy in the Conflict. *International Perspectives on the Gulf Conflict. 1990–1991*. A. Danchev and D. Keohane, eds. London, St. Martin's Press: 106–35.

Hertzberg, A. H. (1984). The Graying of American Jewry. *Survey of Jewish Affairs 1982*. W. Frankel, ed. London and Toronto, Associated University Presses: 148–60.

Hertzberg, A. H. (1989). "Real Anger." *Present Tense* 16: 2 (Jan./Feb.): 9–10.

Hertzberg, A. H. (1991). "Showdown." *New York Review of Books* XXXVIII: 17 (24 Oct.): 23–4.

Hertzberg, A. H. (1992a). "A Lost Chance for Peace." *New York Review of Books* XXXIX: 5 (5 Mar.): 20–4.

Hertzberg, A. H. (1992b). *Jewish Polemics*. New York, Columbia University Press.

Hertzberg, A. H. (2002). *A Jew in America*. New York, Harper Collins.

Hess, S. (2002). *Organizing the Presidency*. Washington, DC, Brookings Institution Press.

Hilsman, R. (1967). *To Move a Nation*. New York, Doubleday.

Hitchens, C. (1992). "Settled: Why Bush Will Yield to Israel and 'the Lobby.'" *Harper's* 284: 1700 (Jan.): 57–60, 62.

Hitchens, C. (2003). "God and Man in the White House." *Vanity Fair* 516 (Aug.): 76–81.

Hoagland, J. (2006). A Perilous Push for Iraq's Unity. *Washington Post*. Washington, DC (9 Apr.): B7.

Hoffmann, S. (1968). *Gulliver's Troubles or the Setting of American Foreign Policy*. New York, McGraw-Hill.

Holsti, O. R. (1996). *Public Opinion and American Foreign Policy*. Ann Arbor, MI, University of Michigan Press.

Holsti, O. R. (2002). Public Opinion and Foreign Policy: Challenges to the Almond Lippmann Consensus. *American Foreign Policy: Theoretical Essays*. G. J. Ikenberry, ed. New York, Longman: 344–76.

Holsti, O. R. and J. N. Rosenau (1990). "The Emerging U.S. Consensus on Foreign Policy." *Orbis* 34: 3: 579–96.

Holsti, O. R. and J. N. Rosenau (1993). "The Structure of Foreign Policy Beliefs among American Opinion Leaders – After the Cold War." *Millennium* 22: 2: 235–78.

Holsti, O. R. and J. N. Rosenau (1999). The Political Foundations of Elites' Domestic and Foreign Policy Beliefs. *The Domestic Sources of American Foreign Policy*. E. R. Wittkopf and J. M. McCormick, eds. Lanham, MD, Rowman & Littlefield: 33–50.

House, K. E. (1991). Where Soviet Jews Belong. *Wall Street Journal*. New York (25 Sep.): A10.

Hunt, M. H. (1987). *Ideology and U.S. Foreign Policy*. New Haven, Yale University Press.

Huntington, S. P. (1989). American Ideals Versus American Institutions. *American Foreign Policy: Theoretical Essays*. New York, Harper Collins: 223–58.

Hurst, S. (1999). *The Foreign Policy of the Bush Administration: In Search of a New World Order*. London and New York, Cassell.

Ignatius, D. (2001). Why Arafat Opts for Bush. *Washington Post* (4 Feb.): B7.

Indyk, M. (1988). The Impact of America's Think Tanks on its Middle East Policy. *U.S. Middle East Policy: The Domestic Setting*. S. Feldman, ed. Jerusalem and Boulder, CO, Jerusalem Post and Westview Press: 40–3.

Indyk, M. (2006). Sharon: From Soldier to "Man of Peace." Brookings Institution (7 Jan.). Online, available at: www.brook.edu/printme.wbs?page=pagedefs/d2ecce14a87aff3f45a3ce1b0a1415cb.xml.

Indyk, M., C. Kupchan and S. J. Rosen (1983). *Israel and the U.S. Air Force*. Washington, DC, AIPAC.

Isaacs, S. D. (1974). *Jews and American Politics*. Garden City, NY, Doubleday.

Isaacson, W. (1982). "Fighting Among Friends." *Time* (4 Jan.): 58–9.

Jacobson, K. (1991). The United States, Israel, and the Middle East. *American Jewish Yearbook 1991*. New York, The American Jewish Committee: 140–76.

Jacobson, K. (1992). The United States, Israel, and the Middle East. *American Jewish Yearbook 1992*. New York, The American Jewish Committee and The Jewish Publication Society: 209–37.

Jacobson, K. (1993). The United States, Israel, and the Middle East. *American Jewish Yearbook 1993*. New York, The American Jewish Committee and The Jewish Publication Society: 119–68.

Jacobson, K. (1994). The United States, Israel, and the Middle East. *American Jewish Yearbook 1994*. New York, The American Jewish Committee and The Jewish Publication Society: 153–83.

Jordan, A. A. and W. J. Taylor, Jr. (1984). *American National Security: Policy and Process*. Baltimore and London, Johns Hopkins University Press.

Kagan, R. and W. Kristol, eds (2000). *Present Dangers: Crisis and Opportunity in American Foreign and Defense Policy*. San Francisco, Encounter Books.

Kaplan, L. F. (2002). "Torpedo Boat: How Bush Turned on Arafat." *New Republic* 226: 6 (18 Feb.): 18–20.

Kegley, C. W. Jr. and E. R. Wittkopf (1982). "The Reagan Administration's World View." *Orbis* 26: 1: 223–44.

Kegley, C. W., Jr. and E. R. Wittkopf (1996). *American Foreign Policy*. New York, St. Martin's Press.

Kemp, G. (1988). The National Security Council's Role in America's Policy in the Middle East. *U.S. Middle East Policy: The Domestic Setting*. S. Feldman, ed. Jerusalem and Boulder, CO, Jerusalem Post and Westview Press: 15–18.

Kemp, G. (1999). Presidential Management of the Executive Bureaucracy. *Domestic Sources of American Foreign Policy: Insights and Evidence*. E. R. Wittkopf and J. M. McCormick, eds. Lanham, MD, Rowman & Littlefield: 157–72.

Kenen, I. L. (1981). *Israel's Defense Line: Her Friends and Foes in Washington*. Buffalo, NY, Prometheus Books.

Kengor, P. (2004). *God and George W. Bush: A Spiritual Life*. New York, Regan Books.

Kennan, G. (1951). *American Diplomacy 1900–1950*. Chicago, University of Chicago Press.

Keohane, R. O. (1971). "The Big Influence of Small Allies." *Foreign Policy* 2 (spring): 161–82.

Kerr, M. H. (1980). *America's Middle East Policy: Kissinger, Carter and the Future*. Washington, DC, Institute for Palestine Studies,

Kessel, J. H. (1984). "The Structure of the Reagan White House." *American Journal of Political Science* 28: 2 (May): 231–58.

Kessler, J. S. and J. Schwaber (1984). *The AIPAC College Guide: Exposing the Anti Israel Campaign on Campus*. Washington, DC, AIPAC.

Kessler, R. (2004). *A Matter of Character: Inside the White House of George W. Bush*. New York and London, Sentinel.

Key, V. O. (1961). *Public Opinion and American Democracy*. New York, Alfred A. Knopf.

Kimche, D. (1991). *The Last Option*. London, Weidenfeld and Nicholson.

Kirkpatrick, J. (1979). "Dictatorships and Double Standards." *Commentary* 68: 5 (Nov.): 34–45.

Kirkpatrick, J. (1981). "Dishonoring Sadat." *New Republic* 185: 19 (11 Nov.): 14–16.

Kirkpatrick, J. (1990). "A Normal Country in a Normal Time." *National Interest* 21 (fall): 40–4.

Kissinger, H. (1982). *Years of Upheaval*. Boston, Little, Brown.

Klutznick, P. M. with S. Hyman (1991). *Angles of Vision: A Memoir of My Lives*. Chicago, Ivan R. Dee.

Kramer, M. (1989). "Playing for the Edge." *Time* 133: 7 (13 Feb.): 26–33.

Kramer, M. (1991). "Nobody Does Nothing Better Than Shamir." *Time* 138: 39 (30 Sep.): 26.

Krasner, S. D. (1978). *Defending the National Interest: Raw Materials Investments and U.S. Foreign Policy*. Princeton, NJ, Princeton University Press.

Kristol, I. (1984). "The Political Dilemma of American Jews." *Commentary* 78: 1 (Jul.): 23–9.

Kristol, W. and R. Kagan (1996). "Toward a Neo-Reaganite Foreign Policy." *Foreign Affairs* 75: 4 (Jul.–Aug.): 18–32.

Kupchan, C. A. (1987). *The Persian Gulf and the West: Dilemmas of Security*. Boston and London, Allen & Unwin.

Kyvig, D. E. ed. (1990). *Reagan and the World*. New York, Westport, CT and London, Praeger.

Lagon, M. (1994). *The Reagan Doctrine*. Westport, CT, Praeger.

Laham, N. (2002). *Selling AWACS to Saudi Arabia: The Reagan Administration and the Balancing of America's Competing Interests in the Middle East*. Westport, CT and London, Praeger.

Leahy, P. J. (1992). It's Israel's Choice. *New York Times*. New York (11 Feb.): A25.

Lenczowski, G. (1990). *American Presidents in the Middle East*. Durham, NC, Duke University Press.

Levey, G. (2006). "The Other Israel Lobby." Salon.com (19 Dec.). Online, available at: www.salon.com/opinion/feature/2006/12/19/israellobby/print.html.

Lewis, S. W. (1988). The United States and Israel: Constancy and Change. *The Middle East: Ten Years after Camp David*. W. B. Quandt, ed. Washington, DC, Brookings Institution Press: 217–57.

Liebman, C. S. and S. M. Cohen (1990). *Two Worlds of Judaism: The Israeli and American Experiences*. New Haven and London, Yale University Press.

Lilienthal, A. M. (1983). *The Zionist Connection II: What Price Peace?* Bullsbrook, Australia, Veritas Publishing.

Lind, M. (2003). *Made in Texas: George W. Bush and the Southern Takeover of American Politics*. New York, Basic Books.

Lipset, S. M. and E. Raab (1995). *Jews and the New American Scene*. Cambridge and London, Harvard University Press.

McGrory, M. (1991). Dems Could Help by Backing Bush on Israel. *Newsday*. Long Island (2 Oct.): 86.

McNeil, K. (2002). The War on Academic Freedom. thenation.com (11 Nov.). Online, available at: www.thenation.com/doc/20021125/mcneil.

Madison, C. (1992). "Strained Friendship." *National Journal* 24: 16 (18 Apr.): 924–8.

Mann, T. E. (1990). Thinking about the Reagan Years. *Looking Back on the Reagan Presidency*. L. Berman, ed. Baltimore and London, Johns Hopkins University Press: 18–29.

Mansfield, S. (2004). *The Faith of George W. Bush*. New York, Jeremy P. Tarcher/Penguin.

Mansour, C. (1994). *Beyond Alliance: Israel and U.S. Foreign Policy*. New York, Columbia University Press.

Marcus, J. R. (1990). "Discordant Voices: The US Jewish Community and Israel During the 1980s." *International Affairs* 66: 3 (Jul.): 545–58.

Massing, M. (2002). "Deal Breakers." *American Prospect* 13: 5 (11 Mar.). Online, available at: www.prospect.org/print-friendly/print/V13/5/massing-m.html.

Martin, W. (1999). "The Christian Right and American Foreign Policy." *Foreign Policy* 114 (spring): 66–80.

Mathias, C. M., Jr. (1981). "Ethnic Groups and Foreign Policy." *Foreign Affairs* 59: 5 (summer): 975–98.

Mayer, J. (2006). "The Hidden Power: The Legal Mind Behind the White House's War on Terror." *New Yorker* (2 Jun.): 44–55.

Mead, W. R. (2004). *Power, Terror, Peace and War: America's Grand Strategy in a World at Risk*. New York, Alfred A. Knopf.

Mearsheimer, J. and S. Walt (2006a). The Israel Lobby and U.S. Foreign Policy. Harvard University, Kennedy School of Government (Mar.). Online, available at: www.ksgnotes1.harvard.edu/Research/wpaper.nsf/rwp/RWP06–011.

Mearsheimer, J. and S. Walt (2006b). "The Israel Lobby and U.S. Foreign Policy." *Middle East Policy* XIII: 3 (fall): 29–87.

Melman, Y. and D. Raviv (1994). *Friends In Deed: Inside the US-Israel Alliance*. New York, Hyperion.

Menges, C. C. (1988). *Inside the National Security Council: The True Story of the Making and Unmaking of Reagan Foreign Policy*. New York, Simon & Schuster.

Merkley, P. C. (2001). *Christian Attitudes Toward the State of Israel*. Montreal, McGills-Queen's University Press.

Milner, H. (1997). *Interests, Institutions and Information: Domestic Politics and International Relations*. Princeton, Princeton University Press.

Mitchell, G. (2001). Sharm El-Sheikh Fact-Finding Committee Report. U.S. Department of State, Washington DC (30 Apr.). Online, available at: www.state.gov/p/nea/rls/rpt/3060.htm.

Moore, D. (2002). Republicans, Conservatives More Supportive of Israelis Then Democrats, Liberals. *Gallup Brain* (17 Apr.). Online, available at: www.brain.gallup.com/content/default.aspz?ci=5836.

Moore, J. and Wayne Slater (2003). *Bush's Brain: How Karl Rove Made George W. Bush Presidential*. Hoboken, NJ, John Wiley & Sons.

Morgenthau, H. J. (1989). The Mainsprings of American Foreign Policy. *American Foreign Policy: Theoretical Essays*. G. J. Ikenberry, ed. New York, Harper Collins: 624–44.

Morgenthau, H. J. (1951). *In Defense of the National Interest*. New York, Alfred A. Knopf.

Morris, B. (2001). *Righteous Victims: A History of the Zionist-Arab Conflict, 1881–2001*. New York, Vintage Books.

Moughrabi, F. (1987). American Public Opinion and the Palestine Question. *Public Opinion and the Palestine Question*. E. Zureik and F. Moughrabi, eds. London and Sydney, Croon Helm: 13–48.

Nakhleh, K. and C. A. Wright (1983). *After the Palestine War: Limits to U.S. and Israeli Policy*. Belmont, MA, Institute of Arab Studies.

Neff, D. (1994). "Settlements in U.S. Policy." *Journal of Palestine Studies* XXIII: 3 (spring): 53–69.

Neff, D. (1995). *Fallen Pillars: U.S. Policy towards Palestine and Israel since 1945*. Washington, DC, Institute for Palestine Studies.

Neff, D. (2005). "An Updated List of Vetoes Cast by the United States to Shield Israel from Criticism by the U.N. Security Council." *Washington Report on Middle East Affairs* 24: 4 (May/Jun.): 14.

Netanyahu, B. (1986). Defining Terrorism. *Terrorism: How the West Can Win*. B. Netanyahu, ed. New York, Farrar Strous Giroux: 7–15.

Neustadt, R. E. (1990). *Presidential Power and the Modern Presidents: The Politics of Leadership From FDR to Reagan*. New York and Toronto, The Free Press.

Newhouse, J. (1990). Profiles: The Tactician. *New Yorker* (7 May): 50–82.

Newport, F. and J. Carroll (2006). Republicans and Religious Americans Most Sympathetic to Israel. The Gallup Poll (27 Mar.). Online, available at: www.poll.gallup.com/content/default.aspx?ci=22063&VERSION=p.

Novick, P. (2000). *The Holocaust in American Life*. Boston, MA, Houghton Muffin.

Novik, N. (1985). *Encounter With Reality: Reagan and the Middle East (The First Term)*. Boulder, CO, Westview Press, for the Jaffee Center for Strategic Studies.

Novik, N. (1986). *The United States and Israel: Domestic Determinants of a Changing U.S. Commitment*. Boulder, CO, Westview Press.

Oakley, R. (1987). "International Terrorism." *Foreign Affairs* 65: 3: 611–29.

O'Brien, L. (1986). *American Jewish Organizations and Israel*. Washington, DC, Institute for Palestine Studies.

O'Neill, T. with W. Novak (1987). *Man of the House*. New York, Random House.

Oldfield, D. M. and A. Wildavsky (1991). Reconsidering the Two Presidencies. *The Two Presidencies: A Quarter Century Appraisal*. S. A. Shull, ed: Chicago, Nelson Hall: 181–90.

Oppenheim, C. T. (1989). "Talking Peace: American Jewry, Israeli Doves and Palestinians." *Present Tense* 16: 6 (Sep./Oct.): 32–8.

Oppenheim, C. T. (1992). Behind the Scenes of the Mideast Peace Process. *Boston Globe*. Boston (31 Mar.): 19.

Organski, A. F. K. (1990). *The 36 Billion Dollar Bargain: Strategy and Politics in US Assistance to Israel*. New York, Columbia University Press.

Orr, J. B. (1973). Theological Perspectives on the Arab–Israeli Conflict. *The Middle East: Quest for an American Policy*. W. A. Beling, ed. Albany, NY, SUNY Press: 335–47.

Orren, G. (1988). The Salience of Public Attitudes on the Middle East. *U.S. Middle East Policy: The Domestic Setting*. S. Feldman, ed. Jerusalem and Boulder, CO, Jerusalem Post and Westview Press: 33–6.

Painton, P. (1991). "Thou Shalt Not Build." *Time* 138: 39 (30 Sep.): 22–5.

Parmet, H. S. (1997). *George Bush: The Life of a Lone Star Yankee*. New York, Scribner.

Perle, R., J. Colbert, C. Fairbanks, D. Feith, R. Loewenberg, J. Torop, D. Wurmser and M. Wurmser (1996). A Clean Break: A New Strategy for Securing the Realm. Jerusalem and Washington, The Institute for Advanced Strategic and Political Studies. Online, available at: www.israeleconomy.org/strat1.htm.

Perlmutter, N. (1983). Domestic Realignments and a Changing Jewish Community: Implications for U.S. Policy. *Israel in U.S. Foreign and Security Policies*. N. Novik, ed. Tel Aviv, JCSS/Tel Aviv University: 5–16.

Perlmutter, N. and R. A. Perlmutter (1982). *The Real Anti-Semitism in America.* New York, Arbor House.

Peters, J. (2002). *From Time Immemorial: The Origins of the Arab–Jewish Conflict over Palestine.* Chicago, JKAP.

Pipes, D. and M. Peretz (1992). "Bush, Clinton & The Jews: A Debate." *Commentary* 94: 10 (Oct.): 15–23.

PNAC (1997). Statement of Principles. Project for the New American Century (3 Jun.). Online, available at: www.newamericancentury.org/statementofprinciples.htm.

PNAC (1998). Letter to President Clinton on Iraq. Project for the New American Century (26 Jan.). Online, available at: www.newamericancentury.org/iraqclintonletter.htm.

PNAC (2002). Letter to President Bush on Israel, Arafat and the War on Terrorism. Project for the New American Century (3 Apr.). Online, available at: www.newamericancentury.org/Bushletter-040302.htm.

Podhoretz, N. (1982). "J'accuse." *Commentary* 74: 3 (Sep.): 21–31.

Podhoretz, N. (1983). "Appeasement by Any Other Name." *Commentary* 76: 1 (Jul.): 25–38.

Podhoretz, N. (1989). "Israel: a Lamentation From the Future." *Commentary* 87: 3 (Mar.): 15–21.

Podhoretz, N. (1992). "America and Israel: An Ominous Change." *Commentary* 93: 1 (Jan.): 21–5.

Podhoretz, N. (1993). "A Statement on the Peace Process." *Commentary* 95: 4 (Apr.): 19–23.

Podhoretz, N. (2002). "How to Win World War IV." *Commentary* 113: 2 (2 Feb.) 19–29.

Pomerance, R. (2006). Two years after Presbyterian vote, church steps back from divestment. JTA.org (21 Jun.). Online, available at: www.jta.org/page_print_story.asp?inarticleid=16741.

Puschel, K, L. (1992). *US–Israeli Strategic Cooperation in the Post-Cold War Era: An American Perspective* [JCSS Study No. 20]. Boulder, CO, Westview Press.

Quandt, W. B. (1973). Domestic Influences on U.S. Foreign Policy in the Middle East: The View From Washington. *The Middle East: Quest for an American Policy.* W. A. Beling, ed. Albany, NY, State University of New York: 263–85.

Quandt, W. B. (1977). *Decade of Decisions: American Policy Toward the Arab–Israeli Conflict, 1967–1976.* Berkeley, CA, University of California Press.

Quandt, W. B. (1981). *Saudi Arabia in the 1980s: Foreign Policy, Security and Oil.* Washington, DC, Brookings Institution Press.

Quandt, W. B. (1984). "Reagan's Lebanon Policy: Trial and Error." *Middle East Journal* 38: 2 (spring): 237–54.

Quandt, W. B. (1986a). *Camp David: Peacemaking and Politics.* Washington, DC, Brookings Institute Press.

Quandt, W. B. (1986b). "The Electoral Cycle and the Conduct of American Foreign Policy." *Political Science Quarterly* 101: 5: 825–37.

Quandt, W. B. (1988). U.S. Policy toward the Arab–Israeli Conflict. *The Middle East Ten Years after Camp David.* W. B. Quandt, ed. Washington, DC, Brookings Institution Press: 357–86.

Quandt, W. B. (1991). "The Middle East in 1990." *Foreign Affairs* 70: 1: 49–69.

Quandt, W. B. (2001). *Peace Process: American Diplomacy and the Arab–Israeli Conflict Since 1967.* Washington, DC, Brookings Institution Press.

Raab, E. (1990). "No Jewish Split on Israel." *Commentary* 89: 6 (Jun.): 46–8.

Rabin, Y. (1996). *The Rabin Memoirs*. Berkeley, University of California Press.

Rabinovich, I. (1985). *The War for Lebanon, 1970–1985*. Ithaca, NY, Cornell Univeristy Press.

Reagan, R. (1979). Recognizing the Israeli Asset. *Washington Post*. Washington, DC (15 Aug.): A25.

Reagan, R. (1983). *A Time for Choosing: The Speeches of Ronald Reagan 1961–1982*. Chicago, Regnery Gateway.

Reagan, R. (1990). *An American Life*. New York, Simon & Schuster.

Record, J. (1981). *The Rapid Deployment Force and U.S. Military Intervention in the Persian Gulf*. Cambridge, MA, Institute for Foreign Policy Analysis.

Regan, D. T. (1988). *For the Record: From Wall Street to Washington*. San Diego, CA, Harcourt Brace Jovanovich.

Reilly, J. E. ed. (1979). *American Public Opinion and United States Foreign Policy*. Chicago, Chicago Council on Foreign Relations.

Reilly, J. E., ed (1983). *American Public Opinion and United States Foreign Policy*. Chicago, Chicago Council on Foreign Relations.

Rice, C. (1990). U.S.–Soviet Relations. *Looking Back on the Reagan Presidency*. L. Berman, ed. Baltimore and London, Johns Hopkins University Press: 71–89.

Rice, C. (2000). "Promoting the National Interest." *Foreign Affairs* 79: 1 (Jan./Feb.): 45–62.

Richman, S. L. (1992). "The Economic Impact of the Israeli Loan Guarantees." *Journal of Palestine Studies* XXII: 2 (winter): 88–95.

Risse-Kappen, T. (1991). "Public Opinion, Domestic Structure, and Foreign Policy in Liberal Democracies." *World Politics* 43: 3: 479–512.

Rosen, S. (1982). *The Strategic Value of Israel*. Washington, DC, AIPAC.

Rosen, S. J. and Y. I. Abramowitz (1984). *How Americans Feel About Israel*. Washington, DC, AIPAC.

Rosenau, J. N. (1966). Pre-theories and Theories and Foreign Policy. *Approaches to Comparative and International Politics*. R. B. Farrell, ed. Evanston, IL, Northwestern University Press: 27–92.

Rosenfeld, S. S. (1983). Israel's Congressional Shield. *Washington Post*. Washington (18 Feb.): A21.

Rosenthal, A. M. (1988). Jews Must Not Break Bones. *New York Times*. New York (26 Jan.): A25.

Rosenthal, S. I. (2001). *Irreconcilable Differences? The Waning of the American Jewish Love Affair With Israel*. Hanover and London, Brandeis University and University Press of New England.

Ross, D. (2004). *The Missing Peace: The Inside Story of the Fight for Middle East Peace*. New York, Farrrar, Straus and Giroux.

Rostow, E. V. (1979). "'Palestinian Self-Determination': Possible Futures for the Unallocated Territories of the Palestine Mandate." *Yale Studies in World Public Order* 5 (spring): 147–72.

Rostow, E. V. (1977). "The American Stake in Israel." *Commentary* 63: 4 (Apr.): 32–46.

Roundtable (1991). "Linkage: Loans, Aid, and Land for Peace." *Tikkun* 6: 6 (Nov./Dec): 31–5, 91–2.

Sachar, H. M. (1992). *A History of the Jews in America*. New York, Alfred A. Knopf.

Safire, W. (1980). Reagan on Israel. *New York Times*. New York (24 Mar.): A23.

Safire, W. (1992). Blaming the Victim. *New York Times*. New York (19 Mar.): A23.

Safran, N. (1978). *Israel: The Embattled Ally*. Cambridge, MA, Belknap Press.

Said, E. W. (1997). *Covering Islam: How the Media and the Experts Determine How We See the Rest of the World*. New York, Vintage.

Schiff, Z. and E. Ya'ari (1984). *Israel's Lebanon War*. New York, Simon & Schuster.

Schiff, Z. and E. Ya'ari (1990). *Intifada*. New York, Simon & Schuster.

Schneider, W. (1992). The Old Politics in the New World Order. *Eagle in a New World*. K. Oye, R. J. Lieber and D. Rothchild, eds. New York, Harper Collins: 35–68.

Schoenfeld, G. (2006). "Dual Loyalty and the 'Israel Lobby.'" *Commentary* 122: 3 (Nov.): 33–40.

Schwartz, S. (2006). *Is It Good For the Jews? The Crisis of America's Israel Lobby*. New York, Doubleday.

Schweitzer, P. and R. Schweitzer (2004). *The Bushes: Portrait of a Dynasty*. New York, Doubleday.

Segev, S. (1997). The Reagan Plan: A Victim of Conflicting Approaches by the United States and Israel to the Syrian Presence in Lebanon. *President Reagan and the World*. E. J. Schmertz, N. Datlof and A. Ugrinsky eds. Westport, CT, Greenwood Press.

Shaheen, J. (2001). *Reel Bad Arabs: How Hollywood Vilifies People*. New York, Olive Branch Press.

Shaheen, J. G. (1997). *Arab and Muslim Stereotyping in American Popular Culture*. Washington, DC, Center for Muslim–Christian Understanding.

Shamir, I. (1994). *Summing Up: An Autobiography*. Boston, Little, Brown.

Sher, H. (2004). Israel and the Middle East: Israel. *American Jewish Year Book 2004*. D. Singer and L. Grossman, eds. New York, American Jewish Committee.

Shirer, W. (1960). *The Rise and Fall of the Third Reich*. New York, Simon & Schuster.

Shultz, G. P. (1986). The Challenge to the Democracies. *Terrorism: How the West Can Win*. B. Netanyahu, ed. New York, Farrar, Straus and Giroux: 16–24.

Shultz, G. P. (1993). *Turmoil and Triumph: My Years as Secretary of State*. New York, Charles Scribner's Sons.

Shultz, G. P. and K. W. Dam (1977). *Economic Policy Beyond the Headlines*. New York, W.W. Norton.

Siegel, J. (2006). Dems Repudiate Carter Book. Forward.com (27 Oct.). Online, available at: www.forward.com/article/dems-repudiate-carter-book/.

Siegman, H. (2003). Has Sharon Set a Trap for Bush? The Road Map and the Settlements. *International Herald Tribune*. Paris (3 Jun.): 8.

Silverman, C. J. (1996). Image vs. Reality: Ethnic Interest Groups in the Foreign Policy Process: AIPAC, a Case Study. (PhD. Thesis) University of Virginia.

Sipress, A. (2002). A Grudging U.S. Policy. *Washington Post* (1 Apr.): A1.

Skinner, K. K., A. Anderson and M. Anderson (2003). *Reagan: A Life in Letters*. New York, Free Press.

Smith, H. (1988). *The Power Game: How Washington Works*. New York, Random House.

Smith, T. (2000). *Foreign Attachments: The Power of Ethnic Groups in the Making of American Foreign Policy*. Cambridge, MA, Harvard University Press.

Smolowe, J. (1992). "Seething over Settlements." *Time* 139: 5 (3 Feb.): 26–7.

Sofaer, A. (1986). "Terrorism and the Law." *Foreign Affairs* 64: 5 (summer): 901–22.

Sommer, A. K. (1994). "Remember the Loan Guarantees? Russian Immigrants Do and They're Boiling Mad." *Moment* 19: 4 (Aug.): 48–9, 66.

Spiegel, S. L. (1984). U.S. Policy in the Middle East, 1982: A Tale of Two Reagans. *Survey of Jewish Affairs 1982*. W. Frankel, ed. London and Toronto, Associated University Presses: 113–29.

Spiegel, S. L. (1986). *The Other Arab–Israeli Conflict: Making America's Middle East Policy, from Truman to Reagan*. Chicago, University of Chicago Press.

Spiegel, S. L. (1990–1991). "America and Israel: How Bad is It? Will It Get Worse?" *National Interest* 22 (winter): 11–22.

Stoler, M. A. (1987). "The Mission Concept and the Role of Ideology in American Foreign Policy: A Historical Assessment." *Jerusalem Journal of International Relations* 9: 1: 45–67.

Suleiman, M. W. (1988). *The Arabs in the Mind of America*. Brattleboro, VT, Amana Books.

Suleiman, M. W. ed. (1995). *U.S. Policy on Palestine from Wilson to Clinton*. Normal, IL, Association of Arab-American University Graduates.

Swisher, C. E. (2004). *The Truth about Camp David: The Untold Story about the Collapse of the Middle East Peace Process*. New York, Nation Books.

Tanter, R. (1990). *Who's at the Helm? Lessons of Lebanon*. Boulder, CO, Westview.

Tanter, R. (1999). *Rogue Regimes: Terrorism and Proliferation*. New York, St. Martin's Press.

Taylor, H. (2001). America's Heroes. The Harris Poll (15 Aug.). Online, available at: www.harrisinteractive.com/harris_poll/index.asp?PID=251.

Telhami, S. (2004). *The Stakes: America in the Middle East*. Boulder, CO, Westview Press.

Tivnan, E. (1987). *The Lobby: Jewish Political Power and American Foreign Policy*. New York, Simon & Schuster.

Tower, J., E. Muskie and B. Scowcroft (1987). *The Tower Commission Report*. New York, Bantam Books and Times Books.

Truman, D. (1971). *The Governmental Process*. Berkeley, University of California, Institute of Governmental Studies.

Tucker, R. W. (1981). "The Middle East: Carterism without Carter?" *Commentary* 72: 3 (Sep.): 27–36.

United Nations (2004). Report of the Open-Ended Working Group on the Question of Equitable Representation on and Increase in the Membership of the Security Council and Other Matters Related to the Security Council. United Nations General Assembly Official Records, 58th Session, Supp. No. 47. Online, available at: www.un.org/Depts/dhl/resguide/scact2006.htm.

USAID (2006). The Greenbook: U.S. Overseas Loans and Grants, Standard Country Report (Israel: Constant Dollars). U.S. Agency for International Development. Online, available at: www.qesdb.usaid.gov/cgi-bin/broker.exe.

Vance, C. (1983). *Hard Choices: Critical Years in American Foreign Policy*. New York, Simon & Schuster.

Viorst, M. (1987). *Sands of Sorrow: Israel's Journey From Independence*. New York, Harper and Row.

Viorst, M. (2002). *What Shall I Do With This People? Jews and the Fractious Politics of Judaism*. New York, The Free Press.

Waltz, K. N. (1971). Opinion and Crisis in American Foreign Policy. *The Politics of U.S. Foreign Policy*. D. M. Fox, ed. Pacific Palisades, CA, Goodyear: 47–55.

Waltz, K. N. (1979). *Theory of International Politics*. New York, McGraw Hill.

Washington Institute's Presidential Study Group (1988). Building for Peace: An American Strategy for the Middle East. Washington, DC, Washington Institute for Near East Policy.

Waxman, C. I. (1996). Weakening Ties: American Jewish Baby-Boomers and Israel. *Envisioning Israel: The Changing Ideals and Images of North American Jews*. A. Gal, ed. Detroit, MI, Wayne State University Press: 374–96.

Weizman, E. (1981). *The Battle for Peace*. New York, Bantam Books.

Wertheimer, J. (1996). Breaking the Taboo: Critics of Israel and the American Jewish Establishment. *Envisioning Israel: The Changing Ideals and Images of North American Jews*. A. Gal, ed. Detroit, Wayne State University Press: 397–419.

Wills, G. (1987). *Reagan's America: Innocents at Home*. Garden City, NY, Doubleday.

Windsor, P. (2002). Cultural Dialogue in Human Rights. *Studies in International Relations: Essays by Philip Windsor*. M. Berdal, ed. Brighton and Portland, OR, Sussex Academic Press: 77–90.

Wolfinger, R. (1988). Structural and Generational Changes in Congress, and the Role of Congress in U.S. Foreign Policy. *United States Middle East Policy: The Domestic Setting*. S. Feldman, ed. Jerusalem and Boulder, CO, Jerusalem Post and Westview Press: 8–11.

Woodward, B. (2003). *Bush at War*. New York, Simon & Schuster.

Wright, C. A. (1983). Part II: U.S. Policy. *After the Palestine War: Limits to U.S. and Israeli Policy*. K. Nakhleh and C. Wright, eds. Belmont, MA, Institute of Arab Studies.

Zakaria, F. (1992). "Realism and Domestic Politics." *International Security* 17: 1 (summer): 177–98.

Zunes, S. (2005). "The Influence of the Christian Right in U.S. Middle East Policy." *Middle East Policy* XII: 2 (summer): 73–8.

Index

Abbas, M. 189, 190, 191
Abdullah, Crown Prince 185
Abourezk, J. 53, 97
Abram, M. 110
Abramowitz, Y. I. 97
Abrams, E. 64, 68, 174, 180, 183
Abramson, P. R. 159, 178, 180
Abshire, D. M. 48
Acheson, D. 34
Addington, D. 180
Aikman, D. 177, 183, 184
AIPAC (American Israel Public
  Affairs Committee): affinity and
  lobby, combined power of 164–5;
  Amitay era 25–7; "anti-Semitism"
  110–11; Arabs, arms sales to 26–7,
  118, 121–2; AWACS sale 71, 73,
  77–83, 87–8, 90–1, 92, 116,
  154–5, 170; and Bush (George
  H. W.) 133, 137, 139–40; and
  Bush (George W.) 180–2; and
  Christian Right 46, 54; civil rights,
  advocacy of 106–7; and Congress
  25, 27, 50–1; Dine era 27–8; and
  Ford 25–6; and government of
  Israel 102–6, 112; Israel, support
  for 24–5, 28, 164–5; Jewish dissent
  107–9; Jewish identity crisis
  106–7; and Likud 103; and limits
  of advocacy 169–71; loan
  guarantees issue 151, 152, 154–5,
  158–9, 160–1, 170; lobby, and
  domestic politics 13, 14, 15;
  organizational expansion 27–8;
  origins of 23–5; and PACs 50;

Palestinian question 109–10, 111;
  and partners for peace 167, 168;
  political coordination 99–102; and
  Presidents Conference 23;
  reorganization 95–9, 164, 170; and
  Republican Party 52, 53, 54–5;
  Revisionist Zionist positions 94–5;
  Zionism, competing brands of 108
Airborne Warning and Control
  System see AWACS
Ajami, F. 135
Allen, R. 62, 68, 83, 84, 85, 88, 90,
  92, 134
Allon Plan 158
American Israel Public Affairs
  Committee see AIPAC
American Jewish Committee (AJC)
  19
American Jewish Congress
  (AJCongress) 19, 156, 157
Americans for a Safe Israel (ASFI)
  35–6
Ames, R. 126
Amitay, M. 23, 25–7, 48, 53, 98, 156
Anderson, I. H. 44
Anderson, J. 44
Anti-Defamation League of B'nai
  B'rith (ADL) 13, 19, 36
anti-Semitism 16; and AIPAC
  110–11; "defense" agencies 19; and
  Jewish population 28; perceived, of
  Bush (George H. W.) 156
Arab League 118
Arafat, Y. 111, 119, 131, 175, 181,
  184, 188, 189, 190

Made in United States
Orlando, FL
02 July 2024

48528764R00146